Patrons of Women

Patrons of Women

Literacy Projects and Gender Development in Rural Nepal

Esther Hertzog

Berghahn Books
New York • Oxford

FOUNDATION®
BOOKS

Delhi • Bengaluru • Mumbai • Kolkata • Chennai • Hyderabad
Pune • Thiruvananthapuram

Published by
Cambridge University Press India Pvt. Ltd.
under the imprint of Foundation Books
Cambridge House, 4381/4 Ansari Road, Daryaganj, **New Delhi** 110 002

Cambridge University Press India Pvt. Ltd.
C-22, C-Block, Brigade M.M., K.R. Road, Jayanagar, **Bengaluru** 560 070
Plot No. 80, Service Industries, Shirvane, Sector-1, Nerul, **Navi Mumbai** 400 706
10 Raja Subodh Mullick Square, 2nd Floor, **Kolkata** 700 013
21/1 (New No. 49), 1st Floor, Model School Road, Thousand Lights, **Chennai** 600 006
House No. 3-5-874/6/4, (Near Apollo Hospital), Hyderguda, **Hyderabad** 500 029
Agarwal Pride, 'A' Wing, 1308 Kasba Peth, Near Surya Hospital, **Pune** 411 011
T.C. 25/ 2731 Lukes Lane, Ambujavilasam Road, **Thiruvananthapuram** 695 001

This edition was published by arrangement with Berghahn Books Ltd.

First South Asia Edition 2013

ISBN 978-93-82264-61-3

Published by Manas Saikia for Cambridge University Press India Pvt. Ltd. and
Printed at Bhavish Graphics, Chennai

For Professor Emanuel Marx:
A fountain of inspiration,
scholarship, and mentorship

CONTENTS

List of Illustrations

List of Abbreviations and Dramatis Personae

Abbreviations

NGOs	Non-governmental Organizations
INGOs	International Non-governmental Organizations
WGOs	Women's Groups Organizers
AOs	Association Organizers
WOs	Women Officers
WOS	Women's Organization Supervisor

Dramatis Personae

Acharya	Division chief, engineering section
Anita	Local consultant on women's empowerment (employed by Tahal – an Israeli irrigation company)
Gupta	Local consultant on farmer participation (employed by Tahal)
Gurung	Head of the regional office of the Ministry of Education
Karki	Caretaker of the bachelors' house
Lama	Head of the agricultural division of the irrigation project
Leon	Tahal's Israeli representative and team leader
Manju	One of seven WGOs
Pandit	Chief of the farmer's organization division
Raju	Leon's secretary
Ranju	Karki's daughter
Samir	Leon's driver
Sam	American development consultant
Thapa	Nepali manager of the irrigation project

Acknowledgments

The inception and growth of this book has gone hand in hand with a series of encounters with people over twelve years, starting with my travel to Nepal in 1997 and lasting until the book's final revisions in 2009. Each and every one of those I have interacted with had some impact on my experiences, thought, and behavior with regard to my Nepali fieldwork. I am deeply indebted to all and this book seeks to express my continuous gratitude and affection.

More than thirteen years since that dramatic episode in my life took place, I consider myself today as a more critical feminist anthropologist. I owe the personal process I underwent to many: first of all to Tahal, an Israeli irrigation company, who afforded me a wonderful and exciting Nepali experience. I fully appreciate the opportunity that Tahal's staff, and those of the local irrigation company provided me with. I am especially grateful to Leon (who I have given a pseudonym, for reasons of discretion), my Israeli superior whom I gradually learned to like during my stay in Bhairahawa and later on while processing my fieldnotes. Leon had to comply with my presence in his temporary home in Bhairahawa, probably feeling uneasy about my invasion of his private territory and my critical insinuations with regard to his attitudes toward the Nepalese who served him there. He and his wife hosted me most generously in their home-from-home in Kathmandu, introduced me to some of their friends there, and showed me around the city.

Indeed, I remember with great affection the many acquaintances I made who worked on the development project that took me to Nepal, and for whom I have again used pseudonyms. Among these are: the local irrigation project manager Thapa, and other heads of the irrigation project: Acharya, Gupta and Pandit. Raju, Leon's secretary assisted me extensively in my daily hardships in the office and I greatly appreciate his kindness and efficiency. I am grateful to the Women's Groups Organizers (WGOs): Sudha, Sharda, Aruna, Shiva Maya, Ranju, Manju, and Laxmi. Although I could hardly communicate with them, I enjoyed their company and warmth very much during exhausting travels to the villages, celebrating together over samosas and Coke in roadside restaurants. Anita, the local gender consultant was my colleague and closest friend during my stay in Nepal. Anita and I shared our rage, disappointments and frustrations over the senior officials' attitude concerning the project. We ridiculed our mutual Israeli "boss" and many of the Nepali men, gossiping about them and comforting each other during our growing disillusionment about the project and its prospect of materializing. Anita symbolized to me femininity: sensitivity, kindness and delicateness. I am particularly indebted to Karki, and Ranju his daughter, the domestic workers at the bachelors' house, who made my stay in the house pleasant and comfortable. Their vulnerability in Leon's presence was hard to bare and I would like to apologize to them for not being able to stand up for them.

The process of analyzing the ethnography took place over nine years and much of it was carried out overseas, where I could get away from routine activities and other demanding commitments. In the summer of 2000 I went to Oxford, where I was a visiting researcher in the Women's Studies Centre, and there I found an outstanding opportunity to exchange views. Shirley Ardener, Lidia Sciama, Maria Jashock among others, became beloved friends, whose good advice and kind hospitality I cherish.

In 2002 I traveled to Manchester, where I was given the generous hospitality of Pnina and Dick Werbner. I am grateful to Pnina and Dick and their charming son Ben, who opened up their home and rich library for my convenience and use.

In summer 2005 I was very generously hosted by Liron, of the Israeli embassy, at her temporary home in Brussels. I remember with much affection the au pair from the Philippines (to my shame I cannot recall her name) who introduced me to her life story and her friends in the local Filipino community.

My next resort for a period of reflection was Vienna, where I stayed during the summer of 2007. I enjoyed a wonderful time in this beautiful city, walking for hours every day in the exquisite streets, museums, palaces, and cafes. No less enjoyable than the tourist attractions were the inspiring conversations I had with Herta Nöbauer of the anthropology department at Vienna University, who enabled my visit to Vienna and became a very close friend. I met some charming people through her, Erica Pöschl, in particular. Erica offered me her home, treating me with much warmth and kindness, and introduced me to many of Vienna's wonders. Sabine Strasser is another wonderful person who provided me with free lodging while she was away in Ankara. I was also kindly hosted by Tirza Lamberger, of the Jewish studies department at Vienna University.

Finally, I spent February 2008 at the Sociology department of Delhi University thanks to the recommendations and efforts of Vandana Joshi and Arima Mishra. I am particularly thankful to my charming friend Vandana, who hosted me at her home and showed me around the city. We had a great time with her sons, and discussed some intriguing issues relating to gender, politics, and economy in India.

In between my overseas stays devoted to writing-up, I was extremely fortunate to have the support of my family, friends, and colleagues. My husband Avraham and my mother Eva, were my main solid sources of support in helping me cope with multiple tasks: teaching, heading the anthropology department at Beit Berl College, and carrying on my social-feminist activities. They have taken on most of the burden from me as our family has grown to include four sons, three daughters-in-law, and five grandchildren.

I am deeply grateful to my professional and personal role model, Emanuel Marx, who has been a most reliable supporter since the early 1980s, helping me pave a way along the *via dolorosa* of academic life. Emanuel has contributed tremendously to the thinking and rethinking of most of my academic work, including this book. Most importantly, he has offered me the reassurance to think and write things that might sound strange when first encountered. I am grateful to Haim Hazan, who offered some exciting comments, and encouraged me to reject "post-ism" theories. I am also grateful to Orit Abuhav, my friend and colleague, who offered some critical comments, and to Ilana Goldberg for the hard work of improving the book's style. Beit Berl College in Israeli has been my professional home base for over twenty years. I thank its management for ongoing support and the librarians, who were exceedingly efficient in providing me with numerous books, for their kind assistance.

My final words of thanks go to the book's reviewers, Sondra Hausner and an anonymous reader, who obliged me to look deeper into the ethnography and to provide a more complex analysis of my Nepali case study of women's development projects.

Foreword

Public anthropology is often criticized for vacillating between a disciplinary commitment to a credible accounting for the experienced reality it studies and an accountability to worthy social causes. This divided loyalty between knowledge and ethics is habitually resolved through an unbending subscription to one or other all-embracing ideology that furnishes both the need for an overarching cosmopolitan morality and the imperative of providing a cogent, well-informed interpretation of the matter in hand. Thus, postcolonialism, feminism, anti-globalism and other -isms of our day are turned, in the name of critical thinking, into indisputable, politically correct tenets of an uncritical, self-indulgent anthropological perspective.

It takes an intrepid, truly critical scholar such as Esther Hertzog to muster the courage of her convictions not to succumb to these trendy regimes of contrived knowledge, and instead to offer a level-headed, disenchanted, yet heartening approach to the study of the so-called underprivileged. The disillusionment lies with the disappointment with false expectations and promises, while the hope rests with the moralistically untainted scrutiny of the unadulterated circumstances of being a disenfranchized woman in a developing country dominated by organizational bigotry and bureaucratic alienation that excludes her even further from any position of power and influence. Indeed, this study bears witness to the far-reaching implications of the experience under study for world economy, political power games and moral agendas; all through the lens of an anthropological discourse free of the airs and graces of contemporary facades of paying lip service to women's rights and to the protest against the exploits of globalization. In this sense this book is a wake-up call from the vagaries of self-righteous do-gooders and political cynics alike.

This book, however, exposes such styles of pseudo-humanitarianism for what they are, namely mere fig leaves to cover ill-intentioned investments and projects. By keeping a dignified distance from, and free of patronizing empathy for, the "natives", Hertzog makes room for their presence and lets their voices come through as persuasive, genuine. and unperturbed expressions of their lived experience. This self-restrained stance enables the author to present an exceptionally lucid and incisive example of an ethnographically informed evaluation study of the built–in subversive forces that turn a socially designated boon into an untoward bane. With impressive vigor and verve, Hertzog took it upon herself to conduct an involved and disenchanted piece of research into an internationally sponsored feat to empower women villagers in Nepal through the introduction of literacy programs.

Drawing on a series of extended case studies embedded in the breadth and depth of contextual analysis of local politics and socioeconomic processes insidiously shaped by overt as well as covert global interests, Hertzog unveils the infrastructure responsible for the aborted initiative. To ascertain the intricacies of the multitude of circumstances and factors implicated in that destined failure to decolonize oppressed women, Hertzog is not beguiled by politically correct postcolonial ideological and pedagogical academic fads offering clichéd, often out of context, blatantly patronizing interpretations. Instead, she resorts to the well-tried ethos and practice of first-hand anthropological observation. She accomplishes that by interweaving the global and the local, thus making sense of what seems to be an apparently paradoxical reality of disempowering empowerment.

Spawning a gamut of interlocked circles encompassing macro perspectives from the operation of world systems, through state rule and legislation to gender relations, Hertzog addresses local cultural knowledge and custom as active, self-aware actors in a worldwide arena of power and interests. All these points of view converge to create a prism through which the studied village scene of ritual, discourse, and interaction is observed and analyzed. This field of action is manifested in the sponsored literacy classes that Hertzog investigated as she highlights their ensuing untoward repercussions in strengthening women's presence and position. With the aim of explaining the almost fatalistic consequences of what seem to be good ideas coupled with the best of intentions, Hertzog employs a spectrum of research methods, ranging from thorough ethnographic fieldwork based on participant observation, through interviews with decision-making officials in government and the funding agencies, to qualitative content analysis of accounts and documentation.

This outstanding wealth of findings allows Hertzog to develop an original and erudite approach to the study of developing societies within the context of the emergence of forms of economic exploitation and gender discrimination under the guise of cosmopolitan ethics and empowering support. This is an unassumingly written, yet powerfully persuasive and immensely disturbing contribution to the anthropological understanding of the place of the Third World in today's global universe.

Haim Hazan
Tel Aviv University

PREFACE

This book is about male domination in international gender development projects, based on research in Nepal. The book offers a feminist critique of the work of both international and local agencies, and shows how they reproduce gender stereotypes and preserve gender inequality. It is based on data I collected while working as a gender consultant for an irrigation company in rural Nepal. The book focuses on male-dominated agencies that manipulate projects intended for the benefit of women. It describes how high-ranking male officials in various agencies in Nepal cooperated in subverting resources allocated to women, while employing a well established rhetoric of gender equality to advance their own interests. Thus, women's marginalization is preserved and further manifested through a dialectic process.

The analysis also elaborates on the hierarchical relations and ethnocentric behavior that emerge from the bureaucratically structured polarization of power between developing and developed, rich and poor, educated and uneducated, urban and rural, employers and employees, men and women, local and expatriate, consulting and consulted, and patrons and clients in Nepal.

Apart from discussing a specific case study of gender relations in the context of the development project in which I was involved, the book seeks to stress the prominence of bureaucratic characteristics in the gamut of development projects. I argue that the processes and social relations that take place in this context should be explicated in terms of power relations that are unavoidably embedded in any bureaucratic setting. Examining the enforced introduction of a women's project into a male-dominated irrigation project reveals unrecognized and denied structured gender power differentials in particular, but it also reveals control mechanisms which are systematically built into organizations. Analyzing development projects in this vein provides a rationale for the persistence of development projects, although they are consistently described as "failures". It seems, therefore, that projects do not "fail" but rather succeed in serving, in complex, indirect, and manipulative ways, the varied interests of organizations and individuals. Analyzing the bureaucratic phenomenon also facilitates the understanding of the paradox that women's empowerment projects mainly serve the interests of male officials. In other words, a look at why a gender project scheduled to be part of a larger irrigation project did not materialize entails the exposure of the gendered structure of the wider society. Both this structure and the women's project within the irrigation project are based on males' domination.

The "gender development program" discussed in this book[1] was scheduled because of pressure that the World Bank put on the Nepali government in the mid 1990s to take upon itself women-centered projects, offering a loan of some $500,000 for their implementation. The Bank claimed that women's advancement would accelerate the pace of social and economic change in the rural areas of Nepal.

As the book progresses it becomes clearer how and why a project intended for women's advancement was used for the benefit of men, and failed to provide women with any of the resources promised. It describes in detail the implicit and explicit interests of all parties: Nepali government officials, heads of the World Bank, and directors of Tahal, the Israeli engineering company. It looks at the tactics they used to prevent the realization of the original aims of the scheme, and at their collaboration in making the funds allocated for women accessible to men. It illustrates the numerous manipulative strategies employed in day-to-day activities and their impact on social relationships, and particularly on gender relations. Moreover, the analysis illustrates how female employees collaborated, although reluctantly and sometimes unconsciously, with the organization's hidden agenda.

The ethnography demonstrates how organizations enhance recognition of the self-evident need for their services, by describing the village women, explicitly or implicitly, as needy and backward. However, the social and economic competence of these women, which is amply documented in the data, contradict this image. The rural women lack economic resources, yet are offered literacy programs that they believe to be only marginally needed for their daily routines. Nevertheless, in reality the developers provide neither literacy skills nor any vocational training or substantial economic assistance. Furthermore, although the village women are well aware of the deceitful game, they cooperate with the developers for their own reasons.

The book follows the growing critique concerning development and gender development in particular, while contributing to the criticism relating to women's development projects. It argues that gender development projects (and development projects at large), contrary to their manifest aims and budgets, do not and cannot contribute to social change in gender power relations (or any other social change). Rather, they serve to support the existing power structures.

However, the book does not offer an alternative discourse or policy recommendations for gender development. Doing so would entail the acceptance of this concept, whereas the book's basic argument is that such projects are all ultimately concerned with power manipulations rather than with social change. Thus, the theoretical analysis elaborates on structured power relations embedded in social organizations. It emphasizes gendered power relations in the bureaucratic setting of the women's project under study. My analysis seeks to contribute to the limited literature in this field, by using reflexive tools of a profoundly involved anthropologist in a women's empowerment project.

The Introduction reviews the literature concerning the main issues that are discussed in the book, among which are: development and gender development projects in bureaucratic perspective; gender relations and feminist theories relevant to development projects; literacy campaigns and Nepali village women. The analysis incorporates insights from feminist, as well as economic and anthropological studies focusing on South Asia.

Chapter 1 analyses some of the dilemmas associated with the role of external consultant in "developing countries." Looking back at my fieldnotes, I reflect on the inescapable hierarchical relations into which I was thrust in my daily interactions with local people. This chapter exposes the constructed patronage and power differentials embedded in encounters between "outsiders" or "experts" and local people, between males and females, and between junior and senior officials in the organization's hierarchy.

Chapter 2 describes the continuous efforts of the representative of Tahal to establish a position of dominance in the project. It analyses the stereotypical expressions and ethnocentric attitudes he adopted toward local people in a drama of power which generated a good deal of antagonism.

Chapters 3 and 4 elaborate on the role that literacy campaigns play in development projects at large, and in the context of the women's project in particular. They describe the negotiations that took place with regard to the conceptualization, budgeting, and implementation of the women's literacy program. The analysis of written documents and field encounters tells the story of the intensive social engagements which ended up without concrete outcomes, for the project provided neither literacy classes nor vocational training.

The detailed description in Chapter 5 focuses on the seminar, a training course for village teachers involved in the literacy program, illustrates how the rhetoric of social change and women's empowerment served male officials in particular, but also the two gender consultants (myself and a local colleague), as a means for demonstrating control. The descriptions reveal the ongoing exposure of women to collective patronization in a male-dominated framework. However, they also illustrate the compliance of the few relatively highly positioned females (the two gender consultants) with the bureaucratic codes and expressions of power relations that prevailed in the project premises.

Chapter 6 exposes the budget as a mere phantom. It suggests that the women's project did not stand a real chance of benefiting the village women from its very inception. In reality, so it transpired, the project was used to "buy off" men in higher positions, at a local and national level. The gradual exposure of the hidden agenda behind the women's development program is connected to a discussion of feminine conduct in a male dominated organizations.

Notes

1. This program, which was embedded in the irrigation project, is referred to by the following terms, interchangeably: gender development project, women's project, women's program, women's activities project, and women's empowerment project. This interchanging use of terms reflects the diverse terms use in daily encounters and in documents.

INTRODUCTION

Development Projects: Persistence Despite Evident Failure

"Development" and "Development Projects": Neocolonialism and the Discourse of Social Change

Gender development programs should be discussed against the wider background of development projects in developing countries.[1] Much of the criticism concerning development discourse and practices in developing countries applies to projects that aspire to effect social change in gendered power relations. Thus, the discussion of a women's development project in Nepal will be linked in this opening chapter to the critical literature about development at large and gendered development in particular.

Various studies draw a parallel between development or aid projects and neocolonialism. Thus, for instance, Chilisa Bagele (2005) argues that "neocolonialism" signifies the dependence of many formerly colonized countries that have gained geographical and political independence, although in practice their "cultural and economic independence was never really, if at all, won. The colonial systems of domination continue ... as the former colonizers continue to economically, culturally, financially, militarily and ideologically dominate what constitutes the so-called developing world" (ibid.: 660). Some scholars claim that development is a form of structural violence (Cowen and Shenton 1995; Des Chene 1996; Rahnema and Bawtree 1997). These studies argue that one of the more conspicuous instruments of neocolonialism is the aid industry, which structures hierarchal relationships and power gaps between countries and communities. These unbalanced relations are anchored in binary categories that differentiate between "givers" and "receivers," development "professionals" and populations "in need of development," between the poor and underdeveloped South and the rich, modern, developed North. Critical research reveals the implied paternalism in these projects and points to development as enhancing economic exploitation in and of developing countries and regions. They expose the hidden agendas behind aid and development discourses and projects. Rather than helping the "weak" and "developing" countries, these studies contend that development programs promote the interests of international aid organizations.

Several salient studies exemplifying this critical trend have been published in the past four decades by Teresa Hayter (1971), Vandana Shiva (1986, 1993), Arturo Escobar (1988, 1995), Graham Hancock (1989), Wolfgang Sachs (1992), Gustavo Esteva (1992), and others. Based on her research on the World Bank, Hayter found that the "purpose of aid is, and cannot be other than, to serve the economic interests of the major capitalist powers, especially the USA, and of the big corporations and banks ... [who] give priority to the interests of their major funders" (Hayter 1971: 88).[2] Arturo Escobar describes "development" as a dream "progressively turned into a nightmare" and defines it as the ideological apparatus at play in global power relations. He maintains that development discourse is governed by the same principles as colonial discourse. Moreover, development has "successfully deployed a regime of government over the Third World, a space for 'subject peoples' that ensures certain control over it" (Escobar 1995: 9). He states that: "Instead of the kingdom of abundance promised by theorists and politicians in the 1950s the discourse and strategy of development produced its opposite, underdevelopment and impoverishment, untold exploitation and oppression. The debt crisis, the Sahelian famine, increasing poverty, malnutrition, and violence are only the most pathetic signs of the failure of forty years of development" (ibid.: 4). Wolfgang Sachs writes that: "Delusion and disappointment, failures and crimes have been the steady companions of development and they tell a common story: it did not work. Moreover ... development has become outdated" (Sachs 1992: 1). Gustavo Esteva argues that two centuries after the social construction of development, it is a reminder, for two-thirds of the people on earth, "of what they are not ... of an undesirable, undignified condition. To escape from it, they need to be enslaved to others' experiences and dreams" (Esteva 1992: 10).[3] Esteva criticizes the conceptual acceptance, by many scholars, of the concept "underdevelopment" as self-evidently "real, concrete, quantifiable and identifiable". Moreover, he argues, "No one seems to doubt that the concept does not allude to real phenomena. They do not realize that it is a comparative adjective whose base of support is the assumption, very Western but unacceptable and undemonstrable, of the oneness, homogeneity and linear evolution of the world" (ibid.: 11–12). For Vandana Shiva, "Development, as a culturally biased project, destroys wholesome and sustainable lifestyles and instead creates real material poverty, or misery, by denying the means of survival through the diversion of resources to resource-intensive commodity production" (Shiva 1989: 72–73). Katy Gardner and David Lewis propose that "development" is "dead," "a non-word, to be used only with the inverted commas of the deconstructed 1990s" (Gardner and Lewis 1996: 1). As far as the practical realities of development are concerned, they assert that by the mid 1990s it became clear that the anticipated benefits of modernization, the assumed outcome of development, were "largely an illusion: over much of the globe the progressive benefits of economic growth, technological change and scientific rationality have failed to materialise" (ibid.: 1).

Following these critiques, I view "development" as well as its derivatives—such as "developing" and "underdeveloped" (countries) and their opposite, "developed"—as representing an obsolete concept, a "non-word," and will refer to it as a term that calls for the use of inverted commas.[4] Therefore, as a contested term, "development" and its above mentioned derivatives are to be read hereafter as if they had inverted commas around them.[5]

Economic and Gendered Critiques of Development and the World Bank

Incisive critiques of development and of the World Bank's policies (which play a major role in the development industry) from the economic perspective have been offered by Graham Hancock (1989), a journalist; Muhammad Yunus (1998), an academic economist and founder of the Grameen Bank, for which he was awarded with the Nobel Prize in 2007; Joseph Stiglitz (2002), who was Chief Economist at the World Bank until 2000; and William Easterly (2006), who was also an economist at the World Bank.[6] These works discuss development mainly in economic and organizational terms, such as the financial assistance (aid) extended by developed countries to developing countries; the economic and political interventions of the former in the management of the latter; the economic dependence, exploitation, and corruption that are embedded in this neocolonialist intervention; the growing and corrupted control of the bureaucratic machinery over budgets intended for the provision of public services; and the one-sided imposition of economic globalization.

Graham Hancock (1989) offers an extensive critique of development aid for poor countries. He provides ample examples of the disastrous impact that development and the aid industry has had on most developing countries that have been engaged in development projects.[7] Hancock analyzes the outcomes of international aid programs in most of the countries that were offered financial assistance by foreign agencies (the most prominent of which is the World Bank) comparing them to countries that either did not receive or stopped receiving aid. Thus, he shows how Africa lost the self-sufficiency in food production that it enjoyed before becoming a chronic recipient of development assistance,[8] whereas countries like Nicaragua have done much better in the spheres of the economy, welfare, and education without development assistance.[9] Consequently, Hancock condemns aid as:

> often profoundly dangerous to the poor and inimical to their interests; financing the creation of monstrous projects that, at vast expense, have devastated the environment and ruined lives; it has supported and legitimized brutal tyrannies; it has facilitated the emergence of fantastical and Byzantine bureaucracies staffed by legions of self-serving hypocrites; it has sapped the initiative, creativity and enterprise of ordinary people and substituted [these with] the superficial and irrelevant glitz of imported advice. (ibid.: 189)

Hancock blames the United Nations, the World Bank, and bilateral agencies for using aid to create and entrench "a powerful new class of rich and privileged people" in the name of the "destitute and vulnerable." "It is aid—and nothing else," he claims, "that has provided hundreds of thousands of 'jobs for the boys' and that has permitted record-breaking standards to be set in self-serving behavior, arrogance, paternalism, moral cowardice and mendacity" (ibid.: 192–93). His uncompromising conclusion is that "to continue with the charade seems to me to be absurd." Thus, he explicitly recommends that the aid industry be wiped out: "the time has come for the lords of poverty to depart. Their ouster can only be achieved, however, by stopping development assistance" (ibid.: 193).

Hancock's extensive study does not relate in any way to a gender perspective on the aid industry. No development projects are mentioned in his book that concern women in the Third World, developing countries, or the "poor countries of the South," nor are they included in the numerous examples he uses to substantiate his claims. Indeed, this drawback can be attributed to the fact that gender was barely recognized or incorporated into development projects before the 1990s. Moreover, even at the beginning of that decade, when women and gender in developing countries gained the attention of international institutions (e.g., World Bank 1990, Murphy 1995) and the absence of development projects intended for women was acknowledged, these were subsequently financed with "small money" in terms of the overall resources available to the aid industry. Indeed, the absence of women's perspectives from Hancock's analysis might imply that, paradoxically, women have probably gained from being excluded from aid projects, avoiding the various harmful effects that could have befallen them. Nevertheless, ignoring women's perspectives in any sociopolitical and economic analysis may be said to entail a basic bias. Overlooking women in his analysis of aid projects, despite the significant role that they play in the economy, at both private and public levels, and their (at least) equal share in worldwide poverty, weakens Hancock's analysis.

A comparison with Muhammad Yunus's "feminist" book (Yunus 1998), in which he describes women's economic participation in South Asia's economy and recounts his own profound engagement with poverty reduction, accentuates this point further. The book tells the story of how Yunus established the Grameen Bank as "a bank for the poor," first in 1976, in Bangladesh, his country of origin, and later in other countries in the region. For reasons of both social ideology and economic rationale, Yunus's initiative targeted women, with the purpose of benefiting and empowering women and their families. Within two decades his enterprise became widely acknowledged and financially successful. From $27 lent by the Bank to forty-two people in 1976, by 1998 microloans had soared to $2.3 billion administered to 2.3 million families.

Like Hancock, Yunus expresses extreme criticism of the aid industry in general and of World Bank policies in developing countries in particular. He argues that the money does not reach those who are meant to be its recipients. Rather, development projects are cynically used as a pretext to benefit more affluent groups in developing countries.[10] He argues that foreign aid becomes "a kind of charity for the powerful, while the poor get poorer" (ibid.: 17).[11] Yunus also confirms Hancock's claim that pressure is put on developing countries to take the loans offered by the World Bank and IMF.[12] He, too, places the blame on the extravagant conduct and corrupt structures of the World Bank and aid agencies; the large number of staff they employ (50,000 altogether in the "aid industry," according to Hancock, and 5,000 World Bank employees, according to Yunus, in Bangladesh alone);[13] their luxurious working conditions; and the squandering of most of the money on needless experts who treat the local people arrogantly. Yunus charges that in all of the projects financed by the World Bank, "their experts and consultants end up virtually taking over. They do not rest until they mould it their way" (ibid.: 14). This external meddling and imposition of policies, he insists, should be resisted, so that local solutions can be cultivated. Moreover, Yunus argues that instead of wasting the money on huge bureaucracies it should be given outright to the neediest: "Just $100 put in the hands of each of the poorest ten million families in Bangladesh would amount to $1 billion that would then either be invested in capital income-earning goods, or, at worst, spent locally on goods and services" (ibid.: 17). Yunus recommends further shutting out the "middle men of the aid industry," so that people can rediscover the human and personal "help" that is tailored to their own needs and aspirations "in line with priorities that they themselves have set, and guided by their own agendas" (ibid.: 193).

Although Yunus shares most of Hancock's criticisms about the aid industry, his book differs in its approach to the role of women in economic policies and socioeconomic change. He perceives women as the main actors in poverty and its eradication. Yunus believes that working for women as borrowers of money, and with women as the Grameen Bank's employees, serves the interests of women, their families' and of the whole society's wellbeing, no less than it serves the Bank's profits. The Grameen Bank, based on microcredit programs, is portrayed as a means for changing gender power relations and promoting general egalitarianism. Thus, Yunus describes his female-centered banking policy and philosophy, which raised his female clientele to 94 per cent—prior to Grameen, women constituted less than 1 per cent of all the borrowers in Bangladesh—as a social revolution (ibid.: 90). In great detail, he describes how he approached potential clients, employing social work strategies to overcome traditional barriers to communicating with women, while convincing them and dissolving their husbands' resistance. Profoundly motivated by his belief in gender equality he confronted the banks' discrimination against women years before he himself became a banker, and later stood up against government officials who objected to the Bank's female-oriented policy. Yunus prides himself for the Grameen Bank's impact on reducing violence by husbands against their wives, by challenging traditional constraints on men, and by communicating directly with village women. He explains the Bank's pro-women policy as follows:

> if the goals of economic development include improved standards of living, removal of poverty, access to dignified employment, and reduction in inequality, then it is quite natural to start with women. They constitute the majority of the poor, the under-employed and the economically and socially disadvantaged. And since they were closer to the children, women were also our key to the future of Bangladesh. (ibid.: 93)

Yunus's conviction of the significance of working with women is embedded in a feminist rhetoric:

> Relatively speaking, hunger and poverty are more women's issues than male issues ... being a poor woman is toughest of all ... When she is given the smallest opportunity, she struggles extra hard to get out of poverty. A poor woman in our society is totally insecure: she is insecure in her husband's house because he can throw her out any time he wishes. He can divorce her by merely saying three times' 'I divorce you' ... She cannot read and write, and generally she has never been allowed out of her house to earn money, even if she has wanted to. (ibid.: 92)

Indeed, this representation of Bangladeshi poor women is rather generalizing and stigmatic. However, it is not unlike the way they are sometimes described in feminist publications as well.[14]

Do Microfinance Schemes Help the Poor and Women in Developing Countries?

Against the background of Yunus's enthusiastic feminist-socialist presentation of his pragmatic banking approach, it is relevant to reflect on a few studies of the Grameen Bank and its microfinance schemes. This will give us some insight into the role of local economic enterprises in developing countries, and especially into women's inclusion and exclusion practices, in the contexts of both economic development projects and microfinance schemes.

In his study of microfinance in the Grameen Bank of Bangladesh, Mahabub Hossain (1988) demonstrates that by providing credit for self-employed activities the Bank has raised the income, employment, asset base, and working capital of borrowers—improving thereby the living standard of more than 90 per cent of borrowers. In addition, the Bank has also been able to reach its target group, the poorest of the poor, who do not have access to formal credit institutions, and has still maintained an excellent repayment record. Shahidur Khandker and Osman Chowdhury (1996) found, similarly, that microfinance programs have helped raise the asset base of poor borrowers, which enables many of them to escape poverty over time. They also suggest that credit programs have enabled beneficiaries to invest more in non-farm activities rather than in traditional farm activities, thus helping to bring about a structural shift in rural Bangladesh.

Focusing primarily on the impact of microfinance on employment generation and return from employment, Rushidan Rahman and Khandker (1996) found enhanced participation rates and employment among credit-program participants. Based on their findings they suggest that credit-financed self-employment can provide good prospects for alleviating the poverty of landless workers.

The question of whether credit programs designed for the poor are likely to be viable over the long term was examined by Khandker, Baqui Khalily, and Zahed Khan (1996). They suggest that it is possible to develop sustainable group-based credit programs in order to alleviate poverty. However, since reaching the poor involves high operational costs for these institutions, there may be a need for an initial subsidy. Khandker Khalily, and Khan found that it took five to six years for the branches of Grameen Bank to break even, and ten years for the Bank as a whole to attain self-sufficiency.

While early studies evaluating microfinance schemes found them to be an excellent strategy for poverty reduction, several recent studies highlight doubts about these optimistic conclusions. One example is a cross-country study in seven developing countries by David Hulme and Paul Mosley (1996), which concludes that the use of microfinance as a strategy for poverty reduction may involve a trade-off between poverty reduction, on the one hand, and overall income growth on the other. Saurabh Sinha and Imran Matin (1998) indicated that microfinance has increased the poor villagers' dependence on traditional village moneylenders. They found that due to the increase in the volume of credit given by the Grameen Bank, contrary to its own claims, microfinance turned out to be an even more expensive alternative to the high-cost loans offered by village moneylenders. In order to keep up with large loan repayments every week, poor households were forced to seek help from moneylenders. Consequently their burden of debt increased, and evolved risky implications for their long-term economic viability.

Aminur Rahman (1999) found that higher debt burden increases tension and frustration among household members, and creates a new form of dominance over women leading to increased violence within the family. Shelley Feldman (1997) and Lamia Karim (2001) report similar findings in Bangladesh. Imran Matin (1998) has noted yet another consequence of greater credit availability. He found that as the amount of credit increased, the Grameen Bank became more interested in the better-off households, who joined the Bank for the first time, as a result of the lure of larger loans.

Most early studies of the impact of microfinance were concerned with its impact at the household level. However, they did not examine its specific impact on women, who happened to be the majority of borrowers in most programs.

Later studies have tried to redress this omission. For example, Ruth Schuler, Syed Hashemi, and Ann Riley (1997) and Lutfun Khan Osmani (1998) found that credit had a positive effect on women's autonomy over reproductive decisions. In her study of the impact of the Grameen Bank's microfinance programs on women, Osmani found that women's bargaining power and their well-being improved, but not in every dimension. She suggests that the reason for this partial improvement probably lies in the disparity between the large increase in the volume of credit and the absence of adequate investment opportunities for women. Women are obliged to enter into a kind of joint venture with their husbands, whereby women secure credit and men utilize it. Since this implies that women have less than complete control over credit, they fail to gain bargaining power to the extent that they otherwise might have. Similar findings regarding women's incomplete control over credit were reported by Anne-Marie Goetz and Rina Sen Gupta (1996). Women's loss of control over credit is attributed by Hulme and Mosley (1996) primarily to the increase in loan size (credit deepening).

It appears, therefore, that since the mid 1990s studies have raised considerable doubts over Yunus's self-congratulatory assessment of the social and feminist success of microcredit. Both poverty alleviation and women's economic empowerment through microfinance programs were found disappointing. That this is the case is not so much due to wrong practices but probably can be explained by shifts in the motivation driving Yunus and the heads of the Grameen Bank. The Bank managed to build up an economic empire based on a social ideology, and survived the first ten hard years of breaking even and attaining self-sufficiency. As years passed, interest in better-off clients, who were attracted by the larger loans, increased, and subsequently the composition of the Bank's clientele gradually changed. In other words, the profit motive has probably overtaken the initial ideological motivation.[15] The shift from targeting the "poorest" clients to the "not so poor" has entailed a trade-off between the goal of poverty reduction, in particular women's poverty, and the Bank's income-generating objectives. Yunus's original aim was to open up economic opportunities for women, especially poor women, by providing them preferential access to credit in comparison with men, and offering them soft lending conditions. However, it seems that over the years, the Grameen Bank lost much of its social and feminist sensitivity. It continuously increased the size of loans and insisted on fixed weekly repayment. Consequently, the moneylenders returned to the front stage of microfinance for the poorest, something that initially Yunus had hoped to change.

Last but not least, one may point to a cynical outcome of this saga. It appears that even the violence of men against their wives was not wiped out by this enterprise. Rather, having lost control over money to their husbands and relatives, who used them to receive loans from the Grameen Bank, and once the pressures of the deepening burden increased, women again became an easy target for violent, frustrated husbands.

It can be concluded, then, that women were used, albeit inadvertently, by Yunus and the Grameen Bank for the Bank's own benefit, no less than other developing agencies and the World Bank that Yunus criticized. It appears that for some twenty years the Bank did indeed help the poor, as Hossain (1988) and others suggest. It is the studies published since 1996 that point to policy changes which have had a negative impact on the poor—and on poor women in particular.

I suggest that Yunus's enterprise, like any new economic enterprise, necessitated reaching out to new groups that had not been previously tapped. Once the new clientele was absorbed into the system, the old rules and terminology of profit, growth, and so on were restored, to facilitate the conventional money-making game. Seen from this perspective women were discovered and exploited as an important potential group of borrowers that had never before been courted by the banks. In fact, they were cheaply bought off, though with passionate idealistic rhetoric. As soon as poor women became captive clients, indirectly serving as access points to their husbands, and had helped increase the Bank's capital and contributed to its credibility, due to their viable payment norms, the women were not really needed any more. More affluent clients were then preferred.

Thus, feminist rhetoric and the terminology of social justice were used to gain public recognition of the social commitment of the Bank. A more sober consideration of the ways in which Yunus conveyed his commitment to changing the situation of poor women in the family and in society at large shows how feminist rhetoric concerning women's collective vulnerability, victimization, oppression, and discrimination can be manipulated. I conclude, therefore, that feminist discourse may be employed in a process in which help offered to women, based on their collective stereotyped weakness, serves to benefit resourceful businessmen like Yunus, as well as various organizations, including non-profit organizations, or even women's NGOs.

The examples and arguments presented above clarify the point that development projects and policies achieve, in practice, the opposite of what they aim to. Instead of social change, progress, improvement, and growth, to which development is supposed to lead, in reality it often signifies degradation, destruction, and regression (of people, communities, and the environment). Similarly, the term "modernization," which is rooted in the discourse of development and planning, and which implies self-evident progress, advancement, innovative thinking and practices, appears to be a misleading term in this development context.

However, despite the growing body of critical studies, certain scholars appear to cling, indirectly and somewhat apologetically, to the notion of "development." The pursuit of an alternative approach to development reintroduces this concept into socioeconomic analyses of neocolonialism and accords it a continued presence. Thus, Escobar, for instance, who maintains that discussing alternatives to development means "remain[ing] within the same model of thought that produced development and kept it in place" (Escobar 1995: 222), suggests introducing an alternative "research strategy." Such an approach would involve ethnographies that investigate "the circulation of discourses and practices of modernity and development" which provide us with a view of where specific communities "are culturally in relation to development" (ibid.: 223).

Gardner and Lewis offer another example for this contradictory argumentation, which is also connected to dilemmas confronting anthropological research. They suggest that development is capable of sustaining all criticisms and undoubted failures because of its conceptual eloquence as a "working tool" for "people discussing global poverty ... even if deriding it philosophically" (Gardner and Lewis 1996: 2). Moreover, they state that, in practice, development agencies impact the world with outputs of billions of dollars a year and that therefore development plans, workers, and policies cannot be simply willed "into non-existence by insisting that they are constructs, however questionable the premises on which they rest may be" (ibid.: 2). These scholars point to a potential collaboration between anthropology and development projects and encourage anthropologists to engage with development. They claim that anthropology and development should cooperate, and that "rather than throwing up our hands in horror ... we suggest that both have much to offer each other ... Anthropological insights can provide a dynamic critique of development and help push thought and practice away from over-systematic models and dualities" (ibid.: 2).

The Comeback of Development Theories

In an eloquent analysis of a "cattle developing project" in Samoa, Susan Maiava (2001) proposes an alternative perspective, which considers development positively at both the theoretical and pragmatic levels. Describing the project in terms of a "clash of paradigms" between traditional and modern Western cultures, her own paradigm, she ventures, would possess "a moral force that could not be disputed." She outlines a theory which "explains development as a creative, dynamic process of interaction, negotiation and response between cultures ... This results in a diversity of manifestations of the development process in variable cultural and historical contexts" (ibid.: 226).

Maiava argues that although the cattle project in Samoa was successful in economic and social terms, its planners and practitioners considered it a failure. Moreover, they attributed this alleged failure to the negative influence of the villagers' traditional customs on the project's potential success. Maiava explains that while the project managers expected the cattle farmers to passively comply with the conventional Western farming practices they were taught, the Samoans, instead, partook selectively in the new knowledge and adapted these practices to suit their own cultural patterns and requirements (ibid.: 215). Thus, Samoan farmers "changed what they wanted to change and retained what they wanted to retain" (ibid.: 213). Maiava indicates that a similar misperception of development-project outcomes as failures is documented by various studies relating to the Pacific region (see, e.g., McKillop 1989), and, hence, a generalization concerning the success of development projects in the Pacific, regardless of the assessments of failure, can be made.

However, as much as Maiava tries to present development projects in the Third World as justifiable and successful, her approach fails to avoid the very same pitfalls of modernization theory and practice which she criticizes. Despite her criticism of modernization theory, she appears to rely heavily on the binary opposition of modern versus traditional. Although she admits that "the practice of development continues to be strongly influenced by modernization" (Maiava 2001: 223), which was based on ethnocentric belief in the superiority of Western culture, values, and technology, she nevertheless advocates the use of development.

Although sophisticatedly expounded, Maiava's analysis seems to rely profoundly on a binary and hierarchal Western conceptualization to which she purportedly objects. This self-contradictory thesis might be attributed to Maiava's unconscious adherence to Western patriarchal thinking, as it emerges from the fact that her whole study ignores gender perspectives or woman's place in the Samoan context. This omission is particularly glaring when she writes that "it is the household and not the village which is the unit of production for income in Samoa" (ibid.: 142), an observation that merely lumps women's contribution in a general way under "household production."

Maiava recommends that researchers and project planners approach development projects with the aim of adjusting them to people, in order to avoid misunderstanding and ethnocentrism, to "simply ask the people … and listen intelligently to their answers" (ibid.: 225). In the course of my fieldwork in rural Nepal, I noted that village women were approached by project planners and asked about their needs and expectations. The women openly (and repeatedly) expressed their preferences, which were included in the reports that were distributed to all those in charge of the project, at local, national and World Bank levels. Yet, all this had nothing to do with the final recommendations and even less with the implementation of the project, a point that will be illustrated later on.

The perceived failure of the "cattle developing" project by practitioners and planners is explained by Maiava as being to do with mistaken conclusions, the lack of a time perspective, the need for a different attitude on the part of planners and practitioners, and so on. However, I would argue that it is the project practitioners' interests which should be explored, as these are likely to account for at least some of the apparent gap between their views of the project's success or failure, versus those of the farmers themselves. Robert Chambers (1983), who is cited by Maiava, highlights this issue. He conceives of political economy, or vested interests, as one of the main contributory factors in perpetuating false views about the success or failure of development projects. However, Maiava declines to accept this explanation in the context of her study, where "intentions were good, even if misdirected" (Maiava 2001: 211).

Nevertheless, if the Samoan cattle project (and other similar projects) succeeded, this happened, so it emerges from Maiava's study, contrary to the project staff's understandings, planning, and implementation. In fact, the farmers' efficient and manipulative use of the project in disregard of the original plans and imposed practices turned the project into something that could serve their divergent needs. This occurred, I suggest, because resources were distributed among farmers, and, apparently the less the project staff interfered the better the farmers could incorporate the additional resources into their economic and social life.[16]

My Nepali experience lends support to this line of argumentation. The irrigation project, in which the women's development program was embedded, was designed to enrich the water reservoir which supplied people's rice fields during the dry season. The project was expected to significantly improve the irrigation system as well as rice-growing conditions. However, the villagers were severely criticized for underestimating the value of the project, for not cooperating sufficiently with the project staff, and for complaining about the need to pay for the water. In 1997, some fifteen years after its initiation—by which time the transfer of responsibility over the project to the farmers was assumed to have been completed—it seemed that utilization of the deep wells' water was far from optimal, as only a partial use of this water had been made. The villagers' response to the ambitious, costly, irrigation project can be also understood as their way of protesting about the processes of privatizing water resources. This explication is indebted to Vandana Shiva's analysis of policies favoring privatization of essential services (Shiva 2002) promoted by the World Bank, the World Trade Organization (WTO), and giant corporations. Shiva argues that this capitalist process creates corporate states that:

> Usurps resources from people for meeting vital needs and puts them in the hands of private corporations for making profits ... Giant water projects have always benefited the powerful and dispossessed the weak ... the beneficiaries have been construction companies, industry, and large commercial farming interests. Donald Worster has called this the "contrived market of the state"—the capitalist state working to facilitate the unlimited accumulation of private wealth. (Shiva 2001)

Shiva blames the World Bank for "Having created scarcity and pollution through the promotion of non-sustainable water use," and adds that, "the World Bank is now transforming the scarcity it has created into a market opportunity for water corporations" (ibid.).[17] The potential water market is estimated by the World Bank "at $800 billion." Thus, Shiva accuses the World Bank of making water a "big business for global corporations that see limitless markets in the growing scarcity and growing demand for water" (ibid.).

However, an indirect, unintended, and unforeseen by-product—an example of what Ferguson refers to as "side effects" (Ferguson 1990: 252)—was noticed (although unacknowledged by the project staff), which profited the population in the villages. The large electricity system and roads that were constructed in order to enable the deep-digging and operation of the wells turned out to be the most outstanding benefit for the villagers in the project area. It follows, then, that the infrastructures that were incidentally provided for the villages in the region contributed significantly to facilitating the life conditions of the population, as well as improving accessibility and communication between villages and throughout the whole region, by enhancing agricultural and social activities. Hence, I argue that investing in basic economic and social infrastructure —such as roads, electricity, cattle, education, and so on—entails (albeit inadvertently) the direct distribution of public resources to large populations. This understanding supports Ferguson's conclusions from his study of development projects and bureaucratic power in Lesotho. Ferguson concludes: "even if the project was in some sense a 'failure' as an agricultural development project, it is indisputable that many of its 'side effects' had a powerful and far-reaching impact on the Thaba-Tseka region". Among these "side effects" he mentions a road "to link Thaba-Tsěka more strongly with the capital … establishing a new district administration" (ibid.: 252). In a similar vein in the Nepali context, Martin Hoftun, William Raeper, and John Whelpton (1999) point to the conspicuous contribution of infrastructures installed by foreign aid agencies to Nepal between 1991 and 1995, as compared to their meager success in terms of a "self-sustaining rise in living standards." Among the most visible results of these large infrastructure projects were "roads and dams" (ibid.: 259 n.3).

Nevertheless, I suggest that while a focus on "side effects" of development reveals a picture of achieved benefits, it also conceals the state's responsibility for providing basic services in poor regions and for handling economic gaps. It blurs people's basic need for direct—rather than mediated (through "instruction" by professionals, for instance)—access to and control over needed resources. It appears, therefore, that "side effects" contribute to preserving power structures, as they provide temporary, negligible solutions for inherent structured inequality and, as a result, they silence protest.

In the following chapters I shall continue the line of critical analysis concerning development and reject the possibility of "alternatives" through an analysis of women's development projects. The discussion will describe and examine the power relations and dynamics involved in a specific case study; namely, a World Bank's initiative to promote the development of women in rural Nepal. The gender development discourse concerning help for illiterate, poor, village women extensively used in the documents and declarations will be shown to play a major role in constructing the image of caring for the women, while in practice development agencies employed manipulative tactics to serve their various interests.

Development and Women's Empowerment Projects

The Construction of Third World Women's Underdevelopment and Subordinated Femininity

An examination of a women's perspective in relation to development and aid projects cannot be separated from a consideration of policy and practices in the general development context. Most feminist writings on this issue strive to accommodate "women" or "gender" within the theoretical and practical sphere of development. However, I suggest that critical analysis concerning the aid industry applies to women's or gender development projects as well. Thus, it is not a matter of applying the "right" discourse, theory, or alternative approach to all variants of modernization theory that are embedded implicitly or explicitly in development projects. Rather, power relations and domination, under various and changing guises, are central to the development context, whether a general or a gendered one. Therefore, development projects and rhetoric, whatever form they take, are part of the strategies used by powerful organizations to dominate weaker countries, communities, and social categories. Hence, they are constructed to preserve dependence and weakness, which in turn "call for" intervention.

In light of my field research, I suggest that both the terminology of "development," "Third World Countries," and "Third World Women", and the aid industry that uses it to establish its own self-evident indispensability, should be unveiled as being manipulated to serve those in power and not those who they claim to be serving and consequently abandoned. Women cannot be helped by development projects, certainly not in terms of changing gendered power structures.

Much of the literature demonstrates that development projects do not change anything basic about women's marginality because they do not break through the barriers of access to credit and other essential resources. At most, some women, either as individuals or as organized groups (mostly NGOs), become part of the hegemonic order. They are co-opted by it and serve it, mainly by complying with women's traditional caring roles and by supporting the gendered, segregated social and economic order. Ranjani Murthy, for instance, points to the tendency of women's NGOs to "strike bargains with patriarchal structures to ensure their day-to-day survival" (Murthy 1999: 177). Similarly, Don Chatty and Annika Rabo suggest that, in the context of the Middle East, many formal women's groups are politically controlled and are: "state run, or owned by political parties or religious organizations ... In general, such organizations are felt to be too dependent on the male controlled power structure" (Chatty and Rabo 1997: 12–13). Reflecting on my experience in the context of Israeli women's organizations, I contend that this claim also applies to the Israeli (and Western) context. Thus, women's NGOs are controlled by governments and manipulated to support and strengthen male dominated regimes.

Nearly four decades of struggle for the recognition of the right of women to be included in development projects and to alter the male bias inherent in development projects have elapsed. Yet it appears that gendered power structures have not undergone any significant change or improvement through the interventions of the development industry.

The recognition of a women's perspective in Third World development discourse and projects emerged with Esther Boserup's work, which was the first to note that development projects deprived women and excluded them (Boserup 1970). Her work was followed and enhanced by demands of feminist development groups to integrate women in development projects. It was against this background that the Women in Development (WID) approach evolved. Embedded in the liberal tradition, it demanded that development projects should aim at and work for greater equality between women and men. Since that time, feminist discourse and the struggle for Third World women has changed the terminology and theoretical focus of these debates, in a dialectic process. The conceptualization of development from a women's perspective was defined and redefined in response to ongoing critiques, focusing mainly on the inherently Western ethnocentric thinking implied in the concept of modernization that drove development projects.

The discourse concerning "Third World women" portrayed "Western," "modern," "developed," and "educated" women as the opposite social constructs of "poor," "non-Western," "non-modern," "undeveloped," and "uneducated" women. The construction of "Western" and "non-Western" homogenized categories of women, which formulated binary relations between two groups and established the weakness, inferiority, victimization, and vulnerability of women in the Third World. As several studies argue, this stigmatizing generalization fostered an image of backwardness that called for the intervention of more affluent, developed countries (e.g., Kabbani 1986; Enloe 1989; Mohanty 1991; Chowdhury 1995). Cynthia Enloe (1989), for instance, suggests that the concept *zenana*[18] plays a major role in the discourse on Third World women. This representation, of veiled women who are "mindless members of a harem" (ibid.: 53), entails a correspondence between images of motherhood and women's "primitiveness."

Geeta Chowdhury (1995) points to the role of the *zenana* representation in constructing the image of traditionalist women in the Third World. Thus, "Third World women are relegated to the *zenana* as housewives, cloistered within the confines of a patriarchal male-dominated environment" (ibid.: 27). She contends that all representations of Third World women portray them as either inferior, subjugated sex objects, or as victims. These images have become inseparable from aid policies and development projects. The implied message of all these images is that Third World women are backward, non-liberated, and need to be civilized, educated, and modernized to conform to the ideal of Western woman.[19] According to Chowdhury, the "welfare approach" that best fits the *zenana* representation is most dominant in World Bank WID policies. This approach conceives of women primarily in their reproductive roles, viewing them as mothers, whose central occupation is child rearing. Such a welfare approach typically focuses on family-planning programs, child nutrition, and pregnant and lactating women.

World Bank documents corroborate Chowdhury's claims. One of the Bank's progress reports advises: "Not all operations in all sectors are equally important for actions related to women. Operations in the area of human resources—education and population, health and nutrition are of prime importance" (World Bank 1990: 14). Moreover: "Six of the eight projects approved in fiscal 1988 and ten of eleven in fiscal 1989 do address such basic matters as family planning, nutrition for mothers and children, and maternal and child health care" (ibid.: 15).

The same document stresses the significant role of women as educators, which necessitates educational projects: "The influence of the mother's education on family health and family size is great—greater than that of the father's education. Maternal education may also have a greater effect on children's learning" (ibid.: 5). A striking statement from a Bank document remarks upon women's "lack of self-confidence, education and basic skills, even for feeding children" (McGuire and Popkin 1990: 13). This characterization clearly emphasizes he Bank's ethnocentric attitude toward Third World women, denying them even the skill of "feeding children."

An observation made by Stacey Leigh Pigg suggests that the World Bank's "welfare approach" is not really concerned with Third World women's welfare but rather in controlling their reproduction. She writes:

> Naively, I hadn`t realized that health in Nepal's development mostly means family planning. I was rather shocked, in fact, to see how much money goes into trying to get these folks not to reproduce. And all this seems so incongruous in relation to the joy and delight Nepalese find in children ... Which goes only to show how pathetically narrow the World Bank's vision is ... Thus I learned something very important about the World Bank in Nepal.[20]

The Gender and Development (GAD) approach that succeeded WID focused on the social construction of gender roles and relations, rather than focusing exclusively on women. This approach introduced the concept of "mainstreaming," which involved the "systematic application of a gender-aware vision to corporate activities, government and agency policies" and the "introduction of routine management procedures to ensure implementation" (Rowan-Campbell 1999: 21). According to Dorienne Rowan-Campbell, GAD "poses a challenge to the operation of patriarchy, its intent being that women's perspectives, knowledge, capacity, and difference become part of the mainstream of development options and national life, thus changing both" (ibid.: 21). Subsequent critiques of GAD suggest that this approach, too, reinforced negative stereotypes of women in the South by emphasizing their homogenized poverty and backwardness. Thus, for example, Chandra Talpade Mohanty argues:

> This average third world woman leads an essentially truncated life based on her feminine gender (read: sexually constrained) and her being "third world" (read: ignorant, poor, uneducated, tradition-bound, domestic, family-oriented, victimized, etc.). This, I suggest, is in contrast to the (implicit) self-representation of Western women as educated, as modern, as having control over their own bodies and sexualities, and the freedom to make their own decisions. (Mohanty 1991: 56)

DAWN (Development Alternatives with Women for a New Era) was another proposed perspective for looking at women and development (see, e.g., Sen and Grown 1987). This approach was also criticized (e.g., Hirschman 1995) for casting these women as victims of the development process and continuing to objectify them as "Third World" women. Similarly, Geeta Chowdhury argues that, "despite this critical stance, and the involvement of progressive feminist groups in the South, such as DAWN, international feminists have neither challenged the issue of modernity nor one of its expressions, colonial discourse on Third World women" (Chowdhury 1995: 35).

Postmodern Feminist Theory Trapped in Development Discourse

While postmodern feminist theory has criticized the concept of "modernity" with respect to the South/North divide, it was also caught up in the paradigm of development, as well as in the illusion of the promise of gender development projects. Postmodern feminists do not reject the concept of development as such. One example of this self-contradictory argumentation can be found in Janet Henshall Momsen's study, which clearly illustrates the failure of development projects in promoting women's equality in the "Third World," and points to the destructive outcomes of modernization, from the point of view of women (Momsen 1991). With reference to the agricultural sphere, she contends that Western experts and the modernization of agriculture have: "altered the division of labor between the sexes, increasing women's dependent status as well as their workload. Women often lose control over resources such as land and are generally excluded from access to new technology" (ibid.: 1). Momsen maintains that even when women are included in development projects, they have scant chances of benefiting from new technological inputs because "local political and legislative attitudes make women less credit worthy than men" (ibid.: 51). Moreover, Momsen argues that there is no such thing as a "Third World Women's" collectivity or identity. She views the concept of *zenana* and the image of women's utter dependence on men as an absurd stereotype and offers numerous examples of divergent situations, places, and contexts in which women are not collectively passive and in which they cannot be described as a homogeneous social category. Momsen highlights Indian women working in paddy fields and making bricks, Brazilian women picking black pepper and processing nuts, Aborigine women hunting and gathering in Australia, and women loading bananas for export in the West Indies. She shows the impact of development on women's roles in agriculture, and on their employment status, which changes "from independent cultivators to unpaid family workers with the expansion of cash cropping in Africa, from independent cultivator to wage laborer in India as landlessness increases, and from permanent hacienda worker to wage-earning rural proletariat in Latin America with the rise of agri-business" (ibid.: 47).

Nevertheless, her analysis notwithstanding, Momsen does concede that correct thinking and planning based on the understanding that "women are central to development" (ibid.: 93) may engender anticipated results. She argues, for instance, that, "despite the apparent lack of change, the United Nations Decade for Women achieved a new awareness of the need to consider women when planning for development" (ibid.: 3). Thus, "awareness" is championed as a substitute for actual, socioeconomic change. Jane Parpart and Marianne Marchand's work offers another example (Parpart and Marchand 1995). They suggest that development cannot be other than what it is: an ethnocentric approach for reinforcing the existing power structure. They argue that: "the discourse of development has often disempowered poor women. This comes as no surprise to those who are critical of the dualistic, patriarchal language and assumptions embedded in Western development thinking." Yet, they pursue a new mode of thinking about women, gender, and development, which "welcomes diversity, acknowledges previously subjugated voices and knowledge(s) and encourages dialogue between development practitioners and their 'clients'" (ibid.: 17). Thus, instead of rejecting development completely, Parpart and Marchand prefer to adhere to the notion of development as it is refracted through postmodern feminist thinking, which addresses development issues in "an increasingly complex, interrelated and unequal world, with its skepticism towards Western hegemony, particularly the assumption of a hierarchical North/South divide" (ibid.: 17).

It follows, then, that postmodern feminism reifies, in essence, the dualistic approach it criticizes, reinforcing it, for instance, with the binary oppositions of "South" and "North," and "development practitioners" and their "clients" (who need to be developed). I suggest that this approach entails, unavoidably, homogenizing "Third World women." Moreover, postmodern feminists emphasize the need to focus on difference and to listen to the silenced and ignored voices of "Third World women". Jane Parpart phrased this approach as follows: "the goals and aspirations of Third World women would be discovered rather than assumed, and strategies for improving women's lives could be constructed on the basis of actual experiences and aspirations rather than modern fantasies imposed by the West" (Parpart 1993: 454).

I suggest that this view not only homogenizes "Third World women," albeit with well- intentioned, idealized rhetoric, it also assumes that these women's goals and aspirations are not known. "They" are so very different from "us," this view implies, that their aspirations and goals distinctively differ from those of women in other parts of the world. The important point is, rather, that women's voices, like those of minorities or disadvantaged groups, are often overlooked, whether they are heard or not. Furthermore, my field data indicate clearly that those "aspirations and goals" in developing countries or in the Third World are indeed being strongly and clearly expressed by women. Their needs, unsurprisingly, are similar to those of people all over the world: to have decent living conditions and fair economic opportunities, to be able to provide for their families, obtain health services, and so on.

A similar point is made by Lauren Leve (2007), who criticizes empowerment theories which "track consciousness verses unconsciousness, agency verses alienation, 'subjectivity' verses 'subalternity', and choice verses constraint." Based on her interviews with rural Nepali women in Chorigaon, she argues that women evaluate their lives in more prosaic terms.[21] They "ask for ease, security, equality of opportunity (including access to education and employment), good food and clothing, some degree of respect for their personal desires—and, as much as possible, some fun" (ibid.: 151). She adds that development, according to their testimonies, "would include water taps, electricity, bridges and roads, and peace" (ibid.: 165 n.43).

The women in the Nepali villages that I visited were asked about their needs and aspirations time and again, by representatives of women's and other NGOs. However, their responses were simply ignored, either by being rephrased in "expert" language, "asking questions in closed or fixed categories," interpreting responses "in ways that fit development's own agendas" (Hausner 2006: 319), or, more importantly and in practice, by inserting them into reports but not considering them as a driver for social change or the allocation of resources.

Although later feminist approaches criticized earlier ones, still they did not reject the validity of development itself, as a sociogeographic concept that presupposes binary hierarchical situations and relationships. Nor did they reject the legitimacy of development projects, women's development projects included. Thus, the various approaches reviewed here accept the need for development as a self-evident truth. Consequently, they provide arguments about how women's perspectives should be addressed in development projects, and to which terminology is more appropriate for overcoming the modernization loop and binary conceptualization criticized by Edward Said (1979), and other postmodernist theorists, feminists among them.

Ambivalence in Discussing the Futility of Gender Development Projects

"Development projects" for women are gradually being recognized as irrelevant and disappointing at best, or as strengthening the patriarchal social order at worst. Recent feminist publications have expressed a growing disappointment and lack of belief in the promise of change through women's development projects. They suggest that these projects, while paying lip service to gender equality, fail to contribute to the eradication of poverty at large and of women's poverty in particular; nor have they contributed to setting in motion any meaningful change in male-dominated structures. Some of these studies imply the futility of theoretical discussions about development programs that encourage women to either work together or separately from men, whichever the case might be. In general, they demonstrate that gender development projects account for no significant change in women's socioeconomic opportunities.

In a tone of despair resulting from the insignificant, disappointing achievements gained in the twentieth century, Dorienne Rowan-Campbell turns her hopes, or rather her prayers, to the new era: "Perhaps the millennium is the moment to begin actively to subvert some of the strategies used against women's empowerment to turn these in on themselves" (Rowan-Campbell 1999: 25). These hopes turned out to be illusions, something which emerges from Janet Momsen's more recent work (Momsen 2004). She claims that although some three decades of gender development policies (mainly WID and GAD) have elapsed, patriarchy is still blocking any significant change in gender power relations, and that, "the work of redressing gender inequalities has only just begun. Gender balance in human rights is hard to deliver. States may pass laws providing equal access to women and men to property rights but these laws may not be enforced at the grass-roots level" (ibid.: 241).

Naila Kabeer (1999) points to the failure of women-specific projects, in particular those aimed at income generation. A decade of experience has shown, she says, that projects intended for women cannot challenge "the marginal place assigned to women within development as long as the norms, practices, and procedures which guide the overall development effort remain fundamentally unchanged" (ibid.: 34). She emphasizes, in contrast, the vital importance of a political agenda, which would focus on the participation of women in decision-making at the policy level and challenge the existing status quo in society.

Fiona Leach (1999) expresses deep disappointment in relation to non-formal education (NFE) and training programs for women, which, instead of compensating them for the failure of the formal system to provide them with marketable skills, have "continued to reflect the same disparities and biases that prevail in formal education." She writes: "IGPs [Income Generating Projects] for women have largely concentrated on support for the provision of goods and services which are an extension of traditional female activity in the home, such as handicrafts or food production" (ibid.: 51).

Reflecting on my own field experience, it appears that informal-education and vocational-training programs funded and set up by NGOs—which, as Leach remarks, "have mushroomed in developing countries" (ibid.: 50)—did not, in reality, achieve much in terms of reducing women's illiteracy or of widening their employment opportunities (be they "traditional" or not). Rather, they served to silence local and international feminist organizations' claims about discrimination. Moreover, these programs were easy to organize on a large scale and, therefore, were a cheap means for buying off the more-educated women in local communities in Nepal. The funds allocated for these programs enabled them to employ some of the women heading local NGOs and to account for the organizations' activities at the same time.

The lack of progress since the 1985 Nairobi World Conference on Women, notwithstanding the institution of development projects and the acknowledgement of women's marginalization, is criticized sharply by Hlupekile Sara Longwe, who states, "Gender policies have a strange tendency to 'evaporate' within international development agencies" (Longwe 1999: 63). She claims that the "patriarchal cooking pot" is "filled with patriarchal bias, implicit in the agency's values, ideology, development theory, organizational systems, and procedures" (ibid.: 75), and concludes that these agencies produce little of value in terms of results. Jo Rowlands (1999) also discusses the growing awareness of the hidden agendas embedded in development projects. These, she claims, are manipulated through extensive use of appealing terms such as "empowerment," "participation," "capacity-building," "sustainability," or "institutional development." She complains that it is tempting to use these terms in such a way that "takes the troublesome notions of power, and the distribution of power, out of the picture. For in spite of their appeal, these terms can easily become one more way to ignore or hide the realities of power, inequality, and oppression" (ibid.: 149).

However, in spite of the extensive critique directed at development projects and development agencies, both at the theoretical and practical level, it appears that they are assumed to be a self-evident reality that must be endured. Rather than suggest, as the critical analysis implies, the need to categorically reject gender development projects (or any other development project, for that matter), most scholars come up with new names for much of the same mechanisms and practices. Deborah Eade's analysis provides one such example: "Given that development agencies exist, and show no signs of being about to self-destruct, it is essential that they should seek constantly to improve the quality of their partnerships. That the whole mission of development may be misguided is not a reason for development agencies to adopt less than the highest achievable standards of integrity" (Eade 1997: 5).

Nevertheless, I suggest that development projects, whether defined generally or as specifically gender oriented, cannot achieve their formally claimed goals. More than anything else, the development discourse serves to construct the self-evident image of a dichotomized, hierarchal social reality of First versus Third World, North versus South, developed versus underdeveloped countries, and modern versus traditional societies, which then calls for international intervention in the "needy," "Third World," "South," or "developing countries." Terms such as "modernization," "development," and "Third World" are used both in the context of gender-specific and general programs to convey an ideological commitment to universal social values. However, in reality they are used to conceal the vested interests of the agencies and organizations involved in the development industry. This dichotomized discourse is a central component in the construction of hierarchal and patronizing relationships. It offers undisputed justification, an "objective" and convincing explanation for discriminating policies, masked by a rhetoric of helping, improving, and developing the lesser, needy others.

Similarly, Chandra Talpade Mohanty's attempt to "move away from misleading geographical and ideological binarisms" by adopting the language of "One-Third World versus Two-Thirds World" in relation to terms like "Western/Third World and North/South" (Mohanty 2003: 506), is an illusion. As much as Mohanty tries to get rid of binary oppositions, it appears that her terminology introduces new ones, such as "social majority/minority," "One Third/Two Thirds," "marginalized, colonized/privileged," "nations/indigenous communities," "haves/have-nots." Despite her efforts, these terms are "seen as oppositional and incommensurate categories" (ibid.: 522). Apparently, these preferred categorizations do not permit the ascription of "ideas about experience, agency, and struggle" to women (ibid.: 527), which feminist scholars like Parpart and Marchand, Eade, and Mohanty eagerly aspire to.

I suggest that gender rhetoric in development discourses serves as lip service for the purpose of appeasing vocal feminists' demands or for concealing ulterior commitments to more powerful partners. Since, for instance, allocated funds for women's projects are easy to manipulate, they can be conveniently transferred to "more important" purposes when negotiating with politicians, powerful corporations, and so forth.

Therefore, the rhetoric concerning development should be examined as an inseparable part of concrete contexts and explored through ethnographic studies. The descriptions and analysis presented in this book offer an example of this crucial nexus, between the concrete context and the role of rhetoric. The case study, describing a project aimed at women's empowerment in rural Nepal, can serve to illustrate the instrumentalization of widely respected terminologies in the realization of extrinsic hidden interests. I suggest that men's interests in preserving power and control, in both the "West" and in the "Third World," leads them to employ the gender discourse while in practice excluding women from vital resources.

Gender, Development and Literacy in Nepal

The "Third World" Image of Nepali Women

Against the background of Nepal's poverty, male-dominated structures and religious practices, it seems almost inevitable that Nepali women are portrayed through the image of the "Third World" woman as poor, vulnerable, oppressed, exploited, and victimized. One example of this image of Nepali women as collectively deprived, passive, illiterate, and so on can be found in a book written by a Nepali feminist, Prativa Subedi. In her book, Subedi paints a portrait of Nepali women's extreme dependency and oppression:

> From her very birth the girl child is discriminated against, often seen as an unwanted addition that somehow must be tolerated until she can be married off. Her emotional growth is suppressed by values imposed by family and society until she is emptied of her most natural human qualities, a girl without a personality or the capacity to think independently ... so she is dependent on her father as a child, on her husband after marriage, and on her son in her old age ... From the very beginning the qualities of shame, fear, passivity and dependence on others are instilled in girls. (Subedi 1993: 1–3)

Moreover, Subedi's book establishes a stereotyped image by over-emphasizing the connection between Nepali women and multiple stigmatic and deviant phenomena associated with weakness, vulnerability, and victimization. These include: violence against women, trafficking in women, women and AIDS, alcoholism, and more. This construction of the miserable Nepali woman's identity offers an inventory that highlights the extremely problematic position of women in Nepal. For instance, the chapter on women and violence (ibid.: 13–22) includes the following subheadings which accentuate the "many forms" of violence against women: child marriage; polygamy; sexual abuse; trafficking of girls and women; dowry-related violence; alcohol and drug-related violence; abuse within the media; caste-related violence; violations of reproductive rights; unequal pay for equal work; wife battering (ibid.: 14). The list of discriminations relating to women and society include: restrictions on educational opportunities; misrepresentation in the media; family control over women's reproductive power; control over women's mobility; control over parental property; discriminatory religious practices; the discriminatory legal system; economic restrictions (ibid.: 7).

Women are indeed extensively discriminated against in almost all countries, including Nepal, to different extents and in multiple ways. However, portraying women as collectively and homogeneously miserable human beings is unconvincing, misleading and even manipulative.[22]

The validity of data concerning poverty rates has been questioned for some time. A skeptical view of women's poverty rates is suggested, for instance, by Diane Elson (2000) and Janet Henshall Momsen (2002). They argue that although women are often presented as constituting most of the world's poorest, "there is no empirical evidence for this statement" (Momsen 2004: 241). A World Bank research report suggests similarly that: "estimating the number of men and women living in poverty is difficult" because "there is no adequate summary measure of individual welfare that can be compared for males and females. The most commonly used indicator of poverty (or current welfare) is consumption. But most household-based surveys collect consumption data for households, not individuals" (World Bank 2001: 64).

Women's collective image as poor, weak, and exploited is diligently (though legitimately) used to develop a feminist awareness and political agenda.

However, in the context of gendered power structures in developing countries, this image is conveniently employed by agencies that profit from women's alleged collective backwardness. The development and aid industry that is oriented to gender issues provides a conspicuous example of the instrumental use of women's collective underdevelopment for establishing the need for intervention and of the need for so-called help, instruction, and development to be provided by "helpers" and "developers." Marianne Gronemeyer's definition of "helping" is relevant in this context: "It is a means of keeping the bit in the mouths of subordinates without letting them feel the power that is guiding them ... elegant power does not force, it does not resort either to the cudgel or to chains; it helps" (Gronemeyer 1992: 53).

The fact that (some) native feminists adopt the image of women's collective victimization and helplessness legitimizes further foreign researchers', consultants', and practitioners' stereotyped images of local women. Thus, they become part of the process which substantiates the need for organized help from the outside. Reports from the "gender development programme" in the groundwater project by Tovi Fenster (1996) and myself (Hertzog 1997) illustrate the point. For example, Fenster enumerates the "social needs" of women (which, allegedly, call for experts' intervention) in the villages she visited as: "literacy needs; discouraging marriage at a young age; preventing women trafficking; preventing polygamy; preventing male drinking and violence in the family; women's financial dependency; etc." (Fenster 1996: 19).

Moreover, the stigmatized image that emerges from describing Nepali women collectively as weak and as victims erases their individual narratives and turns them into human components of an abstract social collective. Also, presenting marginal phenomenon (although truly horrific) as a dominant characteristic of social life may result in losing sight of the complexity of the overall picture as well as the individual nature of women's (and men's) lives. Sarah Cramer makes a similar point: "Nepali women, like other 'third world women' have been homogenized and stereotyped in order to form a single, manageable idea of female oppression for development to attack ... The 'Nepali woman', as constructed by development discourse, is 'ignorant, poor, uneducated, tradition-bound, domestic, family-oriented, victimized, and sexually constrained' because she is a 'third world woman'" (Cramer 2007: 7).

The stigmatic, homogenized image of Nepali women veils the complex and divergent situations of women in Nepal (at any period). It also diminishes Nepali women's active participation and crucial contribution to social and economic life in Nepal. Thus, Subedi's stereotyped descriptions of Nepali women as vulnerable and powerless are undermined when she discusses women and agriculture (Subedi 1993: 75–86). There she incorporates into the picture the positive, active, and significant role of women in their families and society at large. In this context she maintains that "Nepali women make an important contribution to the agricultural activities of the country" (ibid.: 75), contributing 50 per cent of household income. Moreover, she notes that women are overwhelmingly in charge of the production and utilization of food-grains, and that, "Except for plowing the fields almost every agricultural activity—like preparing the land for cultivation, carrying fertilizer, seed sowing and planting, weeding, harvesting, sorting grains, selecting and drying seeds—are particularly the responsibility of women" (ibid.: 76).

The significant role of women in agricultural activity and their essential contribution to household income cannot be underestimated (see, e.g., Dahl 1987).[23] Clearly this activity entails the dependence of other family members (males included) on women for their sustenance and economic provision. It follows, therefore, that Nepali women, in urban and rural regions, are not (and were not) passive, vulnerable, and powerless individuals.

This conclusion gains support in the light of Shtrii Shakti's (a women's organization) study of the socioeconomic changes in the status of Nepali women between 1981 to 1993 (Shtrii Shakti 1995). This study offers statistical data which indicates both the diversity of women's conditions (in rural compared to urban sites, and in relation to specific economic activities), and the significant role of women in agriculture and the labor market. The significant participation of rural women in economic life in Nepal is revealed, for instance, by the fact that their contribution accounts for 67 per cent of the family farm economy and 41 per cent of the local market economy (ibid.: 62). Women's extensive economic involvement includes self-employment enterprises, especially in the field of tourism, and "income-generating activities that are home-based, such as wool and cotton spinning, carding, twining, embroidery and knitting" (ibid.: 137). Although men predominate in most household expenditure decisions, women are far from being passive participants in their households, as some stereotyped images imply. The findings indicate that "women initiated 44.1% of the time, were consulted 32.1% of the time and made the final decisions 28.8% of the time regarding … gifts, loans, travel, religious and social obligations." Similarly, in selling vegetables and fruit, "women act the role of initiator in 45.3% of the cases, and make the decision on 43.2% of sales alone" (ibid.: 91). Even in capital transactions—such as land, buildings, and large animals—women have an input, albeit to a lesser extent. In all rural sites women are the decision-makers in 31.6 per cent of transactions (ibid.: 93).

However, women's crucial contribution to their households, communities, and the larger society is almost ignored by the male establishment and they are often excluded from development projects. Moreover, my ethnography suggests that foreign development agencies cooperate with the Nepali government in excluding women, in practice, from development projects. Thus, while development projects do not bring about social change or poverty reduction in Nepal, they do foster women's marginalization in public life and in economic activities.

Seira Tamang also points to the embedded cooperation between development agencies and Hindu patriarchal domination. She argues:

> The creation of "the Nepali woman" was as much the work of development agencies in search of "the Nepali woman" to develop as it was the result of the active dissemination of state-sponsored ideology. The patriarchally oppressed, uniformly disadvantaged, Hindu "Nepali woman" as a category did not pre-exist the development project. She had to be constructed by ignoring the heterogeneous forms of community, social relations, and gendered realities of the various peoples inhabiting Nepal. (Tamang 2002: 163)

Shtrii Shakti's study makes clear that development, from the point of view of Nepali women, implied a considerable reduction of control over their lives. The increase in cash cropping made them depend more heavily on men, as men more usually appropriate cash. Male migration for waged or service employment has increased women's workload, and female migration for low-wage employment in export-led markets exposed women to social exploitation. Similar arguments, in the wider context, have been advanced by Clare Oxby (1983), Maria Mies (1986), Vandana Shiva (1986), Janet Momsen (1991), and Sumitra Gurung (1994). They all contend that despite the significant role of women in agriculture, forestry, livestock, and maintaining a balance in land and household labor, development has diminished their position. Mies, Shiva, Momsen, and Gurung also blame development for having harmed local ecologies through soil erosion, landslides, floods, deforestation, and wasting water supplies.

The proceedings of an international anthropological conference, which took place in Kathmandu in 1992, further contradict the stereotyped depiction of Nepali women as passive and backward (see Allen 1994). A section in the book on women and power highlights the richness of Nepali women's lives, their resourcefulness, social networks, and the significant roles they play in various aspects of the economy, as well as in the environmental and cultural spheres, and in the political struggle for democracy. Thus, women in Nepal are described as having complex lives, diverse interests, activities, and skills; some are depicted as outstanding leaders and many others as involved in action for social change, as one might expect to find in any human society.

Essays by Sumitra Gurung (1994) and Julia Thompson (1994) can serve to demonstrate this line of analysis. Gurung's anthropological research on Nepali women from a hill region of Nepal reveals that, in contrast to the stigmatic images of development planners and practitioners, these women are resourceful, knowledgeable, and capable of sustainable cultivation of mountain areas (Gurung 1994: 336–37). Moreover, Gurung points to the fact that it is the formal political systems and "the established male-biased model of development" that have "basically neglected women's work, knowledge and potential capacities in sustaining mountain areas" (ibid.: 337). She blames the government for being responsible for reinforcing the gender discrimination which has detrimentally affected the region's ecology.

In her article on resistance among high-caste Hindu women in Kathmandu, Thompson reveals the ways in which these women resist and "actively construct their relationships with others in reference to existing power relations and social structures" (Thompson 1994: 367) despite religious and traditional constraints on their behavior. As a result of their resistance, Parbatya traditions are beginning to be questioned and even challenged.

Indeed, as we will see presently, the conspicuous role played by women in Nepal's Maoist insurgency (Gautam, Banskota, and Manchanda 2001; Leve 2007) offers further evidence of Nepali women's important role in the country's society, culture, politics, economy, and history.

Nepali Women and the Maoist Insurgency

The second half of the 1990s, the period of my stay in Nepal, coincided with the country's Maoist insurgency. This "people's war," which was launched in February 1996, evolved out of Nepal's incessant poverty, its dependence on foreign aid, and the pervasive corruption of its regime (De Sales 2003; Karki and Seddon 2003; Sharma and Prasain 2004). Continuing poverty and a widening gap between the rural and urban sectors (Justice 1989; Thapa and Sijapati 2004; Whelpton 2005), despite four decades of intensive development (Whelpton 2005),[24] were the background to a growing disillusionment with development interventions, and a resentment of the Nepali government and its extensive dependence on foreign aid (Gellner 2003; Thapa 2003; Hutt 2004; Onesto 2005).

The conspicuous participation of Nepali rural women in the rebellion has been discussed extensively.[25] About one-third of all foot soldiers in Maoist strongholds were women. They occupied positions of leadership throughout the Maoist hierarchy, participated actively in village defense groups, and worked as couriers and guides (Leve 2007). According to Gautam, Banskota, and Manchanda (2001), groups of women were involved in guerilla activities. This phenomenon offers an opportunity to examine one of the main issues that this book discusses: the impact of gender development projects, literacy programs in particular, on women's empowerment and on changing gendered power relations.

Some studies suggest that rural women's intense involvement in the dramatic events of the insurgency, contrary to the "traditional" image of their passivity, emerged from their participation in literacy projects. These contributed, whether directly or indirectly, to rural women's motivation to rebel and to set out to change the gendered power division. Gautam, Banskota, and Manchanda (2001) argue, for instance, that development projects, literacy programs in particular, affected women's awareness of their exploitation and discrimination, and served to develop their solidarity.

Defying the growing body of critique that perceives development (in its general and gender-specific forms) as a failure, destructive, violent, and so on, Manchanda (1999) maintains that development has succeeded in rural Nepal. She elaborates on the enormous impact of literacy programs, which have stimulated social networking and collaboration, and suggests that the active support of women in the Gorkha district—a Maoist stronghold—reflects the success of two decades of development work. Gautam, Banskota, and Manchanda further argue that adult women's literacy programs, such as the ones run by an American INGO, had a far-reaching impact on women's presence among the rebels:

> Ironically, it is the success of the adult literacy campaign which has paved the way for women to become active in the public life of the community, for girls to go to schools and for girls politicized in school to be drawn into the armed struggle ... Literacy campaigns ... designed to promote the empowerment of women inadvertently encouraged many conscientised young women to choose subsequent empowerment through armed struggle. (Gautam, Banskota, and Manchanda 2001, cited in Leve 2007: 130)

This argument gains support from various studies that describe the significant influence of literacy programs on nurturing networking, gender consciousness, and so forth, despite the fact that literacy programs have had very limited achievements in terms of their original aims.[26] Thus, Anna Robinson-Pant found that participants have succeeded in transforming the literacy intervention "in spite of, rather than in support of ... project objectives" (Robinson-Pant 2004a: 5).

The implications of literacy courses in terms of unintended social success have been reported by Nelly Stromquist (1994) and Ila Patel and Anita Dighe (1997). Stromquist's study showed that literacy classes in the slums of São Paolo unintentionally offered women participants an opportunity to meet together as a group who were subjected to similar constraints and experiences of poverty and subordination. Following Stromquist, Patel and Dighe suggest that "literacy classes provide an opportunity to a large number of women learners and volunteers to meet, to talk and to share, and break their isolation which is socially structured into their lives" (Patel and Dighe 2003: 223). Dighe's study of a literacy campaign in south Delhi showed that women's literacy classes "provided women learners with a social space, away from home and offered them an opportunity to meet in a group to share their common experiences about work, family, and illness" (Dighe 1995). Gillian Attwood, Jane Castle and Suzanne Smythe (2004), Sujata Khandekar (2004), and Juliet Millican (2004) also stress the social gains, defined as "new spaces," embedded in women's literacy gatherings. This sanctuary provides women with a protected and supportive framework to discuss issues that normally are not addressed in public. Lauren Leve, who interviewed women in Chorigaon in the mid 1990s, and then five and ten years after the conclusion of a literacy program, suggests that, similar to many other literacy courses in Nepal, the effects on the graduates were to encourage "greater confidence and increased self-esteem, less shyness interacting with people outside of the family, and an expanded experience of women's ability to succeed in traditionally male public and intellectual domains. Overall, participants testified to a profound sense of individual and collective transformation" (Leve 2007: 143).

These findings correspond with my observations during meetings with women in Nepali villages. The participants clearly enjoyed the meetings (as described in Chapter 4). They attended them despite the distrust they often expressed in relation to our proposed project. Yet, the empowerment which the women derived from the meetings was clearly revealed even before any of the literacy classes (or vocational training) started. Thus, I contend that the social outcomes of the interactions which took place in the villages were not those intended by the engineers of our development project, but emerged rather as "side effects" (Ferguson 1990: 252), similar to the familiar impact of women's or other organized group activities. The social interactions that evolved from the groups' meetings in the irrigation project's area, which I visited, provided women with a sort of substitute for men's organized economic and political activity— meetings concerning deep tube wells, for instance—through which they produced a form of women's "clubs"—or "social sanction," as defined by Patel and Dighe (1997).[27]

However, this outcome had very little to do with the original aim of advancing women's literacy and economic power and it certainly cannot be considered as the gender development project's success but rather as a coincidental, unintentional outcome (cf. Pigg 1992; Grillo and Stirrat 1997; Leve 2007). Furthermore, developing women's separate frameworks and activities is typically encouraged by dominant patriarchal agencies that ensure women's cooperation and compliance by compensating them with non-formal (inferior) power, at a distance from formal power centers. This understanding corresponds with studies like that of Chatty and Rabbo (1997). Elaborating on women's formal and informal organized groups in the Middle East, they suggest that "where the individual voice is insignificant, where associations that cut across kin groups and tribes are feared" (ibid.: 18), independent women's groups pose a threat to existing institutions. Thus, the strict control over (male and female) organized groups permits only those activities that fit traditional gender roles. Patel and Dighe (2003) argue more generally that as the patriarchal state represents the interests of dominant groups it does not tolerate any collectivization of women's strength.

Thus, I suggest that the massive participation of Nepali women in the Maoist insurgency is better explained by the Nepali government's neglect of rural women's needs and by the Maoists' commitment to support women's equality. I argue, therefore, that although literacy programs could have contributed to women's empowerment and, indirectly, to their massive participation in the Maoist insurgency, they cannot provide an unequivocal nor a major explanation for this phenomenon.

Power, Poverty and Women's Illiteracy in Nepal

Literacy is widely perceived and described by development theoreticians and practitioners as a crucial means for setting in motion social change, and eradicating poverty in particular. The embedded connection between power, poverty, and education has been thoroughly discussed by scholars like Paulo Freire (1971), Samuel Bowles and Herbert Gintis (1976, 2001), and Arnold Louis (1979). In a World Bank position paper, Helen Abadzi (1996) recounts that between 1963 and 1985 many countries introduced literacy campaigns with the help of international organizations and the World Bank. This evolved from the widely accepted belief that "if the illiterate poor learned to read they would have access to information that would improve their lives" (ibid.: 1). Ila Patel and Anita Dighe similarly argued in the late 1990s that: "Illiteracy is typically the plight of poor and powerless people. Illiteracy is essentially a manifestation of social inequality, the unequal distribution of power and resources in society" (Patel and Dighe 2003: 221). Elaborating on the gaps of literacy rates between men and women, they argue that poor women, rural women in particular, face physical and patriarchal constraints in terms of the time and space allocated for, and societal expectations from, education.

Hence, the discourse concerning illiteracy plays a conspicuous role in development projects aiming at social, economic, and political change. Women's basic education—including writing, reading, and numeracy—acquires an additional emphasis. In their "feminine" roles, women are perceived as playing a dominant role in bottom-up processes and as having a great deal of influence on their family members, their communities, and consequently on society as a whole. Therefore, women's education (namely their literacy) is conceived of as a key factor in development projects.

Often presented in international aid organizations' documents as one of the poorest and most underdeveloped countries in the world (in terms of income, health, education, and so on), Nepal seems to exhibit a correlation between poverty, the need to develop its population, the need to advance and empower women, and literacy provided by aid agencies.

The literature on literacy in developing countries often focuses on the necessary and suitable concepts, methods, and training devices that will guarantee wished-for changes (see Patel 1991; Dighe 1995; Misra, Ghose, and Bhog 1994; Rogers, Patkar, and Saraswathi 2004).[28] It is also engaged in discussions about the success and/or failure of literacy campaigns (Manchanda 1999; Ahearn 2004; Leve 2007). Yet another perspective, brought up by some studies, discusses literacy programs as part of neocolonialist interventions in developing countries (e.g., Luke 2003; Lankshear and Knobel 2006; Wickens and Sandlin 2007).

I follow the latter orientation, and Frank Youngman's argument that literacy programs and the aid that sustains them serve to reproduce the class, gender, and ethnic inequalities within society and to legitimate capitalist development (Youngman 2000).[29]

Drawing on examples from a gender development project in rural Nepal, I will point to everyday gendered power encounters, in which the rhetoric concerning the significance of literacy serves high-ranking male officials as a means of concealing the seizure of resources intended for women's purposes. Thus, I will expand on how the documented discourse (on the importance of women's literacy) served the World Bank and Nepali governmental agencies as a smokescreen while taking control over budgets intended for the benefit of women, which eventually served both organizations in various ways. That is to say, an organizational political game was played in which the social, idealistic rhetoric served powerful players to materialize their interests while presenting themselves as virtuous agents who supported women's empowerment, and who served society as a whole through women.

The role of literacy in development projects aimed at women's empowerment and, through them, at the advancement of wider social goals, was revealed in the Nepali context in a large-scale development project, named USAID-Nepal, which was implemented in the mid 1990s. This program enrolled over 100,000 women in six- or nine-month-long literacy courses in one year alone (see Leve 2007: 140). The project document explained that: "the promotion of democracy through women's empowerment is a USAID objective in Nepal. For democracy to be effective at the local level, women must meet their basic needs and the needs of their families ... To organize the family through women's empowerment is to organize society, and to democratize the family is to democratize society" (cited in ibid.: 140). USAID-Nepal explained that literacy programs constitute the starting point for providing women with access to productive resources which will improve their choices. Thus, literacy programs were said to facilitate women's chances to "take jobs which they could not get while illiterate, thereby bringing more income into the household to support their families; they feel more confident to participate in community advocacy and user groups" (ibid.: 140).

However, my ethnography adds weight to doubts that have been raised with regard to the alleged "efficiency" and necessity of literacy projects (sometimes called "adult education"). For instance, even a World Bank position paper (Abadzi 1996) supports these doubts. Its author, claims that, "adult literacy programs have yielded disappointing results worldwide. They generally fail to teach stable literacy skills to the intended beneficiaries" (ibid.: 1). Similar misgivings have been raised by Anna Robinson-Pant, who asks the provocative question: "Are literate women healthier, wealthier and even wiser than illiterate women?" (Robinson-Pant 2004a: 1). She points to the high drop-out rates from these programs, which imply that the assumed link between women's literacy and development can be disputed. Drawing on her ethnography, Robinson-Pant suggests that poor village women have developed the confidence and strategies necessary to survive without literacy, and that those who attended literacy classes, "challenged the assumptions of planners and trainers" (ibid.: 4). Moreover, she argues that the evidence contained in her volume counters the "conventional passive stereotype—a woman who lacks the necessary skills to avoid being cheated or dominated by men, educated or otherwise" (ibid.: 12). Thus, for instance, Brian Street's article on three active, respected, and powerful women from Morocco, Mexico, and South Africa, illustrates how various literacy programs perceive and treat them as "illiterate" and consequently marginalize and deny their local experience (Street 2004). Many of the women from developing countries, depicted in Robinson-Pant's book, are "confident" and "empowered", women who had become active "in public and community activities without 'literacy'" (Robinson-Pant 2004a: 12). Nelly Stromquist (1990) further argues that the gendered, stereotyped messages that are embedded in most literacy programs reinforce values and attitudes that cause women to accept prevailing gender relations rather than question them.

The women in the villages that I visited did not seem to require literacy courses. They were assertive, vital, and socially involved, and they contributed significantly to their families' and communities' economy. Some of them had participated in literacy courses in the past but nothing that was said by these women could support any claim concerning the contribution of these courses to improving their own or their families' lives.

The fact that the development project was ultimately perceived and treated mainly as a literacy program (from which economic activities would proceed), and that eventually even this shrunken format of the gender development project was not implemented (except for a few classes that were used as a showcase for the World Bank, in which all parties cooperated), clearly demonstrates the arguments presented above. It shows that projects aimed at women's empowerment and development do not stand a real chance when stemming from, initiated by, or imposed by a male dominated, patriarchal agent or regime. Rather, they are channeled into the prevailing gendered power structure, to the point of being fully incorporated into it. As the gender rhetoric is so widely embedded in organizational documents—those of the World Bank and Unesco are the most conspicuous examples—and in public discourse, the claim about women's need for literacy skills is easy to "sell" to donating agencies; in Jenny Horsman's words, it is "easier to advocate than other solutions" (Horsman 1996: 65). Moreover, literacy can be portrayed as being moral and just; it is convenient to present (because it is quantifiable); cheap to organize (using volunteers or grassroots trainers); as well as easy to cancel (women do not have the political power to protest).

Being comprised mainly of women, literacy classes can contribute to networking and to gaining other advantages embedded in group formations (as suggested above), but at the same time they can also serve agents and agencies searching for personal and organizational benefits. Women's predominance in literacy classes creates an appeal for organizations that seek to get hold of organized, controlled groups. Due to their collective accessibility and obedient upbringing, women inadvertently provide a convenient target for realizing various interests—among which are "field-banks" offering credit, and NGOs offering training in literacy skills.

Claiming that women, poor village women in particular, collectively require literacy, constructs them in a common generalized image as "uneducated," "underdeveloped," "backward," and "primitive" people in need of help, instruction, and education. Associating the need for women's literacy with their feminine roles, a connection that underpins all "literacy" approaches, serves to justify further the claim of the self-evident need for literacy interventions. Nelly Stromquist (1990) argues in this vein, pointing out that most literacy programs are designed along sexually stereotyped lines that emphasize women's roles as mothers, wives, and household managers. The unequivocal link made between women's literacy and women's roles as a central axis in social change processes is determined in a Unesco document as follows: "The priority attention given to women's literacy is justified not only by the gravity and extent of their inferior position, but also by recognition of the responsibilities they have for the survival and well-being of their children and the key role they play in transmitting knowledge to upcoming generations" (Unesco 1988: 2). My data suggests that the 1970s approach to women's literacy, which perceived their reproductive role as the basis of literacy programs, and thus focused on child health, family planning, hygiene, and nutrition, did not change much, in practice, by the mid 1990s.

Thus, the claim about women's illiteracy is employed to establish and justify the need for development agencies' involvement with women, allegedly for their own and their children's sake. In practice, the access gained through women to their families, communities, and country, serves the agencies' interests rather than the women's and their families'.

Patel and Dighe (2003) argue that literacy classes that aim at empowering women pose a threat to those who benefit from women's unpaid work and docility. My analysis suggests that the men who headed the gender activities program in rural Nepal were not worried about women's empowerment, but were rather interested in taking control of the budgets intended for them. The organizations' control over the budget was solid and stable and no women's program could threaten it.

The women's development project in rural Nepal, namely the literacy program, did not materialize, and within three years of its inception it became a "phantom" project from the village women's perspective, a fullfilment of a dream to travel overseas for Nepali officials, a temporary nuisance for the Israeli irrigation company (and a source of small profit), an opportunity to display its commitment to women's empowerment for the World Bank, and a frustrating but exciting experience (traveling overseas) for me.

In this book I shall describe and discuss the inconsistency between the rhetoric and reality of gender development programs in rural Nepal. I shall suggest that although women's contribution to economic growth at the national level, and to the sustenance of their households at a local one, is formally recognized, in practice it is ignored and underestimated by the men who hold most of the planning and executive positions. I shall examine what happens in reality when development projects are planned and resources allocated for the benefit of women. Drawing on my field data I shall argue that as the situation at all decision-making and implementation levels is controlled by men, the gender programs are transformed and absorbed into the male structure to serve men in positions of power (and a few women, like myself—a "gender consultant" to those men). I shall attempt to show that even projects, which are couched in the most articulate feminist rhetoric stand little chance of benefiting women.

Programs like the one I worked for do not promote women's literacy, do not serve to improve their economic resources and their means of income generation, nor do they develop women's access to credit and other economic resources. The resources that are meant to be allocated to women's activities are eventually turned by Western agencies into resources for bargaining, "buying off" the male heads of the regime, and promoting their own interests. Therefore, those resources contribute to strengthening the ruling elite, fomenting corruption, and expanding Western male patronization.

Methodology

This book was born out of my experience as both a gender consultant on, and critical observer of, a gender development scheme in rural Nepal in the summer of 1997. This scheme was planned to run from 1996 till 1998, as part of an irrigation project in the Lumbini region of Nepal, which had been in operation since the beginning of the 1980s. I was hired by Tahal Consulting Engineers Company, Israeli irrigation specialists, which worked for the Nepali government. The book is based mainly on ethnographic work, most of which was documented in my fieldnotes following encounters with women in the villages, meetings with officials in offices, and socializing with many people of divergent rank and affiliations. I also used documents, especially my Israeli predecessors' and my own reports and project proposals. The analysis developed gradually over some ten years, affected by family and work commitments,

During my stay in Nepal I lived in Bhairahawa (also known as Sidhartha Nagar), where the irrigation project's offices were located. Being located near the far western border with India, about 260 km west of Kathmandu, the city plays an important role in the import and export business.[30] Leon, Tahal's representative, and I shared a two-story house, the bachelors' house. Leon was in charge of the irrigation project in its last phase, shortly before transferring full responsibility over the project to local experts and managers. Spending a great deal of time with Leon, more than with any other person in the field, my relationship with him was extremely complex. Our conversations went on during common meals at the bachelors' house, while walking or being driven together to the project center, at his office at the center, and in various social events. These conversations related to any possible subject: the project's difficulties, the Nepali partners, Nepal's situation, feminism, personal histories, family stories, and so on. Our encounters offered me invaluable food for thought about issues like patronizing conduct, gendered discrimination, corruption, friendship and loyalty, and many other things, in down to earth terms.

While staying in Bhairahawa, I worked closely with Anita, the local gender consultant, who was also hired by Tahal. Pursuing a professional career, Anita left her husband and two small children behind in Kathmandu, where they were taken care of by her in-laws. She visited them every second or third weekend. The two of us travelled to the villages together, discussed the plans and the budget down to their details, including their wording. Anita and I met together with senior officials in the irrigation project's offices and in other offices in town. The two of us travelled to the capital, where we met with the Minister of Informal Education in Kathmandu and with a few heads of women's and international NGOs. We also visited Anita's in-laws' home and met with her husband and children. Sometimes we would go to local restaurants, chatting and enjoying ourselves over local food. Thus, my friendship with Anita grew deeper over time and her company provided me with comfort, amusement, and many refreshing insights.

Although I was the expatriate expert, had a degree and a richer and longer experience in feminist and academic work, Anita was, naturally, much more familiar with the relevant aspects of Nepali culture, language, and life in general. Moreover, Anita was a postgraduate economist who was familiar with development projects and women's NGOs. This situation made clear to me, in a very personal and bothersome way, that in the context of development projects, the not very relevant skills of expatriate experts (like myself) are preferred to those of the local professionals.

Together with several female fieldworkers (called Women's Groups Organizers, WGOs), Anita and I visited dozens of villages in the irrigation project area, talking to the women, listening to them, and suggesting that they join the women's program of literacy classes and vocational training. These meetings with village women took place in the nearby fields. At each meeting, some thirty to forty women and some children would sit on the ground around us, the project people. Much of my field data was collected during these visits to rural villages, and was written down sometimes during the meetings, while Anita and the WGOs were talking with the women, or more often at nights in my room at the bachelors' house. As Anita was fluent in English, and I did not speak Nepali, she acted as interpreter between myself and the village women and WGOs. The WGOs were recruited from villages in the project region and did not speak English. Some of the male officials involved in the project joined us occasionally. The project's jeep, with which we travelled to the villages, turned out to be a tiny crowded space in which we all sweated and socialized. Often, we used to stop on the way back to the office for refreshments, discussing our experiences of the day's meetings and enjoying small talk.

Becoming part of the office staff afforded me countless opportunities of interacting with people who worked on the project premises. Among these were the senior officials: the Nepali project manager and the local consultant on farmers' participation, heads of departments (engineering, agriculture, the farmers' organization), and the junior staff of secretaries and maintenance people. All of the staff members, except for the group who worked for the women's project, were men. The project's building was a two-story house, yellowish on the outside and grey on the inside. It was fitted out with some old furniture and decorated with faded posters. The building's roof was used for social events, such as farewell parties. One of the most conspicuous aspects of daily life in the project's premises was frequent power cuts. This was an irritating experience as the air conditioning stopped working, and the heat and humidity were unbearable. Soon after a power cut began, the noisy generator would start up.

Anita and I organized a training workshop ("seminar") for some ten village teachers, which took place, on nine consecutive days, at the project's center. The daily encounters in and around the seminar added stimulating material to the accumulating data. Our ongoing bargaining with the Israeli and Nepali officials of the project, with the director of the local branch of the Ministry of Education, and others, along with interviews with the seminar teachers, and many interactions with candidates for teaching posts in the villages, were documented and contributed many episodes that enriched the ethnography.

I also became familiar with the ex-pat development community in Nepal during my visit to Kathmandu, where I was hosted by Hanna, Leon's wife, in their home. Hanna took me to a typical "colonial tea party," organized by and for European development workers' wives. This experience provided me with the opportunity of observing the foreign women's style of life and their socializing habits.

In the process of analyzing my data I made extensive use of documents, especially the reports and project proposals prepared by my Israeli predecessor and myself, and which were submitted to Tahal (our Israeli employer), the Nepali government (the Ministry of Agriculture), and the World Bank. I also looked at correspondence between officials, such as Leon's letters to his superiors in Israel, to the Nepali director of the project and his superiors in government, and his letters to World Bank officials and their letters to him.

Photographs taken during my stay—of visits to the villages and interactions with the women; of events I attended; of the streets of Bhairahawa and other places I visited with Anita, the WGOs, and Leon; of offices and meetings with officials—served me as another unintended source for reflection. While in the field I did not realize the impact of this activity on people who attended the situation. It was only much later, when I elaborated on my fieldnotes, that I was able to notice the latent impact of watching people through the camera lances.

I started my study of the women's empowerment project in rural Nepal in almost total ignorance of development and women in the country. The only information I had when Tahal hired me to work for them as a gender consultant was a report that my predecessor had prepared (Fenster 1996). However, although I took this mission upon myself knowing nearly nothing about the place and the professional assignment, as a feminist activist who had studied and taught feminism for many years I was familiar with the feminist literature and with gender development projects. Moreover, having conducted fieldwork in a bureaucratic setting, focused on immigrants from Ethiopia who were treated as Third World migrants, I considered this as a relevant experience for working on a development project. Thus, I was both open to new landscapes and social realities, and at the same time biased with regard to the country and its people, and particularly with regard to women of the Third World and to the supposedly dangerous and poor place Nepal was. I set out as a deeply motivated and idealist feminist, albeit one unaware of the literature concerning the relevant issues, and indeed unfamiliar with any critical studies of development and gender and development.

Although an unintended outcome, this mission offered me a profound lesson of how one becomes a part of organizational life. The compelling and ongoing necessity of making rational compromises between personal, human inclinations and organizational dictates, between adhering to idealistic values and pursuing personal desires, is unavoidable for any person involved in an organization, even a very socially aware researcher. Being absorbed into organizational webs and becoming part of a system, the researcher, like any employee in an organization, adopts willingly or unwillingly its norms, exchanges, and networking techniques. Hence, while in the field, the researcher plays a "dual role of investigator and instrument" of "research tools," as C.W. Watson (1999: 4) suggests. Watson contends that "we rarely step outside ourselves in order to reflect on how our own life-histories are contributing to the perspectives we are accumulating; the reflexivity, if it comes, usually comes later when, self-consciously practicing our profession, we write our ethnographies" (ibid.: 4). Fieldwork is, so it seems, "a work of human engagement" (Ferrell and Hamm 1998: xvii). Thus, my personal involvement as a participant developer offered me an opportunity to observe and reflect on personal and social processes from the "inside" of the organization.

Whereas documenting my daily experiences in my notebook began as a kind of anthropologist's common practice, entering the phase of analyzing the material turned out to be a very slow and complex process. Leaving behind the approach of the adventurer, tourist, and/or fieldworker and assuming routine life entailed engaging again with family commitments, teaching, feminist and social activity, and the like. This transition made it too difficult to proceed with the analysis of the ethnography. Thus, the analysis developed gradually over the course of over ten years, away from home and during academic vacations. Cris Shore's argument (Shore 1999: 26), followed by Eyal Ben-Ari (n.d.), is relevant to this kind of developing analysis. As Ben-Ari points out, "understanding fieldwork implies a range of issues spanning a much longer period than the one actually spent in the field" (ibid.). In a similar vein I suggest that the distance of time and place allows the "interpretative dialogue which goes on within each anthropologist" (ibid.) to create the emotional distance needed for reflection and the re-examination of arguments.

As a visiting researcher at Oxford in the summer of 2000, in a most stimulating intellectual environment, I was able not only to work comfortably on my ethnography but also to acquaint myself with the rich literature that was easily accessible in Oxford's libraries, exposing me to some exciting critical studies of development in the "Third World". World Bank documents I found there provided me with evidence for the critique expressed in neocolonialist and feminist literature. In the summer of 2002, I continued working on the analysis in Manchester, where I came across some further literature on development. The next time I was able to devote myself to reflection was in Brussells, in summer 2005. There I elaborated further on some feminist literature relating to development discourse. I was privileged in obtaining access to Vienna University's libraries in the summer of 2007, where I discovered numerous academic resources on development, gender and literacy, and on Nepal's recent history. Visiting the sociology department of Delhi University in 2008, I came across further literature on development, gender and literacy, in South Asia.

Realizing that my analysis was going to involve me looking at bureaucracy and power structures, I eventually discovered a most significant resource in the library of Beit Berl Academic College in Israel, my professional home. In this final phase of writing I found myself returning to the theme of bureaucracy, with which I had dealt in my study on the treatment of Ethiopian immigrants in Israel during the 1980s. I rediscovered some older literature on bureaucracy from the mid 1950s, such as that of Max Weber and C. Wright Mills, and from the 1980s and 1990s, such as that of Emanuel Marx, Robert Chambers, and James Ferguson. While developing my arguments concerning the gendered components of the development industry I returned to Kathy Ferguson's work on gender and bureaucracy from the beginning of the 1990s and found it inspiring and still relevant.

The basic dilemmas of fieldwork concerning the objectivity and subjectivity of the field researcher, their proximity to or essential distance from their research subjects, the extent of their involvement in the studied society, and the implications of personal exposure, have been pertinent to anthropological research since its inception. Max Weber's approach is most instructive in this context. Weber (1978) used the term *verstehen* ("understanding") to denote a process of subjective interpretation on the part of the social researcher. He argued that, "for a science which is concerned with the subjective meaning of action, explanation requires a grasp of the complex of meaning in which an actual course of understandable action thus interpreted belongs" (ibid.: 9). Moreover, "the interpretive understanding of social action … empathic or appreciative accuracy is attained when, through sympathetic participation, we can adequately grasp the emotional context in which the action took place" (ibid.: 5).

Over the years this approach has gained much support from anthropologists, such as Max Gluckman (1967) and Emanuel Marx (1985), who insisted on the full involvement of the researcher within the social context being studied. Marx stated categorically that "there are no limitations on researcher's and studied people's closeness," and claimed unequivocally that "the closer the researcher gets to the people he studies the more he will learn about them … the anthropologist lives a full life in the field of his study … In this manner he studies himself as part of the wider social context" (ibid.: 139–40). The advantages of researchers' closeness to their researched subjects is well illustrated by studies like that of Marie-Benedicte Dembour (2000). The intimacy that emerged while talking with retired officers who served in the Belgian Congo, but who had left it many years earlier (in 1960), affected her profoundly; so much so, that she was able to question her preconceived beliefs about their evilness and colonialism at large. Eyal Ben-Ari's account of his own conduct as an Israeli soldier in the occupied territories, contrary to his political beliefs, provides another example in the context of militaristic settings (Ben-Ari 1989).

Similarly, being part of a bureaucratic system, playing the roles of a bureaucrat and a consultant myself and reflecting on it from a researcher's position, opened up for me a unique opportunity to question some self-evident beliefs, such as understanding how easily we employ expressions about corrupting power and domineering manners, considering ourselves unattached from and untainted by such negative conduct. This personal involvement enabled me to reveal the powerful sweeping impact of the settings I was part of. I realized how the bureaucratic machine absorbs us and forces us to comply with moral norms that we conveniently denounce when uninvolved with and estranged from the situation.

Ruth Behar's approach to anthropology, which rejects the separation between forms of knowing, between ethnography and autobiography, takes Weber's concept even further. She challenges "reigning paradigms" in scholarly fields that "have traditionally called for distance, objectivity and abstraction" and for which "the worst sin was to be 'too personal'" (Behar 1996: 12–13). Defending[31] "the kind of anthropology that matters" to her from the "surprisingly ruthless criticism of the humanists" Behar claims that "anthropology that doesn't break your heart just isn't worth doing anymore" (ibid: 164). Moved by Renato Rosaldo's ("Grief and A Headhunter's Rage", 1989) "classical work of vulnerable writing" (ibid: 167), Behar urges anthropologists to write vulnerably. That is, to make one's emotions part of one's ethnography and distrust one's own ethnographic authority, as "being constantly in question, constantly on the point of breaking down" (ibid: 21). In short, she advocates "mixing the personal and the ethnographic" (ibid: 22). Writing vulnerably is to "open a Pandora's box" (ibid.: 19), and consequently "new stories" will rush "to be told … stories that tell truths we once hid, truths we didn't dare acknowledge, truths that shamed us" (ibid.: 33).

This challenging of methodological philosophy gains much support from volume edited by Ferrell and Hamm (1998). Taking the personal involvement of the researcher in their subjects' lives even further, the volume's contributors advocate a radical approach to doing fieldwork in the context of crime and deviance. In their introduction, Ferrell and Hamm demand that the researcher should "be willing to abandon in part the security of pre-existing personal and professional identities" (ibid.: 8). Drawing on Michel Foucault's description of confession as "one of the main rituals we rely on for the production of truth" (Foucault 1990: 58), they argue that "'true confessions' of field workers' identities and involvements serve more than academic self-indulgence; they serve as essential components in any full accounting of field research knowledge" (Ferrell and Hamm 1998: 12). Field researchers' confessions are, according to Ferrell and Hamm "an emerging ritual designed to flesh out the fieldwork experience and to produce situated understandings of ... field research findings previously submerged under mythologies of researcher objectivity and distance" (ibid.: 12). There is indeed the risk that these "'confessional ethnographies' and 'ethnographies of ethnography' which are as attentive to researchers' identities, experiences, and emotions as they are to others' ... become accounts of little but ourselves" (ibid.: 12). Thus, Ferrell and Hamm propose that if we balance "reflexivity with scholarly responsibility" we may find that, "in paying attention to ourselves, we are better able to pay attention to others as well" (ibid.: 12). Field research, they argue, should be dismantled "of dualistic epistemic hierarchies which position the researcher over and apart from research subjects, abstract analysis over and beyond situated knowledge, sanitary intellect over and outside human emotion and experience" (ibid.: 14).

The analysis of my ethnography follows the research approach discussed above and derives support from it. I assumed "no limits" with regard to being involved and "merged" in the "field" and no "conceptual barriers" between myself and any "studied subjects." I was one of the officials in the development project, a tourist, a friend, a feminist, as well as many other identities while in Nepal. I tried and hope that I succeeded in examining my own conduct with as much rigor as I used for any other "informant." Thus, I concur with Laura Nader, that "pushing the boundaries is what anthropologists do if they are not trapped in ... hegemonic paradigms" (Nader 2002: 22), and I follow Ruth Behar's recommendation that "what happens within the observer must be made known" (Behar 1996: 6).

Analyzing the fieldnotes, documents, pictures, and the rest of my data brought up several intriguing theoretical themes and personal understandings. One central theme relates to patronizing conduct, which emerged from numerous incidents documented in my fieldnotes, especially with regard to Leon's patronizing and even humiliating attitude to the house and office staff, and to me as well. While analyzing the ethnography I came to realize that patronizing conduct emerges from the situation and position one is embedded in rather than from one's "personality." I realized that once one is positioned in an organizational hierarchy one adopts or complies with its conventions, expectations, dictates, and privileges. Even a skilled and experienced ethnographer would find that "in the field the professional and the personal are fused and we unconsciously engage in the process of making sense by assimilating" (Watson 1999: 4).

The bureaucratic phenomenon was another theme that gained some intriguing insights from reflecting on my documented daily encounters with the irrigation project's personnel. These opened up to me numerous occasions for observing and experiencing hierarchical relationships, the gendered line of command, and the organization's culture, constraints, norms, and so on. I followed and sometimes was involved in producing hidden and overt tensions, in social rituals of regaining human closeness and mutual support. The encounters depicted in my notebooks provided me with numerous illustrations of the nature and development of structured social distance and power relations between local people and foreigners, men and women, people of stratified ranks and so forth, in the bureaucratic context. These encounters also enabled me to reflect on situations and actions that seemed temporarily to crack social barriers, and to dwell on social mechanisms which serve to compensate for compliance, obedience, humiliation, discrimination, subordination, and the like, embedded in structured power gaps, which typically characterize bureaucratic structures. Consequently I learned how people strive and partially succeed in retaining some personal dignity and human solidarity, overcoming the destructive impact of Weber's dehumanizing "bureaucratic machine" (Weber 1978: liii).

Delving into the ethnography brought up the multifaceted subject of development with regard to neocolonialism, gender, social stratification, and education. My documented encounters with officials at most levels of local and international agencies' hierarchies, and in governmental and non-governmental organizations, contributed to my understanding of the specifics and the more general implications of development. They highlighted the subtle mechanisms and manipulative strategies of foreign agencies' intervention in Nepal's economic, educational, and cultural systems. Episodes that I described after they took place, such as the "tea party" and the "seminar," contributed illuminating illustrations of the intersection between gendered conduct and roles, and social stratification and neocolonialism. It is the uncountable accumulated details that were observed in daily encounters, written down in my fieldnotes and later intertwined in the analysis, that tell the concrete story of why development does not and cannot help developing countries and does not empower women there.

Examining the gender development project's documents—the reports and the project proposals—led to many intriguing insights with regard to the "real" picture behind the formal façade of the irrigation project and the women's program in particular. Among these are: the manipulative use of the gender and development jargon; the deceptive use of the budget (included in the women's program proposal); the tricky interchange between "social" and "economic" allocations of budgets; the invisible evaporation of budgets formally intended for women's empowerment; the illusive techniques of cheating women villagers, and the female employees and trainees of the gender activities project; and the channeling of gender consultants into full compliance with the maneuvers of the irrigation project's senior officials with regard to the women's program's budget. All these and more were exposed by digging into the numbers and wording of the documents. Thus, I follow Harold Garfinkel's argument, with regard to the latent value of documents: "the manner in which they [documents] report their consequences and the use to which they are put are all inseparable characteristics of the social order which they describe" (Garfinkel 1967: 201).

It was only at a much later stage of the analysis that I came to realize the meaning of "taking photos" in the context of "exotic" Nepali villages and daily life. Looking at and reflecting on the hundreds of pictures I took brought into focus, sometimes painfully, the banality and ethnocentrism of my view of things as a foreigner and tourist.[32] However, the pictures I took served me unintentionally in several ways. They refreshed my memory regarding forgotten experiences, conversations, situations, sights, and smells. They provided me with many visual illustrations (such as sitting arrangements) of the power gaps embedded in the contexts which I was involved in. Jay Ruby claims that "photographs are always concerned with two things—the culture of those filmed and the culture of those who film" (Ruby 1996: 1345). The photographs I took say as much, if not more, about my own cultural assumptions and the latent stereotypical ideas I held about the places I visited and people I met, than they do about Nepali culture and ways of life.

Indeed, this book does not offer an inclusive discussion of women, gender, and development projects. It is an attempt "to make a contribution to 'the ethnographic record' as 'the central shared heritage of anthropology'" (Adam Kuper, cited in Hirsch and Gellner 2001: 10). The book offers one more example of the pursuit of understanding human conduct in the context of development and bureaucratic organizations. It attempts to contribute to the study of what Nader calls "the culture of power" (Nader 1972, 1997); that is, how the distancing and manipulative mechanisms of hierarchies operate, how they remain invisible, and how cultural constraints are experienced by individuals in organizations. It is also an attempt to contribute to organizational ethnography in relation to women's experience in bureaucratic settings. Hence, the book focuses on officials, organizational processes, power structures, and gendered power relations in the context of an irrigation project in rural Nepal and its sociopolitical surroundings.

Notes

1. The concept of "development" is widely associated with terms such as evolution and socioeconomic change. However, scholars identify Harry S. Truman's presidential inauguration speech of 20 January 1949, in which he referred to the southern hemisphere as "underdeveloped areas," as the historical moment at which the concept was first used to signify gaps between rich, Western countries and poor, non-Western countries—later opposed as

North and South—as well as the efforts to bridge these gaps. Wolfgang Sachs argues that this declaration inaugurated "the age of development," in which the label "provided the cognitive base for both arrogant interventionism from the North and pathetic self-pity in the South" (Sachs 1992: 2). Moreover, he argues that following the breakdown of the European colonial powers, the United States has led relations between North and South, based on the concept of "development" as "that mixture of generosity, bribery and oppression which has characterized the policies toward the South" (ibid.: 1). Arturo Escobar (1995) attributes the emergence of "development" to the "discovery" of "poverty" in Asia, Africa, and Latin America in the era after the Second World War.

2. Hayter has studied the World Bank since the 1960s and published a critique of the World Bank and the International Monetary Fund (Hayter 1971). Hayter writes that initially she believed that "the real purpose of foreign aid was to improve the situation of poor people in developing countries" (ibid.: 88). Hayter's report on the World Bank in Latin America was censored by the Overseas Development Institute (ODI), which previously employed her. The ODI's council consists largely of representatives of the British companies providing money. According to Hayter, although the ODI "claims to be 'an independent non-government body aiming to ensure wise action in the field of overseas development'" (ibid: 7), its council is mainly motivated by its members' strong commitment to the preservation of capitalism. It is financed by "British companies with interests in the Third World, and, intermittently, by institutions such as the Ford Foundation, Nuffield Foundation, Rockefeller Foundation, and the World Bank" (ibid: 8).
3. Esteva discusses the historical emergence, implications, and changes in "development" as a metaphor. He notes the process by which the biological metaphor of development was transferred to the social sphere. Esteva suggests that between 1759 and 1859, "development" evolved from: "a conception of transformation that moves toward the appropriate form of being to a conception of transformation that moves towards an ever more perfect form. During this period, evolution and development began to be used as interchangeable terms by scientists" (Esteva 1992: 8). The historical background of the term "development" is also discussed by Joseph Stiglitz, who points to the connection between development and colonialism. He points out that the World Bank added "development" to its name (becoming the International Bank for Reconstruction and Development) after the Second World War, when most of the countries in the developing world were still colonies. The economic development efforts of one-time colonizers (meager as they were) on behalf of the previously dominated colonies expressed the responsibility of "their European masters" (Stiglitz 2002: 11).
4. This approach derives support from Gustavo Esteva, who criticizes the false conception of "development" and "underdevelopment" held by scholars who perceive them as real. He opposes research which "displays a falsification of reality produced through dismembering the totality of interconnected processes that make up the world's reality and, in its place, it substitutes one of its fragments, isolated from the rest, as a general point of reference" (Esteva 1992: 12).
5. This holds for other contested terms, like modernization and Third World. I shall place inverted commas round these terms only on their first use.
6. Easterly had to leave his job at the World Bank after publishing his book (Easterly 2002).
7. William Easterly's more recent work (Easterly 2006) offers a similar analysis. He blames the "Rich West" for intruding on developing countries through "bloated aid bureaucracies," the IMF, and World Bank in particular. Echoing Hancock's claims he contends that international efforts to stimulate Third World development failed, describing how billions of dollars, pumped into development budgets, nurture byzantine bureaucracies and the development industry.
8. Hancock blames international aid for its disastrous impact on Africa during the past few decades, suggesting that it has become "a continent-sized beggar hopelessly dependent on the largesse of outsiders"; thus its food production "has fallen in every single year since 1962 ... with the result that the continent has the highest infant mortality rates in the world, the lowest average life-expectancies in the world, the lowest literacy rates, the fewest doctors per

head of population, and the fewest children in school. Tellingly, during the period 1980 to 1986 when Africa became ... the world's most 'aided' continent, GDP per capita fell by an average of 3.4 per cent per annum" (Hancock 1989: 191–92).

9. According to Hancock, since all its aid was cut off when the Somoza regime collapsed in 1979, conditions in Nicaragua have improved noticeably during the 1980s. Hancock claims that without "so-called 'help'," the government has succeeded in significantly reducing infant mortality and illiteracy among adult Nicaraguans, and in considerably improving agricultural production and access to medical services. He also notes that the funds "allocated by the Government to both education and health care have more than tripled" (Hancock 1989: 192).
10. Elaborating on development in South-Asia, Sondra Hausner claims, in a similar vein, that, "The glamour, wealth, and elitism of multilateral development institutions in South Asia cannot help but exacerbate the problems of social hierarchy that are responsible for a great deal of the poverty and inequity that development programs seek to alleviate" (Hausner 2006: 320).
11. An Oxfam policy paper makes a similar criticism in relation to a World Bank report produced by the Bank's Development Research Group (Dollar and Kraay 2000). Whereas the World Bank document claims that existing patterns of globalization are inherently good for poverty reduction, the Oxfam report states that the Bank's "current patterns of growth are reinforcing, rather than reducing, existing inequalities in income" (cited in Lechner and Boli 2004: 186). Interestingly, in a World Bank annual development report, the Bank admits the criticism, suggesting that, "Economic growth is crucial but often not sufficient to create conditions in which the world's poorest people can improve their lives" (World Bank 2001: 6). However, the report does not imply the Bank's responsibility for this grave situation. It adopts Oxfam's recommendations and rhetoric as its own. Moreover, it recommends the cooperation of all parties, "developing country governments at all levels, donor countries, international agencies, NGOs, civil society, and local communities" in three priority areas: opportunity, empowerment and security (ibid.: 6). Thus, the responsibility for the failure in reducing poverty is turned away from the Bank's policies to anonymous others.
12. This claim is widely substantiated by Joseph Stiglitz, whose position as Chief Economist at the World Bank lends crucial support for this allegation. He recounts: "The imbalance of power between the IMF and the 'client' countries inevitably creates tension between the two, but the IMF's own behavior in negotiations exacerbates an already difficult situation. In dictating the terms of the agreements, the IMF effectively stifles any discussions within a client government—let alone more broadly within the country—about alternative economic policies" (Stiglitz 2002: 43).
13. Hancock (1989: 50) and Yunus (1998: 14).
14. One example, in the Nepali context, is Subedi (1993), who will be referred to in detail later in this chapter.
15. In his critical study of research on the Israeli kibbutz, Reuven Shapira (2008) demonstrates a similar process in which a conspicuous success of this social framework, which was based on values of solidarity and social equality, declined over the years when capitalist trends took over and financial success brought about the centralization of power, bureaucratization, hierarchization, and autocratic leadership.
16. This argument gains support from an examination of the different absorption policies employed by the Israeli government towards immigrants from Ethiopia and those from the former Soviet Union. The integration of the latter was deemed to be much more successful in economic, cultural, and political terms (see Marx 1996; Siegel 1998). This group of immigrants was offered generous financial aid, put at their disposal with no mediating bureaucratic procedures, whereas the resources allocated for the Ethiopians' integration were distributed through a bureaucratic apparatus that consumed most of the resources and involved daily interventions in the immigrants' lives. Thus, resources intended to accelerate the immigrants' integration into Israeli society were distributed without relinquishing bureaucratic control over them, and at the same time reinforced the immigrants' dependence on the officials because of their need for the resources (see Hertzog 1999).

17. Shiva (2001) also notes that "The water privatization policy of the World Bank was articulated in a 1992 paper entitled 'Improving Water Resources Management.' The Bank believes that water availability at low or no cost is uneconomic and inefficient. Even the poor should pay.
18. *Zenana* is a Persian term originating from *zan*, "woman." The *zenana* designates "woman's space" and implies a dichotomy between domesticity, which entails the confining of women, and the public sphere. Laura Ring, for instance, discusses stereotypical images of women as subjugated and victimized, and associated with the concept of *zenana* in traditional societies, such as those of the Middle East and India. Ring follows the approach of anticolonial movements, who perceive the home (*ghar*) or *zenana* as "sites of cultural authenticity, untouched by the emasculating and corrupt influence of colonial power" (Ring 2006: 3).
19. The private/public dichotomy has been criticized in the Western context as well. Thus, for instance, Lidia Sciama (1981, 1984) questions the perceived opposition of right and left—"private" being associated with the left (sinister, weak, etc.), and "public" with the right (good, strong, intelligent, etc.). She depicts Oxbridge colleges as an example of social milieux in which private and public overlap. Colleges are viewed as male, domestic, yet highly privileged, spheres. They are "private" and exclusive, in as far as women are not welcome. Sciama also criticizes the idea that greater value is attached to public than to private spheres. For example, among Sarakatsani, a group of competitive and often violent Greek shepherds, it is private domestic spheres that are viewed as good and gentle, while the male worlds of the café and the open fields are always charged with hostility and competition.
20. Pigg's remarks are taken from an e-mail dated August 1992, quoted in Escobar (1995: 164).
21. Anna Robinson-Pant's edited volume (Robinson-Pant 2004b) offers a similar approach. Sewells's (1992) concept of "the universality of human agency" fits this approach as well.
22. Collective poverty is often attributed to women in developing countries. It has, for example, been suggested that 70 per cent of the world's poor are women (UNDP 1995: iii). Muhammad Yunus suggests similarly that women "constitute the majority of the poor, the under-employed and the economically and socially disadvantaged" (Yunus 1998: 7).
23. Women's crucial role in agriculture is a well documented phenomenon. To take one example, Dahl (1987) highlights the significant roles played by women in various pastoralist economies and elaborates on the ways in which women contribute to subsistence production. Women here are also represented as a heterogeneous social category with divergent interests and backgrounds.
24. Whelpton suggests that by 1987 aid programs in Nepal, provided by foreign funds, "regularly made up more than half of government's 'development budget' … This dependence peaked in the late 1980s, when the aid component reached around 80 per cent (equivalent to … 14 per cent of annual GNP) … Debt service as a percentage of GDP increased from less than 0.1 per cent in 1974–5 to almost 1 per cent in 1987–8" (Whelpton 2005: 128). Moreover, Nepal's dependency on outside assistance is a long-term one, and thus "in 2000–1 it was still providing around one-third of the government's total budget" (ibid.: 228).
25. Among the many scholars who have dealt with this phenomenon are: Parvati (1999), Gautam, Banskota, and Manchanda (2001), Shakya (2003), Maycock (2003), Pettigrew (2003), Manchanda (2004), Sharma and Prasain (2004), and Onesto (2005).
26. Anita Dighe (1995) found in her study of a group of 100 women living in South Delhi, India, that only 16 per cent of the participants in a Total Literacy Campaign (TLC) were able to reach the National Literacy Mission norm when tested, and that the respondents did not use their reading, writing, and numeracy skills in their everyday lives.
27. Ila Patel and Anita Dighe explain that patriarchal constraints "become at least temporarily inoperative as women come out of their homes and take part in the literacy campaigns with great enthusiasm" (Patel and Dighe 2003: 224).
28. For an overview of the approaches to researching women's literacy, see Robinson-Pant (2004b).
29. Youngman studied the National Literacy Program in Botswana, 1978–1987.
30. Bhairahawa is also known as "the gateway to the birth place of Lord Buddha, the Lumbini Zone" (quoted from: http://www.nepalvista.com/travel/bhairahawa.html. Retrieved 30 July 2010).

31. In her book, Behar (1996) elaborates in detail on the paper she presented in the meeting of the American Ethnological Society in Austin Texas, where "for the first time in the history of this society, border anthropologies and border anthropologists, Latinos and Latinas, will be at the top of the agenda" (136).
32. The development worker's touristic tendency has been highlighted by Robert Chambers (1983).

Chapter 1

THE VULNERABLE PATRON: PLAYING THE ROLE OF A FOREIGN GENDER CONSULTANT

Patronage and Power–dependence Relations

Recounting my experience as a patron in Nepal in the summer of 1997 seems to be a suitable way to begin a discussion about how and why people, men in particular, patronize other people, women in particular, in the context of gender development projects. Studying the dynamics and nature of patronization from a personal, and in my case, a woman's point of view, makes this subject intriguing .and disturbing at one and the same time. Dealing with women's patronization from my own experience enables a better understanding of questions such as: How are people absorbed into the frameworks of local, national, and international development organizations that preserve women's (or others') exclusion and discrimination? How can one explain women's cooperation with mechanisms that, in the name of improving women's opportunities, contribute to women's ongoing marginalization?

Reflecting on my experience from the perspective of a vulnerable participant and observer, and my desire to write about it "vulnerably" (Behar 1996), introduces some thought-provoking insights into situations that are often conveniently perceived in terms of self-evident truths, such as ideological commitments or professional conduct. Using my own experience as a foreign gender consultant, being "myself the principal informant" (Mosse 2005: ix), will enable me to elaborate on these questions from "within." Thus, I will show that being a feminist, a social activist, and a self-conscious anthropologist cannot prevent one from being absorbed into power games and patronizing attitudes when one becomes part of a power structure or "a cog" in the bureaucratic machine (Weber 1978).[1] Moreover, exposing my conduct as both patronizing and pathetic reveals the interchange of control and dependency, which are interwoven in encounters that are embedded with power differentials.

I perceive patronage as a concept which combines power–dependence relations and the rhetoric of help, care, and aid. Patronage, from this point of view, is control and/or domination disguised by the rhetoric of egalitarianism, humanism, feminism, and so forth. The perceived conceptual dyad of patron–client, which signifies power gaps embedded in formalized social structures, is widely discussed in the literature with regard to divergent contexts, social institutions, historical narratives, and geographical locations (e.g., Boissevain 1966; Davis 1977; Gellner 1977; Sharma 1985; Gilsenan 1996; Chaudhary 1999; Keating 2001; Shapira 2008). Some examples of power–dependence relations are: bureaucrats and clients in bureaucratic systems; husband and wife, and parent and child, in family frameworks; patron and client, and feudal lord and vassal, in politico-economic systems; patron and artist in cultural domains; and godfather and protégé in criminal networks.

The use of "patronage" in social analyses has been criticized by scholars (e.g., Gilsenan 1996) for masking the more significant aspects of the societies studied. However, I follow Stephen Lyon's (2004) and Caroline Castiglione's (2005) rejection of this claim and follow their claims that an analysis of a patron–client system can be used as an anthropological and analytic strategy that "renders comparison more feasible" (Lyon 2004: 8).[2] Rejecting Gilsenan's criticisms, Lyon argues that eliminating "the notion of the dyadic, asymmetrical reciprocity of patronage for a more class-based analysis" would deprive social analysis "of a very important tool for understanding patron–client roles beyond the scope of landlord–peasant interaction." Moreover, he suggests that patron–client systems, "should be understood as a system which operates around a set of roles rather than economic positions" (ibid.: 8).

In her book on nobles and villagers in Italian politics from 1640 to 1760, Castiglione reveals that the patron–client conceptual framework is a relevant and helpful analytic tool for drawing comparisons, even across historical periods, as long as mutual dependency and control is assumed. Both Castiglione and Lyon demonstrate the fact that the concept of patronage does not exclude the connotation of mutual power–dependence in the context of asymmetric power relations. Rather, the asymmetry in power relations emphasizes the informal, often unrecognized, and unacknowledged resources, tactics, mechanisms, and channels that are used by those who are perceived as powerless in formal power terms. In reference to James Scott's (1985) analysis, Lyon argues that clients can "restrict their patrons' demands. Patrons have public power mechanisms which are easily equated to the powers that the state tries to monopolize. Clients must rely on other power mechanisms which may go unacknowledged but which nevertheless may have considerable influence on behavior" (Lyon 2004: 8).

Although the terms patronage, paternalism, and patriarchy are rooted in and entail the connotations of male domination, nevertheless, the gender perspective has somehow been marginalized or even omitted from most studies of patronage. Thus, Herta Nöbauer suggests that "paternalism creates relationships based on authority and personal dependence." This is "a (heterosexual) structure of (male) 'patrons' and (female) 'clients'" (Nöbauer 2002: 115).[3] My analysis follows this important understanding, thus emphasizing the male discourse and dominance implicated in the gendered concept of patronage, as well as behind the women's project I am discussing.

Gender Activities within the Bhairahawa Lumbini Groundwater Project

I played the role of a patron during my stay in Nepal in August and September 1997. This image of myself as a patron was established at the outset of my stay in Nepal, staying with me throughout my visit, and it has dominated my retrospective reflections upon my visit there (cf. Shore 1999; Ben-Ari n.d.).

I arrived in Nepal as a gender consultant or expert in the employ of the Tahal Consulting Engineers Company.[4] Tahal hired me to work for them on a development project for women villagers in the region of the Bhairahawa Lumbini Groundwater Project. This irrigation project, which the World Bank financed with loans to the Nepali government, was launched in 1978, and it was aimed at increasing farmers' income by providing them with a year-round water supply. By drilling deep tube wells (DTWs) in this rural area of Nepal and distributing the water through open canals and underground pipes, a new irrigation system was introduced. It was expected that this improved, technologically advanced irrigation system would enable the farmers to diversify the range of crops they grew in the dry season and achieve higher yields per hectare. Moreover, it was assumed that the irrigation project would contribute to raising household income and standards of living (Tahal 1992). By the end of 1998, the process of transferring the irrigation project to local partners was to be completed.

In the mid 1990s, the World Bank was pressing the Nepali government to divert a small portion of the irrigation project budget ($500,000) to women's empowerment programs. This action can probably be explained against the background of a growing awareness of, and emerging feminist trends in Western countries in regard to women's conditions around the world, and in Third World countries in particular. Thus, for instance, Josette Murphy suggests, in a World Bank document, that although efforts to bring out the "invisible" women in World Bank-funded projects started in the 1970s, "progress in moving from rhetoric to action remained slow until the mid-1980s" (Murphy 1995: 1). Nevertheless, the implementation of an operational policy on gender was approved only in April 1994. The 1995 United Nations' women's conference in Beijing, as well as other international UN conferences that took place during the International Decade for Women, might have had a significant impact on this growing feminist discourse and related policies (Murphy 1995; Levy 1996). A United Nations Development Programme (UNDP) statement can serve to demonstrate the influence of this discourse in the Nepali context. It says: "UNDP supports the development of tools and mechanisms that enable Nepalese women to access, participate and benefit from equitable local planning and governance through programmes that are aimed at empowering women."[5]

In any event, at the beginning of the 1990s the heads of the World Bank were already issuing documents maintaining that investment in women might contribute to greater social change than had been achieved during the first two decades of development projects (World Bank 1990). They further suggested that ignoring women's needs, treating men as the main family providers, and working exclusively with male officials had considerable ramifications for the family, the community, and the recipient country. Women's participation in development projects was depicted as essential for accelerating social change, because of their perceived role as mediators between the family and the community, and as having a crucial impact on children (Chowdhury 1995: 32). Development projects at the beginning of the 1990s emphasized the different needs of men and women. It was argued that since planned interventions should be responsive to the needs of the people, a gender dimension must be incorporated into development projects (Levy 1991; Moser 1993).

As a result of the pressures applied by the heads of the World Bank on the Nepali government and the directors of the irrigation project, Tahal decided to send an Israeli woman expert in gender and development to Nepal. This expert was expected to conduct a survey of women's needs in the irrigation project area and to suggest a program that would contribute to social change in the villages. Tovi Fenster, a social geographer by profession, came to Nepal in this role in the summer of 1996. She defined the goals of her proposed program thus: "to provide women (as well as men) in the Project area with skills and means to enable them to increase their standard of living" (Fenster 1996: 17). The target groups of her program were specified by Fenster quantitatively: "27,000 [women in the villages included in the proposed project] are at the ages of 10–65. This is the target population of this plan. This number consists of some 770 women groups (taken 35 women per group)" (ibid.: 17). The program included workshops on gender awareness for the irrigation project staff and a "development package," which would include: literacy programs for women, credit and saving programs, awareness-raising programs, skill-development programs, agricultural and animal-husbandry training, women's marketing groups, and the founding of a women's organization unit.

The following year I was hired by Tahal to continue Fenster's mission, and to implement the women empowerment program. My travel to Nepal was arranged only after the World Bank demanded of the directors of the Nepali Ministry of Agriculture and the local leaders of the irrigation project that they proceed with the gender activities program. A few weeks after my arrival in Nepal, Leon, Tahal's Israeli representative and team leader, told me that I was expected to deliver a report. This came as a surprise to me, because no mention of a report had been made before. Leon presented the request for a report as if it was a self-evident part of my project assignment. As I was acquainted with Tovi Fenster's report, which had been sent to me while still at home, I used her report as a starting point for mine. Thus, following Fenster, I defined the aims of the gender activities program as "increasing the income and economic power of the village women who are at least equal contributors to the village families' economy and to national agricultural production" (Hertzog 1997: 8). My report proposed that some 27,000 women in some thirty villages go through a program of literacy classes, followed by workshops in vocational training.

The following tells the story of the women's empowerment program (sometimes called the gender activities project[6]), the changes that it underwent, and the roles played by the various agencies that were directly and indirectly involved in it. The analysis will offer an explanation of why the women's project was never implemented and will investigate the question of whether it was ever meant to be implemented from the start. It will reveal how the rhetoric of gender development was manipulated by officials and organizations involved in the women's project to enhance their interests. More broadly, the gender activities project will be used to reflect on various aspects of power relations and patronizing conduct (in both, general and gendered terms) which develop around aid projects for developing countries.

Deceitful Hierarchy: Privileged Experts and Low-ranking Paraprofessionals

The first thing I realized upon arrival at the airport in Kathmandu was that my social status was enhanced. I was now a privileged foreigner vis-à-vis most local Nepali citizens. When I left the airport, the driver of Tahal's Israeli representative was waiting for me. The driver had been obliged to return to the airport several times because, due to heavy rains, the flight had been delayed in Bombay for some twenty-four hours. Moreover, the driver had risked his safety, because of a merchants' and students' strike organized by the Maoists that took place at the time.[7]

I was chauffeured to a luxurious hotel in the center of Kathmandu, where I spent the night before flying on to Bhairahawa. That same night I learned that although the Nepali driver had treated me as a privileged boss I was not beyond reproach. Leon, Tahal's representative, called me and gave me a piece of his mind. He made it clear that I had misbehaved. As I had not phoned him nor my husband after landing in Nepal, the two of them had been communicating over the telephone and both were worried at my seeming disappearance.

The next thing I realized was that riding in a car with a driver distinguished between privileged people and others. When I first met Thapa, the Nepali head of the irrigation project, he promised that a car and a driver would be provided for my travel to the villages (to meet with women's groups who were slated to join the women's project). I felt uneasy with this offer. However, the fact that his promise was fulfilled only at a very late stage of my stay, during the last two weeks in Bhairahawa, also entailed some unpleasantness. It implied that my position was rather shaky, and therefore, Thapa did not feel obliged to provide me with a jeep and driver as soon as I started traveling between the villages. Yet, the fact that this advantage was eventually made available for me raises questions about a change in Thapa's attitude toward me. It was not clear whether this happened as a result of his growing trust in me, or as part of a power play between him and Leon. Giving me a jeep with a driver could have conveyed a latent message about who was the real boss of the women's project, and could indicate that I was just as privileged as Leon. My being regarded as his equal was apparently rather humiliating for Leon. Indeed, whenever I accompanied Leon in "his" jeep, or when he traveled in "my" vehicle, he would always sit in the front seat, next to the driver, making me sit alone, sometimes with Anita (the local gender consultant), or sometimes with other project employees, in an overcrowded back seat accommodating more than three passengers.

Reflecting on my behavior during our many visits to the villages brings to mind several illuminating examples of my patron-like behavior. When in Bhairahawa, I visited fifteen villages within the region of the irrigation project. Anita Khanal, my Nepali colleague, accompanied me on all these visits. Obviously, I could not speak or understand any Nepali. Anita mediated between the local women and me, translating what they said, and what I said to them.

Although I opened and closed our meetings with the women villagers, responding to questions that were posed during the encounters, Anita would tell them about the women's project in their own language. Usually she led the discussion that followed our presentation. She would encourage the women to ask questions and express their opinions about and expectations of the gender activities project, and after responding patiently to all the queries, and sometimes criticisms, she would ask them to sign their agreement to be included in the women's program. Clad in traditional colorful gowns, similar to the ones worn by the women, appearing relaxed and self-confident but also humble and empathic, and smiling warmly at the women, Anita gained the women's confidence and easily communicated with them. I watched her admiringly as she interacted with the women, often asking myself what I was doing there.

In all of our visits to the villages, we were joined by Women's Groups Organizers (WGOs). The WGOs, who had usually completed a few years of schooling, were recruited from villages included in the irrigation project. Having much in common with the women villagers, familiarity with their ways of life, and often acquainted with them and their families, the WGOs possessed a substantial advantage in terms of their ability to convince the women villagers to sign up for the women's program. In fact, the WGOs were "field workers" who carried out the most meaningful part of the program. They organized the groups of women in the villages whom we met later on, found a suitable location for the study classes we planned, and identified candidates for the role of literacy class teachers (the final decision was Anita's and mine). The WGOs would also negotiate with the women over rental costs (of huts), salaries, and so on. The classrooms, offered by the village-women, ranged from dark mud-built houses, with tiny rooms and mud floors, to larger and brighter spaces constructed of brick. After Anita and I finished our part of the meeting, the WGOs would carry on talking with the women, circulating among them, approaching each one and persuading her to add her signature to the list of participants. A thumb print (in most cases) on the list expressed a woman's consent and commitment to participate in the literacy class.

My own experience in training paraprofessional workers[8] in the Israeli welfare services from 1979 to 1983 (see Barasch 1986),[9] and my observations and analysis of the role of female instructors (*Somchot*)[10] of immigrants from Ethiopia (Hertzog 1999),[11] suggest some interesting similarities between WGOs in Nepal and Israeli paraprofessional workers. Both are, by and large, female "grassroots" (or "indigenous") workers with limited education and professional skills, who are supervised by higher-ranking women professionals and/or male officials. Introducing the WGOs to the village women's program drew on a similar approach. They were assumed to serve as role models for the village women, as their relationships with them were based on socioeconomic similarities.

I suggest that while the WGOs were offered an opportunity to become part (however low-ranked) of the bureaucratic system, and enjoy its advantages, they were also expected to represent the irrigation project and the organizations behind it (the Ministry of Agriculture in particular) and their contribution to village women's empowerment. Employing paraprofessional workers entailed low costs for the irrigation project, while it generated the benefit of looking good in terms of enhancing women's opportunities in more prestigious, semi-professional occupations, which the WGOs could not enjoy without the women's program. Moreover, since the program did not materialize and even the literacy classes were not opened up, the irrigation project's management could get rid of these women very easily and cheaply. Thus, Weber's argument that, "No machinery in the world functions … so cheaply" as bureaucratic hierarchy (Weber 1978: lix), gains support in the context of the irrigation project.

Apart from generating effective relationships with the groups of women, encouraging them to trust the irrigation and the women projects' staff and forming the learning groups, the WGOs served to create an impression that things were working as planned and that the gender activities program was on its way to achieving "a successful result," as defined by Cris Shore and Susan Wright, who contend that organizations are interested in making "fragmented activities appear coherent, so it can be claimed that an intention has been realized and a successful result achieved" (Shore and Wright 1997: 5).

Despite the substantial contribution of the WGOs to the gender activities program, they were considered to be low-ranking staff and were paid poorly. In contrast, despite my ineffective activity, my poor skills in terms of language, and my lack of relevant background knowledge on Nepal, development, and so on, I was regarded and treated as a VIP, enjoyed a prestigious position and role, and was rewarded accordingly: I was "an expert" (Hancock 1989; Yunus 1998; Maiava 2001; Mosse 2005).

Hence, it appears that "office hierarchy" produces machinery that works very cheaply, as Weber suggests, but not so much as a result of the "expert training" and "a functional specialization" upon which "bureaucracy rests" (Weber 1948: 229). The bureaucracy's success at working very cheaply (and "efficiently") was rather the outcome of employing poorly rewarded (in terms of status, authority, and salary) but highly competent (in terms of suitability and adaptability to relevant organizational aims, vis-à-vis their clients) local workers.

This understanding is equally relevant with regard to the "village teachers," who were women with only a little more education than the other women in their villages. They may have had between five to eight years of schooling and could be as young as fifteen. However, the village teachers' social proximity, like that of the WGOs, to the women "students" or "clients" was found by the irrigation project staff to be very fruitful for the purpose of working with the village women, creating social networks and transmitting their knowledge to them. Contrary to their significant contribution to the organization's aims, the village teachers, like the WGOs, were positioned at the lowest level of the women project's hierarchy, below the WGOs (and paid less than them), and close to the village women.

The advantages of the social proximity between paraprofessional indigenous workers and other people in their neighborhoods, social networks, families, and so on, have been recognized by many social-care organizations. These indigenous workers have been gradually mobilized since the 1960s for the sake of "helping" needy, deprived, deviant, and other clienteles, in contexts such as family therapy, rehabilitating delinquents, teaching assistants, social-work aids, mental health supporters, in-home caregivers, peripheral communities health instruction, and so on (Umbarger 1972; Andrade and Burstein 1973; Etgar 1977; Neipris 1984; Maruna and LeBel 2003).[12] Employing paraprofessional workers in welfare, educational, health, and other social services is introduced into socioeconomically deprived groups and communities in the name of promoting social change. I suggest that while offering local people minor opportunities for social mobility, the stratified hierarchy of social agencies contributes to the power of professionals within it. I would argue further that employing paraprofessional workers benefits social-service systems, and the professionals within them in particular. This practice provides the latter with enlarged authority over subordinate workers, who at the same time serve to absorb social tensions which the professionals and their organizations are designed to alleviate.

The exploitation of paraprofessional workers is rarely acknowledged. One example of criticism is Mark Hunter's article about social-care paraprofessionals (Hunter 2008). Hunter discusses recent developments regarding the "huge swathes of public service that were once the preserve of highly trained professionals, now being carried out by less qualified support staff." He wonders:

> So will the creation of ever-more paraprofessional roles do what it is meant to do—help ease the pressure on overworked qualified practitioners, freeing them from the more mundane of their duties to concentrate on providing quality service in the areas that matter most? Or is it just a stunt to fob the public off with a cut-price service, provided by unqualified, underpaid assistants ready to be made the scapegoats the minute anything goes wrong? (ibid.)

Nevertheless, it has not been claimed, at least not in the domain of social-care services, that this category of workers can provide "unprofessional" services that are in fact more productive and helpful than those of professionals. That is, "professionalism" pretends (or "presents itself," in Goffman's words) to offer services based on acquired knowledge and training, whereas people with limited or no professional training can provide the same or even more relevant services. Moreover, professionals would act in a way that presents their performance as a "sufficiently complex and vital task to justify giving" to those who perform it "the ceremonial and financial reward given to" professionals (Goffman 1959: 28).[13] Thus, paraprofessional workers serve organizations in economic terms, providing low-paid services and, in professional terms, promoting "social inclusion" (Harris 2004), pretending to enhance local or indigenous groups' participation in the running of their communities.

The Compelling Power and Appealing Advantages of the Consultant's Position

On some of our visits to the irrigation project's villages, one or more of the male Association Organizers (AOs) joined us. They would sit on the side and hardly interact with the women attending the meetings. From time to time, a higher-ranking official from the irrigation project staff joined us. On each of the visits some twenty to thirty women attended, sometimes as many as forty. The meetings would typically take place under a tree. In hot weather, under conditions of almost 100 per cent humidity, we would sit on shaky old metal bed frames with straw mattresses, or on the ground. Often a few men and some children gathered around, and sometimes the women held babies in their arms. Livestock wandering around was also part of the scenery.

Very soon I became used to being driven around in the irrigation project's jeep with Anita and the WGOs.[14] It soon felt almost natural to be treated as an all-knowing expert who took center stage at events. Upon arrival, which often occurred later than scheduled, I was immediately offered the best seat by local women as well as by Anita and the WGOs. I had become a privileged person, "encapsulated" (Chambers 1983: 12) in luxurious advantages, such as being chauffeured around and accommodated in a guesthouse (something which it was impossible to reject), and I accepted the gestures bestowed, or rather imposed, on me.

This was my first trip to Nepal. Most of what I knew about Nepal and developing countries was from reading Tovi Fenster's report. I could not speak Nepali and dressed differently from the local women. The fact that I was constantly "observing" the encounters and taking notes, while Anita and the WGOs were busy interacting with the women, emphasized further (unconsciously, perhaps) my physical and verbal otherness. I was probably perceived not only as different looking but also as being distant and preoccupied with other (personal) activities.

One day I was made aware of the impact my conduct had on my surroundings when Raju, Leon's competent secretary, joined us on our tour round the villages. At a certain point he turned to me and suggested that I should write something down. I was rather embarrassed at being caught writing my fieldnotes (which I was doing for my own research purposes, rather than for the women program's sake) and it was only then that I realized my distanced-observer position in that context. Moreover, I realized that I was being observed by other participants in the encounters, and that they were well aware of me documenting what was going on. They might have assumed that I was reporting to "others" in "higher" places what was being said in the meetings. It is also possible that the women were used to meeting "project people," whether foreigners or locals, who took notes while interacting with them, for purposes of surveys, censuses, and so forth. Looking back on that incident it appears to me that I might have felt guilty for using my visit to the villages for my own needs rather than being fully occupied with my assignment. Thus, while Raju and others were probably accustomed to being observed by guests, developers, donors, and/or researchers who would, sometimes, take notes, I was not aware of this and, therefore, assumed that I was "caught" doing something wrong.

It appears, therefore, that assuming the role of an expert, complying with a privileged status and benefits, behaving unconsciously with stereotypic disregard for village people, are unavoidable outcomes of being involved in a hierarchical and bureaucratic setting. This context dictates social roles, expectations, performances, advantages (or disadvantages), and, moreover, the relative positioning of individuals as being affiliated with constructed, stratified categories. It could be argued that the bureaucratic setting imposes codes of conduct on the individual and compels them (me in this case) in a way that does not permit them to "squirm out of the apparatus" in which they are "harnessed" (Weber 1948: 228). However, my ethnography suggests that although social roles and relations are imposed on the individual, they take an active role and join the social encounter willingly and deliberatively. That is, the individual is not a mere "cog" in the system. They are also an active player in the social encounter in which they participate. Thus, complying with my distanced, privileged status as a "foreign expert" was unavoidable, but becoming a distanced observer, or an "anthropologist," was done deliberately.

Manufacturing the Image of a Gender Expert

Playing the role of an expert in a women's economic empowerment project cast me in the role of a benevolent foreigner. One of the ways in which I presented myself as a caring consultant on my first visit to the villages was by expressing my enthusiasm for the village women's handicrafts. Examining my extensive efforts "to demonstrate [my] professional competence" (Mosse 2005: 26), and to be perceived by the village women and irrigation project staff as a gender expert, demonstrates how I strived "to live up the mask" that represented "the self" that I wanted to be (Robert Park, quoted in Goffman 1959: 19). Thus, as Goffman suggests, the "front" of my "performance" during my visits in the villages was aimed at defining "the situation for those who observe[d] the performance" (ibid.: 22). My continuous performance of my role as a gender expert ended well, as it became my "second nature and an integral part of [my] personality" (Park, in ibid.: 19–20). I certainly came to believe that my intentions were idealistic and my expertise was evident.

On my first visit to the villages, some five days after my arrival in Nepal, Leon, two WGOs, Pandit (head of the Farmer Organization Division, and the AOs' and the WGOs' coordinator), and I drove to Khurmundihawa, where we met Manju, a third WGO. When we completed the procedures concerning the literacy classes, I asked to see the women's handicrafts. Soon a few big straw baskets and woolen articles were laid in front of us. The women were very excited to show us their handiwork and the children helped them bring out more objects. Anita asked the women about prices of materials, and they replied that the cost was between 100 and 500 rupees[15] per basket, depending on size.

In the second village I visited, West Bharaulia, a similar event was repeated. I asked to see the women's handicrafts, and again the women and children happily brought out many broad, rounded, and flat baskets of different sizes and shapes. The women explained, in both villages, that the hand-made baskets and woolen articles were intended for their daughters' dowries. However, one woman offered to make a basket for Anita, requesting 100 rupees[16] for the materials.

I revealed my interest in these straw handicrafts repeatedly and persistently by asking many questions about weaving techniques and the materials the baskets were made from, the provenance of the materials, their prices, and so on. Indeed, I also offered to buy some of them. To draw attention to my professional interest, at a very early stage of my visits to the villages, I made suggestions to encourage entrepreneurial initiatives involving straw handicrafts. I included this "original" idea among the recommendations in my final report to the heads of the irrigation project. I also discussed my thoughts about the potential economic value of the women's expertise with Thapa, the Nepali manager of the irrigation project. It appeared that Thapa had his own opinions. He explained that similar ideas had been proposed in the past, but these were found to be unworkable because of the villagers' distance from markets (which made traveling far too difficult and expensive), and also because the low prices paid for the objects made their sale unprofitable. However, this explanation did not put me off, and I compromised by accepting Thapa's suggestion to look out for nearby market sites, instead of Kathmandu.

Toying with this idea of developing a simple money-generating source for the "poor women in the villages" led me to discuss it with Hanna, Leon's wife. While accompanying her husband on his overseas assignments, Hanna had ample opportunity to purchase numerous handcrafted articles. Consequently, she had become an "expert" on Nepali and other South Asian handicrafts. I suggested that Hanna take on a role in the women's project, mediating between the women who produced the baskets and traders in handcraft shops in Kathmandu. She seemed to like the idea and to respect my "professional" initiative. I also discussed with Anita the possibility of developing some kind of marketing initiative as an outlet for the village women's basket ware. I could not be sure if Hanna and Anita really approved of my ideas or were just being polite (they might have felt nothing would come of them). Their response can also be understood as a generous face-saving exercise, supporting me in my efforts to create for myself the image of an expert. Removing my mask of expertise would have left me "caught in a misrepresentation" (Goffman 1959: 244), and would have humiliated me.

The village women themselves, as noted above, did not think it was a good idea to commercialize their handiwork because the basket ware was used for traditional purposes. However, whether my plan was realistic or a flight of fantasy, my eagerness to advance the basket ware business turned out to be useful for my purposes. When, following Leon's advise, I mentioned to Thapa that the search for a potential market in Kathmandu necessitated a weekend visit to the capital in the middle of my visit to Nepal, Thapa authorized it eventually, albeit unwillingly. Thapa quite probably assumed that traveling to Kathmandu amounted to an unacceptable privilege.

On that visit I went to a few handicraft shops in Kathmandu and inquired about potential prices for each kind of basket, and about marketing techniques. Upon my return to Bhairahawa I told Pandit enthusiastically about my inquiries, telling him that one of the shopkeepers had agreed to sell the first twenty items for $1 per small basket. I also suggested putting Manju, an energetic and smart young WGO, who knew some English, in charge of the initiative. Pandit seemed either to like the idea, or he was being careful not to offend me by casting doubts over my enthusiastic suggestion. Anita added a few points on the subject and mentioned that her friends had suggested a few years ago a similar idea. Hanna's name was brought up as someone who had many contacts, and who could contribute to carrying out the handicrafts project. Thus, unwittingly, I developed the issue of handicraft enterprises into a social affair, drawing an increasing number of people into it, while becoming the center of these encounters.

My written report, submitted to the heads of the irrigation project in Israel and Nepal a few days after my return to Israel, also reveals my self-presentation as an expert in developing women's enterprises. In it I wrote:

> Handicrafts Project: Visiting the project area together with Mrs Khanal (local consultant) and women's groups organizers (WGOs), we noticed the great potential of developing existing traditional skills, which are widely practiced (handicraft production in particular). We have seen some beautiful straw baskets, decorative wool works, etc. No extra training is needed (not at this stage, in any case), but what is required to gradually build an income-generating

> project chiefly are: a coordinator, marketing training and purchase of materials. One year at least of financial support for hiring a coordinator, coordinator's travel fares, and material costs … [– are needed]. (Hertzog 1997: 9).

It appears that the handicraft enterprise was used by me as "a sign equipment" and as a way to "dramatize my work" (Goffman 1959: 30–34), to convince my counterparts of my professional skills, and to present myself before them in a way that "incorporates and exemplifies the officially accredited values of the [institution]" (ibid.: 34).

A Tourist in Disguise

Taking photographs was a regular activity of mine during my stay in Nepal, and on the visits to the villages in particular. This activity, which had nothing to do with any professional need concerning my role as a gender development consultant, exposed my hidden urge to make sure that exotic and unfamiliar impressions would be preserved for my own benefit. Being continuously occupied by looking for attractive photo opportunities, I certainly did not behave as a professional expert. This conduct, along with my note taking, meant that I was either acting as an anthropologist, collecting information for my study, or as a tourist, interested in commemorating adventures and impressions related to the local people and scenery. It could also mean that I was doing both, combining anthropological fieldwork with enjoyable trips to Nepali villages. But this kind of conduct is hardly in line with conventional expectations about how experts work. Thus, Chambers's definition of "urban-based professionals" who are involved in "rural development tourism, the phenomenon of the brief rural visit" (Chambers 1983: 10), could be applied to me. David Mosse similarly points to the questionable basis of foreign consultants' knowledge which derives "from short visits after long journeys, [and] sleepless passage through airports" (Mosse 2005: 133).

I took pictures in every village I went to. I particularly liked the pictures in which the women and I were sitting on the ground. Anita was aware of my obsession and often offered to take pictures of the women villagers together with me. My field notes disclose that I was well aware of the hierarchal distance that was established when I was taking pictures of the ongoing interactions. When we were in West Bharaulia we went to see the room that had been suggested as a site for the women's literacy class. It was a small, dark mud hut, used in the mornings for UNICEF children's classes. I wrote in my notes "to my deep shame I was asking to take pictures of myself with the children."

On another occasion, while visiting a school in Shikton, I was photographed with a few schoolchildren, posing like a typical foreign tourist. The children, like the adults, did not object to being photographed by me. Moreover, they complied and cooperated with this intrusion, and "put on their best face and receive[d] the visitor well" (Chambers 1983: 12).[17] Thus, for instance, while I was taking pictures in a class, one of the school girls read for me quietly, without being asked, probably assuming that I would like to take her picture as she was reading. It seemed as though she was accustomed to foreigners visiting, asking questions, and taking photos, and she was aware of what was expected of her. However, my fieldnotes clarify that I felt ashamed for behaving like a voyeuristic tourist (cf. ibid.: 10).

Taking pictures on these occasions illustrates how foreigners, who invade local people's daily life, impose themselves in such encounters. This recurrent situation was in fact a one-sided social encounter, as pictures of the local people were taken then spirited away, serving the visitors, myself in this case, for their own needs. Although in the beginning I asked Anita to request permission to take pictures, later on I took photographs anywhere I liked without feeling obliged to ask for people's consent. In any case, even if consent had been granted, it would not change the hierarchal social distance that was embedded in these unequal situations. In such encounters there is one person (me, in this case) who owns a piece of property—a camera—which is quite expensive by local-village standards. The same person determines how the pictures are taken, their background, framing, and so on. Most importantly, this person takes others' pictures away with them, and in most cases does not send the pictures back to those they have photographed. Certainly none of this would occur the other way round.

The local people did not object to being photographed; often they even seemed to enjoy it and willingly cooperated. However, I tend to think that in these situations they behaved in a way like a captive audience, either because they did not dare to refuse the "VIP" outsiders, or simply because they did not want to offend them. However, even if the villagers enjoyed being the focus of the outsiders' attention, from the latter's point of view it meant that the local people served as objects for their (my) own purposes. It is also possible that the women villagers expected to gain some advantage from these interactions. Clearly, my position as a tourist who returns to her country, family, and friends, and can pride herself in showing such attractive pictures, entailed various social benefits. The pictures could also be used for publications, an even more valuable reward in social terms.

Comparing my Nepali experience to my study of Ethiopian immigrants in an Israeli absorption center (Hertzog 1999), it appears that taking pictures of people in the villages implied a position of power over the situation. Similarly, the American tourists I observed in Israel, who were potential donors to the absorbing agencies, were brought regularly on buses to see the "invaluable and hard work" of the officials with the "vulnerable", "needy" immigrants from Africa. The objectification of people in such situations is reflected in a quote by the center's director, who described the visitors' attitude toward the immigrants as follows: "all they are interested in is to take photos of the zoo." The director was expressing his disapproval of the tourists' behavior and his disgruntlement about the extra work these visits imposed on him, as well as reservations about their low level of interest in the topic of absorption as such. However, his words exposed the latent connotation of animal-watching in that context, which dehumanized the immigrants.

This example is relevant to the context of my visits to the Nepali villages in the irrigation project area, as it also entailed observing others collectively and perceiving them as extremely different from "us." "They," the villagers, were regarded and talked about as exotic human beings in a manner that implied their primitivism. My written descriptions of the scenes and people in the villages often reveal this kind of latent ethnocentricity. Thus, for example, my fieldnotes often dwell on the muddy huts and their surroundings, implying dirt, neglect, and poverty. Following other ethnographic studies (e.g., Shachak 1985; Hertzog 2010b; Mosse 2005), I suggest that attributing uncleanliness, disease, drunkenness, and the like collectively to people, introduces social distance through negative stigmatization. The clean/dirty binary corresponds with other perceived oppositions, such as modern/primitive, and advanced/backward.[18]

The Professional Caretaker

In addition to their development expertise, caring for poor, disadvantaged people is often perceived as necessary part of the consultant's persona. Thus, to be qualified for working with aid agencies and aid projects one is expected to have both a professional background in fields such as education, economics, nursing, social work, medicine, agriculture, and so on, and to be committed to "helping" and "instructing." In Goffman's terms, it can be said that I offered my observers "an impression that is idealized," reaffirming "the moral values of the community" (Goffman 1959: 35). Moreover, as Goffman suggests, this "presentation of idealized performances" (ibid.: 36) is widely associated with social mobility in stratified societies. In most stratified societies "there is an idealization of the higher strata" (ibid.: 36), and efforts to move upward and efforts to keep from moving downward involve sacrifices "made for the maintenance of front" (ibid.: 36). Thus, presenting myself as both professional and caring served my endeavor to convince my audience of my relevant skills and social commitment.

Like many other consultants, volunteers, NGO and development organization workers, I assumed this double role as soon as I entered the irrigation project site in Bhairahawa. Concerning myself with the empowerment of women became my proclaimed expertise alongside my human and feminist deep commitment (which, in fact, had been part of my feminist identity for many years). The role of a caring expert in women's affairs was embedded in all my encounters during my stay in Nepal. Acting as a representative of women's interests was an inseparable part of every encounter with officials in and outside the irrigation project, of my various social engagements and, indeed, of the meetings with the women villagers.

This professional, caring identity was at the fore at a meeting which Anita, three WGOs, and I held with three local officials from the veterinary ministry in their office. We came to talk about the animal husbandry training program for the village women, which formed part of their literacy classes. After summarizing the program, which focused mainly on husbandry and health instruction, and after presenting the budget to the three male ministry officials, one of them asked us to stay for tea. I replied that "Anita is the boss and she decides." The laughter of all the participants spoke volumes of who really was considered to be the "boss." The men asked again, and Anita agreed to stay for tea. When all were quiet I started "to explain" the gender activities project.

Elaborating on the potential influence of the literacy classes on some 9,000 women and on their social surroundings, I demonstrated both my mastery of the subject and my concern for women's empowerment. When I realized that I had taken over the conversation, I apologized for "lecturing." Anita commented half jokingly that talking was my profession, and that I was doing it well. It appears that I had assumed the role of representing the women's project, although I had only become acquainted with it a few weeks earlier and was, practically speaking, an outsider to the place and to the women's project. Moreover, although Anita and the WGOs were much more familiar with the project than me, none of them tried to speak about it. They behaved as if it was natural or self-evident that I should represent the women's project.

My focus on women's affairs colored the whole conversation. Hence, when Anita did speak, she asked the officials if women had ever participated in vocational training courses organized by the ministry. One of them responded that only a few women had participated in such courses. His reply provoked me to "lecture" again. This time I was indirectly reprimanding the officials. I said: "Why have not more women been included in these courses? Are the women not the ones who do most of the work in the fields?! Why should they not be included in the training just like the men?" The man replied, "this is because of the culture." That reaction elicited open criticism on my part, and I referred to my study of Ethiopian immigrants in Israel. I explained to them that Israeli officials had used the rationale of the immigrants' culture to justify their discriminating practices in relation to women's vocational training opportunities. I argued that these claims were not substantiated by facts, as in Ethiopia women worked in both the fields and in their homes. "Denying women the opportunity to undertake vocational training meant, in fact, their discrimination", I stated, and the men agreed (perhaps out of politeness). The fact that the men seemed to agree with me encouraged my outspoken preaching, and thus I suggested: "It is in the hands of state officials who are in charge and in control over budgets and who are authorized to recruit people to training courses. They can decide that 50 per cent of all participants will be women and they are able to implement it."

My extensive efforts to enforce the implementation of literacy classes also afforded me with countless opportunities to display both my gender expertise and my feminist devotion. As none of the 900 literacy classes commenced before I left Nepal, I became a nag, continuously, although carefully, pestering the heads of the irrigation project to implement the classes. But it became clear to me from a very early point in my visit that the local heads of the irrigation project were not keen to begin the classes. They would rather have them implemented, at most, on a limited scale. Insisting that the proposed budget be sent to his superiors in the government and to the World Bank for approval, and that the training courses (seminars) for village teachers be started at once, were part of the daily pressure I exerted on Thapa, on other local officials in the irrigation project, and on Leon, Tahal's representative.

Only much later, when I looked back at my fieldnotes, did I fully realize that they had all cooperated in ensuring the postponement of the literacy program (and, consequently, of the whole gender activities program) to the point that it would not happen. This late revelation could imply that throughout my stay in Nepal I was reluctant to admit that the irrigation project's leadership objected to implementing the women's program, as this would have implied the end of my mission there. Ignoring the signs of rejection could also have been the outcome of the successfully misleading performance of the irrigation project's heads, working as a team marked by familiarity, solidarity, and common secrecy, making sure that "secrets that could give the show away are shared and kept" (Goffman 1959: 238).[19] While they were pretending to show interest in the women's program, and confidence in my professional performance, they might have been pulling strings behind my back to bring about the program's termination.

The frustration and disappointment I felt appear to be a common experience of foreign experts in the wider context of development projects. This understanding emerges, for instance, from David Mosse's study of a British aid project in rural India. For example, Mosse writes that "members of our consultancy team universally expressed frustration at their inability to have any influence over project practice" (Mosse 2005: 135). Mosse suggests distinguishing between "project practice" and "policy theory." Thus, while foreign experts' practice can evidently be considered a failure, the production of "project models of great clarity for the donor (and beyond)" can be claimed to be successful (ibid.: 135). I contend, however, that this dialectic argument can be better understood as being about bureaucracy and bureaucrats' success. That is, bureaucratic power (of donors, aid agencies, governmental departments, and so on) effectively and elegantly overcomes the efforts of professional foreigners to bring about any significant social change. It manipulates experts and turns them into collaborators who are compensated for their efforts in terms of material advantages (such as travel and wages) and, indirectly, by mobility in their academic careers. Moreover, these experts are not really needed for bringing about social change but rather for the purpose of refraining from it, by focusing on "a huge number of visit reports, progress reports, annual reports" (ibid.: 134). This is what transpired in my experience.

In the Name of Women's Empowerment

One of the excuses used to postpone the implementation of the women's project, while concealing this intention from me, was a demand that the village teachers, who were invited to participate in a preparatory seminar, provide their husbands' or fathers' written consent. When I talked with Pandit and Gupta, some three weeks after my arrival in Nepal, about starting seminars for village teachers the next day, the two reacted with complete surprise and started talking between themselves in Nepali. Their conversation went on for some time, and after waiting patiently I asked them if there was a problem. They explained that forms of consent and commitment for attending the seminars regularly must be signed before they began and that this would take some time. They then went on talking again in Nepali. When I asked why not have the women sign the forms when they arrive on the first day of the seminar, they explained that it was not clear that the women would show up at all and that there was a chance that the women might not be allowed to come. Therefore, they would all have to be notified again.

Surprised but also disappointed, and to a degree resentful, I argued that all of the women had been notified already and that all of them had agreed to participate in the seminar. The discussion continued, and the two men turned to talk with Anita in Nepali. The two WGOs, present in the room, were listening and smiling now and again, probably when jokes were made (naturally, I wondered if they were at my expense).

It appears, then, that my seemingly superior position as a foreign consultant, representing the Israeli irrigation company, professionally responsible for a program which enjoyed the support of the World Bank, did not entail me being able to implement the program when confronting reluctant local officials. At most, polite gestures were made and superficial respect afforded, but not much beyond that. This became evident when one morning I entered Pandit's room, which was crowded with the irrigation project's employees (including the WGOs), as usual. Everyone, except for three WGOs, left the room. Anita got off her chair and went to share a chair with one of the WGOs. Next, another WGO got off her chair and left it for me. Despite the superficial respect I enjoyed, it became apparent that in practice the local people and I, the outsider, were on opposite sides. Even the women, who were supposed to be interested in getting the women's seminar and literacy classes up and running, seemed to join forces with the men. They did not express any objection, at least not openly, about the postponement of the courses. This could be explained by the fact that the men were their direct employers. Also, their Nepali male superiors were there to stay, whereas I was just passing through.

Eventually my campaign had a certain impact, and a date for starting the seminar was suggested; nevertheless I expressed my disappointment. Anita asked: "Is it not good that the Seminar will begin next week?" I replied instantly: "It is not good because I shall not be here when the literacy classes start." I meant that if the ten-day seminar ended later than I had planned, the literacy classes which were to follow would not begin while I was still in Nepal. Thus, the delay in beginning the seminar would prevent me from attending the opening of the first twenty literacy classes.[20] We entered lengthy negotiations, and I cautiously demanded that the earliest possible date be set for the start of the seminar. The men consulted between themselves and with Anita (in Nepali) while examining the Nepali calendar on the wall. When they suggested starting on Sunday, I expressed my disappointment. After checking other options they agreed to run the seminar on the Saturdays as well, which is the day of rest in Nepal. Eventually, in an attempt to please me, they suggested starting on Thursday. That was the best deal I managed to strike. They concluded the debate, saying "now it is necessary to go to the villages, to talk to each and every one of the village teachers and with those responsible for them and sign them up."

Applying pressure to start the seminar and literacy classes was indeed part of my self-presentation as a devoted professional and feminist. Yet, it appears in retrospect that my primary concerns were my own constraints and needs, such as my flight schedule on the one hand and a need to show tangible results to my employers on the other, although they did not really care about the implementation of the women's project (as I suggested earlier). I did not object to the suggestion of including Saturday as a study day for the village teachers. Yet, as a feminist, I should probably have been aware of the extra burden these intensive studies would put on the women, who had to come all the way from their villages to the irrigation project center in Bhairahawa.

This relative achievement did not satisfy me, and I went on playing the feminist role and raising "provocative" questions. I asked Pandit and Gupta: "Why should guardians sign for the women instead of the women signing for themselves, why is it not enough that the women sign the consent and commitment form? Is it not the purpose of the women's project to empower women and to relate to them as independent persons?" Gupta explained to me patiently and gently: "Here the social structure is different from that in Israel, and here the parents and the husband must give their consent for women's work, otherwise there are going to be problems. The woman may get married and go to her husband's place and stop working. But if the parents are responsible they will make sure that she conforms to her commitments. It is necessary to explain to the parents that their daughters will be paid some money and then they will understand the importance of the issue." I asked Gupta if the same applied to boys. Gupta replied that it is not the case with boys unless they are less than eighteen years old. I tried to push my agenda further and said: "You are the ones who decide on the matter, of course, but why not follow the same practice with girls as for boys, and in this way the women's project will contribute to promoting social change?" He repeated his explanations very patiently. Although I realized that I had lost the case, I asked again: "What will be done if the woman quits teaching despite having her own and her husband's or father's signature? Will she be sued?" The two men smiled and dismissed that option. In the end I retreated, saying: "Ultimately you know very well what is happening and indeed you are the ones who decide what should be done." The outcome of the consent-form affair seemed to sort itself out shortly after Anita spoke with the irrigation project accountant. She informed me that the consent forms were only a formality, and that the women teachers themselves would sign the forms of commitment to teach upon their arrival at the seminar.

The requirement of consent by male guardians appeared to serve as an excuse for local heads of the irrigation project to delay the opening of the seminar, following which the whole women's project could easily be postponed and then canceled. Once the officials were sure that only one seminar would be held (and that by the time it ended I would be gone), they could give way to my pressures. Moreover, as the only seminar that was to be implemented necessitated a very small budget, the "traditional," "cultural" explanations were rendered unnecessary, and that is probably why the officials relaxed the requirement about male guardians' signatures. If this is true, it implies that the insistence on acquiring the father's or husband's signature was a tactic used to deal with my pressures, and that the real reason for the officials' objections to the implementation of the women's project was disguised.

This understanding should not come as a surprise, as cultural and/or traditional narratives are widely assumed as self-evident, and therefore are easy to manipulate (Hertzog 2001).[21] The use of culture and tradition as an explanation to justify the postponement of the women's program demonstrates how male officials ensured their ongoing control over resources, policies, and discourse. Confronting my efforts to carry out the women's program, or even to become part of the decision-making team, they managed to exclude me by using the Nepali language in my presence, and by indicating that I was an outsider who was not familiar with local customs and social norms. Similarly, Mosse argues that labeling knowledge as Western serves local project staff as a strategy "for handling foreign experts and keeping [them at a] distance" (Mosse 2005: 133–34) when they want to reject foreign experts' knowledge. I suggest that more rather striving to reject foreign experts' knowledge, the local staff is interested in rejecting the foreign experts themselves, and probably in expressing latent reservations with regard to foreign experts' interventions.

Nevertheless, the point I wish to stress is my ongoing application of pressure and my repeated attempts at bargaining so as to ensure the start of the literacy classes, in the name of the women's empowerment. I identified with and adopted the role of a women villagers' advocate: I stood up for them, and faced local males in authoritative positions who obstinately objected to projects intended to serve the women. In the name of professionalism and feminism, I became a nuisance to the local officials, who had to put up with my pressurizing only as long as I was present in the region.

Confronting Men's Chauvinism

Despite the fact that the problem of the consent form seemed to have been resolved, the following day it transpired that this was not the case. The ongoing encounters concerning the disputed forms afforded another opportunity to display my professional and feminist stance. A couple of days later, when Anita and I went down to Pandit's room to find out if everything was ready for the seminar, Anita showed me two forms which had been signed by village teachers and their husbands. She also said that Gupta had spoken to three other village teachers and their husbands, but had not secured their signatures yet. When I discovered that things were going in the "wrong" direction, I said to Pandit: "I wish to state my protest." In reply, Pandit again used sociocultural jargon and said: "We are talking about a social structure in which the husband domineers and the wife is dominated." I replied:

> Yet, it is in our control, at least to some extent. We know that we have some power and influence. If we ask only the women to sign the forms of commitment, quite probably no one will ask us why we did not ask the husbands or fathers to sign them. It is likely that the men don't even think about having to sign the forms. And besides, they are not stupid and they also know that it is just a matter of formality and has no real meaning in any case, whether the husband signs the form or both husband and wife sign it.

In stating my wish to protest, my patronizing "professional" position was expressed antagonistically. However, it is apparent that as much as I was shown respect for my professional positions as a gender consultant, in fact, the local officials carried out only what suited them, and did not hesitate in changing decisions regardless of what they had promised and agreed upon. They endured minor demands of mine, those which they perceived as temporarily unavoidable but which could be changed later on.

I succeeded, however, in forcing many officials to discuss the gender implications of having males sign the commitment form. Following Pandit's explanations concerning the requirement that men approve the women's participation in the seminar, Anita commented that she was surprised about this state of affairs. She stated that things were quite different in Kathmandu (where her family and permanent home were). Pandit then asked her why she had said nothing about the matter before. I said that she had not been given a chance to react, and that they (the men) had decided on the matter. Pandit reacted defensively to my criticism and asked Anita if she was obliged to ask her husband for his permission to come out to Bhairahawa. She admitted that she did ask for her husband's approval and Pandit looked triumphant.

Not wanting discussion of the subject to end here, I asked what would have happened in the reverse case: Would her husband have to ask for her permission? Anita replied that her husband would have told her that he was going away. Then I admitted: "In Israel, too, the wife is normally the one to ask, explain, and beg for permission, and the husband would just announce that he is going away as a matter of fact. But this is different in every case and depends on the couple's relationship and it is also relative to specific situations and places." Using comparisons with Israeli society in particular was a favourite means of mine to convey my arguments and my "professional" approach. This enabled me to introduce "advanced" feminist attitudes from a presumably more equal and less ethnocentric position. However, from the officials' reactions it was apparent that this tactic did not fool them. They still seemed to think that I was referring to some irrelevant context, very different from their own. Their reactions were apologetic and evasive, pointing to their own social context as totally different from mine. The modern versus traditional opposition was thus implied in those conversations, both by the local officials and myself.

The intense conflict over consent forms demonstrates clearly that the senior male officials had their way. No technique or calculated strategy that I employed had any bearing on the outcome. This happened regardless of whether my verbal, practical, professional, or any other kind of performance, was skilful or poor. This conclusion emerges clearly from other studies of gender projects in the context of development (e.g., Chambers 1983; Oxby 1983; Gurung 1994; Kabeer 1999; Mosse 2005).

Patronizing Anita

Taking on the role of tutor to Anita was another way of displaying my professional superiority. This became apparent during a conversation we had about the consent form. We were eating sweet yogurt in a local restaurant where we used to sometimes go after our meetings with the irrigation project's officials or people from other offices. Anita referred to the demand for a male's signature on the form, and expressed her surprise again. I replied:

> It is very important to insist on your position and to stick to one's principles. This is something I've learned from my experience in struggling for women's equality. I learned that we have to insist and not give up, without getting overexcited or aggressive, but nevertheless to stick to one's principles and aims. The surrounding society, those in powerful positions in particular, do not want to change their habits and concepts, nor would they relinquish their positions of power. They would surely prefer to preserve the existing situation. Those in charge often use excuses to justify their conduct and decisions, as in the case of the males' signatures.

Following this, Anita said that she would not have noticed these things had I not pointed them out. Flattered by her comment I continued to wax philosophical: "With self-awareness and a lot of attention, as well as familiarity with feminist studies, it becomes natural to observe these things, which it is very important to transmit to the WGOs. You can use such events (like the signature affair) in your talks with them to illustrate your ideas." This blunt preaching was not the end of my overbearing, patronizing manner. Lecturing Anita about how to enlighten "her" WGOs in regard to gender awareness, I again brought up my research on Ethiopian immigrants in Israel. I reiterated how officials prevented women from receiving vocational training, justifying their discriminatory practices by invoking the immigrants' culture. I said: "They would claim that in Ethiopia the woman worked indoors taking care of children, although she worked outdoors, in the fields, as well." I concluded my "professional" talk by asserting that in the coming seminars the women should be the ones to sign the consent form.

My patronizing attitude was also evident in my use of professional and feminist jargon. On one of our visits to the villages, the women firmly demanded that their teacher be a married woman, rather than the one preferred by the WGO. They also disagreed about the location of the intended class. Anita was displeased with the women's objection. Yet, I expressed satisfaction at the women's behavior, arguing that "it is encouraging that women are collaborating to pursue a common cause." Another key phrase I often employed was "to build on local forces." I used that expression, for example, when Anita and I met the American head of a literacy NGO on a joint visit to Kathmandu (in fact, both the NGO person and I used it). Such terms conferred an impression of possessing the essential professional background and knowledge expected of a foreign consultant who was sincerely concerned with empowering the poor, weak, disadvantaged, and discriminated against Nepali people. Expressions like "developing women's solidarity" and "forming women's collective interest groups," often used by me in daily encounters, also exemplified the role of jargon in establishing a convincing image of myself as an expert in gender issues. This terminology was always employed in a self-confident tone.

One such example was an informal meeting that I initiated at the bachelors' house, the place where Leon, I and Tahal's employees boarded at one time or another. Anita and the WGOs, who were invited to the party, were offered refreshments, and we were carrying on a friendly conversation. I began by saying: "I consider it as most important to have a solid, reliable group that meets regularly to discuss personal and general matters in relation to the women's project. It is also essential to form a framework that can contribute to the self-enrichment of all involved."

By taking center stage, and acting like a source of "authority" and expertise in relation to gender issues, I unintentionally pushed Anita aside and positioned her as inferior to me in this situation and in many others. Since I was playing the role of the expert, she became my trainee, or my junior assistant. That state of affairs was incompatible both with feminist and development values. Thus, for example, when the two of us came out of a meeting with some people from a health NGO that was held in Thapa's room, I "advised" Anita to be more assertive and to voice her opinions. Realizing that I had taken control of the conversation with the NGO people, I said to her: "It is most important that you speak out your ideas, and not let me shut you up. It is crucial not only so that people will listen to what you have to say and respect you, but also so that men will become used to listening to a Nepali professional woman like yourself." Indeed, this advice exposed my hidden stereotype of Nepali professional women as people who lack self-confidence and need (an outsider's) reassurance to speak up.

On another occasion I presented myself as a role model to convey to Anita appropriate professional conduct. In response to her doubts about the prospects of the women's project being carried out, I said: "I would resign if the project turned out to be a fake." Encouraging Anita to resign if she discovered that the women's project was a sham exposed the pretentious attitude behind my expertise and professional integrity. It was easy for me to suggest that Anita resign as I was going back to a secure position at home. My conduct, then, illustrates Goffman's claim that "as performers we are merchants of morality" (Goffman 1959: 251). I was, indeed, "concerned with maintaining the impression" that I was "living up to the many standards" according to which I assumed I would be judged. Moreover, I was "concerned not with the moral issue of realizing these standards, but with the amoral issue of engineering a convincing impression that these standards are being realized" (ibid.: 251).

Complying with Expectations about Patronizing the Village Men

The image of expertise I established was apparently so convincing that a short while before leaving Nepal to go back to Israel Leon came up with the idea that I should meet the male villagers and give them a talk. It was suggested that this initiative take place at one of the final ceremonial events, at which the management of the wells was transferred to the local farmers. During one of our regular communal breakfasts at the bachelors' house, Leon said: "It is very important that you meet with the men, who are the other side of the equation. So far you have only met with women. You can talk to them and explain the importance of women's advancement." I replied that I liked the idea but that it was rather unlikely that Thapa would favor it.

However, Leon did not give up and later on he put the idea to Gupta. Gupta was anything but thrilled with the proposal, and hesitantly explained that these meetings were very messy and noisy, and that the men do not care to hear about women's issues. He added that on these occasions only practical matters concerning the transfer of the wells were discussed. I knew from Leon's stories that a recurring issue at these events was the complaint made by the villagers about the need for them to pay for the electricity for operating the wells once the running of the wells was transferred to them. These reservations did not convince Leon and he went into detail, describing to Gupta the important things I could tell the men. I flattered him and said that he sounded as though he was very familiar with feminist thinking. Gupta gradually changed his mind and suggested that we ask Thapa. Eventually, Leon informed me that Thapa had agreed that I could speak to the men at the ceremony, which was scheduled to take place that same day. Leon reported to me: "I said to Thapa, 'There are two options: One is that Esther will attend the meeting, sit there quietly and watch it. The other option is that she will talk to the men'. Thapa replied: 'Why not? Let her talk.'"

At the gathering, Leon sat at the speakers' table, in front of an audience of some forty men. He was protective and patronizing toward me. While Gupta was introducing me, Leon asked him whether I should stand up or sit down. Gupta responded that I could sit down and he would translate what I said to the men in the room. Leon told me to speak to the men. My talk was patronizing and pretentious. I told them about the gender activities project and expanded on its far-reaching potential in terms of economic and social change. I highlighted the significant advantages that their villages would enjoy as a result of women's empowerment. I mentioned the Scandinavian model of gender equality as an example of the embedded connection between women's equality and social justice in wider society. At the end of my speech I added that they, as leaders who are responsible for the welfare of their communities, could enhance women's participation in leadership.

Using the Scandinavian example, challenging the men as leaders regarding their attitude toward their female counterparts, and emphasizing the values of gender equality were all a way of displaying my expertise. My lecture revealed my ethnocentric view of my audience as less advanced, less informed, and even backward in terms of their understanding of the meaning of social change and gender issues. A passage in my notebook demonstrates this point: "At the end of the meeting I added the most difficult thing," meaning my appeal to the men to share the leadership and management of the wells with the women. Thus, my assumption was that the idea of sharing leadership with the women would be problematic and threatening for the men, although my information about them was based mainly on the irrigation project officials' stereotypical descriptions.

Leon's efforts to have me lecture the village men could be understood as stemming from his appreciation of my expertise, and his sincere desire in wanting to raise the men's gender awareness. But it could also be explained as serving his own and Tahal's interests. Tahal was interested in employing foreign consultants as a means of creating profit for the company (a point I will return to at a later stage). Displaying my professional mastery of the subject and my demonstrated skills in communicating with the villagers (even with the men) could later serve to convince Thapa and the other Nepali heads of the irrigation project to hire my services (through Tahal) again. This argument also explains Leon's desire to take center stage in the events that signified the termination of the irrigation project. Tahal's essential part in the irrigation project had to be stressed constantly to the local project leaders.

Patronizing Male Officials

Patronizing the male officials was an inseparable part of my interactions with them. Even on my last day at the irrigation project offices, when a second farewell party was organized for me, I revealed this attitude. Leon, Gupta, Pandit, Anita, and I were present in Acharya's room, talking about the informal farewell party. I used this opportunity to talk again about starting the literacy classes and said, in a somewhat dramatic tone: "You are the ones in charge and have the authority and the power to do things. It is easy for all of us to be content with what duty requires of us, but we can do meaningful things when we possess authority."

On that occasion I also belittled Anita, although inadvertently. As we were discussing the future of the women's project, Acharya suggested that as there was not enough money for carrying out the whole project it would be necessary to revise the budget and implement it only partially. Anita whispered to me, "every woman will enjoy, in fact, only a very small amount of money." I announced that Anita had something to say. Adding, "there is no chance that a woman will be able to speak out to a male crowd of people," I started to repeat what Anita had told me discreetly. At this point Leon interrupted me, saying that I should not speak for Anita but rather let her speak for herself. While I was presenting Anita and women at large as weak and vulnerable, Leon reprimanded me, exposing my own arrogant behavior. He responded to Acharya's statement about the necessary cuts in the budget by remarking that the gender activities project was too important to be scaled down. I reacted by saying that I was proud of Leon "for insisting on the full implementation of the women's program, even more than myself." Thus I presented the women's program as mine, and myself as being in charge of it, while treating Leon as a naive person who could be easily placated. The people I perceived as not appreciating the women program's importance were reprimanded (Acharya, for instance), while those who appeared to comprehend the women program's value (like Leon) earned my approval.

Using compliments and preaching to the male officials present produced a pattern of interaction in which I assumed the role of an authoritative educator who seeks to instruct the misbehaving trainees. This attitude entailed, as the above encounter illustrates, the infantilization of the other participants.

Similar dynamics recurred on other occasions, such as the more formal farewell party that was organized for me by the heads of the irrigation project before I left. The party took place on the rooftop of the office complex, in the open air, where people sat in a wide circle. Refreshments were served, including cold drinks, fruit, and samosas. Some forty people attended this event, among which were most of the WGOs, some of the AOs, Raju (Leon's secretary), Anita, Thapa, Gupta, Acharya, Pandit, and myself. Leon called me to join Thapa, the senior officials and himself at the front and to give a short speech. He introduced me, saying that I had come to Nepal with the purpose of empowering women. I began with a short description of the women's program. Referring to Leon's introduction, I said: "Leon told you that I came to empower women but, as a matter of fact, I was empowered by the women I met in the villages."

In my short talk I used two examples, the first of which concerned one of the participants in the women teachers' seminar. This woman, who used to arrive at the seminar with her baby, came from a distant village but hardly missed a day of the whole seminar. I said: "If she could come despite the tough conditions, while having to leave her children behind to carry out the routine tasks at her home, and yet managed to arrive regularly at the seminar with her baby, it means that women can overcome many hardships on their way to improving their situation and acquiring education and professional training." My second example referred to an incident that took place at the ceremony that marked the conclusion of the teachers' seminar. All the heads of the irrigation project attended the event and a few local representatives of the Ministry of Education were also invited. The panel of speakers consisted of Thapa, Gupta, Leon, and the ministry official. Following an offensive remark made by one of the speakers toward a seminar participant, another seminar participant had stood up and supported the offended woman. Elaborating on that episode I said: "That woman's courage offers us a very important lesson: that only when women support each other and struggle together will we be able to change the situation and promote gender equality."

I then complimented the WGOs for "showing a profound devotion" and being "real feminists." I concluded my talk with praise for Thapa, saying that he was "a strong man" and that "many of the (irrigation) project employees think highly of you, and therefore much depends on you regarding the implementation of the women's project." Thus, my self-presentation as an expert on gender issues and women's empowerment, offering "empowering" evaluations about other women's devotion to feminism and judgmental statements regarding men's behavior towards women, served to legitimize and establish my professionalism.

Veiled Vulnerability

Nevertheless, behind the authoritative disguise, my vulnerability was exposed at both the farewell parties put on for me. My performance as a foreign expert was not very convincing. It was made clear to me, implicitly and explicitly, that I did not belong there and that my expertise and feminist agenda were not welcome. In short, I was given to understand that as soon as I was gone my ideas would be gone with me. At the formal farewell party held for me the situation was especially embarrassing, at times even humiliating. Such was the case when Thapa asked to speak right after Anita finished her talk. He said that I had referred to discrimination against women, but then countered: "You don't know that at home the women can control the men." He continued his criticism, suggesting that I was not familiar with Nepali culture, which differs from Israeli culture. He then used the seminar incident, which I had mentioned in my talk (concerning the woman who defended her offended friend), to illustrate his point. "You see", he said "you thought that the woman was offended but Nepali people do not get offended that easily." Thapa's reservations in relation to my work and views became even more explicit following Leon's comment. When Thapa complimented my work, Leon used the opportunity to suggest that the irrigation project would bring me back to Nepal. Thapa instantly replied, smiling, "I am not sure about that."

The language also played a role in unmasking my vulnerability, as an outsider who could not speak or understand Nepali. Before addressing people, I asked for someone to translate into Nepali what I was saying. My request was refused and it was explained that the participants understood English. This was not true, as only a few of those who were attending the event spoke some English. I went on speaking, knowing that most of the people did not understand what I said. Anita spoke right after me. She spoke in Nepali, so I could not understand what she said, although she briefly told me later what she had said. Thapa, however, spoke in English. It appeared that he was directing his comments at me (and at Leon too), and probably did not care that the lower-ranked employees could not understand what he was saying. The message came out loud and clear: I was not one of them, I had presented myself as an expert but I knew nothing about Nepali culture and mentality. As most of my arguments referred to the gender context, and repeatedly offered comparisons between Nepal, Israel, and the Scandinavian countries, his criticism trivialized my proclaimed expertise as pretentious.

The farewell party, which was meant to show respect and gratitude for my work, became, inadvertently, a humiliating event for me. Reflecting on this clarified for me various incidents that had taken place before the party. Bargaining over refreshments, the timing of the party, and the number of participants to be invited—this was not hidden from me, and it indirectly conveyed the same message: the heads of the irrigation project did not sincerely regret my departure. I was asked to participate in ongoing discussions over details of organizing the party. One morning Leon handed me the printed invitations for my ("formal") farewell party and told me to distribute them among the WGOs. He also informed me that he had agreed with Thapa that some ten people would be invited to the party, and that refreshments would include two samosas per participant, cold drinks, and fruit. At first I thought that Leon was handing me my own invitation. However, when he asked that Anita and I get the WGOs to sign receipts acknowledging their invitations (to make sure they would attend the party), I realized my mistake.

On yet another occasion I was made to feel uncomfortable when Leon and Thapa were discussing a suitable time for the party while I was present. Thapa suggested that the party should be in the early afternoon, to enable the WGOs to get back to their homes before dark. I then went to Pandit's room to give him the invitations for the WGOs. He was surprised and said he knew nothing about the party.

I went up to Leon and told him of Pandit's reaction. Leon claimed that Pandit had attended the meeting with Thapa when they talked about the party. I then went to Thapa and told him that Pandit did not know about the party, that Leon had asked me to invite the WGOs, and that I felt embarrassed about the whole affair. Thapa smiled and explained calmly that the invitation (as well as the party) was initiated by Leon and that he (Thapa) had personally invited the irrigation project's people already. I said that I would go back to Pandit and ask him to invite the irrigation project's staff. Thapa suggested: "Perhaps Anita will notify the people." My total vulnerability was exposed when I blurted out: "You can thank God for getting rid of me." He reacted politely: "Oh no, we will be glad if you stay in Nepal."

Reluctant Patron, Vulnerable Foreigner

Apparently my presence and conduct evoked covert and overt reservations. I seemed to provoke antagonism, especially among the higher-ranked officials. However, as much as my behavior may be described as ethnocentric and pretentious, I do not suggest that I was more arrogant, patronizing, and ethnocentric than most people are or may become under similar circumstances, or even in daily encounters. I suggest, rather, that the role I took on and the situation itself had a dramatic and inevitable impact on my behavior. Once I accepted the position of consultant in the women's project, I was obliged to play the expert role that was indirectly imposed on and expected of me. The point here is that my behavior should be understood in general and structural terms, rather than in personal ones. Moreover, I have tried to demonstrate that my confident authoritative self-presentation was in reality fragile and misleading. It became apparent that I did not really have any substantial power or influence. Rather, I was a transient visitor who depended on permanent local officials for recognition, acceptance, and respect.

Although Thapa expressed subtle hostility toward me, he was never offensive outright. I found out soon after my arrival in Nepal that he objected to my being hired by the irrigation project, and that prior to my arrival he had expressed his reservations explicitly to the heads of Tahal in Israel. His objection (about which, as I mentioned above, I did not know) delayed my visit for some time. Leon claimed that Thapa had objected to having any foreign gender consultants on the irrigation project.

Thapa's reluctance toward hiring gender consultants became clearer when Leon came out of Thapa's room one morning, looking very agitated. He told me angrily that Thapa had demanded that he make instant financial arrangements (through Tahal's consultants' budget) that would enable the urgent recruitment of a specific marketing expert to join the irrigation project. Leon said:

> He wants me to provide him, here and now, with the consultant's CV, and employ him on the spot. But later on the matter will be set aside for a year, just as it happened with the women's program. It took him such a long time

> to approve the hiring of Tovi Fenster [my predecessor], and then he would not accept anyone but her coming again. So I told him that she had broken her leg, and that she could not come because Tahal did not want her to come again as she had demanded she stay in a hotel and it was not good enough for her to reside in the bachelors' house. He [Thapa] said then that he did not approve of your CV, as a consultant for development projects. Do you think that this was the real reason? That was an excuse to delay the implementation. And do you think that he needed Tovi? But as the World Bank was pressing him to make progress with the women's program and he had no choice, he agreed to have Tovi again. But when Tovi could not come he conveniently used the excuse that your CV was not appropriate.

Thapa's implicit and explicit reservations toward me can be explained, at least partially, by his generally negative attitude to foreign consultants. They were probably perceived as parasites, who profited professionally and economically from development budgets at the expense of local, low-paid officials. Yet, Thapa's unequivocal demand that Leon arrange the immediate hiring of a marketing consultant rules out this interpretation as a sole explanation. Thapa's resentment can be better understood in relation to my explicit feminist position, which questioned his control—as a dominant male in Nepal, of the irrigation project, and at home as well. The underlying theme of the social exchange between the two of us, as well as between other heads of the irrigation project and myself, related to gender inequality and the need to change it. Therefore, I must have presented some sort of threat to men like Thapa who held high positions, were the superiors of women in the work place, and provided for, and thus economically dominated, their wives at home.

My overt criticism of male domination and the exclusion of women probably provoked resistance and defensive postures amongst the irrigation project managers. I would argue that the reason for objecting to my position and my presence was related mainly to my stubborn insistence on implementing the women's program and starting the literacy classes. This was not only a nuisance for the heads of the irrigation project. Rather, it exposed their resentment at the enforced obligation to transfer some of the World Bank's loan to the women's program, which they perceived as irrelevant to the irrigation project. The women's program was manipulated to the point whereby it was established as irrelevant to the "real" project, and this was done by demonstrating its unsuitability in terms of Nepali culture and its impracticability in terms of its time frame. Consequently, the $500,000 budget allocated for the implementation of the women's program turned out to be "free money," unallocated from the point of view of the irrigation project's officials. Therefore, this money could easily be perceived and treated as available to them for their own purposes.

In the next chapter I shall focus on Leon's patronizing behavior and try to illustrate the impact that domineering social settings have on personal conduct.

Notes

1. Weber perceives the extent of bureaucratic power over the individual as something that "reduces every worker to a cog in this bureaucratic machine" (Weber 1978: lix).
2. In his anthropological study of a Pakistani village, Lyon proposes three definitional points about patron–client relations: they are systematically personal and dyadic; patron–client roles are voluntary and reciprocal; and the embedded friendship in these relationships is "instrumental" rather than "emotional" (Lyon 2004: 262).
3. Nöbauer follows the definition of "paternalism" in the *Metzler Philosophie Lexikon*: "[a] specific claim to legitimize economic and political domination, which is constructed in analogy to the position of the family patriarch and which stresses, in addition to the punitive power of the father of the house, of an enterprise or of a country, his social and 'welfare' duties. Paternalism always refers to both these aspects of the deployment of domination and production of obedience" (Metzler 1996: 382).
4. The Tahal Group is an international engineering concern. Founded in 1952, Tahal is involved in the planning, development, and management of water resources in Israel, and has carried out projects in over fifty countries on five continents.
5. Source: http://www.undp.org.np/gender/projects/mgep/index.php?ProgramID=32 Retrieved 17 September 2010.
6. See note 1 in the Preface.
7. The Maoist guerrilla insurgency was launched in February 1996 by the Communist Party of Nepal-Maoist.
8. The category "paraprofessional" emerged in the US in the 1960s as a strategy to reduce social tensions by co-optation of indigenous/non-professional workers by social services. This practice was based on the concept of "new careers for the poor," developed by Arthur Pearl and Frank Riessman, who called for transforming "receivers of help (such as welfare recipients) into dispensers of help; to structure the situation so that receivers of help will be placed in roles requiring the giving of assistance" (Pearl and Riessman 1965: 88–89; see also Riessman 1968). Edward Brawley and Ruben Schindler, meanwhile, define "paraprofessional social welfare personnel" as "those persons who are engaged in the provision of social welfare services to individuals, families and communities, but who do not have professional social work education" (Brawley and Schindler 1986: 165). In another publication, they use the term "paraprofessional" in reference to a broad range of paid front-line social-welfare and social-development personnel who have received limited or no training for their jobs (Schindler and Brawley 1987).
9. My own experience in the paraprofessional field stems from founding the Israeli Association for the Development of Paraprofessional Manpower in Social Welfare Services (ASI) in 1979, initiated and funded by the Ministry of Labor and Welfare and JDC Israel, which I headed until 1982.
10. The concept and role of paraprofessional workers was adopted by the Israeli welfare services in the mid 1970s from the US. When immigrants from Ethiopia arrived in Israel in the 1980s and 1990s, they were sent to absorption centers run by the Jewish Agency. The *Somchot* were recruited to instruct and assist the newcomers in their integration into local society. The role of the *Somchot* was conceived of as a female occupation, based on homemaking and childcare (Etgar 1977; Jewish Agency 1984; Neipris 1984). In practice they transmitted to the immigrant women the social values that prevailed in the larger society and imposed social control through the embodiment of female identity (Hertzog 2001).
11. In 1983 I prepared a course for paraprofessional workers who instructed female immigrants from Ethiopia in absorption centers, run by the Jewish Agency.
12. Sally Andrade and Alvin Burstein (1973), who describe the introduction of indigenous non-professionals in mental health services in Texas, elaborate on the rationale for such usage, arguing that non-white, non-middle-class clients, frequently a majority in community clinics, are likely to relate more readily to helpers of similar socioeconomic or cultural background. Maruna and LeBel propose employing paraprofessionals to work with ex-convicts to combat

their social exclusion and stigmatization. They suggest that this paradigm "calls for opportunities for ex-convicts to make amends, demonstrate their value and potential, and make positive contributions to their communities" (Maruna and LeBel 2003: 97).

13. Erving Goffman demonstrates this phenomenon through the example of American medical organizations' dilemma of administering anaesthesia by nurses. This takes place "behind the front," which involves "ceremonial subordination to doctors and a relatively low rate of pay" (Goffman 1959: 28).
14. The role of transportation and other advantages in creating distance between local (rural) people and visitors has been indicated by Robert Chambers (1983). Visitors are of divergent affiliations and backgrounds, including government officials, specialists, academic researchers, staff of voluntary agencies, journalists, diplomats, politicians, consultants, and so on. In Chambers's words, visitors are "encapsulated first in a limousine, Landrover, Jeep or car and later in a moving entourage of officials and local notables" (ibid.: 12).
15. Thus, one basket would cost between approximately $1.7 and approximately $8.6 (as $1 dollar's value was approximately 58 rupees).
16. That is approximately $1.7 (see previous note).
17. Robert Chambers contends that "whatever their private feelings, (indifferent, suspicious, amused, anxious, irritated, or enthusiastic), the rural people put on their best face and receive the visitor well" (Chambers 1983: 30).
18. My own study points to the use of "uncleanliness" and "disease" in constructing images of Ethiopian immigrants to Israel in the 1980s and 1990s, and to the representation of them as weak and needing guidance (Hertzog 2010b). The connotation of primitivism, manipulated by politicians and officials, is also evidenced in Shachak's study on the inhabitants of a development town in Israel, inhabited by immigrants from North Africa, who settled there in the 1950s (Shachak 1985). Mosse suggests that in the Bhil society alcohol was connected "to ill-health, debt, social conflict and, most seriously for women, with domestic violence," and that alcohol has been "a core symbol of Bhil underdevelopment" (Mosse 2005: 216–17).
19. Goffman suggests that within the walls of social establishments there are teams of performers "who cooperate to present to an audience a given definition of the situation." Establishments are divided, so he argues, between back and front stage. The front stage is "controlled in order to prevent ... [the] outsider from coming into a performance that is not addressed to them" (Goffman 1959: 238).
20. My departure was scheduled for 24 September. Therefore, my attendance at the start of the literacy classes would necessitate them starting before the 24 September and ending the seminar by 22 September.
21. This argument is illustrated in my work on the bureaucratic treatment of Ethiopian immigrants in Israel (Hertzog 2001), where I describe how officials employ cultural explanations to justify their discriminatory practices toward women with regard to vocational training and employment prospects.

Chapter 2

INSTRUMENTAL PATRONAGE: LEON AND HANNA

Leon as a Bossy Patron

If physical appearance can reflect one's societal role or status—as Edward Gifford (1929: 3), Marshall Sahlins (1963: 288), and Paula Brown (1990: 97) have suggested—then Leon's appearance presents a stereotypic "caricature" (Sahlins 1963: 289) of a colonial patron.[1] Comparing political structures in Polynesia and Melanesia, Sahlins points to differences between the types of leaders of these two societies, which even their physical bearing reflects. The Melanesian "big man," he says: "seems so thoroughly bourgeois, so reminiscent of the free-enterprising rugged individual of our own heritage. He combines with an ostensible interest in the general welfare a more profound measure of self-interested cunning and economic calculation. The historical caricature of the Polynesian chief, however, is feudal rather than capitalist. His appearance, his bearing is almost regal" (ibid.: 288).

Leon was a tall man, had a respectable (not too big) belly, gray-white thin hair, which was receding at the forehead, a tanned face, and an overbearing look of contempt. However, Leon seemed to me to embody a colonial patron not only in physical dimensions. His characteristics were manifest in "bearing, appearance and manner—in a word personality" (ibid.: 288). Leon's attitude was communicated in the way he talked, in his gestures, in the way he walked, and in the demeaning remarks he made with regard to local people, and of others (Israelis, for instance) as well. I often felt that Leon despised the local people, their customs and manners, and that he gave them very little, if any, credit for their integrity, competence, proficiency, and sincerity. He seemed to treat the local employees of the irrigation project, the junior ones in particular, as his inferiors, and seemed to view most senior government officials with whom he had to deal with as collectively corrupt, selfish, and primitive.

Brown has noted that the physical size and strength of leaders "has often been mentioned especially where leading warriors are politically important" (Brown 1990: 97). Although this argument relates to the Melanesian context, I suggest that in Western societies the physical dimensions of leaders—whether they be political, military, or whatever—is of significance. I suggest that leaders do not "happen to be" physically big, but are probably preferred, through certain social mechanisms, to "small men," and more importantly to (small and big) women. The latent link between leadership and the "big man" implies a gendered connotation that is ignored in most discussions about the "big man". Simon Harrison (1993) points to the gendered implications of physical differences, latently associated with the role of violence and warfare. He suggests that the symbolic idealization of men's power constructs a community that is "externally bounded against 'enemies' and internally structured by inequalities of age and gender" (ibid.: 148). Following Harrison, John Gledhill notes that Sambia men of Papua New Guinea justify their dominance as necessary for defending society. Their dominance "rests on a peculiarly male essence, *jerungdu*, which is a life-force substance embodying uniquely masculine qualities of bodily and spiritual strength" (Gledhill 1994: 34).

Indeed, perceiving Leon as representing colonial, male dominance embedded in an individual's body is a far-reaching idea. However, Leon's bodily presence, body language, non-verbal expressions, and strong voice all had an impact on his counterparts. It is not clear whether he was aware of it and if he consciously used his physical attributes to impose his views and demands on others, but it seems that these masculine components could not be ignored. Thus, Leon's relative height was conspicuous in his interactions with local men and women, most of whom were shorter than him. Thus, for instance, Leon used a "manly," harsh, cold voice, which sounded threatening, especially in his encounters with women and subordinates.

Nevertheless, despite his arrogant airs, his prejudiced remarks, and offensive manners, sometimes Leon would reveal different features of his personality. On such occasions he would show sensitivity, express feminist views, and expose himself as vulnerable. Clearly, as any behavior should be understood against the background of its relevant social context, the extreme shifts in Leon's style of communication across diverse social scenarios can be understood by referring to the specific encounters in which he engaged, and the constraints they entailed. Goffman suggests that an individual's social identity is related to a performance "which regularly functions in a general and fixed fashion to define the situation for those who observe the performance" (Goffman 1959: 22). In this vein I suggest that the colonial arrogant (male) patron, which Leon seemed to be, was a role played and changed by him, adapted to specific situations, to other participating actors' self-presentations, and reflected his own compliance with the role he assumed.

This perspective introduces the essential need for ethnographic descriptions of complex situations and of the intricate behaviors of participants, which provide a detailed choreography of events and of their multifarious human nuances. Thus, I will use the detailed descriptions of encounters Leon was engaged to enable me to draw a portrait, from which a more complex understanding of a colonial male patron can be derived.

From my very first contact with Leon, when he phoned my hotel room in Kathmandu (described in the previous chapter), Leon established his superior position in our future relationship. By reproaching me for not calling him and my husband to inform them about the delay in the flight from Bombay to Kathmandu, and by using a hostile tone to address me (although he had never spoken with me before and had not yet met me), he made me feel irritated and worried. I became very anxious, and I worried about having to live in the same house as this unpleasant person while I was in Nepal.

Leon's animosity during our first telephone encounter may have stemmed from his sense of responsibility for my safety, and his genuine concern for me as a foreigner in the country. However, I was left with a lingering feeling that his concern was insincere, possibly reflecting his own worries about the anticipated outcome of my imposed presence, and having a total stranger invading his privacy (as he was at the time the only person living on the premises). Yet, a couple of weeks later, after sharing living quarters in Bhairahawa, taking our meals together, walking or driving together to the office of the irrigation project, sharing office space, and engaging in friendly conversations, we became closer and he felt at ease with me, as I did with him. This closeness encouraged Leon to trust me and consequently to consider me a suitable partner for sharing gossip and judgments on other people. Thus he felt free to tell me about his bad experience with my predecessor, Tovi Fenster, using certain crude expressions to describe her "snobbish" manners. According to him, they had had several hostile interactions, following which she left the house and moved into a local hotel.

Leon's negative experience with Tovi Fenster could explain, at least partially, his initial antagonism and reservations towards me. However, in light of various encounters that I witnessed, an alternative explanation can be given regarding his frequent use of intimidating verbal and non-verbal communication. His aggressive, domineering style was predominantly evident in his interactions with local people of lower social status, including those who worked for him at home (in Bhairahawa and Kathmandu) and in the Project office. It is plausible that because Leon wanted them to serve him to the best of their ability and not to mess around, he felt that a strict, unequivocal attitude toward his staff was required. His bossy attitude, from this perspective, was rational and practical. Therefore, separating work relations and personal relations, "eliminating all purely personal, irrational, and emotional elements which escape calculation" (Weber 1948: 216), was probably perceived by Leon as an inevitable part of maintaining good working relations, for his benefit and for the Project's sake. Thus, "the more perfectly the bureaucracy is 'dehumanized'" (ibid.: 216), the better it serves to ensure domination over the staff.

This argument is also applicable to our first telephone conversation. Leon's aggressive tone was instrumental in making clear from the very beginning who was the boss. It was most important for him to make me recognize his dominant position and my relatively lower standing, so as to preserve complete control over "his" Bhairahawa home. This is compatible with some of the comments he made about Tovi Fenster, being someone who took pride in her academic status, which irritated him. In other words, I was implicitly warned to act humbly and respectfully.

Presenting himself as an all-knowing expert was a conspicuous feature of Leon's domineering attitude. In our numerous discussions, Leon repeatedly revealed that he enjoyed playing the role of expert in relation to the women's development project, as he elaborated authoritatively on the women villagers' literacy competence and needs. Thus, for instance, his interventions in the process of hiring teachers for the training course of village teachers,[2] during which he pretended to be knowledgeable about literacy teaching, were sometimes irritating and sometimes ridiculous. Leon's behavior, which was probably intended to convey an impression of his command over the situations he was part of, could sometimes become amusing. This happened, for instance, after a meeting that took place at the Projects' meeting room, where I presented the women's program to the WGOs and the AOs. The presentation was prepared by Anita and me, and was translated by Anita into Nepali. As soon as Anita and I entered his office, Leon addressed us both with his critical comments. He told me that I should not have spoken about the program with the Project junior employees, while Anita was criticized for speaking too fast, thus making it impossible for people to follow her, and also for using Latinate words that they could not understand. He claimed that he knew enough Nepali to notice her use of words that were not part of the vernacular. It may be that Leon was venting his resentment at my "unauthorized" encounter with the junior irrigation project's staff. The fact that Anita and I did not consult with him about my presentation was probably annoying and an affront to his expectation of having full control. Leon expected his subordinates to show respect, obedience, and complete loyalty.

Thus, Leon's posture and familiar conduct could be easily perceived as arrogant, patronizing, pretentious, and sometimes even wicked. However, his social performance was more complex, and it also contained humane gestures and responses. In Marie-Benedicte Dembour's terms, he was not a "baddie" (Dembour 2000: 202). Exploring domination in the former Belgian Congo, Dembour realized that the retired officers she interviewed were not the "baddies" she had expected encountering. In the course of meeting them and analyzing their narratives, she confronted her own prejudices and "disgust for colonialism" (ibid.: 202), a situation which revealed to her the complexity of colonialism and of individual colonialists. I conclude that Leon's personality should be understood in more complex terms than "arrogant colonialist" or "domineering boss," and that, like the Congo, the irrigation project "was a place inhabited by people 'like those we meet everyday.'" (ibid.: 202).

Complying with Hanna's Dominance

Leon's behavior towards Hanna, his wife, as I witnessed it on a few occasions, provides another example of his context-dependent domineering conduct. Hanna stayed in the couple's rented house in Kathmandu, which was paid for by Tahal. She joined Leon in Bhairahawa only once during the three years of his stay in Nepal. Every Thursday at noon, Samir, Leon's driver, would take him to the airport to catch a flight to Kathmandu, where he would spend the weekend with his wife. Returning on Monday morning, Samir would pick him up and bring him back to the office.

Hanna seemed to be a very different person from Leon. She was friendly, pleasant, and very hospitable. Nevertheless, it seemed to me that in her relationships with her staff (a cleaner, a cook, a driver, and a gardener) she took up the matron's role very convincingly, although she did not employ the same harsh manner as her husband. This difference can be explained, apart from personality differences, by the fact that Leon, but not Hanna, was engaged in organizational performance, holding an authoritative position. This meant, probably, that Leon assumed he was expected to display his unquestionable control over his employees. Because he was more dependent on the staff than she was, he had, or thought that he had, to make it constantly clear to all that he was the boss and that he expected everyone to serve him to his satisfaction. Moreover, as an outsider, without knowledge of the local language, he had to be on his guard with respect to any possible resistance or opposition, which could cast doubt over his authority.

Hanna's basic dependence on the local staff, on the other hand, was more limited. She needed the cleaner and cook for domestic chores, but could do without them from time to time when they left her. She also needed the driver to take her shopping in the local bazaar, a significant activity of hers in Kathmandu. However, because I spent much more time with Leon than with Hanna, my characterizations should be considered tentative rather than conclusive. Thus, for example, it is possible that Hanna treated her employees no better than her husband.

Furthermore, as the irrigation project approached its end and Leon remained the last Israeli representative in Bhairahawa, it became evident (certainly to the local people around him, but possibly to himself as well), that he was not really needed and had made hardly any substantial contribution to the project. If so, Leon's tendency to present himself as vitally important and in control can be understood as a reaction to these changing conditions. Bossing others around was, therefore, a means to enforce his presence and convey the impression of his indispensability. This understanding derives support from Goffman's (1959) emphasis on the impact of a participating audience on the individual's self presentation, and from ethnographic studies carried out, for instance, by Emanuel Marx (1976), Eyal Ben-Ari (1989), Gideon Kunda (1992), and myself (Hertzog 2007).[3] These case studies demonstrate how people adjust their performance to changing circumstances, and how they utilize social skills and physical advantages to convince the audience what they should think about them and how to respond. Leon's rough behavior suggests that he had to work hard to impose his unwanted presence on senior and junior local employees of the irrigation project.

While Leon was struggling over recognition of his control in Bhairahawa, Hanna was engaged in socializing and shopping for "folklore" in Kathmandu. In fact, she became a competent expert in local handicrafts and her house was furnished and decorated with exquisite taste, with beautiful ornaments and genuinely artistic items. A considerable part of Hanna's life was devoted to socializing with other women, mainly the spouses of diplomatic representatives and professional staff, most of whom were from overseas. Hanna can be described as an "incorporated wife" (Callan and Ardener 1984), a personal dependent of her husband, and "ranked solely in terms of the status" (Gartrell 1984: 166) held by him. Being a high-ranking official's wife, she was a "materially privileged woman" (Callan 1984: 3). She clearly extracted as many benefits as she could from her socioeconomic position, in terms of luxury, comfort, and a "kind of glamour," in Lidia Sciama's (1984: 64) words. In her account of academic wives, Sciama describes the advantages that were enjoyed (or expected) by incorporated wives at Cambridge University: "They did hope to reap their rewards on this earth—and rewards sometimes did come with their husbands' achievement of senior positions which granted the women too, some active involvement in the inner circles of the 'good society'" (ibid.: 64). It appears, therefore, that Hanna had "a life of her own" (Ardener 1984: 41), enriched with social activities and personal enjoyment.

When I went to Kathmandu, Hanna invited me to accompany her to one of the women's garden parties that took place at the luxurious Shangri-La Hotel in town. The party was presented as a charity event intended to raise money for the poor in Nepal. Most of the women present were the wives of diplomats or of foreign consultants, and some were volunteers in NGOs. We paid a 100 rupee[4] entrance fee, which also entitled us to light refreshments (samosas and biscuits), served in the lovely garden under colorful parasols. The event looked like a typical colonial tea party (reminding me of similar ones I had seen in movies). The women were beautifully dressed, holding their teacups, chatting with an authoritative air about the situation in Nepal and its poverty.

I integrated very easily into these conversations, many of which were about local social topics. I assume that my questions, and the fact that I was new to the place, presenting myself as a hired gender consultant, provoked these topics. Two other Israeli women also attended the party: Rina, who had arrived the day before from Israel for a one-month stay to help out the Israeli embassy with some communication problems; and Yael, the wife of the security person at the embassy. While I was eating my samosa, Yael questioned me about why I was in Nepal. Before receiving a reply, she explained: "So much is done for the Nepali people but nothing is changing … So what is really being done? What can be done to change things?" I started to explain patiently what I was doing, and what I wished to do. I revealed to her my ideas about developing handicraft production with an entrepreneurial project, but she was not really listening. When she noticed one of her acquaintances she seemed very pleased to have found an exit, and she rushed toward her friend and never came back to continue the conversation with Hanna and me. This type of small talk went on for some time, until it started to rain and everybody left in a hurry. Hanna invited me to join her for dinner, which was cooked and served by her cook and servant. The driver waited for me outside until I left the house, and took me back to the hotel.

That garden party reflected the social distance that exists between foreigners and Nepali citizens. "Real" Nepal was, for those women, far away from their daily affairs. The "whiteness" of this group of privileged foreign women highlighted the ethnic distance between "natives" and people from overseas. Thus, the tea party and others of its kind contributed, indirectly, to symbolic "racial" stratification (Gartrell 1984: 166–185), in which male foreigners' wives were incorporated into the (neocolonial) development system through socializing with their expatriate female peers. This argument finds support in studies of colonial wives, like that of Janice Brownfoot on memsahibs in colonial Malaya. She argues that the *mems[ahibs]* "played a distinctive part in both the colonial order and its demise" (in Hillary Callan's introduction 1984: 6). Studying British wives in colonial Uganda, Gartrell similarly found that officials' wives contributed to racial exclusiveness "passively by providing a self-contained society for white men, as much as actively through their behaviour towards colonized people" (ibid.: 6). Being involved in charitable activities provided colonial women personal satisfaction and they filled "part of their leisure time by good works: starting baby clinics for Africans, teaching literacy classes, Red Cross work" (Gartrell 1984: 176).

Apparently, doing charitable work for the distant, unseen poor, and avoiding close contact with them, suited these "incorporated wives" very well. Hence, Hanna could live in Nepal and not live there at the same time. She lived, in fact, in her own sheltered house, beautifully decorated with Nepali works of art, and enjoyed a comfortable routine. Her lifestyle resembled that of rich upper-class people anywhere else in the world. She was served from early morning until late at night by poorly paid local employees, often went shopping to find bargains, socialized with the wives of high-ranking foreign officials at garden parties, and hosted guests (like myself) generously, with the help of her servants' labor, at home. Thus, unsurprisingly, Leon was anxious to get back to this "civilized paradise," and to get away as often as possible from the "wilderness," where he had to bear the intensive, close presence of local people. Also, coming back to Kathmandu meant, from Leon's point of view, joining Hanna, with whom he probably did not have to worry about threats to his authority. Indeed, Hanna was the "ideal colonial wife,"[5] and as such she fulfilled supportive roles, such as facilitator "of tensions reducing informal socializing…" (Gartrell 1984: 172), and similar to colonial wives, she provided unpaid and unrecognized services to her husband.

When the two of them were together Leon appeared to be a courteous person, showing Hanna respect and care. It was apparent that in their (publicly displayed) relationship Hanna was the more dominant. Leon did not oppose her in anything and always seemed eager to please her. She was the one who decided what to buy for their Kathmandu house, what to eat, with whom to socialize, and so on. When I went to Kathmandu, Leon and Hanna invited me to join them for a tour of the vicinity and for lunch at a restaurant in one of the most beautiful locations in the region, overlooking the city from the hills. Hanna took care of all the details: our itinerary, the duration of our visit to the tourist shop, and what the two of them would eat. Leon uttered not one word of disapproval. It seemed very clear who the boss was.

When in Bhairahawa, Leon would phone Hanna every other day and have a long talk with her. To me it appeared to be a sort of ritual. While on the other days we remained chatting for some time in the dining room, after having finished the meal, on these evenings Leon would finish his dinner on time to leave for his telephone conversations with Hanna. Then he would shut himself in his room and talk with Hanna, sometimes for hours. He was not seen until the next morning. Hanna provided, so it seemed, "companionship, the reduction of loneliness" (ibid.: 168).

Sometimes Leon would tell me about his conversations with Hanna. It was always evident that Leon profoundly respected Hanna's advice, and he often used to quote her. One of Leon's oft-used expressions was, "Hanna said I did not come to save Nepal." He used this expression, for instance, when I stated that, if it turned out that the heads of Tahal did not really intend to implement the women's project, I would consider returning to Israel. My spontaneous statement came as an emotional outburst when I was taken by surprise by Leon's announcement about the poor chances of realizing the women's project (this will be described in detail at a later stage).

Alarmed by my reaction, he tried to calm me by quoting Hanna's magic phrase that we cannot save Nepal. This expression suggested that Nepal's situation was hopeless and there was no chance of bringing about any meaningful change through one's work and expertise. It also implied that since it was, in any case, impossible to save Nepal, one should rather limit oneself to matters over which one had some control, renounce wider responsibility for the outcomes of projects of which one is part, and look out for one's own personal interests. However, the main point is Leon's adherence to Hanna's professed understanding of both his personal problems and of real life. She was the only person with whom Leon could discuss "the day's doings in his own idiom" (ibid.: 168).

Hanna's life in Nepal and her relationships with Leon offer an illuminating example of a "colonial service" context. Although the two were part of a postcolonial era, living in the contemporary bureaucratic context of development projects in poor countries, the resemblance between the patterns and norms of this situation and the colonial past is striking. I suggest that these similarities are related to the power structure embedded in both situations. This structure involves the construction of a categorical separation, in seemingly different organizational contexts, of foreigners from local people and of men from women. Gartrell notes that the "organizational type" of colonial rule can be compared to other organizations, such as corporations, the military, and the diplomatic service, in all of which "a predominately male body of employees is hierarchically organized" (ibid.: 166).

Leon and Hanna were part of a "colonial" setting, which obliged them to comply with given gendered roles, status and etiquette, enabled them different spheres of activity, and rewarded them accordingly. Whereas Leon received a high salary and position, and relied on his wife for companionship and moral support, Hanna enjoyed social advantages and a glamorous life, and depended on her husband for her economic needs.[6]

The Betrayed Patron

A clash between Leon and Sam, a foreign consultant, concerning the salary of Raju, Leon's secretary, offers another example of how Leon relied on Hanna's advice and reassurance in stressful circumstances. Sam, a young American and Leon's friend, had attempted to intercede on Raju's behalf, supporting his claim for a raise in his salary. Leon explained to me that Sam had betrayed him and expressed his contempt for him. He announced that their friendship had come to an end and that he would never meet Sam again. However, according to what Leon told me, Hanna advised him not to be so hasty in ending his friendships. "After all," she said, "how many friends do you have?" To this she added a warning: "And to whom can you turn to when something happens to you?" Indeed, Hanna's practical advice revealed her awareness of Leon's isolation.

Apparently, Leon felt that he was alone among strangers who could not, and perhaps would not, like to help him were he to end up in trouble. Moreover, he may have suspected that they might even endanger him. Hanna's common-sense advice offers an example, drawn from daily-life interactions, of Emerson's analysis of "balancing operations" (Emerson 1962: 35–40) for reducing power differentials in social relationships. Attaining an alternative social contact, which provides one with the goal one desires, reduces one's dependency on the sole person who possesses the needed resource and that person's control over one at the same time. As Leon did not have any alternative meaningful relationships with anyone apart from Sam, he therefore depended heavily on Sam for his friendship.

It was obvious that in Leon's and Hanna's minds, local Nepali people could not be considered "real," reliable friends, and so Leon could trust only an outsider like himself as a close friend. Sam, a foreign English-speaking man, was the suitable person to befriend. Indeed, this assumption could have been the outcome of not being made welcome by the local people, especially not in Bhairahawa. This seemed to be the case, as Leon's local acquaintances were people with whom he was working, who either responded to his bossy manners in kind, or simply preferred to keep their relationships with him formal and limited to professional matters. The fact that Sam was able to develop closer relationships with the locals suggests that people distanced themselves from Leon because of his perceived arrogance. Leon's complaints about not being invited by his Nepali colleagues to their homes implied that he was hurt by their reserve. However, it appears that he nevertheless preferred to keep a clear distance between himself and local people, and refrained from maintaining relationships with them outside of work.

There is, however, another possible interpretation regarding the issue of Leon's apparent contradictory modes of behavior: his arrogant attitude towards Nepali people on the one hand, and his warm, respectful attitude toward Hanna on the other. Leon's need for Hanna's support and friendship seemed to be very basic, as she offered him unconditional and continuous support. Hanna was there for Leon, providing him with "the nurturant and restorative functions widely ascribed to wives, who were expected to provide solace for the stresses of organizational life and to send their men back ready to work with renewed vigour" (Gartrell 1984: 168). Hanna also provided Leon with a sense of belonging, furnishing him with a family base and a stable marriage, which, "… the confidence placed" in it "is generally well-founded" (Callan 1984: 22). She created "a place of trusting and giving" (Bourdieu 1996: 20) for Leon, which enabled him to endure the tensions of life in Bhairahawa.

Thus, Leon profoundly depended on Hanna, and was therefore obliged to be respectful, generous, and compliant to her. Conversely, Leon's job with the irrigation project was secure and anchored in a written contract by Tahal, and which explicitly stated the duration of his assignment in Nepal. Hence, he did not depend on local officials, neither the junior nor the senior ones, for his contract, or work conditions. They had little or no impact at all on his employment status. These were secured in his contract with Tahal. It follows, then, that Leon depended on Tahal and was obliged to them by his contract with the company. As a permanent employee, sent by Tahal to development projects in other countries in the past, Leon was committed to, and relied heavily on, the company for most of his professional career and employment.

Obviously, therefore, Leon's dependence on his Nepali counterparts (in terms of essential daily needs in Nepal) was relatively limited. This could account for his apparent arrogance towards them, especially towards the junior employees. Yet, senior officials in the irrigation project could complain about him to his superiors in Tahal and also to the World Bank officials. They could also have had some impact on work conditions in the office. This partial dependence forced Leon to take into account these officials and any reprisals they might make, should they disapprove of his conduct.

Although Leon's outward behavior can be described as that of a bad-tempered authoritarian, he was, nevertheless, vulnerable at the same time. The conflict with Sam reveals this perspective. The heated row with Sam started (or so, at least, I thought for some time) from a friendly conversation I had with Raju,

Leon's quiet, dedicated, and competent secretary. One day when Leon was out of the office, Raju told me that he wanted to go to India, his country of origin. When Leon heard this, he reacted angrily and demanded that Raju not leave, insisting as well that he continue working for him until his return to Israel. Raju told me that his son lived with his parents in India, and studied at a good school where Raju himself had studied as a boy. His wife, a Nepali woman, also wanted to go to India, although her family lived in Nepal. Raju assumed that they could both find secretarial work in India, and he felt that people were nicer in India than in Nepal: "They are not like the Nepali people whose only interest is money. Without money they will not do anything for others, just as human beings. Poverty is less terrible in India, and here in Nepal men treat women badly and there are a lot of drunken men here." Raju was very bitter and told me that even after ten years of living in Nepal he had not succeeded in acquiring Nepali citizenship. Consequently, he could travel only to India.

When Sam came to visit me one evening, while Leon was away in Kathmandu, I told him Raju's story. We were having a couple of beers and chatting openly about the usual things—the irrigation and literacy projects, the corruption of Nepali officials, how they were being bribed—and comparing this state of affairs to Israel and the United States. Feeling at ease, I told Sam about Raju's intention to go to India and work there.

The next morning when I came back from a meeting I found Sam leaving Leon's office. As he left the room, Leon was angrily muttering something about Raju's misbehavior. Raju did not understand, or pretended not to understand. It took me some time to realize that Leon was referring to Raju's intention to stop working for him and leave for India. At first I thought that Leon had found out that "his" jeep had been used a few days earlier, when he was away in Kathmandu, to take Raju's mother-in-law to the hospital. For a few minutes I felt concerned for myself, because Raju had asked me for permission to borrow the jeep (as Leon left the keys with me), and I had no choice but to grant it. But when Leon spoke, it became clear that he was furious about Raju's intention to leave him, and I felt relieved. Nevertheless, at the same time I felt guilty and ashamed for having given away Raju's secret. (Later on I found out that this was an ongoing issue, but at the time I did not know this.)

Raju was in a panic and kept apologizing for his "misconduct." Leon told him repeatedly and coldly that he had to announce his intention to leave one month in advance of his departure, and said: "You cannot just get up and leave, like your sister-in-law did" (she had worked for Leon before Raju). Leon also frequently reminded Raju that when he started to work for him he was very inefficient, but that thanks to his guidance, Raju's work had improved considerably. Raju brought up the issue of his salary, saying something about being offered better pay somewhere else. Leon reacted aggressively: "Everyone is entitled to look for better pay … Please yourself and go … But let me know one month in advance." Raju seemed anxious. He said that he did not mean to leave

Leon and that he knew he had to announce his resignation one month ahead. Leon replied to Raju's talk about his salary by saying that he had already raised his salary considerably, and that Raju's salary was higher than anything paid in other places in Nepal for similar work.

This dialogue went on for two days, with minor nuances. Leon sounded very angry and hurt. As I thought that Raju's troubles had started because I stupidly revealed his secret to Sam, I apologized whole-heartedly to Raju for telling Sam about his intention to leave for India. Raju did his best to reassure me, insisting that it was not my fault and that the information had come from Sam, with no connection to me. When I saw Sam, I told him quietly that he should not have told Leon what I had told him about Raju. Sam was embarrassed, and he denied that he had brought up my information about Raju when he had talked to Leon.

The affair demonstrated Leon's way of producing an atmosphere of anxiety and caution around him. He conveyed a sense of threat to people who interacted with him. While Leon and I were walking to the office one morning (due to a strike organized by the Maoists that prevented Samir from driving us there), I used the opportunity to defend Raju's behavior. Doing so also served to ease my guilty feelings for having caused Raju his troubles. I explained to Leon, very carefully, that Raju had simply expressed a wish to live in India, and had not mentioned any concrete intention to quit working for Leon. I went on to explain that Sam had inadvertently misinformed him of things. Leon tried to calm me down, saying that no one had suggested that I was the cause of the conflict. I was evidently acting out of anxiety and concern about a potential reprisal by Leon, as a consequence of taking sides against him.

Leon, so it seemed, reacted to the tension I was experiencing, but preferred to ignore the main problem behind the affair, namely Raju's request for a higher salary. Leon's behavior revealed that he was annoyed and felt betrayed by someone he considered a close friend, and was furious over the fact that any employee of his would dare to threaten his entitlement to administrative services (good secretarial services, for instance). Out of my own anxiety, I responded to his interpretation of the situation by saying: "I am not worried that people will know that I was the one who revealed Raju's story, but rather feel bad that I might have caused Raju's problems." Leon was surprised and asked if it was I who had brought up the story. I confirmed that I had, adding that when Sam came to visit me I had told him, confidentially, about Raju. He did not seem to be surprised about Sam's part in the story, as the dispute over Raju's salary had probably begun before I became involved in the affair. Leon said that it would never be the same between him and Sam. "I gave him so much and Sam gives back so little, if anything at all, in return. Our relationship will never be the same again. What happened is that when Raju brought up his demand for a raise in his salary he said that everybody, even Sam, was telling him that his salary was low. Sam knows, as he is an American, that in America nobody reveals any information concerning his salary to others."

Imposing Discretion for the Sake of Dominance

Secrecy concerning salaries is an important means of controlling employees. By obstructing their access to this vital information, delegitimizing the essential act of comparing wages, employers ensure their employees' compliance with prevailing working conditions. From Leon's point of view, quite probably, Sam had undermined this strategy, and consequently failed to identify himself with Leon's side in the power structure. The fact that Sam was a friend must have annoyed Leon in particular, because if he could not trust even a close friend to be loyal, then his sense of security must have been threatened.

The crucial role of secrecy in constructing and preserving elites' interests and power is highlighted by David Vincent (1998). Analyzing the pervasive culture of secrecy in Britain, Vincent suggests that the social changes brought about by industrialization in the nineteenth century forced the British ruling elite to replace its codes of behaviour in which formal rules were not required because an individual's status depended on the approval of his close acquaintances. The "control of knowledge", served to guarantee "Historic identity, security, and income" (Vincent 1998: 51). This argument supports Robert Merton's (1973) insiders'/outsiders' doctrines (ibid.: 99–138). Merton claims that the contemporary problem of "patterned differentials among social groups and strata in access to knowledge" (ibid.: 102), is a long-standing problem in the sociology of knowledge. Doctrines of the insiders, based on class, race, ethnicity, age, sex, etc., include the claim that the outsider has a structurally imposed incapacity for access to knowledge. Outsider doctrine involves claims of access to knowledge grounded on the assumption of socially based detachment.

Discretion and other bureaucratic means, such as "bureaucratic language" (Ferguson 1984: 40), were obviously essential to the irrigation project in order to preserve the privileges of the privileged and to sustain the hierarchical structure, which reflected the differential division of economic benefits, mainly in terms of salaries. As long as those at the top could ensure that people kept quiet about their salaries, they were able to maintain control over their employees. This is true for both poorly paid and better-paid individuals. Guaranteeing the discretion of the former was essential for avoiding the emergence of collective awareness concerning working conditions, following which an organized action to improve them might arise, by "coalition formation" balancing operation (Emerson 1962: 37).[7] The discretion of the better-paid group was essential in order to avoid ongoing pressure over pay aimed at the heads of the irrigation project, which would have impinged heavily on the budget. Obviously, this state of affairs ensured people's dependence on those who controlled the budgets, some of whom were subordinate to Leon, and others to Thapa.

Naturally, every employee (at any rank) strived for a higher salary. Bargaining over raises and buying-off people's compliance could work only in an individualized system by ensuring the ongoing one-sided dependence of employees on their employers. Besides imposing discretion, employees' dependency could be maintained by preserving a fairly uniform low wage for most of them. Indeed, any collective pay rise would have a far-reaching impact on the budget. Also, the irrigation project heads could pay their low-ranking workers in informal ways. For instance, Leon had an arrangement with Raju that every morning he would come in at 9 A.M. (Leon arrived some fifteen minutes later), open the windows, and empty the bin. He used to pay Raju for this service an additional sum of 300 rupees (about $5.00) per month. Leon had another arrangement with a man that was in charge of serving tea in the irrigation project offices. The man brought a jug of water every day to Leon's room, and was paid 100 rupees (less than $2.00) per month.

Leon seemed to believe that the local employees needed less than he did. This perception was apparent not only in relation to Raju, who, although poorly paid, was nevertheless paid better than other low-ranking employees who performed similar secretarial work. Gupta's salary, as an employee of Tahal, was much higher than that of the local employees. In fact, after Thapa, his earnings were second highest among the local employees of the irrigation project. When he asked for a raise, Leon reacted antagonistically. This came up when Leon and I were walking home from the office on one of the many strike days. Gupta walked with us part of the way until we reached Buddha's Square (a small traffic island in the center of town with a statue of the Buddha in the middle), where he turned on to another road leading to his home.

Continuing our conversation from the morning, I asked Leon about Gupta's salary. Leon said it was 67,000 rupees (about $1,100) per month. He then complained that he had raised Gupta's salary considerably in the last year and a half. I asked Leon what Gupta would do with such a substantial amount of money (in local terms). "Would he buy a car?" I asked. He replied: "They keep the money for old age, by then they cannot enjoy it any more. Gupta would not even pay 10 rupees for a rickshaw to come and visit the bachelors' house." Leon's reply obviously reflected his annoyance over pay-bargaining encounters, his bitterness about the fact that Gupta refrained from socializing with him, as well as his lack of respect for the Nepali people. However, it also demonstrated my own ethnocentric view regarding the subsistence needs of local people.

The cost estimate of the women's project, which I submitted for approval to the heads of the Ministry of Agriculture and the World Bank, demonstrates the considerable gap between wages among employees, depending on who their employer is—Tahal or the Nepali party (the department of irrigation in the Ministry of Agriculture). The budget proposal recommended the employment of two "Women's Groups Coordinators (WGCs)"[8] explaining that:

> at the moment the coordination and supervision of the project and of the women's group organizers is done by Mrs Khanal [Anita's surname], who is paid by Tahal. However, as the project is about to be enlarged significantly (from some 60 active groups up to 300 groups) it necessitates the

> employment of at least two Women's Groups Coordinators. The two WGCs salaries are calculated for a 17 month period, starting from January 1998 (when some 240 groups will be added gradually to the project) (6).

In practice, Anita was the only coordinator employed by the irrigation project, and her salary was $72 per month. She was also provided with accommodation in Bhairahawa. Tahal paid Anita's salary, as the Project's local consultant. The difference between her salary and mine was conspicuous. My salary was approximately $3,500 per month; that is, fifty times more than Anita's salary. But that was only part of it. I was also paid an extra $290 per month for working overtime or on Jewish or local holidays. Also, for each day of my stay at the bachelors' house I received a sustenance allowance of $75, all of which added up to an extra $2,500 (for my whole visit). In addition, an extra sum was paid to cover days when I traveled (from and back to Israel, and my three nights and days in Kathmandu). Health, life, and luggage insurance were also paid for.

Significant wage gaps between local and foreign employees were not unique to the irrigation project. This state of affairs is embedded in the development industry generally. In the Nepali context, Judith Justice reports: "For a foreign staff member or advisor in Nepal, the United Nations Development Program budgets $75,000 per year, or 1 million rupees, excluding agency overhead. By contrast, the official cost to the government for a Nepali officer is between 20,000 and 30,000 rupees per year, yielding a ratio of one foreigner for every thirty to fifty Nepali counterparts" (Justice 1989: 38).[9] Hausner reports that a "local hire, a Nepali contractor, will earn half the rate of an internationally hired contractor, even with identical credentials, and often more experience" (Hausner 2006: 326).

Nevertheless, Anita's salary was twice the amount of the WGOs. According to the cost estimate I submitted, the WGOs, who were employed by the irrigation project, "will be employed until its termination in May 1999. Their salaries are thus calculated on the basis of 21 months, starting in September 1997." Each of the eleven WGOs earned $37 per month. The program recommended recruiting another nineteen WGOs to "carry out the task of organizing 300 women's groups." The total for salaries of the village teachers was calculated on the basis of $13 per teacher per month. The 300 teachers that the program recommended recruiting were "village women with basic education (8–10 classes)," and they were expected to teach two hours a day, six days a week, for nine months.[10]

Control of information about employees' salaries—by means of secrecy, taboos, one-to-one bargaining—was apparently employed by Leon to maintain his dominance over people who depended on him in the project, and at his homes in Bhairahawa and Kathmandu. Leon's endeavors to prevent leakage of discreet, insider information are an example of Weber's concept of the "official secret," a "specific invention of bureaucracy," and which is "fanatically defended by the bureaucracy" (Weber 1948: 233–34).[11] Secrecy, so it appears, divides "insiders" from "outsiders," employers from employees, and most importantly those who control access to the organization's resources from those who do not. It follows, therefore, that secrecy is crucial to the preservation of dominance and the privileges it entails.

Serving Tea and Power Differentials

Obtaining social power necessitates the presentation and preservation of hierarchal distance. Consequently, bossing people about and introducing strict social distance between himself and others was a predominant feature of Leon's daily encounters with the people around him, especially with those who worked for him. One such example was connected to serving hot drinks: who should serve them and who they were to be served to. Leon used to prepare hot drinks for himself a few times every day. Feeling uneasy about making coffee only for myself on one of my first days in the office, I asked Leon and Raju if they wanted me to make them coffee. Leon accepted my offer but reacted with hostility in regard to my intention to make a drink for Raju: "No! You are not offering him coffee." I was surprised, and Leon explained that it was wrong for me to serve Raju, as he was expected to serve Leon and myself and not the other way round, and that I should not mess up the hierarchy.

On another occasion, while offering Leon a cup of coffee I dared to say: "I want to offer coffee to Raju too. It is very hard for me not to do that." Leon repeated his objection to such a gesture, saying uncompromisingly: "Soon he will think that he deserves to be served coffee." Leon was clearly annoyed and disturbed by any seemingly trivial matter that was probably perceived by him as undermining the order of things in the office, thus posing a threat to his self-evident position as the boss. Bound by Leon's instructions I felt like a collaborator, and hence when Leon was away I apologized to Raju for not offering him coffee in Leon's presence. However, when Leon was not there I used to offer Raju coffee, but Raju would never accept the offer.

It appears, then, that assuming a superior attitude and creating clear social distance was, in Leon's eyes, an inevitable practice necessary for maintaining his dominant position. Hence, his behavior was deliberate and not just a matter of bad manners. From my point of view, as a temporary visitor, his behavior was unbearable and seemed to bespeak his evilness. However, unconsciously I took advantage of this situation by presenting myself as Raju's ally. Moreover, I used this issue to gain Anita's respect and trust. Talking with her over a cold coke I told her that Leon would not allow me to serve Raju coffee: "I find it difficult to manage in a place where such a distance between people prevails." She responded warmly. Identifying with my approach, Anita brought up her own bad experiences with superiors in one of her previous work places. At another place, she recounted, which was "very different" from the irrigation project, friendly working relations prevailed between junior and senior employees. That is to say, revealing my feelings about Leon's insistence on maintaining social distance indirectly and unintentionally served my interest in getting closer to Anita.

Leon's attitude in relation to serving hot drinks in his office was apparently a departure from the prevailing norms concerning tea drinking on the Project's premises. Serving tea was usually carried out by a specific person, who was considered as occupying the lowest position in the Project's hierarchy. More importantly, drinking tea reduced social distance between people belonging to different social categories, based on professional status, bureaucratic position, gender, and so on. Tea was generally made with cooked milk (chai) rather than boiled water (which was how it was drunk in Leon's office). Drinking chai was an integral part of any meeting or social gathering within the irrigation project's premises, whether with people from the project or those coming from the outside. Whenever people came for meetings with officials in the office, chai was immediately ordered.

However, the more interesting phenomenon in relation to drinking chai was the habitual social gatherings which took place every day in the officials' rooms. The daily gatherings in Pandit's room were, probably, the most noticeable ones. Whenever I came down to Pandit's room (his office was on the first floor, beneath Leon's office, which was on the second and top floor of the irrigation project's building) it felt as though I had arrived at a noisy party. The room was almost always crowded with some five to ten people, cheerfully chatting and joking. As the space was rather small and chairs were few, people often used to share seats. The people in Pandit's room were mainly his own staff, lower ranked workers such as the male Association Organizers (AOs) and the female women's groups organizers (WGOs). Senior officials like Gupta would also join the cheerful group occasionally. Sometimes even the chai-man would join the party. Nevertheless, hierarchy was maintained there as well, although in a more subtle way. Pandit always sat at the head, behind his desk, while the others sat around. The male AOs usually sat to Pandit's right, whereas the female WGOs sat in front of him and were usually the ones who shared seats. When I entered the room the atmosphere invariably became more formal, and a seat was offered to me by one of the WGOs.

In bureaucratic terms the "tea-parties" could be considered a waste of time, lacking efficiency, causing a break-down of the hierarchical order, and even jeopardizing the organization's goals. However, it appeared that although illegitimate from the point of view of formal organizational rules, these social encounters were indispensable events, contributing significantly to the irrigation project's sustainability. As people were very poorly paid and their employment conditions were shaky and temporary, the informal socializing and friendliness could somehow alleviate feelings of bitterness, frustration, and helplessness. Being aware of the approaching termination of the irrigation project on the one hand, and of its questionable contribution to the villages they were working for and of which they were part on the other, these enjoyable meetings offered them opportunities to talk and joke. These encounters clearly reduced the personal tensions and frustrations of junior employees, but also brought together higher and lower-ranked people, reintroducing human, egalitarian components of friendship and solidarity into the hierarchical and alienating context. This social networking event possibly also contributed to everyday mutual help, though I cannot be certain of this. As "class relations are both captured and disguised within bureaucratic networks" (Ferguson 1984: 40), the "informal" gatherings of the irrigation project's employees "dissipated power" (ibid: 17) and eliminated formalism. My sudden entrance into this set up, a foreigner unable to speak Nepali, and identified with the irrigation project's superiors, seemed to disrupt the social mingling. Nevertheless, I do not see these social encounters as anecdotes of a "latent function" (Merton 1957: 68) in organizational life that indirectly contribute to its ongoing efficient and steady functioning.[12] Rather, I suggest that these events were inseparable from the organization's everyday operation, and fly in the face of the Weberian concept of the formalized, hierarchical, and rational structure of organizations.

The Jeep: Symbolizing and Contesting Superiority

Leon's efforts to maintain a hierarchal structure, with himself at its apex, were clearly demonstrated in relation to "his" jeep. He would never sit anywhere else but in "his" seat, beside the driver. The only exception was in the few cases when he rode in Thapa's jeep. On occasions when Leon allowed me to use his jeep, if he himself was using Thapa's vehicle, it was implied that he was doing me a favor, signaling approval of my behavior and upgrading my status. And permission to use his jeep would usually entail some preconditions. On one occasion, Leon instructed me as follows: "You can have the jeep, but there is a problem. There is an empty gas container in it, which has to be filled up, and another smaller container. You can drive to the gas station, fill it up, and then bring it to the bachelors' house. After that the jeep will be available to you." When I complained that what was being asked of us would take too long and would considerably reduce the time we had for traveling to the villages, he compromised, and instead told me to leave the empty container at the filling station. On another occasion, at which Thapa was present, Anita asked Leon if she could have "his" driver. Leon replied: "As soon as I know what happens with your employment [i.e., if her contract was to be extended by the local irrigation project's manager], then I shall have no objection to you using my driver." Thapa instantly interfered and, referring to the jeep that was provided for the women's project, told Anita: "You have your own vehicle and you don't need to depend on any other vehicle."

Providing us with a vehicle and a driver was, or so it seemed, an arena for competition between Leon and Thapa concerning who had seniority in the irrigation project. Leon was willing to consider our use of "his" jeep when he realized that Thapa had offered us his vehicle and driver. On the other hand, Thapa's decision to provide us with his vehicle and driver was prompted by our discussion with Leon about whether or not we could use "his" car and driver. The car was promised by Thapa soon after I arrived at the irrigation project premises, but did not materialize until the abovementioned encounter some weeks later.

The jeep, so it seems, was a symbol of—and a means for establishing—status and power, a means of manifesting control over people and property. Making clear that the jeep and the driver were "his" and were there for his use enabled Leon to consider himself and to be considered by others as a powerful person, competing only with Thapa over the highest position in the irrigation project. In a way, the jeep with the driver signified Leon's extended embodiment. The symbolic function of a vehicle, provided to senior officials for their personal use, as signaling status and organizational power is discussed by Reuven Shapira (2008) in his study of moral leadership on kibbutzim. Shapira argues that the privilege enjoyed by activists and leaders of having an "attached car" in the formative period of the kibbutz played a major role in symbolizing their high status. The "fancy American chauffeured cars" of the main leaders, he argues, "clearly negated their preaching and stood out in a society where private cars were very rare" (ibid.: 61).

Leon behaved as if the jeep belonged to him and therefore was not available for other people's use as well. Whenever he was asked by the irrigation project's employees to give them a lift, he showed his resentment openly. Leon seemed irritated by their requests and for being obliged to stop on the way or sometimes to go out of his way for them. He spoke about them as impudent, as taking advantage of his property, and as imposing on him, leaving him no choice but to let them join the ride. Indeed, his readiness to give someone a lift would vary according to the person who asked for it. Offering Gupta a lift was another matter altogether. Leon was explicitly glad to have him in his jeep. However, this warm welcome for Gupta was exceptional, as Leon did not like to bother with either higher or lower ranking passengers.

The hostile exchange Leon had with one of the irrigation project's engineers demonstrated that the relative status of a project employee would not move Leon to offer them a lift. During one of our regular breakfast chats, Leon told me about an irritating incident with one of the project's local engineers. The previous day he had given a lift to a few people. When he arrived at the bachelors' house, he found out that two men were still in the jeep, one of them the engineer. Leon was furious and told him angrily that this should never happen again. That was not the first confrontation Leon had had with the engineer over giving him a lift in his jeep. Leon told me that some time ago he had given the engineer a lift when he was returning home at night from a party. Leon told the driver to take the engineer home first, which meant that "we had to go through the fields and I got home half an hour later." Leon resented feeling exploited by the engineer, or by anyone for that matter. For him, using "his" car, "his" driver and "his" time to bring anyone home was unforgivable.

The only gesture Leon considered acceptable was to take people part of the way, dropping them off en route to wherever he was going, although he grumbled while doing it. This was done more willingly with higher-ranking workers (Gupta, in particular) than with others, but in no case was it acceptable to go out of his way, at any time, to take people home, whether higher or lower in rank than him. In this matter, as with tea drinking, Leon's attitude was in contrast to local people's norms. Thapa, who also had a project vehicle, would always take other people with him, and send his driver with other workers to carry out their assignments.

The seating arrangement in the jeep also signified for Leon the level of personal importance. Leon would always sit to the left of Samir, the driver. The only exception to this was when he was with Thapa, in Thapa's vehicle. Furthermore, the "appropriate" seating order had to be kept not only in Leon's presence. He insisted that I too made sure that I got the "better" seat in the vehicle. His instructions on how to behave according to my status took place when he joined Anita, three WGOs, and myself in the women's project jeep on our way to meet women in the villages. When he was seated in the front seat next to the driver, Leon asked me sarcastically if I would permit him to have the front seat. Indeed, there was no other option for me but to "allow" him to sit in "my" seat. Moreover, until that moment I had not noticed that he had seated himself in the front seat. This act seemed so "natural" that only following his comment did I realize that he conceived of occupying the front seat, by the driver's side, as the self-evident right of a boss. As I had previously paid no attention to the symbolic meaning of the seating arrangements, preferring always to sit behind with the WGOs and Anita, it was only then that I realized that he had, as far as he was concerned, pushed me away from "my" privileged seat, and therefore felt uncomfortable. Taking the front seat without permission might have reflected his covert ideas about a woman's place, for if a similar encounter were to take place in a non-formal setting Leon would quite probably offer me, as a woman, the more comfortable front seat while taking the back seat for himself. I suggest that the symbolic importance attributed to a specific seat depends on the specific socio-cultural context, and indicates structured power relations.[13] According to European etiquette, for instance, respect is revealed to those at the back side of the car. Thus, the back seat is offered to guests, who are being chauffeured by a driver at the front. The host would sit next to the driver at the front or with his guests at the back, However, in this case, taking the front seat does not emerge from Leon's good European manners. "Pushing" me to the back of the car is explained by his need to get control over the "better" seat, as a way of signaling his formal superiority (and, hence, his entitlement for a better position in the car).

Leon's rhetorical question probably reflected a conflict between acknowledging the obligation to respect status privileges, mine in this case, and his urge to appear to have a higher status than me, in terms of both the irrigation project and gender relations. As I sat behind, feeling crowded between Anita and the other three WGOs, I made a move to go to the back of the jeep, behind the four of them. Leon was infuriated and said to me "the one who renounces honor will not be honored." I replied instantly "the one who chases honor, honor runs away from him."[14] He did not give up and responded cynically. Then he turned to the other passengers telling them determinedly that on the way home he had to go to the travel agency. However, we did take Anita home first.

Using "our" vehicle to go to the travel agency to get his ticket for his regular Thursday flight to Kathmandu meant that, although he acknowledged the fact that the vehicle was not "his" but "ours," he still allowed himself to use it for his own purposes, ignoring the other passengers' needs and/or wishes. Thus, Leon's behavior suggests that he perceived the women's project and the women working for it as inferior to him.

As much as Leon tried to protect his monopoly over his jeep, he failed to achieve complete control over it when he was away. For example, on one of his weekends in Kathmandu, Raju phoned me to tell me that his mother-in-law was hospitalized and that he and his wife wanted to visit her. To do so he wanted to use Leon's jeep, and as Leon left the keys with me when he went to Kathmandu, Raju needed my cooperation. He asked me to send Samir, the driver, with the jeep to his home, and begged me not to tell Leon anything about it. I agreed and asked him how long he would need the vehicle for. He said that the visit should take around an hour and a half. Then he asked me if my computer was okay (the previous day he had helped me repair it), although I had told him that morning that the computer was working fine. He added instantly that if any problem came up with the computer over the weekend I should call him and he would gladly come and help me out. He gave me his neighbor's telephone number, in case I needed to get in touch with him.

Raju needed my cooperation to ensure that Leon did not find out about his use of the jeep, as Leon never allowed anyone to use it but himself.[15] Thus, Raju and Samir could be considered thieves for taking Leon's property without his permission. My complicity in their act was acknowledged by Raju's offer to help me out with my computer, an offer made to reward me for my cooperation. This example demonstrates how junior employees reacted to Leon's attempts to exert total control over things. The power relations that Leon nurtured indirectly motivated people to lie and cheat in order to get out of him what they considered to be project property. It is likely that from their point of view Leon was using the project property illegally. Leon had effectively requisitioned a project vehicle for his own private use and had forbidden others to use it, unless they were serving him.

Raju and Samir may have been manipulating me as well, assuming that I would be unable to refuse Raju use of the vehicle for an emergency. They could have used the car for any purpose whatsoever without my knowing it. If that were the case, it would emphasize further the strategies adopted by the workers to get even with their domineering boss, and exercise some ownership over property that they might have considered as belonging in some way to them as well. Thus, Leon's anxiety about being "exploited" by local people had a basis in reality, and such exploitation in fact took place without his knowing it. This was a two-sided situation, in which Leon had control over people and property on the level of overt, formal reality, and low-ranking employees had their own ways of obtaining latent control and advantages. Gaining forbidden access to the jeep, which symbolized to a heightened degree Leon's status and power, undermined the secure and orderly world that Leon strived to create.

The fictitious nature of Leon's perception that he was in control of what he viewed as his employees and property echoes with other studies that reveal misleading images of "control" (e.g., Burawoy 1979; Strauss et al. 1981; Greenberg 1982; Kunda 1992). Tannenbaum's assertion that "organization implies control" (Tannenbaum 1967: 3) conveys an impression of self-evident stability, the "formalization, codification, and enforcement of rules and regulations" (Kunda 1992: 220).[16] This conceptualization of organizational life ignores dynamic aspects, which are essentially embedded in organizations, and which render elasticity and vagueness to the meaning of organizational power and control. Thus, for instance, Strauss et al. (1981) suggest that organizational control is related to ongoing negotiations between participants in an organization, and Michael Burawoy (1979) suggests that consent is not automatic and must be worked out. Challenging Goffman's (1961) argument that dichotomized power differentials between officials and clients are essential for achieving organizational goals, Ofra Greenberg (1982) argues that even in institutions where power differentials are extreme—such as prisons—control is neither absolute nor stable, and needs to be negotiated daily through informal exchanges between prisoners and warders.

Stressing his control continuously must have involved considerable effort on Leon's part. However, I suggest that the protective boundaries that he worked hard to construct around himself and his self-proclaimed property were, in fact, fragile and penetrable.

A Ridiculed Patron

This double-faceted reality of power-relations, whereby they were both exerted and undermined, was revealed in other ways as well. Most people who interacted with Leon, including myself, seemed to experience considerable stress and unease. People were obviously scared of the man. Thus, in Leon's presence, reactions to his intimidating behavior ranged from uneasy laughter and smiles to frozen silence, hesitant mumbling, and ingratiating comments. However, behind his back the lower-ranked employees never missed an opportunity to mock and ridicule him. Such was the case when Anita and Raju used Leon's momentary exit from the office to laugh at him. I was curious to know what they were laughing about. Anita explained that a few minutes earlier, in Leon's presence, Raju and she were talking on the telephone in Nepali with someone who did not speak English. Leon did not allow them to speak Nepali in his presence and, therefore, talking with someone from outside the irrigation project office in Nepali meant that they where ignoring his demand, and this implied their ability to disobey him.

The advantage of their common language enabled Anita and Raju to get even with Leon. The two of them turned Leon into their common enemy. They clearly had a mutual interest in belittling Leon, who was domineering toward both of them. Their resentment over Leon's humiliating expressions made them allies, and encouraged them to break down the structured distance between them. Resisting Leon's domination covertly, by ridiculing him behind his back, Anita and Raju regained some of their self-esteem, enabling them to perceive themselves as empowered and less vulnerable, while Leon was stripped of his power and importance. However, belittling Leon occurred by way of trivial matters, such as speaking Nepali in his presence. This indicated his subordinates' relative lack of power, certainly their lack of formal power. On the other hand, Leon's formal power was found to be worthless in situations where he was not present, and in his own office too his perceived control could be easily ridiculed.

Writing about the resistance displayed by subordinate groups to domination, James Scott (1985, 1990) has analysed acts of "everyday resistance" and the "weapons" employed by relatively weak groups. The weak may use simple means to resist those who dominate them—such as slowing down, faking illness, false consent, theft, falsely claiming ignorance, sabotage, and so forth. In this form of class struggle, the weak refrain from direct symbolic confrontation with the authorities and with the norms of the dominating elite.[17] I suggest that tactics, such as the ones used by the irrigation project's employees—and similar to ones used by the women immigrants whom I have previously studied (Hertzog 1999)[18]—should be called "latent resistance" rather than "everyday resistance." This proposition follows Feierman's (1990) claim that if everyday resisters want to be effective they cannot reveal their intentions openly, because the authorities are too powerful for a vulnerable group to confront directly.

Anita tried to let me join their discreet coalition, although she did it cautiously. When Leon left the office later (after the abovementioned encounter), Anita and Raju were smiling at each other like accomplices to some mischief. I asked why they were smiling and Anita said: "We are afraid of him". "I know what you mean", I replied, and she asked: "What do you know?" Obviously, she was testing me, trying to find out how far I would go in my criticism of Leon. Anita had to be careful with me, especially after my unfortunate role in the dispute over Raju's salary. As much as I tried to be her friend and not just her co-worker, Anita had to take into account the fact that I had intensive interactions with Leon and was directly under his supervision in the office and at the bachelors' house. Indeed, Leon and I had a common employer and shared the same nationality, language, and the like. These factors inevitably affected my relationship with Anita and made the social distance between the two of us sometimes seem unbridgeable.

When Anita disclosed to me her secret that she was staying with her aunt in Bhairahawa instead of in the house provided for her by the irrigation project, she asked me not to tell Leon about it. Trying to help her, I suggested talking it over with Leon and asking him to allow her to stay with her aunt. She reminded me of Raju's bad experience with my good intentions, and claimed that if Leon knew about the matter he would reduce her accommodation allowance. Living with her aunt was not only nicer and more comfortable; it was also a way to save some extra money. It appears, then, that in order to achieve their objective—be it regaining self-esteem, using the jeep, increasing their salary, or whatever—employees used secrecy, deceit, and other such strategies no less than their employers, who themselves strove to preserve their power and its advantages (Vincent 1998).

It follows that the suppressed power conflicts built into bureaucratic settings, between those who possess formal power and those who lack it, introduce unconventional, delinquent, violent (Marx 1976) and other socially or legally forbidden acts. This applies to both the oppressed and their oppressors, employees and employers of all ranks. Following Ferguson, I conclude that bureaucracies are "political arenas in which domination, manipulation and the denial of conflict are standard operating procedures" (Ferguson 1984: 17).

Abusing the Defenseless at Home

The most blatant expressions of Leon's offensiveness were revealed at home, in the bachelors' house. The more vulnerable the people around him were and the more they depended on him for their sustenance, the more likely they were to be offended by him. Humiliating his house staff—the caretaker and his daughter in particular—was an integral facet of his social interactions. Karki, the caretaker, was a short, thin man in his middle sixties. He had heart problems as a result of a heart attack he had suffered some years before, which had left him with speech difficulties and a limp. He spoke very little and in a kind of mumble which was very difficult to understand. One morning, at the dining table, while serving breakfast to Leon and me, Karki handed Leon a list of the items he had to shop for that day. This was a routine occurrence. Every few days Karki would approach Leon, waiting for him to go over the list and approve or change it. Upon returning from his purchases, he would regularly hand over the receipts to Leon to be reimbursed. When Leon saw the list that morning he looked at Karki and said harshly: "Here, nobody buys oil". Then he turned to me and asked, in a cold voice: "Do you want your food cooked in oil?" "No," I replied instinctively, as Leon probably expected of me, and added, "but the mashed potatoes we had yesterday were cooked in oil, and were very tasty." Leon sneered. "That was only mashed potatoes," he said.

When checking the receipts Karki handed him, Leon used to spend a considerable amount of time inspecting every item and every figure, making sure there was no mistake whatsoever. Whenever he found the smallest mistake, even if a few rupees were missing in Karki's tally of all his receipts, he would reprimand him angrily. Leon presented these inspections as a legitimate necessity to ensure the honest management of his money. These instances, in which Leon treated his staff like servants, showed him to be a wicked boss. Watching these scenes silently made me feel like Leon's collaborator, taking advantage and enjoying privileges on account of the helpless, obedient staff. My insignificant attempt to support Karki by complimenting him on the mashed potatoes, and my usual silence in relation to Leon's offensive behavior against Karki, accentuated my acquiescence. Although Leon's behavior was hard to bear, I nevertheless accepted it.

Ranju, Karki's daughter, was a pleasant and nice-looking woman in her mid forties. She used to come regularly to help her father out and cook for Leon (and for me, when I was there). She too was often humiliated by Leon. One night, when Ranju served us dinner, Leon suddenly called Ranju in a very loud, scary voice. I was startled. "What's happened? Are there any ants in the salad?" I asked. Leon replied sharply: "Taste it and find out." Ranju came in, very anxious, and Leon shouted at her angrily for putting a sour-sweet spice in the salad. Ranju froze. The incident made me feel sick, and for some time I refrained from talking to Leon.

Trapped in an extremely unpleasant situation involving a marked imbalance in power, and identifying with the offended while being associated with the offender, all I could do was to engage in passive tactics. I searched desperately for a rational explanation for Leon's outburst and employed the protest sanctions of a powerless participant, such as avoiding verbal communication with the offender. Leon's offensive treatment of Karki and Ranju seemed to illustrate the most extreme instances of his domineering ways. As Leon's collaborator, albeit a reluctant one, I could not even be perceived by Karki and Ranju as someone in whom they could confide or to whom they could reveal their feelings. With no clue as to how the two reacted when we were not present, but cognizant of their apparent fear and instant compliance with any of Leon's demands, I tend to think that their reaction to their subordination must have been different from that of the irrigation project's junior employees. In other words, subordination is complex and relative; thus Raju's, Anita's, and others' resistance to Leon's aggressiveness was likely to be significantly different from that of Karki and Ranju. Had Leon treated the irrigation project's employees like he treated those who worked for him at his home, he would probably have paid dearly for it.

Reflecting on Leon's aggressive attitude toward Karki and Ranju may raise some doubts concerning Sherry Ortner's claim that "the dominated too always have certain capacities, and sometimes very significant capacities, to exercise some sort of influence over the ways in which events unfold" (Ortner 2006: 143–44).[19] It does make one wonder whether explanations of resistance have gone too far, blurring the implications of cruelty, exploitation, and other dehumanizing forms of power that emerge in oppressive situations and structures. Guita Grin Debert offers a similar critique. She argues:[20]

> Drawing inspiration from Gramsci, [studies of resistance have] focused on the resistance strategies that organized social practices among the popular sectors. [These have] produced a new kind of romantic view of popular culture in which power, counterhegemony, and resistance are central analytical categories. However, insofar as these categories are used pervasively to approach all domains of social life in the same way, they run the risk of becoming empty concepts. (Debert in Nader 1997: 726)

I argue, however, that settings, which are distanced from the public's eye and separated from the public arena entail a much greater potential for inflicting injustice, exploitation, and other perils on individuals.

Bribery, Drunkenness, and Ethnocentrism: Cooperation and Mutual Dependence

Allegations about Nepali officials' corruption were a favorite subject of Leon's at our common meals at the bachelors' house. Nevertheless, although he spoke about corruption with obvious contempt, he never acknowledged any responsibility that might be attributed to Tahal or to any other foreign organization engaged in projects with the Nepali government. One story that illustrates one end of the spectrum of corruption involving development projects concerns the presents Tahal used to give to senior officials. Bottles of Johnnie Walker whisky were the standard gift that Leon used to buy with Tahal's money for senior heads of the Ministry of Agriculture.

The issue of the whisky pay-off came up when a local holiday was approaching and Leon had to buy some bottles. He sent a letter to his superiors asking how much he should spend. When no reply arrived, he sent a fax to the head office in Tel Aviv, requesting urgent advice about the specific amount of money he could use for purchasing the bottles. He recounted the episode as follows:

> Some time ago … the general director of the Ministry of Agriculture wrote me a letter saying that it was not acceptable that senior officials be offered cheap whisky [red label Johnnie Walker]. He made it clear that they should only get black Johnnie Walker, which cost some $40 a bottle. Then he sent me a long list of more than sixty people that should receive two whisky bottles each for the holiday. Luckily enough, he did not demand green Johnnie Walker, which is the most expensive whisky. I wrote to Tahal asking them what I should do and they replied that I should get red Johnnie Walker and add some conserves, such as tuna, for each person. Only the most senior officials should get black Johnnie Walker.

Naturally, Leon ignored the fact that corruption necessitates the participation of the givers of bribes, and that he was on the bribing side of the exchange. When the Nepali officials were bribed by him and his employers, they evidently were just as corrupt as the Nepali officials. Like other overseas agencies and NGOs working in developing countries, the Israeli company used personal payoffs to senior officials so as to allow them to secure their position in Nepal.

Scholars like C. Wright Mills (1956), Scarlett Epstein (1973), William Jansen (1978), and Robert Chambers (1983) have recognized the institutionalized perspective of corruption since the 1950s. Mills argued that although "there may be corrupt men in sound institutions," nevertheless, "when institutions are corrupting, many of the men who live and work in them are necessarily corrupted. In the corporate era ... the executive feels less personal responsibility. Within the corporate worlds of business ... the higher immorality is institutionalized" (Mills 1956: 343). Mills pointed to the connection between corruption, "corporate worlds of business, war-making and politics" (ibid). More recently, Carolyn Nordstrom has argued in a similar vein: "corruption is about transnational profiteering—it entails a highly cosmopolitan, twenty-first-century form of international warlordism ... It's not just the story of bleeding a country. It's about owning it" (Nordstrom 2007: 57–58). In the development context, it has been suggested by Peter Griffiths that bribery is inevitable for consultancy firms that want to work with Third World countries, and "there is not a lot the consultancy firms can do about this: they pay or go bust" (Griffiths 2003: 243). I suggest that the corrupt practices of foreign agencies working in Nepal is morally as problematic as those of the Nepali officials, because both parties collaborate in illegal activity. On both sides the officials functioned allegedly as individuals, but were, in fact, backed up by their organizations. Indeed the disguised terminology, calling the whisky bottles "presents", suited both sides.

The exchange of whisky is also suggestive of certain socially denigrating connotations. Discussing the stigmatism associated with alcohol in the context of a Self-help Groups (SHGs) project in Bhil villages in India, David Mosse suggests that "Abandoning alcohol was often ranked as the most significant change brought about by the project" (Mosse 2005: 216). He argues further that the SHGs appeared to "morally delegitimise social capital mediated by alcohol ... After all, alcohol has long been a core symbol of Bhil underdevelopment, and renouncing *daru*[21] a Brahmanic virtue and idiom of progress and modernity..." (ibid.: 217). An implied connection between bribing the officials with whisky and the alleged social problem of alcoholism emerges indirectly from Fenster's gender activities project proposal. She writes:

> Alcoholism is one of the major and severe problems in the area and is the first problem to tackle if the objective of the Project is increasing the level of living. This is a common problem in most of the Project Area. This problem affects families both financially as most of their income is spent on drinking and it also affects the increase of violence in the family. There are legal means to help these women but the problem is social and cultural ... But it is obvious that in-depth action must be taken in order to combat this phenomenon. (Fenster 1996: 9–10)

While the Nepali senior officials received whisky, with its connotations of drunken natives, ill-health, debt, social conflict, and underdevelopment, Tahal received profitable deals, pretending to have obtained them due to their professional competence. This state of affairs fostered the image of polarized encounters between the sober and the drunken, West and East, rich and poor, patrons and clients, and expressed the degrading dependence of the Nepali people on foreigners' aid.

These "presents" symbolized the inferior position of the Nepali government, like many other governments in developing countries. They have to comply with the World Bank's constraints and demands concerning the companies they should work with, accepting foreign consultants instead of hiring local people, complying with their relatively high salaries, and so forth. Discussing the pressure exerted by the World Bank and other development funding agencies, Susan George (1988), Mark Smith (1998/2001, 2007), and Wickens and Sandlin (2007) emphasize in particular the World Bank's interventions in education and literacy policies, which "seem to rest so heavily on the work of foreign, Northern scholars and agency staff" (Smith 1998/2001). These interventions are born of economic conditions which face many countries of the South. Economic dependence on loans and grants by international agencies, such as the IMF and the World Bank, has allowed those agencies to dictate economic and other policies to recipient countries. It has shifted control of education and literacy programs "from national governments to the agencies themselves" (Wickens and Sandlin 2007: 289).

However, the expectation of, and demand for, presents can also be understood as a reminder of the dependence of foreign agencies (Tahal in this case) on the Nepali government for permission to carry on their activities in Nepal. The need to negotiate over the number and kind of whisky bottles to be offered to Nepali officials, over the number of people who should receive them, as well as the need to purchase the bottles, put Leon in an extremely vulnerable position, of which he was fully aware and which made him furious.

To conclude: Leon's persona combined a number of facets. He seemed to enjoy relating to people as his inferiors, domineering "weaker" others and insulting them when they failed to please him or disappoint him; at the same time Leon also revealed friendliness, warmth, and even vulnerability. Which aspect of his character Leon embodied in a specific situation depended on how he perceived the people he was interacting with, whether they were considered more or less powerful than him, whether they were people on whose help, support, or cooperation he depended, whether or not they had access to things he wanted, and so on.

The following chapters build on the foregoing analysis and suggest that Leon's hostile attitude was not coincidental, and nor was it a matter of bad temper. It will be showed that Leon's attitude to others, and that of other senior irrigation project officials, had little to do with personal characteristics or inclinations, but rather emerged from their hidden agenda, their reluctance toward the women's program, and from their role in the organization. They did not want the women's program to materialize.

Notes

1. Edward Gifford wrote that in Polynesia people would say sometimes: "Don't you see he is a chief? Look how big he is!" (cited in Sahlins 1963: 288). Differentiating Melanesian self-made leaders from ascribed chiefs, Paula Brown, meanwhile, suggests that "physical size and political prominence are conceptually linked in some areas and languages" (Brown 1990: 97).
2. These interventions will be described at length in the Chapter 4, which focuses on the village teachers' seminar.
3. Analyzing the social context of violent behaviour, Emanuel Marx (1976) proposes the term "appealing violence" to signify the part played by the audience in violent encounters. He argues that the assailant's aim is "to appeal to other persons for a way out of his impasse" (ibid.: 63). The sense of playing a role which is adapted to situational constraints is well illustrated by Eyal Ben-Ari (1989), who describes "Soldiers with masks", who flexibly adjust to situations that impose conflicting demands from the perspective of their ideological views. He offers an illuminating example of the seeming paradox of Israeli men who are peace activists (like himself) participating in oppressing Palestinian civilians in the occupied territories, while fulfilling the role of officers. Kunda's expression "presentational rituals" illustrates the instrumental aspect of playing organizational roles, defined as "occasions for enacting, enforcing, and reinforcing the display of the managerially sanctioned member role and are thus a mechanism for mediating normative demands and normative responses" (Kunda 1992: 159). My own study of bureaucracy offers an example of the roles people play in daily life, trying to convey manipulated impressions to their social surroundings (Hertzog 2007). Bureaucratic staff invest great effort in producing an appearance of formal power in order to achieve recognition of their roles, their professional skills and authority. However, these are exposed as rather limited in reality.
4. Which was equivalent to less than $2.00 (One dollar's worth was about 58 rupees).
5. Gartrell (1984: 172) argues that the "ideal colonial wife" contributed to the British colonial system in various ways.
6. Hanna's position puts me in mind of Margaret Mead's account of *taufo* in Samoa. According to Mead a *taufo* is "a princess title" (Mead 1973: 75). Her privileges include the receipt of "gifts, dancing and singing for her benefit … when a visiting village comes" (ibid.: 76). Moreover, the wives of titled men take "their status from their husbands … The wife of the highest chief receives the highest honour, the wife of the principal talking chief makes the most important speeches. The women are completely dependent upon their husbands for their status in this village group" (ibid.: 77–78).
7. Emerson suggests four "balancing operations" which "operate through changes in the variables which define the structure of the power relation as such" (Emerson 1962: 35). "Coalition Formation" is "Operation number four". It "increases the power of weaker actors through collectivization… coalition formation is the one most commonly recognized as a power process… the coalition process is basically involved in all organized group functioning… this illuminates the role which power processes play in the emergence and maintenance of group structure in general" (ibid.: 37).
8. "Women's Groups Coordinators" ("WGCs"), is another title for "local gender consultants" (as Anita was). This term is used in my report (page 6), suggesting to hire two local consultants instead of one.
9. These amounts are derived from Shrestha (1983: 1).
10. Quoted passages are taken from my report (Hertzog 1997: 6).
11. Max Weber further suggests that "bureaucratic administration always tends to be an administration of 'secret sessions': in so far as it can, it hides its knowledge and action from criticism" (Weber 1948: 233–34).
12. Adapting Freud's terms "manifest" and "latent," Robert Merton distinguishes "between the end-in-view and the functional consequences of action" (Merton 1957: 62).
13. The social implications of seating codes and arrangements have been analyzed by several scholars. Jules Henry (1963), for instance, demonstrated the connection between row arrangement in the American classroom and power relations between teachers and students.

Analyzing the connection between caste and symbolism in South-Western Ethiopia, Gunnar Haaland (2004) points to the manifestation of the "up-down schema" in seating arrangements "for members of different castes, for example in the market place, and in the side members of different castes will take when they meet each other on a path; the higher caste person will take the higher ground" (84). Marc Forster (1998) elaborates on the symbolic implications of seating arrangements in early modern German Catholicism. He writes: "Conflicts over seating took place at several levels… over who should determine seating arrangements…" (69). Robert Tittler (1992) writes about "Seats of Honor, Seats of Power: The Symbolism of Public Seating in the English Urban Community, c. 1560–1620." It appears that seating arrangements and norms entail far-reaching implications in terms of class, ethnicity, race and gender. One important example is the segregating arrangements concerning seating in public transportation, as Rosa Park's story unfolds. Park's refusal (on December 1, 1955) to move to the back of a bus in Montgomery, Alabama, became the symbol of the the modern civil rights movement. An example from the Israeli context is the separation imposed in public busses that drive through orthodox neighbourhoods, between men and women, and the distancing of women to the back of the busses.

14. These phrases borrow from Jewish traditional writings. The original phrase says: "the one who chases honour, honour runs away from him and the one who renounces honour, honour chases him."
15. Leon's offer to let me use his jeep to travel to the villages took place against the background of the power struggle between him and Thapa, as suggested earlier.
16. Arnold Tannenbaum argues "it is the function of control to bring about conformance to organizational requirements and achievement of the ultimate purposes of the organization" (Tannenbaum 1967: 3).
17. Lila Abu-Lughod (1990) suggests that acts of resistance carried out by powerless groups disclose larger processes of social power.
18. The pronounced power differentials between women immigrants from Ethiopia and their paraprofessional welfare aides (*Somchot*) provides a similar example (see Hertzog 1999). Although the *Somchot* rudely invaded the women immigrants' lives, the latter were not completely passive and vulnerable. They used to react indirectly by gossiping, and ridiculing and criticizing the latter's enforced patronizing manners while they were not present. Ignoring the *Somchot*'s demands and interventions the women immigrants could regain their self-esteem and collectively overcome the humiliation.
19. Sherry Ortner suggests that resistance is a form of "power-agency" which "includes everything from outright rebellions at one end, to … a kind of complex and ambivalent acceptance of dominant categories and practices that are always changed at the very moment they are adopted" (Ortner 2006: 144). Laura Ahearn's study of Magar villagers in Western Nepal (Ahearn 2001) offers another example of suppressed people's potential power to resist oppression. Ahearn discusses "marriage by capture," a practice of low cultural value involving kidnapping the bride, as a way of overcoming parents' authority. This act of resistance undertaken by youngsters exposes the unstable control of parents despite the traditional system.
20. This is Debert's comment on Laura Nader's lecture at Sidney W. Mintz Lecture for 1995 (published in *Current Anthropology*, December 1997).
21. *daru* is distilled liquor (according to Mosse's [2005] Glossary).

Chapter 3

Marginalizing Economic Activities, Profiting from Literacy Classes

Literacy and Economic Resources

Empowering women in the rural area of the Lumbini region was the basic rationale of the Gender Activities Program embedded in the Bhairahawa Lumbini Groundwater Project (BLGWP), an agricultural enterprise. Located in the Rupandehi district in the Tarai, the irrigation project extended over 20,800 hectares of irrigable land. A formal document states that by 1999, when it was slated for completion, the irrigation project was intended "to raise the standard of living of the rural population living within its boundaries, most of which are farmers, and the status of women in particular, so as to enable them to contribute more effectively to the economic development of the area" (Tahal and the Ministry of Water Resources 30 January 1997: 1).

In this chapter and the next I will describe and analyze the negotiations that took place in regard to the conceptualization, budgeting, and implementation of the program during 1996 and 1997. I will refer to two sets of sources: my predecessor's and my own project proposals, which will be delineated in this chapter; and the documentation arising from my visits to the villages, which I will consider in the next. In analyzing the programs' proposals, reports, and cost estimates I follow Harold Garfinkel's (1967) argument that documents reveal much more than they explicitly suggest. It will be demonstrated how both the written documents and my field encounters entailed intensive social engagements and effectively ended up without results. The reports Tovi Fenster and I submitted to the Israeli irrigation company, the Nepali government, and the World Bank were found to be invaluable in terms of the project partners' interests in preventing the project's implementation, and deceitful in terms of the manifest purpose of the project's aim of empowering women in rural Nepal.

I suggest, more generally, that development project reports can be manipulatively used while being presented as genuinely needed for promoting social change. The implication of the self-evident need for reports emerges indirectly from various studies. One such example is Judith Justice's study of health development in Nepal, in which she discusses the different kinds of information planners need about the recipient country (Justice 1989). She stresses the fact that government and donor agencies produce many kinds of reports, "often voluminous: background papers, feasibility studies, annual reports, progress evaluations, and project proposals" (ibid.: 112). Nevertheless, although she indicates the reports' limitations and weaknesses, she firmly recommends another kind of information that should be sought in planning social programs—that is, "detailed cultural information" (ibid.: 111). I would argue that it is not a matter of ensuring that the "right" kind of information is prepared that explains the conspicuous role of reports in development agencies' operations, but rather it is the latent organizational needs involved in negotiations over contracts and in the ways agencies can extract profits. Thus, the written documents of the women's project were needed for pursuing policy makers' aims "rather than [to] inform" (Apthorpe 1997: 43).

Bargaining over content, essence, extent, timing, and so on was a dominant feature of daily encounters involving the women's project, which took place in various settings: in the irrigation project offices, in the bachelors' house, in the villages, and also in random locations. Two foreign consultants— my predecessor Tovi Fenster, who worked for the women's project in 1996, and myself, who did so in 1997—played the chief role in the women's project affair. We both submitted reports, including recommendations for implementation, to Tahal, to Nepal's Ministry of Agriculture, and to the World Bank. Fenster had also carried out a survey of village women's situation and needs.[1] Both of us traveled to dozens of villages, meeting the women there, listening to their expectations, and writing them down. The two of us presented our ideas and proposals to the women in the villages concerning their literacy potential and economic opportunities, and responded to their queries. We were involved in daily interactions with the irrigation project's managers and staff, representing our ideas and the women's responses, struggling continuously over acknowledgement and cooperation.

Although we differed with regard to the conceptual and financial emphases that should be placed on various activities—mainly in relation to literacy and the economic sphere—we both ended up recommending a vast project of literacy classes for some three hundred groups in the irrigation project area. Only ten classes were established. Tovi's main achievement was a gender awareness-raising workshop for high-ranking officials of the irrigation project and others from local government offices and directors of women NGOs. She also succeeded in recruiting eight Women's Groups Organizers (WGOs). The WGOs gathered together some thirty groups of women, who were expected to join the women's program. My only substantial achievement was a course (the seminar) for a group of ten women from villages in the region, who were candidates for teaching literacy in their villages. Hence, the Gender Development Project turned out to be a fantasy, existing mainly in Tovi's and my own reports. Having come to Nepal motivated to contribute to women's advancement, this revelation shocked me. This phantom project, and the story of the literacy classes for women as it emerges from various documents, is the focus of the present chapter.

Recommending Literacy: Fenster's Report

As self-evident as the gender activities project's purpose might appear to be, its purpose was ambiguous. Comparing Fenster's and my own definitions of the women project's aims, it appears that these entailed a certain vagueness and ambiguity. Fenster wrote: "The main objective of this Program is to find out ways and means to increase the standard of living in the Project area by looking at the needs of the population as expressed by women, as they are the producers, reproducers and maintain community roles" (Fenster 1996: 6). She also wrote, "The aim of the plan is to provide women (as well as men) in the Project area with skills and means to enable them to increase their standard of living" (ibid.: 17). Thus, at one point Fenster conceives of women as facilitators of economic improvement for the whole society, and in another place women's (and men's) needs are more explicitly expressed.

In my own report I stated, "The Project aims at increasing the income and economic power of these village women, who are at least equal contributors to the village families' economy and to national agricultural production" (Hertzog 1997: 8). Thus, Fenster defines her target as increasing the whole population's standard of living, and women are perceived as mediators in realizing this target. That is to say, from Fenster's point of view, women are treated by the plan mainly as a means for achieving wider social change. My own plan's rationale defines women as the main "target population" and the women's program sets out to provide them with the rights to which they are entitled, as equal partners and contributors to their families, communities, and country.

Both plans—Fenster's and my own—reflect the rhetoric used in many other similar programs, literacy programs in particular, which assume that access to education entails significant benefits. Among the anticipated outcomes are, for example, "community, self and socioeconomic worth, mobility, access to information and knowledge, rationality, morality, and orderliness" (Graff 1979: xv). Lawrence Summers, chief economist of the World Bank, stated that "the 'vicious cycle' of poverty could easily be transformed into a 'virtuous cycle' through the intervention of women's education" (Summers 1993: vii), and Robinson-Pant indicates that "Women's and girls' education has been taken up by many governments and development agencies as the key to improving the lives of poor families" (Robinson-Pant 2004: 1). Similarly, Mark Smith describes the anticipated benefits from informal and non-formal education programs in the South as the cultivation of: "a skilled work force to contribute to economic development, national unity and social cohesion, and in some countries, popular participation in politics. For the individual, it promised an escape from poverty, greater social prestige and mobility, and the prospect of a good job, preferably in town" (Smith 1998/2001[2]). Nevertheless, these assumptions and expectations were already recognized as the "literacy myth" (Graff 1979: xv) by the end of the 1980s.

Interestingly, a project document, which was distributed to NGOs, invited them to propose the provision of "services for the promotion of women economic activities through the provision of women development programs" (Tahal 1997). However, the two reports and their budgets had little to do with "economic activities". On the formal, declared level, the women's project seemed to relate to and include both the economic needs of women and their "social and educational needs." However, the written documents (mainly Fenster's and my own reports) as well as the field data indicate that the latter were more readily acknowledged and favored by those in charge of the women's project—the Israelis, the Nepali officials, and those at the World Bank. The importance attached to "social and educational needs" becomes apparent from Fenster's report. Emphasizing the main concept of women's development, she suggests: "Poverty eradication in the Project area can be carried out only if special attention is paid to social, educational and health needs together with economic and agricultural needs" (Fenster 1996: 17). She also states:

> Initially, the basic assumption underlying this study was that efficient involvement of women in economic activities is one of the major means of alleviating poverty in the Project area. However, after a few weeks of fieldwork we realized that alleviating poverty in the project area could be achieved *only* if development includes social, educational and cultural components together with economic and agricultural aspects. We are now certain that putting emphasis on the efficient involvement of women in economic activities only is not sufficient to alleviate poverty in the area. (ibid.: 4, original emphasis)

It follows that the consultant's original understanding that the essential practice needed for alleviating women's poverty necessitates their "involvement in economic activities" had been dramatically changed. This shift in her analysis gained no support from her own study. The emphasis on "social, educational and cultural components" recommended by Fenster (interestingly writing in the first person plural) does not emerge from the "extensive work of the Project WGOs and AOs and the meeting held by Expatriate Expert [herself] with some twelve women groups from the three stages of the Project" (ibid.: 8). Rather, the evident conclusion that stemmed from numerous encounters with the women villagers was that "In all discussions held with the groups, economic needs were the first to be expressed" (ibid.: 8). Fenster also admits that: "An important factor in increasing the standard of living in the Project area is in increasing the yields of the crops and improving techniques of animal raising. This is also the request of many women in the groups. Since agricultural training is part of the Project activities it is recommended to carry out [*sic*] as many training programs as possible for women" (ibid.: 20). Yet, "agricultural training" is very poorly budgeted (it is about 14% of the whole budget: $60000 out of $438475). This becomes even more striking in describing the economic needs, explicitly designated by the women as their main needs:

> *Agricultural activities and animal raising*: all women expressed their needs and interests in having agricultural training. The areas of training that they wished to acquire were mainly: cropping and vegetable growing, animal husbandry, poultry keeping, and goat rearing. *Credit*: the need for credit was universal. All women expressed their interest in obtaining credit and complained about the very bureaucratic process of receiving credit from the banks. *Non-agricultural activities*: several women groups expressed their wish to have training in sewing and cutting. (ibid.: 9)

Moreover, the main part of the budget, as it appears in the estimation, allocates most of the funds to "development packages." This vague category obscures the fact that literacy classes were the core of the program and budget: some $300,000 out the $440,000 total. When the additional sum of over $40,000 is added to this amount—allocated, whether directly or indirectly, for hiring the expatriate gender consultant, who stayed in Nepal for some two months during the summer of 1996, a sum which does not appear in Fenster's report—the figures suggest that a much smaller proportion of the budget and the program was allocated for economic projects. In fact, only $60,000 was allocated for any economically oriented activity, namely animal keeping. Apart from development packages and animal keeping, other sections in the budget were: group formation, salaries for WGOs and Women Officers (WOs), bicycles for the WGOs, gender workshops, stationery and supplies, refreshments, and 10 per cent for miscellaneous expenses, which amounted to about $40,000.

A deeper look into Fenster's explanations of the "development packages" brings the centrality of literacy into clearer focus. She explains, "Literacy programs are the bases for any desired change in lifestyle and any attempt to increase the living standards of the population in the area should start with such a program" (ibid.: 19). Considering the centrality of the literacy classes to the women's project, the meager and generalized information about the extent of female illiteracy provided in the "demographic characteristics" of the irrigation project area is unconvincing. Fenster claims that "there are no accurate figures as to the female/male proportions among literate and illiterate people" (ibid.: 7). However, she extrapolates from a socioeconomic survey of 1992, which states that over 50 per cent of people in the irrigation project area are illiterate, as well as from some obscure "national figures" that only 25% of the literate population are women. (ibid). I suggest, therefore, that no evident need for literacy was established through conclusive data, nor had it been definitely requested by the women.

Focusing on literacy served to ignore the economic needs and public services that the women articulated as essential for their livelihood. In other words, the village women's struggles with regard to poverty, scarcity, and the forces of hegemony were more significant, from their point of view, than those concerning the lack of reading and writing skills. The process of shifting from economic needs to literacy can be explained by Fenster's, and my own, unintentional compliance with our employer's (Tahal) and host's (the Nepali heads of the irrigation project) expectations.[3]

The prominence of "social and educational" needs is constructed in Fenster's report by referring mainly to the "social needs" of village women. The heading "literacy needs" appears at the top of the list. Other headings listed under "social needs" are topics which were hardly mentioned by the women (according to Fenster's study), among which were: marriage at a young age, women trafficking, polygamy, male drinking and violence in the family (ibid.: 9). The latter is described in great detail. This generalized emphasis on grave social malfunctioning is enhanced by enclosing it in a box. Fenster's conclusion is: "Women's needs and interests in the Project area are not only in Agriculture. Most of them face problems of male alcoholism and violence in the family, lack of basic health facilities and need advice in family planning" (ibid.: 8).

Thus, the "social rationale" behind the proposed program is found to be a generalizing, stigmatizing assessment, which implied the backwardness of local society. It follows therefore, that the gender development project aimed, from the point of view of Fenster's proposal, at a kind of social change that would advance a problematic, traditional, patriarchal society toward a literate, modern, egalitarian social order. This perspective implied the essential need for professional intervention, namely for experts trained in solving "special social problems".

The processes of attaining public acknowledgement of special social problems that call for the allocation of public funds and professional intervention have been discussed in several studies. To cite a few examples: Joseph Gusfield (1980) pointed to the connection between the construction of public problems—drinking and driving in this case—and the hidden interests of institutions. Lea Shamgar-Handelman (1986) described the process by which the status and categorization of Israeli war widows is constructed and public resources are allocated for dealing with the special problem, as well as the systems of "special care" and the interests of workers and organizations that develop in this context. Dina Siegel (1989) discussed the process by which the problem of battered women comes to be seen as a "severe social problem," thus constructing groups of allegedly violent men, to serve the social services' interests. In my own study of the absorption of Ethiopian immigrants into Israel (Hertzog 1999) I described how the "caring" stance and "professional" approach of the absorbing agencies serve as rationales for their patronage over Ethiopian immigrants and control of the resources allotted for their "treatment". Finally, David Mosse describes how development consultants develop "a professional overview of the domain" in which they have expertise, thus insisting that their project is "dangerously ill-informed" and in need of "additional research or data collection for 'proper planning'" (Mosse 2005: 135).

These studies suggest that "special care" does not necessarily help the needy group. Very often it creates the "problem." James Ferguson's (1990) study, for example, clearly points to this. He argues that the constructed "problematic" situation of Lesotho was employed to indicate the self-evident need for aid intervention. The World Bank's funds and expertise were enlisted to develop and modernize Lesotho's "traditional peasant society" which was "virtually untouched by modern economic development" (ibid.: 27). The outcomes of that "development" initiative did not, in fact, benefit Lesotho. Rather, it has enfeebled it.

This implied connection, between publicly acknowledged "social problems" on the one hand, and the consequent need for assistance and the self-evident necessity of expert intervention on the other, becomes evident in Fenster's report. Recommending the nomination of "Women Organization Supervisor [WOS]", and "Local consultant" (Fenster 1996: 21), she suggests that the "expatriate expert" (herself) "will visit the project every few months for assessment of the Program" (ibid). Although she recommends that a WOS should be hired by local heads of the irrigation project, and that a Nepali "woman professional" should be hired by Tahal as a "Local Consultant", Fenster nevertheless recommends that an "expatriate expert" be employed as well. Also, the difference in terms should be noted: the relatively lower status ("a Women Organization Supervisor") is associated with the woman to be employed by the local heads of the irrigation project, whereas a higher status is attributed to the Nepali woman who will be employed by the overseas heads of the irrigation project (a professional "local consultant"), and the highest status ("the expatriate expert") is attributed to an overseas person who will be hired by heads of the irrigation project overseas. Thus, a hierarchy of prominence and prestige is constructed, in which professionalism and prestige are equated to varying degrees with locality versus foreignness.

Examination of the third heading of "women's needs", namely "health needs," offers another example of Fenster's manner of stigmatizing the population. Under the subtitle "health care" Fenster writes: "The population in the Project area suffers from many diseases and therefore complained about the lack of basic services. They need a doctor's visit at least once a week and a nearby clinic. The nearby Hospitals for the Project people are Bhairahawa and Butwal. Maternity care is also absent at these villages" (ibid.: 10). Stating that the population suffers from many diseases as a taken-for-granted fact and tying this to women's explicit request for improved health services exposes a latent bias. Thus, the lack of proper health services in rural parts of Nepal, which women complained about and which was probably the outcome of "bad governance, oppression, corruption and marginalization of people, especially women" (Sharma and Prasain 2004: 164), becomes secondary in Fenster's discussion to the "many diseases" the village population is alleged to suffer from.[4]

Although Nepali women are discriminated against (see, e.g., Bennett 1983; Subedi 1993; Acharya 2001; Bhattachan 2001), the effect of portraying them as a helpless collective of victims, apart from homogenizing them (Tamang 2002),[5] conceals the central role of state policies in failing to provide basic services and its responsibility for discriminatory practices. Fenster's description of poor hygienic conditions which the people endured, their negligence and wretchedness, fosters a stigmatized image of the population, their weakness, inferiority, and need for help. Moreover, emphasizing the diseases of the villagers establishes a social and hierarchal distance between them and those who study and treat them. In other words, when Fenster describes village populations as "suffering from many diseases" they are portrayed as collectively needy and her position is identified, consequently, as a professional, distinct and superior "other" who provides the crucial help.

Judith Justice's study of the cultural dimensions of primary health care in Nepal (Justice 1989) supports the argument that the problem of providing basic health services can be understood in terms of Nepali government's and international health agencies' policies and practices rather than the rural population's inherent and collective weakness. Justice argues that "many features" of health programs are not adjusted to "local conditions and cultures" (ibid.: xi–xii). She claims that "one central problem in providing the best possible health care to rural Nepal is the communication gaps between the cultures involved" (ibid.: 151). However, I suggest that the problem of providing poor services to rural Nepal is connected to organizational and personal preferences and interests (as Justice's book demonstrates) rather than to cultural gaps. Although Justice acknowledges this understanding, arguing that donor agencies often take "a course of action that has more to do with their own needs than with the needs of their beneficiaries" (ibid: 151), she perceives this conduct as the outcome of "the demands of the administrative structure and culture" (ibid). The "two major cultural boundaries" between international health policy and its outcomes are the ones that "separate the Western 'rational' bureaucratic culture of the donor agencies from the Westernized bureaucratic culture of the Nepal government, with its traditional roots; and the other separates the Nepal government from the traditional village cultures" (ibid.: 151–52). This "Westernized" versus "traditional" dichotomy, which reintroduces the concept of modernization, has been discussed in the Introduction and was rejected as ethnocentric and, more importantly, as legitimizing neocolonialist intervention in developing countries.

Illiteracy and the Invocation of Foreign Expertise: My Own Report

A similar analysis can be easily applied to my own gender activities report (Hertzog 1997). The first and central part of the two main sections of my estimation of the program costs refers to literacy classes, with the second section devoted to development projects. It appears that Fenster and myself were aware in some way that the economic activities part of the women's project was of secondary importance at best, and that these activities were invoked in a token manner. The most striking example of this is the footnote attached to my work plan (ibid: annex 2.1). This detailed the proposed stages of program implementation month by month from September (when I left Nepal, and when none of the literacy classes yet had commenced) to December 1997, and from January until March 1998.

This footnote states that "Economic Development Activities [are] to be added at a later stage (January 1998 at the latest)" (ibid). It follows that by the time I completed my report I was well aware of the fact that implementation of the economic activities had been postponed until after the literacy classes were completed. Moreover, the fact that this part of the women's project was mentioned in the footnotes (of an annex) suggests that it became clear to me that the economic activities should not be taken seriously. Furthermore, in my introduction to the cost estimation for the women's development and economic activities program, I report that "in discussing the issue of content to be offered to the groups of women, with Mr Thapa and Mrs Khanal, it has been decided that literacy training will be ... the focus of the Project at the first stage" (ibid.: page 1 in annex 1). Thus, I explicitly acknowledged and accepted the prominent role of literacy classes. However, the decision, which implied a significant shift from the main purpose of the gender activities project, clearly undermined my main position, as mentioned in the recommendations section of the report. I state there that, "the project aims at increasing the income and economic power of these village women, who are at least equal contributors to the village families' economy and to the national agriculture" (ibid.: 8).

Another additional emphasis in my report relates to the firm justification of the need for the services of a foreign consultant. In the last part of my recommendations, I suggest:

> It is recommended that [an] expatriate consultant should visit the Project for monitoring, assessment and supervision purposes. The consultant's first visit in December 1997 will serve to assess the implementation of the program during the first four months of its implementation by the local consultant, WGOs and AOs, as well as for discussing with them their experiences and problems in the field. This visit will also serve to supervise the preparation activities carried out prior to the widening of the Project targets, from 70 literacy classes by the end of 1997 to the opening of some 270 new literacy classes in 1998. Preliminary evaluation of literacy training outcomes and progress should also be done in this visit, thus to enable changes and adaptations of the concept and methods of training. Moreover, the December 1997 consultant's visit is recommended for the purpose of supervising the first stages of economic activities implementation, scheduled to start in the second quarter of 1998.

> The second visit of the expatriate consultant is suggested to take place in March 1998. At this stage an advanced assessment of the program's implementation should be made and the economic activities should be reassessed and supervised, in regard to the extent, content and timing of preparations carried out towards the full implementation of the program. Both visits, in December 1997 and in March 1998, are considered as important in terms of offering encouragement, professional support and advice to local consultant and WGOs in particular, and also to others in charge of the program, officers and field workers alike. (ibid.: 10–11)

It is indeed interesting that I present myself as an expert not only for literacy classes, gender issues (in particular), and development (in general), but also for planning, assessing, and supervising economic activities of the women's project. Most importantly, I suggest that this text is perfectly adjusted to the "correct" rhetoric of development, and in particular it is adjusted to my employers' expectations. It clearly reflects both Fenster's and my own acknowledgement of, and compliance with, their intentions—that is, that none of the economic activities would in fact take place.

The vital need for visits by a foreign consultant to the women's project gains additional support in Leon's letter to Thapa, attached to the beginning of my report. The entire letter focuses on my recommendation of additional visits by the expatriate expert to the women's project. In the last and longest paragraph of his letter, Leon writes:

> We would like to draw your attention again to Mrs E. Hertzog's recommendations on pages 8 to 11 of the report in general and to her last recommendation on pages 10 and 11 regarding two (2) visits of an expatriate consultant, in December 1997, and in March 1998, for the purpose of monitoring, assessment and supervision of the implementation of the work plan suggested by her for the empowerment of women in the BLGWP Area.

This letter hints at the hidden agenda behind the over-emphasized importance of the foreign expert's visits to Nepal. Leon's firm encouragement and insistence that I should include that recommendation in my report reveals the fact that something more than a matter of professional requirement was involved. I complied reluctantly, having my own reservations concerning the need for a foreign consultant and feeling that it was not appropriate for me to recommend myself, either directly or indirectly. My instinctive response exposes further the manipulative use of the foreign expert role in the project, "disguised as technical expertise" (Mosse 2005: 266).[6]

Moreover, by the time I wrote my report I was well aware of the fact that employing expatriate experts was crucial to Tahal's profits. This was explicitly revealed to me in one of my chats with Leon. When I asked him how Tahal would benefit from the women's project, he replied that Tahal's sole profit is based on Anita's and my own employment, through per-diem costs. Thus, Tahal's and Leon's core interest in the women's project was connected to the profit made by hiring experts. As my salary was much higher than Anita's, employing me entailed greater income for the irrigation company. Therefore, my visits to Nepal were crucial from Tahal's financial point of view.

A final point of comparison between the two reports can be made regarding the budget. Two conspicuous differences emerge when comparing Fenster's cost estimation and my own: the difference in the proportional allocation of the budget for literacy classes (or "development packages" in Fenster's terms) and economic activities; and the difference between the total sum of each budget. In Fenster's budget, economic activities (more specifically, animal keeping) are allocated $60,000 out of the $440,000 total budget. In my own budget, the economic section is allocated $130,000 out of a total of $288,500. This substantial difference in the proportion of money allocated for economic and literacy activities can be explained in terms of our different assessments of the relative significance of the two spheres of activity. More important is the considerable difference between our estimated total costing of the project: Fenster's grand total is $440,000, and mine is $288,500. Nevertheless, even my own, smaller, budget was hardly spent on the women's program. Moreover, although the literacy program was, as suggested above, the core of the women's project, and although its budget was reduced considerably, only a small part of it was actually implemented.[7]

The differences of cost and emphasis between our budgets can be explained in relation to the point in time at which Tovi Fenster and I played our role in the gender activities project. When Fenster came to Bhairahawa, Tahal's involvement in the irrigation project was greater because the company had about two more years left before withdrawing from it and transferring the constructed irrigation system to the villagers. This enabled Tahal's representative a greater measure of negotiating power when facing the local managers of the irrigation project. By the time I arrived in Bhairahawa, Tahal's mission was nearly over. This situation explains the intense pressure that Tahal's representative exerted on their Nepali partners in order to extract some additional benefits for Tahal out of the women's project, before the irrigation project contract was terminated. It follows that the longer the Nepali party could defer the implementation of the women's project, the better their chances of canceling the women's project and using the money for their own preferred purposes.

This conclusion clearly emerges from letters I received from Leon and Anita a couple of months after I left Nepal. Having no idea about what happened with the literacy classes, I received a letter from Leon in November 1997, in which he wrote that eleven literacy classes had commenced and were running smoothly. He added that "the nine-day Seminar which was planned to train twenty village teachers and the consequent opening of twenty literacy classes has been delayed because of lack of funding."[8] Anita's letter, which arrived not long afterwards, informed me as follows:

> Our ten literacy classes are running nicely. The ten teachers are taking their classes very seriously. There are thirty women in each class. All women appreciate the studies. We took their first exam on Dec. 11. We provided them agriculture training from November 9 to November 12 with the help of Mr Lama, Chief of Agriculture Division, and gave them free vegetable seeds. Veterinary training was held on November 23 to 28 for ten literacy classes.[9]

I still do not know which of the reported number of classes—ten or eleven—is the correct one. More important is the conclusion that in the end the women's program involved a lot of commotion over almost nothing.

Successful Negotiations and Stalling for Time

It appears that the entire gender activities project was not meant to succeed. The existence of the women's project was, therefore, mainly virtual—it existed in the reports and in budgets, but it was not really about to be implemented, whether geared toward economic development or toward educational and social change. However, arguing that none of the parties involved intended to carry out the women's project from the start paints only a partial picture. Tahal's motivation and efforts at realizing this project were explicitly articulated, although only with regard to employing experts, which benefited them (as suggested above). The World Bank may also have been genuinely interested in implementing the women's project, which could serve to demonstrate its contribution to women's empowerment. As the World Bank did not have to allocate any additional budget for it—the Nepalese were expected to siphon off a portion of the World Bank loan for the irrigation project to the women's project—the women's project must have appealed to it. The Nepalese were the only party that voiced implicit and explicit objections to the women's project from the start.

The Nepali party, it would seem, succeeded in preventing the realization of the women's project, while ostensibly negotiating its implementation with the other two partners. Nevertheless, while striving to achieve their goals, the heads of the irrigation project probably changed their views and adjusted them to the ongoing dynamic situation. I suggest that the precise goal of their interventions was not completely clear to any of them while negotiating over the women program's budget. I assume that eventually both partners, the Israeli and especially the Nepali, gained more than they initially desired.

I would argue that the parties involved in the women's project—the Nepalese, the Israelis, and the World Bank—were only concerned with providing village women with economic resources and/or literacy only insofar as doing so paid lip-service to international gender trends that had to be endured.

This understanding emerges, I have argued, from examining the various documents. It was also exposed verbally by the heads of the irrigation project on several occasions. One example concerns the encounter Anita and I had with Thapa, when we returned to the irrigation project center on the first day of our visits to the villages. Describing our impressions and ideas, I said that living conditions in the first village we visited (Ekala) were harsh and that the proposed options for literacy classes were inadequate. I then raised the idea of constructing huts. Thapa rejected this idea instantly, claiming that the World Bank would only approve budgets for instruction and definitely not for infrastructure. However, he suggested that people in the villages could construct study huts themselves. He seemed to fancy this idea and developed it further, proposing a competition be held and explaining that "a healthy competition between the two political groups in the village would motivate people to compete over the chance to construct the hut, if we promise that the winning group will earn the literacy class as a reward." Hence, both Thapa, the Nepali director of the irrigation project, and the World Bank people would not consider investing in facilities for village women, as these cost much more money than paying local women instructors.

Despite Thapa's objection, I went on trying to convince him that the irrigation project should construct study huts, arguing that they would also benefit the UNICEF children, who had unbearable study conditions. He ended the discussion by saying that the matter would be taken care of. However, to my surprise, Thapa willingly accepted Anita's idea of offering the women students certain perks, such as refreshments, remarking that, "it is possible to buy some biscuits." Thapa also seemed to support my suggestion of establishing a small fund, in which small amounts of money would be saved, for the women's use after they completed the literacy classes. He proposed that I include that suggestion in the proposal to the World Bank. Thapa also accepted the idea of purchasing sewing machines, though not before I assured him that they would be for collective use in vocational training courses and not for personal use. All these meant minimal costs and delayed implementation.

My idea of marketing women's handicrafts in Kathmandu was also rejected by Thapa. He said:

> Let's run the courses first and only afterwards will it be possible to talk about marketing. Marketing products in Kathmandu does not have the slightest chance to succeed, because of the high costs of delivery and their low market prices. Besides, I have tried a few times to market agricultural products, potatoes for example. It never worked. But in the future we might try the local market.

Thapa's reservations with regard to encouraging private, small-scale ventures, finds support in John Whelpton's analysis of Nepal's development economy between 1951 and 1991 (Whelpton 2005). Referring to a 1991 government report, he argues that, "The cottage-industry training programme had been of doubtful value because, even if equipped with adequate skills, the home producer was often not able to compete with mass production" (ibid.: 149). However, Thapa's comment—"Let's run the courses first and only afterwards will it be possible to talk about marketing"—is the significant part of his response to my proposal. That is, literacy courses were the main activity he was willing to consider, rather than any economic enterprise.

Unsurprisingly, Thapa was very pleased with Anita's suggestion of incorporating lectures on health, family planning, and so forth into the literacy classes, and also with her ideas about enrichment activities for the WGOs. He added that we should include in our plans enrichment activities for village teachers, because they should be empowered. Thapa's approval of Anita's ideas can be readily understood as him conforming with then current views on gender issues, in line with the policies of UNESCO (1988) and the World Bank (1990), and with early 1990s literature, such as discussed by Elizabeth King and Anne Hill (1993). King and Hill suggest: "A better educated mother has fewer and better educated children. She is more productive at home and in the workplace. And she raises a healthier family since she can better apply improved hygiene and nutritional practices" (ibid.: 12). The dominant approach to women in development (WID) in the 1990s viewed women as mothers whose central occupation is child rearing and, consequently, this approach typically focused on family planning programs. Robinson-Pant claims that this approach remains unchanged and that "the reason for promoting women's literacy (and girls' education) is still to contribute to their roles as mothers and workers" (Robinson-Pant 2004: 16). Discourses and practices that ignored women's autonomous agency were criticized by scholars like Stacey Leigh Pigg (1992), Geeta Chowdhury (1995), Fiona Leach (2000), and Priti Chopra (2004).

However, Thapa's support for Anita's ideas can also be seen as the outcome of his and other irrigation project heads' desire to keep Anita and me busy with literacy and family health instruction, issues that were as remote as possible from the irrigation project and its economic activities. Thapa's reactions in the meeting with Anita and me, and Pandit's supportive attitude during our joint visits to the villages and during discussions over various difficulties involved in the implementation of the women's program, may still suggest that both were genuinely interested in implementing the women's project, and the literacy program in particular. Pandit promised to help open the literacy classes. He offered his help in guaranteeing that the needed books would be purchased on time. He also engaged enthusiastically in Anita's and my deliberations concerning suitable classrooms in the villages. Thapa similarly conveyed the impression that he sincerely considered the literacy program as important and feasible. When we met, following our first visits to the villages, he responded pragmatically to each and every one of our suggestions, whether in the affirmative or in the negative. Thapa seemed to treat the women's project as if he had to make technical decisions regarding a program that was to be implemented shortly.

Yet, in examining Thapa's attitude to the women's project on other occasions, the impression emerges that Thapa did not intend the project to be realized. Thapa avoided hiring foreign consultants for a very long time, and in fact he did everything in his power to prevent it. Moreover, Thapa rejected not only the overseas experts, he also ensured the long delay in hiring the local consultant. Eventually he capitulated after heavy pressure was put on him by the World Bank and Tahal, who demanded that he hire both the expatriate and local consultants. It is reasonable to assume that Thapa enjoyed the support of his superiors in the Ministry of Agriculture. This conclusion gains support from Leon's comment that the Nepali authorities were reluctant to "do things" unless they were forced to.

The reluctance of the Nepali officials, and their hostility toward expatriate experts, is also mentioned by Judith Justice (1989) and John Whelpton (2005). Justice reports that "the flood of foreign advisors and representatives" were considered by Nepali officials as "part of the aid package," "one of the 'penalties' of aid," "too abundant," and that it was impossible to cut back their numbers. Nepalese, she recounts, "questioned the high cost even for those whom they considered most helpful" (Justice 1989: 37–38). Whelpton describes the reluctance of the Nepali government toward American advisors in the 1950s and 1960s, who attempted to "urge reform within the administrative system" (Whelpton 2005: 129).[10]

The Nepalese did not object to the irrigation project. However, the women's program was perceived and treated differently, and the Nepalese objected to it. A comment made by Gupta, the local consultant on farmers' participation employed by Tahal, further supports this line of argument, and illustrates the reservations the Nepali directors of the irrigation project had with regard to the gender activities project. In conversations held between our visits (which he joined a few times), he said to me:

> They [the village women] do not believe that anything will come out of this project. What can we do? The people in high places are not interested in the projects for women. We are dealing with irrigation, what do we have to do with women development? That is why I always tell people [the female WGOs and the male AOs] not to promise anything and explain that the project will be implemented only later within half a year. All we need is to start one group to break the ice.

The fact that Gupta was a local high-ranking official, and was at the same time employed by Tahal, makes his comment indicative with regard to both the Nepali authorities and the Israeli company. Thus, the "people in high places" were reluctant regarding the women's project and Tahal was clearly aware of this. Indeed Gupta's expression, "All we need is to start one group to break the ice," exposes the deceitful intentions of the Nepalese. As far as Tahal's people were concerned, they were either indifferent or shared similar reservations, as is apparent from Leon's comment following our visit to Ekala. He said to me that the women's project did not stand a real chance, because:

> as you have seen, these women, they cannot really read. In any case this is not serious, these women cannot learn to read and write within the planned course of time of the classes, especially since they are going to be very tired, when coming home after working all day in the fields. Think about children in Israel, how many years they study. And besides, this teacher, she can hardly read herself, how can she possibly teach other women?

Leon made similar comments often. As Tahal's representative, his reservations seemed to echo his employer's attitude towards the women's project. If this view reflects the basic attitude of the decision-makers, whether Nepali or from Tahal, it follows that the women's project was imposed on the Nepalese, while Tahal was scarcely inclined to struggle for the project's implementation beyond hiring its consultants. Therefore, it was only a matter of time before the women's program fell apart. In this context, Thapa's encouraging remarks during his meeting with Anita and me can be explained as a manipulative tactic to gain time until the women's project could be disposed of completely. His cooperative behavior could have also stemmed from a fear that the World Bank would succeed in imposing the program on the Nepali government and hence he was maneuvering over the minimum amount to be carried out.

While expressing their objections about the women's program, Leon, Gupta and Thapa—together the Israeli and Nepali heads of the irrigation project—employed various arguments to persuade me, Anita, and probably themselves as well, that the project was not feasible. Their arguments pushed responsibility away from themselves and onto the village women, women "who cannot really read … and are tired," who "do not believe that anything will come out" of the women's project, and who are not relevant to an irrigation project. They also blamed people "in high places" who "are not interested in the projects for women." These arguments implicitly justified women's exclusion from men's spheres such as irrigation, their denial of resources, and their stigmatization as backward and ignorant.

The apparent pressure the World Bank exerted on local heads of the irrigation project to move ahead with implementation could be seen as reflecting the Bank's sincere interest in women's development. It is also clear that local officials seemed eager to satisfy the World Bank and to show progress. However, it appears that the World Bank would not or could not provide sufficient pressure to ensure the realization of the program. Moreover, Thapa's gesture—hiring the one and only class teacher with his own money, a very unusual act in itself—reveals the covert indifference of the World Bank concerning the implementation of the literacy program (and certainly of the economic activities part of it). Apparently, the Nepali officials knew that they did not need to demonstrate any real progress and that what became known as "Thapa's class" was, in David Mosse's words, just "a paradoxical ritual" (Mosse 2005: 166)[11] which was good enough to satisfy the World Bank's representatives. This episode revealed the deceitful aspect of the whole women's program, and symbolized the collusion of all three parties—the World Bank, the Nepali government, and the Israeli company—in pretending that the literacy program was on its way.

It is inconceivable that the World Bank's staff were unaware of the fact that more than a year after the start of the women's project only one class (out of some 300 originally planned) had been opened. This means that they colluded in the charade. I assume that if I was able to discern the true state of affairs on my first visit to the villages, the World Bank's people could have assessed the situation just as well. For their own reasons, they seemed to consider the only class that was operating in Ekala as representative of the women project's progress. Moreover, the conditions in which learning took place, which were noticeable to the World Bank delegation, did not seem to disturb them, as no comment was made in the Bank's letter concerning the tiny, dark, and muddy hut in which the women were expected to acquire their literacy skills.

Project Reports, the Social Order, and Developers' Compliance

Garfinkel's argument, that documents are inseparable characteristics of the social order which they describe" (Garfinkel 1967: 201), finds much support in the analysis presented above with regard to the two women project's reports and the irrigation project heads' discourse. Analyzing these seemingly straightforward professional reports and some of the dialogues relating to the women project's implementation exposes concealed organizational and personal interests of the people and organizations involved in the women's project. It reflects the irrigation project's hierarchical structure and reveals the adherence of the authors of the women project's reports to wider discourses and practices concerning gender equality, development ideology, social change, and so forth. However, the reports were more than "inseparable characteristics" of the social order; they also demonstrate how and why people, idealistic and committed as they may be, succumb to organizational dictates, demonstrating "obedient compliance" (Weber 1948: 229) to the "moral discipline" of authorities which imply the "self-denial" (Weber 1948: 95) of their moral and professional self-declared positions.

Moreover, examining the figures, categories, priorities, and certainly the terminology contained and employed in these reports unveils the "secrets" of the women's project: the papers served to impose agreement and acceptance on resisting participants at all levels. The written papers testify to Fenster's and my own tacit agreement to substitute (higher budgeted and more concretely implemented) economic needs with a (flexibly changed) obscure budget for literacy classes; they signal an acceptance of the Nepali party's fait accompli and the unquestioned need of Tahal's expertise for the women project's maintenance and success. Hence, the reports played a significant role in overcoming resistance to the imposed cooperation: the gender consultants' potential reservations with regard to the changing of emphasis in their professional understanding of the women's project and the Nepali officials' resistance with regard to accepting Tahal's professional intervention. The reports and the daily encounters that took place with relation to them enhanced the belief that something was really happening and endorsed the women's project into the ongoing organizational bargaining.

In what follows I will use ethnographic data, collected during visits to villages in the area of the irrigation project, to describe this bargaining process concerning the women project's purposes and prospects in the field. Analyzing some of the encounters that took place in the villages, and the interactions that followed them in the irrigation project offices, reveals the women's project to have been a deceitful social drama.

Notes

1. Fenster's study focused on "identifying both existing constraints and assets in order to formulate a plan which will meet the needs of the people in the Project Area" (Fenster 1996: 6). Her study is based on discussions with twelve women's groups, and interviews with the irrigation project officials, state officials, and NGO activists.
2. Source: *infed* http://www.infed.org/biblio/colonialism.htm (Retrieved 29 September 2010).
3. A more detailed discussion of this point will be presented at a later stage.
4. Lack of proper health services in rural parts of Nepal are extensively discussed by Justice (1989). Sharma and Prasain argue that the conflict between the Maoists and the state "has behind it a long history of bad governance … The government has been at best a remote entity for most rural women, and its programmes have not been responsive to their needs and aspirations" (Sharma and Prasain 2004: 164). They suggest that rural women's massive support for the Maoists is better understood against this background.
5. Tamang criticizes the homogenization of Nepali women in development discourse, the denial of the heterogeneity of women's lived experience, and the Panchayat elite's "unifying national narrative … to legitimate their rule over a heterogeneous populace" (Tamang 2002: 170).
6. Mosse discusses the manipulative use of foreign consultants by development agencies. He argues that consultants are "contributing to a broader relationship of donor power and patronage" (Mosse 2005: 266 n.6).
7. According to a letter written by Anita ten classes were opened after I left Nepal, whereas Leon's letter mentions 11 classes.
8. Letter from Leon, 10 November 1997.
9. Letter from Anita, received by fax, 19 December 1997.
10. Latent and sometimes outright resentment toward foreign experts is discussed in various works (see esp. Yunus 1998). In the context of education programs funded by the World Bank, Mark Smith (1998/2001), for example, points to the indignation of the South toward the World Bank's policies and pervasive influence in education, which rest "heavily on the work of foreign, Northern scholars and agency staff." *infed* http://www.infed.org/biblio/colonialism.htm (Retrieved 29 September 2010).
11. According to Mosse, "paradoxical rituals" are events "in which the power of the donor over the project is publicly acknowledged but practically denied" (Mosse 2005: 166).

1. Main street in Bhairahawa

2. “Little Buddha” at the center of Bhairahawa

3. A village scene

4. A village scene

5. A tea-party of the expatriate functionaries' wives in the Shangri-la hotel

6. The project's jeep stuck in the mud

7. At a meeting with village women

8. At a meeting with village women

9. Meeting women in the village

10. Thumb print – village women approving their acceptance to be included in a literacy course

11. Eating samosas with the WGOs

12. Cool drinks at a kiosk – Two of the WGOs

13. WGOs

14. Gathering in a project office

Chapter 4

The Role of Economic Activities in Negotiating Consent

Development Tourists and Village Women

On my second day in Bhairahawa I became acquainted both with the landscape on the way from the irrigation project offices to the villages, and with the ritual encounters that were part and parcel of visits to the villages. Leaving Bhairahawa, we drove on wrecked roads, sharing them with animals carrying wagons, old bicycles, and vehicles—a typical countryside scene. Green rice fields made a lovely sight to watch during the uncomfortable ride. On the muddy banks of the wide river Dno, many men were digging deep into the mud, probably looking for useful construction materials. The way to the villages required shifting from the main roads onto muddy, bumpy paths, which made the drive almost unbearable. The visits to the villages were characterized by some routine activities. The women were either gathered before we arrived or were called out by the WGOs to meet with us. The meetings would last for an hour or two in each place. After checking the women's names off against a list to confirm their participation in the literacy course, we would then tour the village, the local school, and other public locales, including Tahal's wells. Sometimes the women brought out their handicrafts to show us, and occasionally we would come across religious event, a local market, and so forth.

Robert Chambers's cynical description of the "standard route" visitors of "rural development tourism" (Chambers 1983: 16) take easily fits our travels to the villages. Chambers perceives these tours as a "show" for visitors in which "The same people are met, the same buildings entered" (ibid.: 17); "Buildings, machines, construction works, new crops, exotic animals, the clinic, the school, the new road, are all inspected" (ibid.: 12). Similarly, Celayne Heaton Shrestha calls these visits to project sites a "showpiece," "painstakingly staged performances" (Shrestha 2004: 13) for donors. However, it appears that beside the tourist element of these encounters, meeting the village women also had ethnocentric and patronizing implications. The kind of power relations encountered in development settings are perceived by some (e.g., Manzo 1995; Gardner and Lewis 1996) as "guardianship, found to have been characteristic of colonial relations" (Shrestha 2004: 12). Yet, the women and other people we met in the villages interacted willingly and even took advantage of these encounters.

Ekala: Literate Developers meet "Illiterate" Villagers

On my first tour of the villages in the project area, the first we came to was Ekala. It was a typically hot and humid day, and there were six of us traveling in Leon's jeep: Pandit, Leon, Anita, two WGOs and myself. A few male Association Organizers (AOs) joined us later.

Traveling in a relatively large company of some ten people (beside the WGOs, Anita and I, there were senior male officials and AOs) seemed to me to imply that the irrigation project employees were not overloaded with work, and thus could easily join our trips to the villages. Although it was not the norm on all our trips to the villages, they could nevertheless be described as social events. The impression that project employees, whether junior or senior, had a light work load was also clearly conveyed in the daily gatherings of AOs and WGOs that took place in Pandit's office, meetings that were sometimes joined by senior officials.

Leon had decided to join us on our first trip when he found out that the local engineer could not attend a meeting with him that had been scheduled for that morning. His decision could have also been influenced by the fact that Pandit decided to join our trip. Presenting himself as the boss of the women's project, Leon did not want to have his position usurped in his absence.

The journey to Ekala lasted about half an hour. Approaching the village, we passed a filthy pond, in which children were bathing, while large insects and mosquitoes buzzed overhead. Upon arrival, we entered a school class of girls, studying in a small dark muddy hut. Some twelve girls, aged 8 to 16, were sitting around the hut's walls studying Nepali and mathematics from text books. The girls were deeply absorbed in their books, and seemed to be unhappy about being distracted from their work (or about being observed by a group of strangers). The teacher, an old woman, answered the many questions addressed to her by the WGOs. I also asked her many questions, which Anita helped translate. The men, except for Leon, did not enter the hut. Leon asked about boys' and girls' education in the village. He was told that the girls do not go to the nearby school because their mothers need them to stay at home to help with the babies and in the rice fields. Then I turned to one of the students and asked her to read. She tried her best but had difficulties reading to us. The teacher explained that the girl had missed a few lessons and therefore was experiencing difficulties.

Behaving as the source of authority and knowledge, "literate" people confronting "illiterates," our dominance was accentuated all the more by our physical position, standing, as we did, in the low-roofed hut high above the shy young girls sitting on the ground. It was not only the girl who stumbled over her reading who was shamed by us. The teacher too was put on the defensive, having to explain and apologize for her student's failure, which also meant her own failure.

Later on Anita told me that the class in Ekala was privately funded by Thapa. Soon I found out that the Ekala class had a unique story. I later heard from the division chief of the engineering section that the year before the head of the World Bank, James Wolffenson, had visited the project. That visit made the local heads of the project anxious, feeling that the project (and they themselves) had to look good. Driven by the anticipated visit of the Bank's delegation, Thapa, the Nepali manager of the project, had opened a literacy class in Ekala. This he did with his own resources, paying a woman from the village to start teaching the first (and apparently almost the only) class in the project. The Bank's delegation arrived at Ekala by helicopter and visited the women's literacy class. Thapa's initiative was a success, as was made clear in the World Bank report on the delegation's visit to Ekala. Leon showed me an excerpt from a letter the Bank sent some time later, which stated the satisfaction of the delegation with the progress made in implementing the project. However, the letter also included a demand from the local heads of the project for the hiring of a new local coordinator for the women's program by March 1997, as the previous coordinator had not been replaced for a long time. Leon commented: "It is only the Bank's pressure that makes things move here." In fact, the new coordinator was Anita, who was hired as a result of the World Bank's remote and limited control over the local heads of the irrigation project.

After the encounter in "Thapa's class," we went to see the village school. It was a single-floored, ugly, gray-looking building constructed of bricks with a few attached huts, located on the outskirts of the village. We entered one of the classes where some ten boys and two girls were sitting on the floor with their bags next to them. The English teacher, who did not seem to know much English, answered our questions. Within the two dark huts we saw some tens of boys sitting on the floor studying. It was explained that the children, aged between 6 and 10, had studied there daily from 8.00 A.M. until 2.00 P.M., for some four to five years. We were also told that the girls who attended school came from more affluent families, who could afford to do without their labor at home and in the rice fields. Close to the school some twenty women were standing in the shade of some trees. A small group of women was sitting on the ground, some of them holding babies, and some were nursing them. On that day children were receiving polio vaccinations. A nurse from the Ministry of Health approached us and explained what was going on. She told us that she came to the village every month and that the health ministry's professionals used to visit the village regularly and offer the women lectures about health issues. This practice took place in all villages in the region.

In considering our interactions with the villagers, it appears that we were mainly interested in educational matters, asking questions "drowned in statistics" (Chambers 1983: 17): years of schooling, gender differences in rates of school attendance, and so on. This bias disclosed our attitude to the children and women in the villages, as well as toward the entire village population. Focusing on quantitative measurements of children's and the women's schooling hints at our latent prejudice about their poor intellectual skills and levels of attainment. Our perception of the self-evident worth of schooling (efficiently installed in our minds from the first day of attending school) made us blind to more complex and relevant elements in the children's and women's lives. Moreover, implicit in this ethnocentric attitude was a sense of the villagers' backwardness when compared to our own intellectual achievements and superiority. In any event, that is how things appear to me from the observations and impressions recorded in my fieldnotes.

Khurmundihawa: Intruders meet Locals

The visit to Khurmundihawa, the next stop after Ekala, further illustrates our intrusive methods and arrogance. However, my account of the visit to the second village also highlights the women's assertiveness in responding to our presentation of the women's project. Khurmundihawa was in many ways similar to Ekala, though it looked even poorer. It was in Khurmundihawa that I first met Manju, a WGO. I was deeply impressed by her charismatic character, typical of foreign visitors who, according to Chambers, tend to be impressed by the "charisma" of local people who are regarded as "exceptional leaders" (Chambers 1983: 17). She was an intelligent, energetic, and charming woman in her early thirties. The group she organized gathered around us, conveying a pleasant welcome. Manju explained that the original group had split into two as a result of political disputes, one group identifying with the Communist Party and the other with the Congress Party. In each of the groups there were some thirty women.

The two spokeswomen explained that the women expected to receive 1 to 2 rupees (about $0.017) per day for lunch while attending literacy classes. I asked if this was a prerequisite for attendance and received a positive reply.[1] We went on asking many questions and the women cooperated willingly, especially the spokeswomen. The village women were obviously aware of our desire to gain their confidence and, more importantly, their participation in the literacy project.

Manju informed Anita and me that she had found a teacher for the literacy class in that village, and this woman was also willing to rent us a room in her house in which the classes could be held. On our way to check out the potential classroom we passed through some animal mud-huts, which had dung stuck to the walls (for cooking purposes). The brick constructions[2] were used for people's accommodation and the mud-huts were used for cooking and storage. The animals seemed integrated in the living houses. This impression finds evidence in Tahal's socioeconomic Survey (1992) of the irrigation project area. The Survey's findings suggest that "About 74% of the households are having separate animal shed. The remaining households keep their animals in any corner of the living houses" (ibid.: 32).

The room we were shown, intended for the twenty-five or so women who were expected to attend the literacy class, was around two by three meters. It smelled bad and was dark. A bed with no mattress on it occupied most of the space. When I commented that the room was too small and dark the woman rushed us into another room, where some big stones were laid out. This other room was bigger than the other one; nevertheless, it too was appalling. I asked if it was possible to study outdoors, in a shady place, and also urged Pandit and Anita to consider constructing study huts. These could be used for the women's literacy course and to house the Unicef class, which we had visited on our way to the teacher's room. The Unicef class was housed in a small, dark hut, although there was a school building nearby. Their teachers were employed by Unicef, who, we were told, would not pay for anything except the teachers' wages. Observing the children in the dark room, it occurred to me that a specially constructed classroom could serve the children in the mornings and the women in the afternoons. When things seemed to be finalized I asked to see the women's handicrafts. Baskets of different sizes, decorated fans, and home ornaments were brought out.

It appears that in my visits to Khurmundihawa and Ekala I reacted with simultaneous feelings of revulsion and compassion. My awareness of the prevailing conditions in which people lived motivated my urge to do something about it. This ambition was naive and pretentious, but it was also a way of justifying my intrusion into local people's lives, part of group of who were scrutinizing the villagers' way of life. Moreover, my perception of the living conditions as repulsive revealed my latent, alienated, attitude to the place and the people. My mixed feelings—embarrassment (at inspecting poor people's lives), alienation and revulsion (from the "primitive" life conditions of local people), compassion (for their misery), admiration (of "charismatic" local people)—were all part of my daily encounters with the village women, though this uncomfortable state of mind was always hidden behind a professional mask and my seemingly self-confident air of expertise.

My written descriptions of village encounters reveal the ethnocentric attitude of a foreigner. Certain expressions concerning village life and its recurring scenes disclose my unconscious disdain and aversion. At times I even expressed my emotional attitude explicitly—using, for instance, the term "appalling"—to convey my impression of a room offered to us as a classroom. I often described roads, paths, and huts as "muddy," considering them too disgusting to walk or drive on, or live in, or "filthy" to denote the lack of basic hygiene, when referring, for example, to children washing in the river. In alluding to diseases associated with flies and mosquitoes, I revealed my distanced and judgmental position. Focusing on the close quarters humans and beasts shared in the villages, and on the dung stuck on the (mud) walls of the huts, discloses an aversion to the way of life and probably towards the people as well. It appears that I perceived this way of life as unbearable and inconceivable for "normal" people like me. The associated images of disease, dirt, and proximity to animals on the one hand, and of weakness and poverty on the other, recorded in some of my descriptions of the villagers, created a perceived unbridgeable distance between "me" and "them." From this perspective, comparing Fenster's reports and my own, I can see that whereas Fenster exposed her latent stereotyped views by writing about the "many diseases" of the local population, I revealed my latent stereotypes in my fieldnotes.

West Bharaulia: Procedural Rituals and Challenging Stereotypes

The alienated attitudes were reinforced by our visit to the next village, West Bharaulia. The scene there was similar to the one we encountered in the other two villages: huts, muddy and dirty surroundings, cattle and people mingling together. We sat in the shade of some trees and were gradually joined by women, children, and men. One man was urging his wife to join the group and to sit next to us. Again, old iron beds with straw mattresses were brought out for us to sit on, while the village people sat on the ground. We were offered water, which came from the nearby hand pump. This time I refused to drink the water because Leon had warned me, after having tried the water in the previous village, that it was not safe enough to drink.

Similar questions to those raised in the previous villages were raised here. An assertive woman mediator, who seemed to take control of the meeting, told us that many of the women in the village had taken a sewing course, which was organized by the rural development department of the Nepali government. The women asked that the women's project provide them with sewing machines and with further training in sewing. Literacy training was also requested.

While inquiring about the women's expectations of the project, Manju interacted with the women cheerfully. They responded to her warmly and confidently, while she signed them up for the literacy class, which most women did using their thumb. Some twenty-four names and signatures were eventually collected. During the conversation, which was mediated by Manju, the woman leader said that she hoped that a female teacher would replace the male teacher in the local school, thus enabling parents to send their daughters there. While the process of signing up the women was going on, Leon chose to gather some "statistics," asking Manju to find out how many of the women's husbands could read and write. She told him that only one or two of the men did.

Signing the women up for the literacy classes appeared to take the form of what Gideon Kunda calls a "presentational ritual," "a mechanism for mediating normative demands and normative responses," and used in developing "an organizational culture". (Kunda 1992: 159). The process began with small talk with the women, establishing personal contact and winning their confidence. Then Anita's or my presentation of the program followed. We described in detail the women project's objectives and schedule to the women sitting around us. Next the women would ask questions and we—Anita in particular—patiently answered all questions and tried to appease doubts. The lists of women thus obtained indicated the WGOs' good work in preparing the women for committing to the literacy classes, and also attested to Anita's and my success in convincing the women of the project's importance and seriousness. The lists served as a kind of contract between the women's project and the village women, perceived by the latter as the project's commitment to provide them with literacy and, more importantly, to deliver anticipated material resources and benefits, such as refreshments, vocational training, and sewing machines. The dramatic moment of counting signatures and informing other project members of the results turned the list of signatures into a symbol of professional and personal attainment.

While discussing with Pandit how we might find a suitable location for the literacy class in West Bharaulia, he said that it might be possible to use the well site, which was near the village. After concluding the enrollment process we went to see the place. Pandit explained authoritatively that we could take advantage of the fact that the well was soon to be transferred to the local people. We agreed that the well site could accommodate the literacy class. En route to the site, a male villager approached Manju, asking her to hire his wife as a teacher. Manju agreed willingly and assured him that in any case his wife was the one she had intended to recommend for teaching the local group, since she was the most educated woman in the village.

Just as I had done in the other villages we visited, I asked the women about their handicrafts. Again, many pieces of work were quickly brought out which the women and children were excited to show us. Nevertheless, we were told again that the handicrafts were not for sale.

In retrospect, my encounter with the women in West Bharaulia clarifies the superficial and stereotypic picture I had in my mind when I engaged with the women and while later writing up my experiences in my fieldnotes. Clearly the overall impression that I had of the villages and their inhabitants was a product of my distant, alienated position. While this attitude is probably clearest in my initial impressions of the villages, it could also have been latently present throughout my visit to Nepal and afterwards. Nevertheless, my initial and unacknowledged images of the village women did not correspond to their actual self-presentation, as it emerges from the ethnography. The women were obviously very aware of the fact that we needed their cooperation, and openly expressed what they expected from us. As they had attended a sewing course in the past, they expected to benefit from the project in economic terms. Moreover, although many of the women were illiterate and could not even sign their names, they were capable of learning and apparently could manage their lives without recourse to formal education. As the women's handicraft skills made clear, they were able and capable of producing objects that were not intended for subsistence. My eagerness to see the women's products appears to be stereotypical tourist behavior; the women villagers, meanwhile, contradicted my representations of their poverty and weakness by refusing to selling their handicrafts.

Structured Social Distance and Men's Marginality in the Village Encounters

Social interactions between project people and village people assumed the pattern of dichotomized encounters. The theme of "us" versus "them," "outsiders" from the town versus "locals" from the village, "literate" versus "illiterate," was the most prominent feature of many of our visits. We came to the women's villages, sometimes into their homes; they awaited us, sometimes for hours on end because of delays. They would gather round us, seated on the ground, most of the time listening or reacting to our directed conversation and questions, while we sat on seats offered by them. The hierarchal social distance created in these encounters was even more conspicuous in relation to Leon and me. We did not know the local language and had to rely on Nepali-speaking colleagues to interpret for us. Yet, our disadvantaged position in communicating with local people never prevented us from taking front stage during the encounters, thus pushing the Nepali employees of the women's project into a secondary position, serving us in their role as mediators and interpreters.

Leon's presence and my own seemed to introduce formality and social distance into the encounters. Our foreign, Western appearance must have contributed to fostering social distance between local employees and the two of us. This distance was enhanced by imposing the use of English on all participants in the situation. This imposition of a "stronger" foreign language on the locals can be viewed more positively by taking into account the fact that both parties (speakers of Nepali and Hebrew) were obliged to use a non-native tongue to communicate, thus introducing into the encounter a sense of mutual disadvantage.

Thomas Ricento's (2000) collection offers support for this line of argument, suggesting that an interactive and subtle influence occurs in interlinguistic encounters and processes. Martin Hoftun, William Raeper, and John Whelpton, meanwhile, describe how English was politically employed by Nepalese in reaction to India's dominance in the 1990s "to stress their linguistic independence" (Hoftun, Raeper, and Whelpton 1999: 277).

However, although the mutual disadvantage of language (greater even for the Israelis, who had no recourse to the local language) brought the higher-ranking Nepali officials and the Israelis closer, it clearly created a social distance and alienation between those, on the one hand, who did not speak English—the villagers and the junior officials—and those who did. Thus, I consider Robert Phillipson's (1992) perception of English as an important component of neocolonialism relevant in this context. This interpretation finds support in Anna Robinson-Pant's comment, that "the need for English language in Nepal has been initiated by foreign development agencies rather than by government administration" (Robinson-Pant 1995: 5). Robinson-Pant stresses further that the "need for funding" enforced the use of English on local NGOs. Hence, most literacy reports, studies, evaluations, and so on produced until the mid 1990s were in English, written "primarily for a Western rather than a Nepali audience, the majority being written for donor agencies such as UNICEF or the World Bank" (ibid.: 4).[3]

These hierarchal encounters also involved a gender component, which effected a reversal of the usual pattern of gender stratification. In most meetings with the village women, a few men were present, but they usually sat at some distance. This could mean either that they were curious to hear what was going on in the meetings between their wives and the "important," urban, and foreign, project people; or, alternatively, that they were suspicious and reluctant in relation to the possible outcomes of these encounters. Yet another alternative interpretation is suggested by Fenster. She reports that the "presence of men enabled women to express themselves freely" (Fenster 1996: 8), indicating that men's attendance gave the women confidence when facing project people. This explanation suggests that the women were in some way vulnerable in their interactions with project people, and portrays them as needing men's protection. However, I would question this observation. Although it is true that the meetings placed village women in an inferior position, the women did not behave as either helpless or in need of men's protection.

Moreover, my impression was that the men were made marginal in these encounters, while the women's project people invested a great deal of energy in pleasing the women. As women's empowerment was the focus of these encounters, men were almost entirely ignored and excluded. Furthermore, from speaking to some of the men I inferred that most of them were also illiterate; thus, the fact that only the women were offered literacy courses implicitly discriminated against men. Similar observations have been made by scholars like Naila Kabeer (1994), Anita Dighe (1995), Alaka Basu (1999), and Anna Robinson-Pant (2001). Robinson-Pant, for example, argues that the common focus on women as participants means that "even non-literate men often feel reluctant to join a class".[4] Moreover, she adds, the "common focus on women as participants" and the "feminisation of literacy programmes" that exclude men limits their potential to initiate social change, particularly in the area of HIV/Aids prevention, family planning, and gender equality (ibid). Ila Patel and Anita Dighe (2003) also point to the feminization of literacy programs in terms of facilitators, participants, and curriculum, which tend to focus on subjects seen as belonging to "women's domain." Thus the potential for social change and changes in gender relations are probably diminished, as these require men's participation.

Another possible explanation for the men's attendance at these meetings is their interest in making sure that any potential advantage offered by the women's project is not missed. That is to say, by attending the meetings they could be involved in bargaining over prospective benefits. One example of this is the occasion when one of the husbands asked Manju to appoint his wife as a teacher in their village. Whatever the men's motivation was in attending the meetings, their presence never seemed to imply reservations about the program, but rather the opposite.

Another aspect of the gendered dimensions of the village encounters was the passive, cautious participation of the women project's male employees (the AOs).

I suggest that although the meetings took place in an informal setting and manner (a countryside location, sitting close together on the ground, in an informal arrangement), status and gender differentials emerged. This was demonstrated not only by the domination of proceedings by Anita and myself, an artifact of our central positioning, but also by the formation of distinct groups and their different relative positioning, such as the visible exclusion of men from the women's circles. Those attending the meetings regarded themselves, and were regarded by others, as belonging to distinct gender groups, and were identified by their formal job titles (which were in English and not in Nepali).

The marginalized place of the men and their seemingly reduced prominence in these encounters indicate the latent, although definite, impact of project staff on gender and power relations. Their attendance and conduct indirectly influenced the villagers' patterns of socializing, the groups' clustering, the prominence in groups' discussions, the voicing of opinions, according to gender. It appears, therefore, that structured hierarchal distance and gendered group formation, introduced by the presence and conduct of project staff, have the potential to influence gender power relations, even reversing them at times. Moreover, the influence of project staff fosters gender division even though no formal means are used.

The Village Women's Assertiveness

Although some of the descriptions of the women in my fieldnotes, especially those from my first visits to the villages, paint a picture of women as compliant and passive, they were in fact nothing of the kind. Viewing the women villagers as vulnerable, helpless, or ignorant ignores the ample examples which point to the opposite. Moreover, the use of the blanket stereotype "illiterate women"—implied in Fenster's report, documented in my fieldnotes, and often expressed by officials—reveals the ethnocentric thinking of developers rather than the reality of women lives.[5] Robinson-Pant makes a similar point, using case studies of women "who are confident, [and who] have developed other strategies to survive without literacy" (Robinson-Pant 2004a: 4). She also argues that "women are not powerless because they cannot read or write" (Robinson-Pant 2004b: 28).

When project people entered the villages they were perceived to be backed by formal authority, professional advantage, and anticipated budgets, and these fostered social distance between the women villagers and the project people. Nevertheless, the interactions described above reveal many of the women to have been assertive, self-confident, politically-minded, and even suspicious at times. They were certainly not, at least not in any generalizable way, powerless or ignorant.

Manju was probably the most remarkable example of a young, liberated, and self-confident village woman. She had completed twelve years of schooling, was a mother of two, and had her own motorcycle. Before being recruited by the project, she used to go around the villages, helping needy women with groceries they could not afford and encouraging other mothers to send their daughters to school. She proudly told Anita and me that her husband used to share responsibility for the household and helped care for their daughters. My perception of Manju as a "charismatic leader" (Chambers 1983: 17) may be criticized as an example of a (romanticized) biased perception which underestimates rural deprivation and poverty (ibid.: 1–23). However, I contend that this kind of argument implies a generalization of poverty, rural poverty in this case, in a way that erases numerous narratives of individuals. Manju was a very impressive person indeed, but she was definitely not an exception but rather an example for some of the young Nepali village women.

Most of the women we saw in the villages were dressed in lovely colorful fabrics that they seemed to keep clean although they were long enough that they trailed on the ground. The longer the meetings went on, the more the women would open up and chat freely and cheerfully with the Nepali-speakers among us. At moments when Leon and I were less involved, and when communication was centered on Anita and the WGOs, the conversation seemed to be more fluent and personal.

Women villagers were not only assertive, self-confident, neatly dressed, and friendly, some of them also conveyed an evident air of dominance. In many of the villages—as in the account of our visits to Khurmundihawa and West Bharaulia—we met spokeswomen who mediated between the WGOs and others from the irrigation project and local women. They represented other women in negotiations over the study venue and the choice of teachers. They also bargained on behalf of their companions over the possible benefits that could be obtained for those who joined the literacy classes. The spokeswomen were in a position to advance their own interests, as occurred in Khurmundihawa, where the spokeswoman expected to profit from the women's project by renting a room and being employed as a teacher.

It appears that these women leaders knew that they had some bargaining power in negotiating the terms for hosting the literacy classes in their villages.[6] They realized that the women project's employees needed their approval of the literacy classes. This awareness empowered them to demand certain benefits, such as lunch money. Being so confident of their bargaining power, sometimes the women presented their demands as ultimatums. The women's project employees, the WGOs, and Anita in particular, depended on the women's signatures, indicating their agreement to attend the literacy course. The longer the list of signatures, the more evident was the WGOs contribution to the program. In fact, they probably depended more on the village women than vice versa, for the enrollment lists meant that they would continue to be hired by the irrigation project. In response to their demand that they be given an allowance for their lunch, Thapa instantly agreed that "refreshments" for participants in the courses would be included in the budget. Thapa understood quite well the significance of the demand and the need to buy-off the women, giving them something in return for their consent to be included in the women's project. This bargain was very good from his point of view because it involved minimal costs.

The women in West Bharaulia were no less assertive, asking for advanced training in sewing to supplement the course they had finished already. They also openly requested being provided with sewing machines, which would enable them to put their training into practice and make some kind of living from it. The women in Ekala signed up for the literacy course, assuming that further training and assistance in purchasing sewing machines would be provided if they joined the course. Anita and I did not say anything to cast doubt on their expectations, mentioning vaguely that the women's project did indeed aim to provide for "economic needs" at some later stage. The woman leader in West Bharaulia was also cognizant of the potential of cooperating with the women's project, and tried to get project staff to agree to help the local school obtain a female teacher so that villagers would be able to send their daughters there, assuming that it was in the project's power to do something about the matter.

The men in the villages also seemed to be aware that the introduction of the literacy program would entail various benefits. This was illustrated by the men's behavior in both Khurmundihawa and West Bharaulia. Encouraging his wife to join the women's group, the man described in the account of our visit to Khurmundihawa must have assumed she would benefit somehow from participating in the literacy course, thus indirectly benefiting their family. The husband, who asked Manju to appoint his wife as a teacher in West Bharaulia, was clearly aware of the advantages of being a project employee, in terms of both a salary and social prestige for his wife and indirectly for himself. If these two husbands represent the village men's general attitude to the women's project and to their wives' educational advancement, than it appears that their wives' advancement did not pose a threat, but rather the opposite. Men's passive attendance at our meetings in the villages can be perceived as their endeavor to make sure that their wives took full advantage of what the women's project had to offer. If so, then the argument about traditional constraints on women's progress, and on promoting gender equality (in the villages in particular), which were often used by the irrigation project's heads and by directors of other local organizations, was not substantiated by the men's actual behavior. Hence, those arguments were clearly excuses used to justify the project leaders' reluctance to implement the women's project.

Bhawarabari: Women Leaders and Economic Issues

The second round of visits, which took place two days after the first, foregrounded many of the features previously observed. However, some further understandings emerged from interactions in the villages and from unique episodes we experienced there. These meetings also revealed the women's assertiveness as they expressed their wishes and objections, while drawing on their past experience with development projects. The women's interest in economic issues, in particular, was pronounced during our encounters. Moreover, the village women's entrepreneurial spirit was clearly apparent, indicating their essential need for access to financial and information resources. As with the previous round, three villages were visited. Once again it was very hot and damp, with six of us in the pickup truck, four crammed in the back seat. One of the passengers was a professional instructor in agricultural training.

Our first stop was Bhawarabari. Women, girls, small children and babies gathered gradually, as Aruna, the local WGO, and the other WGOs went to call the women to join the meeting. We were told by Aruna that about half of the girls in the village attended the nearby school, some 2 km distant, while the others were forced to stay at home and help with household chores. The WGOs, Anita, and I sat on a thin straw mattress laid on an iron bed. Some fifteen women villagers were seated, with a few small children at their side, on sackcloth spread on a thin layer of straw, which had been brought in by an old man. Some time latter he brought a mat for another four women who joined us with their little children. The man then sat next to the woman who was leading the meeting, listening to her very carefully. A few men joined the group, sitting behind us on another bed. Pamela, one of the WGOs, encouraged more women to approach, while Anita explained to me that those women were shy and did not dare to join us. Many of the women were wearing a golden nose-ring and some of them had a traditional red mark on their foreheads.

The women told us that they were interested in raising sheep and goats rather than breeding chickens, as these had been causing them trouble, consuming their neighbors' crops. They also asked if the literacy class could run for two hours a day, instead of three. Meanwhile, Pamela wrote down the women's names quietly, bending down to get closer to the women so that they could stamp their thumbs next to their written names.

While we were chatting and collecting names, one of the women was trying to cope with her son's jealousy as he persistently harassed his baby brother in her arms. The group grew steadily and some young men and a few more women joined the event. More than thirty women were gathered eventually. Three girls, aged about seven years old, who were standing nearby arm in arm, requested that they be given a basic education. They added that this learning would allow them to know what kind of vocational training to seek. Some of the women at the meeting expressed a desire to have kitchen gardens, for cultivating vegetables. They expected the project representatives (presumably addressing, indirectly, the local agriculture instructor who was accompanying us) to provide them with a solution to the problem of water shortages. The women villagers were probably hoping that they could gain access to the new irrigation system of deep wells introduced by the irrigation project. The small wells that were dug by families, and from which they drew water using a hand pump, had dried up. Pamela explained that due to water shortages, cultivating vegetables was unfeasible and, therefore, some of the families used drinking water for growing vegetables.

The local women's leader, dressed in a turquoise sari with pink flowers, a red traditional spot on her forehead, and wearing a gold nose-ring and earrings, seemed to be in control of things. Having had a high-school education, she was, undoubtedly, the most natural candidate for teaching literacy in her village. The woman was an activist in a women's organization and had headed a group that participated in an agricultural training course some six months earlier. She explained that the three-day course, which she regarded highly, offered training in vegetable and fruit cultivation, in basic health care, and in marketing. She also told us that she liked to help people with traditional medication and agricultural activities, and that she had done so before joining the agricultural course. A few women mentioned that family-planning training should be provided for women with more than five children. The leader asked us to consider her home for the literacy class. When I suggested an open, shaded place to study, assuming that her place would look like the other rooms we had observed before, the women objected, saying that the children would disturb them.

The agricultural course that the women had previously taken had included training in growing red beans, which at that time were very expensive (around 75 rupees per kilo [that is about $1.3]). Following that training, the women grew a large quantity of beans, by which time the local market was flooded with them and their price had dropped to 33 rupees (that is about $0.6) per kilo. Consequently, the women did not sell their entire crop and stored the beans at home, preferring to sell their stock as seed during the sowing season, something which would bring a good price. The leader explained that in order to facilitate the women's use of their stock of beans to generate income, all they needed was some basic instruction in marketing the beans, mainly packing techniques and selling practices. When the women told us that they also grew potatoes, Anita suggested selling them as potato chips.

Sewing was another economic option discussed at the meeting. The group leader said that providing the women training in sewing would enable them to sew uniforms for factory workers, and also to sell some of their products elsewhere. Moreover, it was suggested that while some women sewed others could be in charge of sales to markets and factories. I was curious to know how the women would obtain the sewing machines needed for this enterprise. When Anita posed my question to the group leader, everybody listened carefully. She replied that the village women's group had savings of some 25,000 rupees (about $431). Every woman had to pay 5 rupees (less than $0.1) per month into the savings fund and was entitled to obtain a loan at an interest rate of 2 per cent. The money had to be repaid within a month, thus facilitating the fund's continuous growth.[7]

The option of selling the women's traditional handicrafts was also raised, as in previous encounters with the women in the villages, but the women rejected the idea spontaneously. The leader explained that the items were designated for their daughters' dowries. Nevertheless, she added that the women could produce different items for commercial sale. On our way to see the place offered for the literacy class, one girl showed us a colorful basket that had been made by her mother. The leader explained that they would be prepared to sell such a basket for some 70 rupees (about $1.2). Producing a basket of that relatively small size involves two hours work per day for a whole working week, paying its maker about 5 rupees (about $0.09) per hour. By comparison, factory workers earned about 6 rupees (about $0.1) per hour or 40 rupees (about $0.7) per six-hour work day.

After I had taken some photographs, something I did at each village meeting, the leader took us to her home to see the room she had offered to rent out for the literacy classes. The room was small and dark but the attached balcony was suitable for studying. At that time it was being used for an animal husbandry course, in which some twenty-five men participated. The room would become available for the literacy classes as soon as the men had finished their course, which was to run for twenty days.

At the time of the visit I failed to notice the fact that only men were participating in the animal husbandry course. However, I became aware of women's absence from this and many other agricultural training courses later on. Being fully aware of the discriminatory implications of women's exclusion, Tovi Fenster reported as follows: "Although women contributed a significant share of the agricultural work and the households' livelihood, they were often excluded from governmental development programs. They were widely excluded from training programs provided by the Irrigation Project" (Fenster 1996: 15). Noting the conspicuous absence of women from the irrigation project farmers' training programs, Fenster asked "why women farmers' participation in training programs is relatively low in spite of the fact that they are doing at least half and sometimes more of agricultural work" (ibid.: 15). Tahal's socioeconomic survey of the irrigation project region offers some quantitative evidence for women's significant cobtribution to what it calls "farm operation." It states that the division of labor in "farm operation" between males and females was as follows: land preparation and irrigation: 5% done by women and 95% by men; planting and processing: 70% by women and 30% by men; weeding, harvesting and storing: 55% by women and 45% by men; threshing: 30% by women and 70% by men (Tahal 1992: 34 "table 3.7.1: Stage III Area – Proportion of Female and Male Labour in Farm Operation").

The biased perception of gender, including the sexual division of labor, that prevailed in the irrigation project, and in development projects in Nepal more generally, was particularly conspicuous when compared to information on Nepali women's significant role in agriculture and the labor market. A study carried out by Shtrii Shakti, a women's organization,[8] for instance, indicates that women contribute 63 per cent of the family farm income in the rural sector, and produce 35 per cent of agricultural farm products in the local market economy (Shtrii Shakti 1995: 197–8). Prativa Subedi contends that women are definitely "those who are most involved in the production and utilization of food grains" (Subedi 1993: 85). Moreover, "except for plowing the fields," women are responsible for almost every agricultural activity, "like preparing the land for cultivation, carrying fertilizer, seed sowing and planting, wedding, harvesting, sorting grains, selecting and drying seeds" (ibid.: 76).

It appears that although women were assertive, ambitious, capable, hard-working, significant contributers to the family and national economy, the heads of the irrigation project did not consider them as relevant participants in agricultural training courses and only minimally included them in running the irrigation activities. It follows, from the situation of both the irrigation project and devlopment in Nepal more generally, that the government and developing agencies play a crucial role in gendering the national economy, and more specifically in denying women fair access to public resources and inflicting relative poverty upon them.

Brindban and Sikatahan: Banking NGOs and Village Women's Enterprises

The next village we went to was Brindban, where we met the local WGO, Sita. During our visit Sita needed help with interpreting because a different Nepali dialect was spoken. The women were already waiting for us when we arrived, sitting on the ground between two huts. Some fifty people were gathered there, among them women, men, and small children. A baby was crying. A soft breeze was blowing and made the dreadful humidity somewhat more bearable.

A representative of a credit NGO, who had come to discuss loans to the local people, was there, sleeping peacefully nearby. He woke up when things started to heat up, and credit programs were debated. The village men came nearer and discussed the issue of loans and interest. It was explained that loans were based on repayment of the borrowed amount within five years, while the interest had to be paid starting from the end of the first week after receiving the loan. The rate of interest could be as high as 16 per cent per annum. Anita explained to me that people did not like the lending conditions of the organization. They did not like the high rate of interest, and nor did they like having to begin repayments immediately, because, they said, this prevented them investing in a serious venture. Therefore, the people preferred to take modest loans and to use them for their daughters' dowries, and for purchasing hand pumps for the household.

The women in Brindban were also interested in agricultural training, such as instruction in growing vegetables and animal husbandry. While we were leaving we met the village school teacher, a 16–year-old girl who had completed six years of schooling.

We were one hour late arriving at the next village, Sikatahan. The local WGO was Aruna. When we arrived, an unusual event, from my point of view, was taking place: in the center of the village setting a "field bank" was operating. Two men were sat on the ground in front of some thirty women, and buffalos ambled around between them. One of the men was taking money from the women, who were queued up in front of him. Piles of bills accumulated at his feet. When women handed the man their money, he jotted down the relevant details in their savings books. The two men represented a credit NGO, which lent village women money at an interest rate of 25 per cent per annum, the loan to be repaid weekly.

While waiting for the money transactions to end, we chatted with the leader of the women's group in a nearby tea house, which the leader owned. Her home of some nineteen years sat outside the village on the hillside. As it was rather hard to make a living in that area, she had to come down to the village to earn her livelihood. While we were watching the field bank in operation, the leader explained that its loans were only offered to women. Repayments of 10 rupees per 100 rupees (about $1.7) loans had to be paid monthly, and the entire loan (with interest) had to be repaid within fifty months. Most of the women took the loans to start small enterprises, such as the small tea house we were sitting in. Sometimes the money was used for agricultural needs. Loans could amount to as much as 300,000 rupees (about $5172). She mentioned an example of a woman who had bought a taxi with a loan, making a profit from running it while at the same time repaying her debts.

As we talked, the leader expressed reservations with regard to the literacy classes. She argued very persuasively that there was no point in offering literacy classes to everybody because some of the women were old and had difficulties with their vision. Anita explained to me that the leader was trained at teaching birth-control techniques, and that she was involved in distributing contraceptive devices provided by one of the NGOs that was active in the region. She also used to accompany women to clinics to have contraceptive devices installed, and sometimes to sterilization procedures at the hospital. According to the leader, some 200 to 300 women were using birth-control pills while a similar number preferred to have an injection that prevented conception for about three months.

From where we were sat we could hear the women praying loudly together. Anita explained that as there was no other way to guarantee that the women repaid their loans, their commitment to repay the money was based on this collective ritual prayer. When the money lenders eventually left, we joined the group of women.

Anita was given a bench to sit on and I sat on a chair that was brought out from the tea house especially for me. Buffalos approached us from time to time, and were chased away by an old woman with a stick, assisted by a little boy. I was suffering so much from the heat and humidity that I could hardly follow the exchange between Anita, the other two WGOs, and the village women. Desperately exhausted, I sat there waiting for the meeting to end and did not bother Anita with questions for the women.

A little while later, when the topic had changed and the lists for the literacy classes were being signed, the encounter became informal. Anita and I came down to sit on the grass. A woman in her late 70s came to sit beside me, and waved a fan at my face to relieve my noticeable suffering. She was very amused by my visible distress, and made, so it seemed to me, jokes at my expense. She leaned her head towards mine, as if to show we resembled one another on account of us both having white hair, and patted my feet, thus causing her friends' unconcealed excitement at her daring gestures. Anita suggested taking pictures of the old woman and me, and then of all the women who had attended the event. Later, she told me that that village was relatively advanced (referring to the tea house and other small enterprises as proofs of this), and that some of the women had gone through literacy classes already. The school we visited also seemed relatively more "advanced." The classrooms had blackboards, and the girls sat on chairs next to tables.

On our way back to Bhairahawa the familiar sights could be observed: children carrying wood parcels on their heads; women working in the paddy fields, their feet immersed in water; cattle walking around; wretched mud huts scattered along the way (described in my fieldnotes as "disgusting"); dirty-looking ponds with buffalos bathing in them. The hour-and-a-half drive to Bhairahawa seemed to last forever. The vehicle was unbearably cramped, with three of us at the front, and when another WGO joined us there were four people in the back of the jeep, all sweating heavily. A large dead snake lying on the road broke our exhausted silence, eliciting some excited comments from the people crowded in the jeep. The light rain that started to fall, and the drinks I bought for everyone a short while before arriving back at the project's site, made it a bit easier to endure the heat.

Manipulative Development: Ignoring Women's Wishes

The main insights derived from the second round of visits to the villages are compatible with the conclusions from the previous round. The women were very clear in stating what kind of activities they preferred. Economic enterprises, material needs, and health services were the ones they described as the most important for them. They clarified their preferences in detail: training in vegetable cultivation, animal husbandry, marketing, and sewing; access to resources such as water supplies; better credit facilities; and improved health services. However, the women's stated needs and desires were practically ignored by all parties involved in the gender activities project, including officials from the World Bank, the Nepali government, the local irrigation project administration, and Tahal's representatives, Leon, Tovi Fenster, and myself. Thus, literacy studies, which were, in fact, the core of the women's project, had very little to do with what the women explicitly stated they wanted.

A similar situation, involving an imposed bargain on female peasants in rural El Salvador, is described by Julia Betts (2004). In her study of the relationships between "dominant constructions of the 'illiterate' female peasant" and "actual gender constructions and processes within rural communities" (ibid.: 68), Betts asserts that the figure "who stands 'out there' in the land, waiting to be classified and 'made literate' in the name of the greater good … exists only as a phenomenon created through discourse" (ibid.: 81). It seems that the women in both contexts—Nepal and El Salvador—were aware in some way of the fact that "literacy skills do not represent a direct means to social status or a channel to dominant codes of communication," and that "these routes lie elsewhere … in experience, history, relationships and local constructions of social power" (ibid.: 82).

I do not mean to suggest that the women did not want literacy classes, although more than a few objected to it, but rather that literacy was not presented as a salient need by the women. Moreover, as literacy classes were the only thing offered, it follows that the women were made to think that the classes were the best they could hope for. This was explicitly voiced by an older, energetic woman in one of the villages we visited, who said: "We are not interested only in literacy, but in more practical things". It seems that the women assumed that once they became involved in the women's project, the other more attractive benefits might follow. In fact, as I suggested earlier, in our talks we made it quite clear that when the literacy classes ended the women's desires would be addressed. Furthermore, even when women did respond positively to the offer of literacy classes, they often stipulated certain conditions, the most common of which had to do with the place where the classes would take place. Demands for refreshments, and for a local, experienced, and respectful teacher, were additional preconditions brought up by the women.

Sales of handicrafts were another example of imposing an idea, though one that was clearly rejected by the women. Certain that marketing handicrafts would be relatively easy and profitable for the women, Anita and I repeatedly suggested the idea to the groups we met, despite the women's explicit rejection of this and their insistence that their handicrafts were not intended for commercial but rather for social and traditional purposes.

Our conversation with the women of Pakadihawa offers a further example of our belief that we knew better than the women themselves what was good for them. When we arrived at the village we saw a woman knitting a small decorative table cloth with one needle. My instant reaction was to find out whether this kind of object was commonly produced in the village. It did not take long for the woman's little daughter to bring us a few more samples of her mother's handiwork. Anita commented that she has seen similar examples at the regional market. I asked if the village women knew about the market. A local woman who followed our conversation replied that similar handcrafts were sold at a nearby market, but that the women were not interested in selling their works. She explained that this was due to practical reasons, and not just because of cultural norms, namely the high price of the raw materials. Producing one article would cost around 400 rupees (about $6.9).

Moreover, the women not only knew what they wanted and needed, and well informed about marketing options, they were also capable of empowering themselves through initiating independent entrepreneurial ventures. Given the necessary capital, the women were resourceful and capable—as the examples of the tea house and taxi business in Sikatahan demonstrate. The cooperative fund, which the women in Bhawarabari founded, also serves to show how resourceful women could be when they gain access to credit, and then using it for different ventures. Some of the women in the villages volunteered in women's organizations and were involved in helping other women. This feature of the village women's way of life was evident in both the first and the second rounds of visits. The women had been organized for mutual help and other social activities before the women project's representatives (the WGOs in particular) started to work in the villages, and even before the government's agricultural training projects were introduced into the villages.

I contend that the women's enterprises, whether economic or social, had nothing to do with the irrigation project. These were self-organized, economically focused initiatives that had emerged regardless of Tahal's irrigation project and the introduction of the gender-oriented rhetoric and projects of the mid 1990s. Tahal's groundwater project, the BLGWP, which was inaugurated in 1978, did not contribute much to the village women's economic opportunities nor to their advancement. A few women entered the agricultural training programs provided by the irrigation project after 1986. According to Fenster's report, only 19 per cent of the 1135 farmers who participated in the training program that took place from January to June 1996 were women (Fenster 1996: 14). Moreover, the agricultural division of the project, which was in charge of training the farmers, only employed male technicians. Furthermore, at the tube-well meetings, women comprised only 2.2 per cent of the participants (12 out of 540), because most of the water-user groups, where decisions concerning water use were made, did not include women.

The kind of gender system detailed here—both with regard to villagers' everyday lives, and the perceptions and biases of developers—is not unique to the rural Nepali context. David Mosse's analysis of Bhil society in rural India describes a similar gendered economic reality. He reveals that "the structure of gender responsibilites produces an unequal distribution of tasks and workloads" (Mosse 2005: 63) and, moreover, "despite the fact that women share agricultural tasks, exert decisive influence over farm management based on distinct interests, deploy specialist knowledge, expertise and skill in key areas … their roles are socially constructed as unskilled, manual, ancillary and low status, as menial 'housework' which does not imply technical skill" (ibid.: 64). Furthermore, the men are the "holders of knowledge, decision makers as farmers or herdsmen," and they "dominate interactions with the market, moneylender, input supplier, cooperative, bank…" (ibid: 64). However, the reason for this extremely inequality and these discriminating practices is perceived by Mosse to emerge from "cultural ascriptions of women as dependent labour" (ibid: 64). Yet, in a note Mosse hints at an alternative explanation: "Officially promoted 'farmers' groups are typically understood as male groups, while the activities of women's groups do not emphasise their roles as farmers" (ibid.: 258 n.45). Mosse contends further that women's roles "are socially constructed (by themselves as well as by men)" (ibid.: 64). Thus, the construction of gender inequality has its roots in the society itself. Bracketing out those who engender gender inequality lends vagueness to the process. Thus, it seems that Mosse neutralizes the role of development and other bureaucratic agencies, such as the Indian government and the development project who employed him. A final point in this regard relates to Mosse's argument that, "The gender division of labour is an ideological structure that naturalises gender-based inequality rather than a functional allocation of tasks" (ibid.: 64). However, he does not disclose whose ideology is being pursued in this context.

A similar picture emerges from Dorothy Hodgson's study of the cultural politics of development among the Maasai (Hodgson 2001), although she offers a different explanation from Mosse's. Hodgson reveals the role of development, as well as commoditization, in empowering Maasai men and displacing Maasai women "from their former rights and roles," and by producing "separate male-dominated domains of the 'economic' and 'political', as opposed to the female domain of 'the domestic'" (ibid.: 271).[9]

My own study suggests that gender inequality and discriminating practices in development contexts are closely connected to the organizational policies of development programs. The irrigation project ignored women's significant role in agriculture, and thus succeeded in "naturalis[ing] gender-based inequality" (Mosse 2005: 64), partly by denying women access to resources, which were provided solely or mainly for men. As a result, women's position and participation in decision-making processes and their access to available resources diminished.

Foreign Agencies and the Takeover of State Responsibilities

My impressions from the second round of visits reinforce another conclusion, namely that state agencies were not only capable of carrying out agricultural training, in fact that they were doing it quite efficiently, although unequally, whenever and wherever they were involved in providing basic services to the population.

This observation is backed-up by studies such as that of Hoftun, Raeper, and Whelpton (1999). They point to the large-scale educational reforms which were carried out by the governments of the 1950s and by the National Education System Plan (NESP) from 1971. The reforms "brought schools under government control and the use of Nepali as the medium of instruction was made compulsory ... [A] standard national curriculum was introduced, including subjects relating to national culture and history. The aim of this was to further integration between Nepalese belonging to different communities and different social classes" (ibid.: 221). Although Hoftun, Raeper, and

Whelpton consider the NESP's implementation a failure, they admit, however, that it ensured "an explosion in the numbers of children receiving a primary education" (ibid.: 222). In 1942, Hoftun, Raeper, and Whelpton report, the literacy rate in Nepal was only 0.7 per cent; by the end of late 1980s it had risen to nearly 40 per cent (ibid.: 220).

It appears that the problem of social (gendered included) stratification lies mainly in an unequal distribution of resources, in particular with regard to rural regions, as compared to the urban parts of Nepal. Thus, for instance, both Deepak Thapa and Bandita Sijapati (2004) and John Whelpton (2005) point to the economic dualism of Nepal. They suggest that economic development has benefited local elites and deepened poverty and the exploitation of the poor (Whelpton 2005: 128). Furthermore, Thapa and Sijapati claim that economic policies work in favor of the rich and the urban sector, and that,

> even if the government verbally commits itself at every opportunity to the progress of society as a whole, most of the organized activities and modern facilities are concentrated in the urban areas ... poor people in rural areas are asked to match government investment in irrigation, electricity distribution, and other types of infrastructure while these facilities are installed in urban areas without any direct costs for urban dwellers. (Thapa and Sijapati 2004: 60)

A similar picture of Nepal's economic dualism emerges from my ehtnography. In one of my converations with Leon's friend Sam, an American consultant living in Bhairahawa, he compared Tahal's irrigation project with another agricultural project for which he was working. He claimed that Tahal's project could have been considered a good one had it been labeled "a project for constructing roads and electricity." However, he added,

> as an irrigation project it is not efficient. It would have been better to dig more wells which are smaller in size and closer to each other, for the benefit of the smaller farmers, whereas the main concern of the project planners and practitioners is directed toward the bigger farms. The 'small' farmers cannot organize in groups and also cannot pay for the electricity, and therefore the usage of the water is limited.[10]

Nevertheless, I argue that the assistance of international and local NGOs was not really needed to provide large-scale services for the rural population, women included. Providing basic services for nationwide populations, urban and rural alike, obviously necessitates large scale policies and practices, as well as massive budgets.

I conclude again, therefore, that the Nepali government did not need to import professional expertise, clearly not for literacy training, nor for vocational training such as sewing. Employing foreign consultants is an important part of development projects and it absorbs a substantial portion of a project's funds. Thus, the Nepali government's desire for financial resources, in the form of overseas aid, carried with it a price tag in terms of economic dependence and vulnerability. This dependency was embedded in wider neocolonial processes. Thus, Mark Smith, for instance, argues that, "Given the scale of indebtedness and the lack of internal funds for education and social programmes, Southern countries have become particularly dependent on assessments and perspectives made by key international and national agencies in the North" (Smith 1998/2001).[11]

I suggest that development projects aimed at social change entail long-term involvement, probably longer than projects that introduce technological changes and infrastructure, which are subject to a relatively strict and formal schedule. Projects such as literacy programs are "easier to advocate than other solutions" (Horsman 1990: 65), and can be conveniently presented to donors in appealing terms to describe the aims and methods that are involved in their implementation. This means that organizations and agencies involved in projects which aim to effect social change can present their aims in somewhat vague and manipulative terms, "mobilizing metaphors ('participation', 'partnership', 'governance') whose vagueness, ambiguity and lack of conceptual precision is required to conceal ideological differences so as to allow compromise and the enrolment of different interests" (Mosse 2005: 23).[12] The instrumental component of social programs, literacy programs in particular, is exposed in the extensive use of the ideological terminology of "development vocabularies" (Chatty and Rabo 1997: 10), which include numerous buzz words, like people's participation, structural adjustment, and community involvement (Chatty and Rabo 1997; Pfaff-Czarnecka 2004). Chatty and Rabo argue that concepts like "growth, social development ... and sustainable development have riddled development debate. Concepts such as production, basic needs, people's participation, and structural adjustment, have been used as both catch-words and solutions for all major Third World difficulties" (Chatty and Rabo 1997: 10). The manipulative terminology clearly "bears a high legitimating potential for those who claim that they are facilitating the process" of negating "physical distances and power differentials" (Pfaff-Czarnecka 2004: 186). Once in the field, development agencies can claim that additional, more advanced programs are required (Hertzog 1999).[13] They can also easily claim the need for extending the implementation phase.

Introducing overseas expertise in the field of social issues into local social services accentuates the colonial tendencies of development agencies. Reflecting critically on the meaning of foreign expertise in social matters makes one wonder what kind of advantage these experts can offer in terms of socio-cultural structures, relations, habits, norms, and so forth. They seldom know the language; most of them are hardly familiar with the local social, economic, political, and cultural contexts; and they are usually "passers-by," short-term visitors, and always "foreigners" (Chambers 1983: 10–12). Discussing the implications of foreign consultants' role and conduct in the context of a development project in western India, Mosse points to the "fragmented experience" consultants had of their project, being "disengaged from the day-to-day routines and the pressing demands of relationship building. Their knowledge of the project derived from short visits ... within busy itineraries that connected thinking about the project to other intellectual endeavors ... for other clients" (Mosse 2005: 133). Mosse also highlights the instrumentally constructed distance between foreign experts and local people, the short visits of the former mediated by project staff.

In my case, the role of expatriate consultant that I assumed emphasized the fact that I could offer no real expertise whatsoever, nor could I contribute to any social change. My background as a feminist activist in Israel was clearly not relevant to the Nepali context, and in any case there were numerous local feminist activists much better equipped and suitable for dispensing advice in the context than I was. It should also be noted that I was never asked by Tahal about my knowledge concerning Nepali society, history, and so forth. Nor was I advised to prepare myself on the subject.

Incorporating agricultural training for women, aimed at socioeconomic change, but not directly connected with irrigation, into the irrigation project suggests that this extended sub-project of the gender activities project enabled Tahal to prolong its stay in Nepal. Moreover, agricultural expertise, as suggested earlier, was effectively provided by the Nepali authorities, thus proving that Tahal's involvement was essentially unnecessary.

The fact that numerous women's NGOs were extensively engaged in such enterprises all over the country, including the rural regions, underscores the needlessness of overseas expertise in gender matters and in projects aimed at changing gendered power relations. The extensive presence of women's and other NGOs in the irrigation project area became clear during a visit by Anita, the WGOs, and myself to the local office of the regional development ministry to obtain a list of active women's organizations in the region. We received a list of some 200 NGOs, 100 of which were women's NGOs. I suggest that the intervention of outside agencies in the subtle, complex social webs of Nepal, as well as in other countries, entails inevitable neocolonial connotations, and is doomed to be resisted.

Assuming that the Nepali government and its officials were well aware of these entailments, the question arises of why they continued to accept this kind of foreign intervention, which could only be superfluous and detrimental? I suggest that the Nepalese authorities were trapped in the aid and development web, which necessitated compliance with excessive overseas demands. The heavy dependency of the Nepalese government on international aid, which started as early as 1952 (Whelpton 2005), is described by Hoftun, Raeper, and Whelpton as follows: "it is the developed countries which provide most of the foreign aid and loans on which the Nepalese government is heavily dependent. Assistance is generally provided either directly from government to government, or, more importantly in recent years, through international agencies such as the UNDP or World Bank" (Hoftun, Raeper, and Whelpton 1999: 280). Whelpton further suggests that by 1987 aid programs in Nepal were provided by "sixteen individual countries and six international organizations" (Whelpton 2005: 135).

Craving international financial help forced Nepali governments to allow the massive entrance of foreign actors into spheres of state responsibility, over which the latter often took control. The World Bank's loans to Nepalese governments, including the loan for the irrigation project in the early 1980s, became fiscally important in the early 1970s (ibid.: 128).

It is possible that the low visibility and non-threatening nature of interventions in social matters that development projects entail made it easier to accept them. Moreover, as these socioeconomic projects focused on the poor, and probably politically weak populations, governments could easily ignore the infiltration of outsiders into national territory. In other words, weak populations are relatively easier to submit to foreign influence because they are not considered to be an essential asset or as possessing significant political power that should be taken into account by politicians in power. Indeed, this conclusion applies in particular to social categories such as women and children, rural women and children even more so. Another relevant perspective in this sociopolitical game, within the context of literacy and other programs for women, is the fact that although there were numerous women's NGOs in the field, they appeared to have no substantial political power. Thus, the government could ignore their contributions in the spheres in which foreign NGOs and other agencies stepped in and took over parts of their ongoing activity.

By 1997, Whelpton estimates that the number of Nepali NGOs was between 20,000 and 30,000 (ibid.: 228). The substantial increase in the number of Nepali NGOs involved in aid programs is attributed by Whelpton to foreign donors' preference for cooperating "with Nepalese non-governmental organizations rather than with government departments" (ibid.: 135). The channeling of funds from a foreign governmental or non-governmental organization to a Nepali NGO has grown significantly since 1980. Whelpton suggests that local NGOs "were registered and regulated by the Government's National Social Services Co-ordination Council ... but generally operated more flexibly than the civil service" (Whelpton 2005: 135). Hence, I suggest that the preference of foreign donors for cooperating with local NGOs could be attributed to their weakness as compared with the governmental establishment. Thus, foreign NGOs were less controlled and had greater freedom to operate from a more powerful position in the field.

This weakness of local NGOs was no less relevant to local women's NGOs, as became apparent in the context of the women's program. Thus, local and national women's NGOs were dependent on our willingness to turn to them, and there was no doubt as to who occupied the leading role in the field. Literacy classes and sewing training were provided for women villagers by both governmental agencies (such as the Women's Training Center, the Women's Development Division, and the Rural Development Department) and Nepali women's NGO's (such as Mothers' Club and Didi Bahini). From what Anita told me, based on the experience of her previous work place, development projects initiated by the government (the Ministry of Agriculture, in this case) could benefit village women in terms of literacy, agricultural training, and access to credit. It follows that governmental organizations are potentially more capable and more committed to providing necessary services to their citizens, since they are not geared to the profit motive. While banks are interested in making money, and most NGOs are interested, in practice, in generating paid jobs, the government is more oriented toward providing services for the population. The fact that governments are extensively exposed to internal and external criticism is another reason why the state fosters a deeper responsibility for providing basic services to its citizens. The state must be publicly accountable for their performance, to a much greater extent than private enterprises such as banks or NGOs. It emerges, then, that projects aimed at women's advancement could be organized by national, regional, and local Nepali agencies with no need for outside intervention.

I suggest that because the Nepali government was eager to obtain international investment it used women as a social resource for bargaining over financial aid. Thus, by virtue of being a socially and politically weaker group, women were gradually left out of national projects and vocational training practices while becoming more accessible to non-governmental agencies, whether Nepalese or foreign. The fact that children in the villages were also part of these non-governmental, foreign initiatives (Unicef's in Ekala, for instance), provides further evidence for the argument that the weakest groups in society, like women and children, were used as a bargaining chip in negotiations over financial aid with powerful and rich international organizations.

The practically invisible character of overseas involvement in social-change programs can be illustrated by Tahal's case. No governmental agency connected to education, either national or local, was aware of and certainly not involved in Tahal's Women's Development Program. This was made clear in all our interactions with local and national representatives of the Ministry of Education, whether in relation to supplies for the literacy classes and teachers' seminar or to the employment of village teachers. When we met with local officials of the ministry, the director and his assistants said they were pleased to become involved in "our" project and to offer us any assistance they could. This attitude was revealed repeatedly and in various ways. It seemed that they were pleased that we had approached them and appeared to have no qualms whatsoever regarding the fact that we were doing "their" work, and breaking into their field of expertise. They did not even seem to think that we should have considered them as the responsible party in education projects. Indeed, we were involved in informal education and their main responsibility was for formal education. This once again illustrates the fact that relatively socially and politically weak groups (such as "the illiterate") are easier to ignore and to marginalize.

Moreover, this lack of awareness of foreign initiatives taking place in the field of education was also revealed by heads of the Ministry of Adult Education. When I phoned the national supervisor of the ministry and asked to meet with him in Kathmandu to talk about several issues concerning the literacy program, he said he was very willing to meet me, yet his reaction clearly indicated that he was surprised to hear about our project. It also transpired that the ministry was running a literacy project in the same region. He argued, therefore, that we should coordinate our involvement in the villages in parallel with the ministry's own efforts. Thus, the government officials in charge of adult literacy appeared to be the last ones to hear about our project. This state of affairs suggests that government agencies have to compete with outside organizations, consultants, and local NGOs over control in a field that is clearly under their jurisdiction. It is reasonable to assume that as the government lacked the required budgets to provide adult literacy studies for all parts of Nepal it welcomed any additional resources and the sharing of responsibility.

On this background, of growing governmental dependency on outside financial resources, "neocolonialism within educational contexts" (Wickens and Sandlin 2007: 278) emerged, and, moreover, education operated as a form of neocolonialism (Milligan 2004). Murray Thomas (1993) and Murray Thomas and Neville Postlethwaite (1984) suggest that schooling within any country be assessed by considering it in relation to "a continuum where complete control by foreign powers is at one end of the continuum and complete control by independent nations is on the other" (as phrased by Wickens and Sandlin 2007: 279). Assessing the Nepalese adult education system according to Thomas's continuum, it seems that it has not moved toward "political, economic, and cultural independence," and cannot be described as having "self-determination [regarding] the purpose or role of education, curriculum and instructional methodology, and the financing of the education system" (Wickens and Sandlin 2007: 286).

The absence of cooperation between foreign agencies and state authorities, and the absence of state monitoring of enterprises that take place inside Nepal and which involve its citizens, convey an impression of political chaos (Hoftun, Raeper, and Whelpton 1999: 228).[14] This implies a situation in which the country has rendered itself vulnerable to unwanted consequences by failing, on the one hand, to adopt a coherent social policy, while, on the other, encouraging individuals and organizations to promote their own interests at the expense of the larger Nepali society.

The Appeal of Village Women's Groups to Financial Agencies

Another issue that emerges from the description of the second round of visits to the villages relates to the field bank. Well-organized women's groups seemed to appeal to field banks and other financial institutions as a captive market. Though these were clearly money-making organizations, they did provide women with access to credit, effectively giving them the economic opportunity to improve their own and their families' socioeconomic conditions. In a way, the women villagers became an asset for many organizations, banks as well as NGOs, who behaved like "private consultancies rather than advocacy organizations" (Hoftun, Raeper, and Whelpton 1999: 135). These organizations discovered that women were good clients, and could be relied on to pay back their loans, even though the rate of interest charged was high.[15]

Women's NGOs were also involved in these financial ventures. For example, the Women's Development Organization used to offer the women in the villages sewing and agricultural courses. Eventually it ceased this activity, because, as one of its heads said, "We found [the courses] ineffective for the purpose of increasing family income." Consequently, the organization began to offer credit to the women, acting as a mediator between banks and the women themselves. Although the organization still provided some instruction in health care and family planning, that sort of activity had become marginal, and the organization's primary focus was on organizing women's groups for the purpose of obtaining cheaper rates of interest from the banks.

As Anita and I were planning to create a credit fund as part of our women's program, we approached the head of the Women's Development Organization for information about credit procedures. In response she explained: "first, you have to organize the group and see what they want to do with the money. Then the group comes into the organization's office and the women are asked to express their commitment to pay the money back, by signing a document." After the members sign the commitment form, the organization files a request to the bank on the group's behalf, and adds its own recommendation. If things run smoothly, seven days later the loan should be available for the women's use. Our informant added that the rate of interest for these loans was 12 per cent, and "this is cheaper than the usual 18 per cent rate of interest. In this way the women can start to earn some money, from raising livestock, for instance."

The extent to which women appeal to banks and mediating organizations as consumers of loans was also made clear during a meeting with the manager of the Grameen Bikas Bank in Pokara.[16] When Shova (a WGO), Anita and I met with the manager he was most welcoming. The meeting was arranged through Shova's relative, who worked for Grameen Bikas. The manager met us without delay, offered us coffee, and joined us. We chatted with him for over an hour and a half, during which time he showed genuine attentiveness. He made it clear that the bank would be very interested in taking part in the women project's economic enterprises, that is to say, in offering loans to groups of women in the villages. From the bank's point, five women could comprise a group. The manager clearly set out the terms for loans: in the first year every woman could have 5,000 rupees, increasing to 10,000 rupees (about $172) in the second year, and 20,000 rupees in the third. For the third loan, the woman would also needed her husband's signature. Repayments commenced in the first week, and the weekly payment (of the big size loan) would be 510 rupees (about $8.8), which equals an annual interest rate of 19.5 per cent. At a later stage the interest rate would drop to 10 per cent.

In response to my question concerning the method of repayment, the manager explained that the best arrangement for repaying a loan was to do it on a local basis, by sending Grameen's people to meet the women in the villages. I wondered why the coordinator, appointed by the group of women to represent them, could not be responsible for the repayments. The manager explained that the coordinator might not always want or be able to come to town to take care of the other women's payments, and subsequently the debts might pile up, resulting in the women getting behind in their repayments to such an extent that it would be impossible to overcome this. His eager interest in gaining access to "our" village women became obvious when he stated that the Grameen Bikas Bank would be very willing to incorporate the villages included in the project's region within the branch's reach, although the Lumbini region was not part of its territory. The manager addressed Anita primarily, speaking Nepali, which made me feel that he assumed, correctly, that Anita was the woman to be won over as she was the person who would be responsible for contacts with the village women in the future.

As the three of us were leaving the bank, Anita commented that the lending conditions sounded horrific and that the demand that repayments begin within a week of receiving the money was unfair. Then she told me that governmental officials who worked for the agricultural development department, with whom she had worked before, used to encourage women to establish independent credit groups. The department offered loans for a reasonable rate of interest, she said. Anita explained that the villagers in the region where she had worked were very successful tea farmers, and she added that women had comprised at least half of those benefiting from the department's loans. That night I told Leon about our meeting in the bank. He calculated the annual rate of interest that they charged, and claimed that it was about 40 per cent per annum, which he called a "murderous" rate. The village women were well aware of the profits generated by banks from their loans, and one woman said: "a lot of NGOs [who mediate between women and the Grameen Bikas Bank] come here. They give us small amounts of money but make a good profit for themselves."

The practice and implications of exploiting people's poverty for making easy profits are documented by Yunus (1998), and in fact they motivated his initiative in founding the Grameen Bank. Thus, he quotes one of his interviewees in a "street-survey" carried out in Jobra (Bangladesh): "... the money-lender would demand a lot. And people who start with them only get poorer... Sometimes they charge 10 per cent per week. I even have a neighbour who is paying 10 per cent per day!" Yunus' conclusion is: "Usurious rates have become so standardized and socially acceptable in all third world countries that not even the borrower notices how oppressive the contract is." (ibid.: 6). Trying to understand the quoted rates (in the context described above as well as in others) I realized how hard it is. It turned out that they were confusing and perhaps misleading.

The social framework of a village, in which people are embedded in extensive social webs and dependencies, offers attractive opportunities for shrewd operators, who can take advantage of cooperative groups set up by social activists, community workers, and various organizations. Women in the villages partook in a variety of daily interactions, while working in the fields, in their social engagements and in child-care activities, as, for example, the gathering of many women in Ekala for the polio vaccination in Ekala, described above. In many villages, women's organizations and other NGOs were a visible presence, forming groups for the purpose of providing women with services, training, and so on. The literacy programs were a conspicuous example of initiatives offered to groups of women (and men) villagers by outside organizations. The gatherings of women provided a convenient access to organized groups of women for organizations and individual entrepreneurs who were interested in pursuing both, social and economic goals. Rather than dealing with individuals they could negotiate with groups' representatives who organzied the women for them and mediated between the organization and the other women.

When the project people arrived in the villages of the Lumbini region, women's self-organized groups were well rooted in most of them. Thus, the women could be easily organized into functioning groups, facilitating the provision of various services and programs, such as the literacy program, to large populations. The women could also be conveniently accessed and targeted for extracting financial profits. Women's groups were evidently observed and exploited by banks and mediating NGOs (Hachhethu 2004).[17] It appears that women in the villages were easy to access, easy to persuade, easy to manage and, therefore, an easy source of profit. A term I used in my fieldnotes discloses this aspect of the women groups' attractiveness from the perspective of organizational interests. Following one of our visits to the villages I wrote in my notes that when we arrived at the meeting place in the village, and the village women were not present, "the WGOs went out to search for 'prey'." This term cast us as hunters on the trail looking for suitable objects to serve our needs. We needed the women's groups to establish our project's value and relevance, while the banks and NGOs needed them for their interests, whether for the sake of money-making or for various organizational purposes.

In the case of the field bank, the exploitative undertones of the encounter involved a gender perspective as well. The encounter between the bank's men and the village women underscores the gendered power differential between these two parties. The encounter suggests that the village women were vulnerable and naive in their relations with the men, and the men in turn were out to exploit the women and make easy profits from them. This representation of the relationship is echoed by the ritual that took place when the transactions were over. Thus, the men were portrayed as cynically manipulating the women's religious beliefs by sanctifying their commitment to repay the money, in order to benefit the bank and themselves. Moreover, the women were not perceived and treated as adults when it came to financial procedures. They were not obliged to repay the loan by signing the relevant forms, as men would have been required to. Rather, the women were treated like intimidated children, instilled with the fear of a sacred power.

The Appeal of Village Women's Groups to NGOs

As soon as it became known that our project planned to spend a considerable amount of money on literacy studies, the project area became a popular destination for representatives of different NGOs, including literacy and health training organizations. One such NGO was involved in health training. Some ten days after my arrival at Bhairahawa, one of this organization's representatives showed up at the irrigation project office and offered to assist Anita and myself in planning and implementing the women's project. They were interested in particular in carrying out health training for the women in "our" villages. A few days later, two people from another local health-training NGO appeared in Thapa's office (while Anita and I were present) offering their services to the women's project. The men stated that they were interested in taking charge of implementing the entire project, as they had the volunteers and the expertise to do it best. Anita and I had previously approached the head of this NGO, a medical doctor, and proposed that he give some lectures on health care to the village women, to be done in conjunction with their literacy studies. Approaching Thapa directly meant that the men were very interested in getting involved in the women's project and they showed up to apply pressure and try to ensure that this would happen.

After the meeting in Thapa's office, Anita and I asked the two men to produce a cost estimate for a program to train the WGOs as health-care instructors. In response, they asked if we could tell them our budget ceiling before submitting a proposal. The negotiations with that organization's representatives dragged on for weeks. In fact, they went on almost until I left Nepal. The doctor and his colleagues came to the irrigation project offices every few days; sometimes, they arrived unannounced and found that we were not there. They seemed interested as long as they thought that they could get a slice of the women project's budget for their organization. Complying with our changing financial and professional demands, the NGO was ready to accept a substantially reduced role in the project, and with it a much lower payment than they had originally asked for. Because Anita and I had to comply with Thapa's instruction to reduce the budget significantly, we offered the health NGO the task of training the WGOs as health-care instructors. The NGO accepted this reduced remit, probably because they hoped that, because of the women project's scale, if their organization were to become involved in it, the project would provide their employees with some extra income.

A representative of another NGO, who approached us in an attempt to gain entry to the women's project, offered to train village women in sewing and literacy. One day we found a short, thin woman waiting for us in Pandit's room. She had not made an appointment, and Anita and I had just returned from a meeting with the local head of the Ministry of Education. The woman told us that her organization owned four sewing machines, and that they trained groups of about twenty women for some six months each. In the past she had taught literacy to some 300 groups. We asked her to send in a proposal, which arrived a few days later, but we never invited her to another meeting.

A head of a regional women's organization, involved in literacy training and charity work for women, also tried to gain access to the women project's funds. Anita and I met the woman in a village bazaar that had been set up by her organization. It took place in a two-story, poor-looking building. Women's dresses and colorful nylon fabrics, as well as cheap ornaments and decorative items, were offered at low prices. The woman came up to Anita and me and told us enthusiastically and in great detail about her organization's voluntary activities in helping poor women. Before we left she pulled Anita aside and spoke with her for some time. Later on, Anita told me that the woman asked her why we (the women's project people) had not let her organization run the literacy classes. Anita replied that the classes had not yet started, and that if we found out that we could not manage the literacy program by ourselves we would let her organization organize some of the classes. Anita smiled mischievously and added: "They want too much money. Thapa is right in claiming that these organizations want a lot of money."

Anita and I were clearly perceived as being in control of a large-scale project with a substantial budget, though this was far from being the case. Anita's comment regarding Thapa's reservations about women's NGOs makes clear his underestimation of the work of these organizations and our willingness to represent the deceitful practices of the irrigation project's heads.

Anita and I seemed to enjoy our advantageous position. We acted as if we were in control of things and clearly enjoyed the fact that we were sought out by various organizations who looked up to us, eagerly asking to cooperate with us. However, this pretentious game was soon over. Even before I left Nepal it was already quite evident that if anything came of the women's project it would only be a very limited version of it. Meanwhile, the local NGOs were there to stay and continue their work, for better or worse.

Considering the vast number of active NGOs in the region (and beyond it) that work in the fields of literacy, health, and vocational training, the question arises: What is their actual contribution to improving social services, social mobility, economic opportunities, and so forth? The evidence concerning the effectiveness of literacy programs in Nepal is rather dubious. Whelpton suggests that "at least some of the NGOs have been making valuable contributions" in raising literacy levels in Nepal, and "at village level they are providing opportunities to local people for upward social mobility" (Whelpton 1999: 228). However, this assessment seems overly positive when one considers the significant gap in literacy rates between rural and urban areas (Hoftun, Raeper, and Whelpton 1999: 222), and indeed between males and females—in 1991, the literacy rates for men and women were respectivley 56.2 per cent and 23.5 per cent (ibid.: 96). It therefore follows that literacy was restricted until at least the early 1990s to "a small elite" (ibid.: 222).

My data suggests that literacy studies were offered repeatedly by both NGOs and government organizations in the same villages. As information on the extent, content, and value of earlier courses is unavailable, their contribution to changes in literacy in the villages remains obscure. Moreover, as Whelpton (1999) claims and my ethnography suggests, literacy initiatives carried out by NGOs were hardly monitored. Furthermore, reliable information concerning the proportional contribution of governmental and non-governmental agencies to increasing literacy rates in the villages is unavailable. Also, since "the impact of education on adult women, as compared to schooling, has not been disaggregated" (Robinson-Pant 2005: 3), and "the links between literacy and development have not disaggregated youth from adult literacy" (ibid.: 1), the connection between literacy and social benefits is difficult to substantiate.

Based on an extensive review of the literature on this issue, Robinson-Pant concludes: "The social benefits of literacy have been shown to be enhanced when literacy programmes are accompanied by supportive interventions, such as credit facilities, skills training, and in the health context, access to family planning facilities or maternal child health centres" (ibid.: 12). Such integrated, well-budgeted programs, were clearly not provided by the irrigation project. Moreover, even the much-reduced literacy program that remained following the hopeless round of negotiations between the irrigation project heads and myself was not carried out. It remains, therefore, to find out what actually did take place in lieu of the literacy program for women villagers.

The Village Women: Neither Naive nor Passive

Our paternalistic encounters with the women villagers became a game, in which Anita and I played the role of benevolent and professional persons in possession of desired resources. The seemingly powerful position that we pretended to have was a short-term affair. Moreover, the encounters with the women villagers were clearly more complex than a picture of one-sided power relations conveys. My notes from the second round of visits to the villages reflect the interplay of all the participants in the meetings and the shifts in power that took place. The women villagers seemed to enjoy interacting with us. In most cases they were clearly willing to cooperate, and sometimes, when they became aware of our eagerness to obtain their cooperation, they were openly enthusiastic and would take control of the situation.

From the village women's perspective, the encounters often seemed like a social gathering in which they had the opportunity to meet unfamiliar faces. This possibly made these events more exciting and diverting than the habitual round of social activities and gatherings. The idea that this kind of meeting was an opportunity for socializing, networking, and enjoyment is echoed in other studies of literacy classes. Juliet Millican, for example, speaks of classes that were designed to promote functional literacy but which turned into opportunities for "social and personal contacts" (Millican 2004: 204), and Sujata Khandekar sepaks of a similar context as a "mental and social space and a platform for the sharing and ventilation of grievances" (Khandekar 2004: 217; cf. Dighe 1995; Patel and Dighe 2003)[18]

The recreational aspect of the village meetings is illustrated, for instance, by the incident in which the old woman used my looks to amuse her friends and draw attention to herself. That is to say, Anita, the WGOs, and, particularly, myself (because I could not understand Nepali), were also treated as objects in a cultural performance. Thus, while we perceived the village women as potential (needy) clients, the women themselves probably perceived us, aside from representing the authorities and carrying potential benefits, as a sort of social distraction from their quotidian routines. The fact that the meetings in the villages were pleasant social events for all—the village women as well as the men, children, WGOs, and AOs who joined the visits—was very noticeable and repeatedly described in my fieldnotes. For example, in recounting our meeting with some thirty women in Mazitihwa, I used the words "tranquility" and "peaceful" many times. While watching the ongoing interaction, I wrote:

> The women with a few children at their sides, the WGOs, and the AO who joined us from the tube well (which is close to his little house), and his wife, are in a good mood; they seem very relaxed, as though having fun. A baby was peacefully sleeping on his mother's knees and she gently passes him to her friend's arms when she gets up to sign the lists of women interested in joining the literacy class. All this time a pleasant conversation is taking place among the WGOs, the AO and the women … It seems that all are enjoying themselves and are not keen to end the meeting and leave the place. I am sitting nearby, on the grass, close to a small water pond, writing in my notebook. Opposite me an old man is leaning against a poplar tree, very peacefully, watching the ongoing scene. The tranquility is all-embracing, with the animals, brown and black buffalos, goats and sheep, eating the grass calmly. The women and children are sitting completely relaxed … Some 30 meters away from us near a straw hut a young man is giving a haircut to a boy, sitting in front of the hut under a shadowed bush with yellow blossoms.

The women not only made fun of us and enjoyed the large social gatherings, they were sometimes blatantly critical about our women's project and other similar projects. They were far from being naive. This clearly came out, for instance, when we visited Pakadihawa, where Shiva Maya was the WGO in charge. We found out that the department of agricultural development had formerly organized a literacy class in the village and most of the people there knew how to read and write. A vigorous woman, dressed in a pink blouse and sari, seemed to tease and ridicule us sarcastically. Anita translated her comments, and she explained that the woman and others did not believe us. They had already met projects' people "some fifteen times," asking them about their willingness to participate in literacy and vocational training. And then "nothing happened."

The women in Pakadihawa did not hurry to meet us, and after waiting some thirty minutes for them we sent our driver to get them to come and see us. The woman with the pink sari also told us that the women's literacy class used to take place in the evenings. When at one point the teacher decided to hold the classes in the afternoons, the women stopped coming to the class. She added that some people had come to the village, taken pictures, and then gone away.

The women did not hesitate in voicing their critical views of organizations they had dealt with, and expressed their awareness of the benefits they expected to gain from them. This was also apparent in our visits to East Khungawa and to Madhuwani. Sumitra was the WGO attached to these villages. While chatting with the local women in East Khungawa, one of them complained bitterly about the loans they had been given. She said: "many NGOs are coming here, they give us some money but they themselves make a lot of money." Anita explained that the Grameen Bank could lend them 5,000 rupees (through mediating NGOs), and that they had to repay 110 rupees (about $1.9) a week.

Women in Madhuwani complained that schoolteachers were recruited on the basis of their politics rather than their professional qualifications and performance.[19] The women said that since the teachers lacked basic training and experience they would tell the children to study by themselves. This evaluation of the standard of Nepali schoolteachers is backed up by Whelpton, who writes: "politicization after 1990 has eroded discipline and commitment among the teaching staff … Although there certainly are some dedicated professionals among them, teachers are often appointed because of their political connections and often concerned principally with politics" (Whelpton 2005: 227). However, I would suggest that teachers anywhere are often used as scapegoats to hide the state's educational failures. In other words, blaming teachers for the education system's failure is a manipulative strategy to move attention away from dominant classes' role and the state's responsibility for children's poor educational achievements (Bowles and Gintis 1976, 2001)[20] as a result of restricted school budgets, poor wages for teachers, maintaining over-crowded classes, and so on (Hertzog 2010a). Moreover, governments tend to serve the hegemonic groups in society, which often are not interested in social change

(Carnoy 1974). In any case, whether the women's criticism was justified or not, the important point to make here is that the women clearly responded to public discourse, were interested in public affairs and political debates, and voiced their views.

The women in Madhuwani also commented sarcastically that politicians were like "buffalos," presumably meaning that they were lazy, and exploited others' work. During our visit to Pakadihawa, when one of the women commented ironically that, despite numerous visits by development project staff, "nothing happened," another noted that in the previous year Tovi Fenster had arrived at the village with Elka (Anita's predecessor), and that this time we had showed up instead. Raju, Leon's secretary, who joined us on some of our visits, commented ironically: "Who will come here next year?" Anita replied: "Next year they will throw stones at us and not just show us unpleasant smiles."

It follows, then, that although the women villagers could be easily accessed, because they lived in a relatively confined geographic and social setting, and because they were easily organized as a group, this did not necessarily entail the women's automatic acquiescence. Moreover, the fact that the women were collectively organized must have afforded them some reassurance, as this gave them a support network and an extended source of information. Even their involvement in loan arrangements with the banks (mainly through mediators), which appeared to be exploitative and cynical, cannot be considered as being due to the women's vulnerability. It appears that they were fully aware of the banks' conditions, procedures, and large profits. They had, quite probably, entered these transactions consciously, because these provided them with certain advantages, as limited as they were, that they could not obtain otherwise. The enterprises that were set up by the women serve to reinforce this argument.

In conclusion, the women in the villages were far from being naive or vulnerable. They extracted what they could from meetings with development staff. These events turned the tables on those who represented seemingly established, powerful organizations. From my viewpoint as a participant-observer, the women seemed to me to reverse, albeit momentarily, the picture of powerful officials stood before weak peasants: the former had to leave their strongholds and came out of their way to the villages; there they were hosted by the women, depending on them for their cooperation, and even made themselves susceptible to the women's criticism and mockery.

The women in the villages we visited lacked economic resources, yet our women's project and other similar projects mainly offered them literacy programs that were hardly needed for the demands of their daily lives. Indeed, literacy classes had previously been run in many of the villages we visited. Nevertheless, if the villagers were deemed to need further literacy training, perhaps this meant that literacy was not a basic requisite of people's daily lives, and that despite the fact that they had been given lessons the literacy skills they had already acquired had not been used and had consequently been forgotten.

What we were offering did not seem particularly useful, and the women appeared to use the negotiations over literacy classes as an opportunity to extract other resources from the women's project.

Illiteracy and the Image of Women's Collective Intellectual Failure

The village women's assumed or real illiteracy was an essential component of the development projects that were offered to them. Development organizations and their representatives assumed women's ignorance and backwardness, and this was seen to necessitate their need for professional help. These embedded assumptions in planners' and implementers' perceptions and writings about the women villagers clearly emerges from Fenster's report, as indicated in my analysis (see previous chapter).

The embedded image of the village women's "backwardness" was often revealed in comments by project staff. For instance, on our way to Madhuwani, a male AO who accompanied us commented sarcastically that "in our next village there are twenty-five women with 450 children." Anita added that the village was very backward. It emerged from these remarks and from many others that a village would be considered advanced if there were fewer children per family, if the village women practiced family planning, if the girls attended school, if classrooms were equipped with chairs and desks, and if local enterprises were operating. Sikatahan fit this description: many of the women in the village had gone through sterilization operations, some had installed intrauterine devices, several hundred were on the contraceptive pill, and some received a contraceptive injection every three months. "Advancement" implied, therefore, women's compliance with technological interventions in their bodies, which drastically affected their reproductive potential. Literacy and education were also major indicators of "advancement," as Anita's comment implies: "This is a relatively advanced village, some of the women have had literacy classes."

These indicators of "advancement" entail three things. First, that Western concepts of modernization, including control over reproduction, literacy rates, and compulsory formal education, are embedded in the ideological background of development projects, such as the one described here. Development projects, therefore, differentiate between the developed-literate and the underdeveloped-illiterate, the latter assumed to need the former to instruct them. Second, that gender development projects are aimed at female populations, which implies that women are less educated, less literate, and therefore less advanced, or conversely more backward. Considered collectively illiterate and overly fertile, it was implied that the village women in the Bhairahawa Lumbini Groundwater Project area needed instruction and supervision. Third, focusing on women's "backwardness" distracts attention from governmental agencies' responsibility for and failure in providing basic universal services, such as education and health. This is particularly the case in Nepal (Thapa and Sijapati

2004; Whelpton 2005). Thus, women's collective failure to adapt to the modern way of life is established.

Two anecdotes can serve to highlight, from another perspective, the ethnocentric and stereotyped attitude involved in the encounters I witnessed and took part in with the village women. There was in place among project staff a set of oppositions by which modern, educated, advanced people were opposed to uneducated, backward, traditional villagers, and this was used to distinguish between foreigners and Nepalese, and between the Nepalese themselves. Gupta, the local consultant on farmer participation, joined us on a visit to the villages a few days before I left Nepal. It was a holiday and Gupta had brought along his wife. Raju, Leon's secretary, also joined us that day. As we were discussing the literacy project and its vague implementation plans, Gupta told me proudly that his two daughters, quite contrary to the prevailing norms in rural Nepal, were studying at university: one was doing her Ph.D. in India and the other was studying for a B.A. In their family, he explained, girls were treated similarly to boys with respect to educational opportunities. Gupta clearly viewed himself and his family as "advanced" and as an exception to the general situation in rural Nepal, probably even the whole of Nepal, in terms of women's educational opportunities. Thus, Gupta considered higher education a valued social ideal and a legitimate aspiration for young women.

This view, however, was inconsistent with the way he perceived the women in the villages and their families. According to Gupta, the women did not really share or deserve the same high aspirations and chances. He did not seem to conceive of any connection between his daughters' academic career opportunities and the irrigation project's obligation to contribute to village women's educational and professional opportunities. This is apparent from Gupta's claim that the decision-makers "in high places" were not interested in women's projects, and from his description of the women as easily manipulated by pretending to open up classes ("breaking the ice") instead of fulfilling promises made to them. Promisses to the village women, so it emerges from Gupta's expressions, could be easily ignored. Irrigation, too, from his perspective, had nothing to do with women. It was evidently men's business.

Raju's comments on the same day introduce another dimension into my discussion of representations of the village women. Throughout the visit to the villages, which took place on a holiday, a few days before I left Nepal, Raju was diligently interpreting to me what the women were saying. He told me that they insisted on not telling the WGOs their husbands' names, because doing so might inflict death upon their husbands. He added: "You should write this down in your notebook." Raju probably assumed that I was interested in "exotic" behavior and thinking that demonstrated the women's superstitions and, hence, their ignorance. It follows that Raju considered the women to hold superstitious beliefs—that is, primitive ideas—and thus that they were irrational and quite different from himself and others in his social surroundings. Perceiving me as a Western, educated, rational person, and perhaps taking into account my anthropological background, Raju assumed that I would appreciate the chance to learn about women's traditional, irrational thought. In fact, he was not far from the truth, as a comment I made in my fieldnotes following our visit to Sikatahan reveals: "At long last, after all the countless hardships in the 'advanced' village we returned to the 'big' city of Bhairahawa." My use of inverted commas discloses my ethnocentric views regarding village life, implying that the women of Sikatahan were not really advanced but, rather, were pretending to be so, and that Bhairahawa was not really a big city but was perceived as one by its (uncivilized, unmodern) inhabitants. I suggest that the ethnocentric, dichotomized categories that characterized my own and others' discourse were the outcome of the structured social distance and hierarchy constructed by the project.[21] This constructed power differential, associated with a range of oppositions—such as village/city, rural/urban, illiterate/educated, farmers/professionals, traditional/modern, women/men—facilitated the project heads' denial of their obligations toward the village women.

The foregoing analysis of the village encounters reinforces the conclusion drawn in the previous chapter. That is, the women's project was focused on literacy classes, whereas economic activities, which were clearly preferred by the women, were marginalized, and only ever used to gain the women's trust and cooperation.

In the next chapter I describe the seminar. This, together with Tovi Fenster's workshop, Thapa's privately funded literacy class, and ten other classes, opened after I left Nepal, was among the few negligible concrete outcomes of a project that aimed at providing 300 village women's groups with literacy training.

Notes

1. Similarly, Mosse reports that fieldworkers' accessibility to villagers depended on "benefits they could, or promised to, deliver" (Mosse 2005: 81).
2. Tahal's (1992) socioeconomic Survey differentiates between two categories of villagers' homes in the irrigation project area: "permanent, and semi-permanent," explaining that "(a) Permanent Structure – made of brick/cement or mud with tint/tile roof. (b) Semi-Permanent – made of brick/mud with thatched roof." The survey reports that "all sample households reported having their own houses…" 64% of the farm households "Have semi-permanent type of houses while about 36% of the households have permanent type of houses…" (Tahal 1992: 32).
3. Robinson-Pant suggests that "unlike in neighboring India … most Government letters and reports are still written in Nepali only" (Robinson-Pant 1995: 5).
4. This quotation, from Robinson-Pant 2001, is in the following link (a document titled: 'The Social Benefits of Literacy'): http://portal.unesco.org/education/en/files/43483/11315414221 Robinson_ Pant.doc/Robinson_Pant.doc. (retrieved 30 September 2010).
5. In the introduction to a volume on women, literacy, and development, Anna Robinson-Pant questions "the stereotype of the 'illiterate woman' which has informed most policy on literacy development" (Robinson-Pant 2004a: 2).
6. A reversal of power relations between visitors and locals in the village setting is demonstrated also by Shrestha with regard to relationships between NGOs and International Non-Government Organizations (INGOs). She argues that in the field, "the direction of power

seemed reversed—or at least, more easily reversible—as lack of INGO competence was highlighted" (Shrestha 2004: 12), and concludes that "if donors were generally in a position of power in relation to NGOs, this power was not always and everywhere experienced as irreversible or ineluctable … [T]he view of NGO–donor relationships as 'exchange of deference and compliance for the patron's provision', is inaccurate" (ibid.: 14).

7. This is a common financial system, often referred to in the literature as ROSCA (Rotating Savings and Credit Association). Shirley Ardener's and Sandra Burman's edited volume (1995) on women's ROSCAs, for example, contains a wide range of studies on this topic. Ardener points to "its wide distribution, its variety of forms and functions, and its relative durability in situations both of high financial insecurity and of prospering industriatilzation." The ROSCA can be placed "within a broad set of institutions which provide credit and mutual aid" (Ardener 1995: 1). Ardener (1964) proposes a comprehensive and basic definition for ROSCAs, which may "isolate the common elements: … an association formed upon a core of participants who agree to make regular contributions to a fund which is given in whole or in part to each contributor in rotation" (ibid.: 201).
8. According to its web-site Shtrii Shakti is working "towards women empowerment". Its declared goal is "To find practical and innovative solutions to social problems to contribute effectively to the empowerment of women, men and youth from under-served communities, victimized individuals and so on." Source: http://www.shtriishakti.org/ (retrieved 1 October 2010).
9. Hodgson argues that the impact of development on gender roles and power relations is related to modernist ideologies of individualism, rationality, and progress which have empowered Maasai men "through such categories as taxpayer, head of household, and livestock owner" (Hodgson 2001: 271).
10. This argument finds support in Muhammad Yunus' (1998) critique of irrigation projects (in Bangladesh and beyond it). He writes: "Because of their heavy operating costs, deep tubewells have proved highly inefficient, with corruption and wastage... Accordingly, almost half the deep tubewells sunk at the cost of millions of dollars had fallen out of use. The rusting machinery in abandoned pump houses was a testimony of a technology transfer initiative that was simply not relevant to the farmers. Yet another scandal, another failure of misguided development" (ibid: 48–49).
11. An extended discussion of power–dependence relations between neocolonizers and the colonized is offered in the Introduction.
12. Mosse's analysis of the manipulations of terminology in the development context draws on Li (1999) and Dahl (2001).
13. The vocational training offered to Ethiopian male immigrants in Israel in the early 1980s is one example of this (see Hertzog 1999). Most of the courses provided for the male immigrants involved basic carpentry and car mechanics. They took place in old workshops containing outdated equipment. A decision was soon made to provide the immigrants with an "advanced" course, as the first one was recognized as being insufficient (meaning: a failure). Later on the various additional courses were also declared a failure and another stage was suggested. These courses drew on the vocational training system for unemployed and disabled people, which were already recognized as inefficient and outdated.
14. A similar impression stems from Whelpton's comments regarding flourishing local NGOs. He suggests that "fears are also expressed that the state's capacity to co-ordinate and direct development activities is being undermined" (Hoftun, Raeper, and Whelpton 1999: 228).
15. Muhammad Yunus was well aware of this fact when he established the Grameen Bank (see Yunus 1998).
16. Modelled on the Grameen Bank methodology, the mission of PasGBB (Paschimanchal Grameen Bikas Bank Ltd) is "to generate self-employment through micro-credit to the rural poor at their doorstep to reduce poverty level in the western region of Nepal." The PasGBB "was established as a Regional Rural Development Bank in 1995 through a joint collaboration of the government of Nepal, Nepal Rastra Bank and Commercial Banks." Source: http://www.bwtp.org/arcm/nepal/II_ Organisations/MF_Providers/Paschimanchal_Grameen_Bikas_Bank_Ltd.htm (retrieved 3 October 2010).

17. Thus, it is not surprising that one of the forty demands of the Maoist United Peoples' Front, submitted to the government in February 1996, a few days before they began their armed action (Hachhethu 2004: 58), was that "the invasion of colonial and imperial elements in the name of NGOs and INGOs should be stopped" (quoted in Hutt 2004: 285).
18. Millican (2004) offers a critical analysis of the Muthande Literacy Programme for adult women in Durban, South Africa. Khandekar (2004) examines the collective activism that emerged as a consequence of literacy learning among untouchable (Dalit) women in a slum of Mumbai, India. Dighe's study focuses on the Total Literacy Campaign by the Delhi Saksharata Samiti in Ambedkarnagar, a resettlement colony in south Delhi.
19. A similar criticism of teachers' meager performance is often made in regard to schoolteachers in poor neighborhoods and in state-funded public schools in other countries. Two examples from the Israeli context are relevant here. Elias Mazawi (1995) suggests that the Israeli government is responsible for politicizing Arab schooling, and consequently for the low quality of its teachers. Meanwhile, in his work on the social mechanisms that enabled the preservation of class stratification and hegemonic vested interests in Israel in the 1950s and 1960s, Arnold Lewis (1979) argues that poor children's failure at school was closely related to their teachers' poor performance. Lewis also argues that this was an outcome of the structured marginalization of the school, the town, and its population.
20. Bowles and Gintis (1976, 2001) perceive the role of egalitarian ideology as a "smokescreen", veiling the political construction and preservation of class stratification through schools. Following the Marxist theory they claim that the egalitarian ideology serves to hide the inequality of opportunity which is a central characteristic of the capitalist educational systems. According to them: "... beneath the façade of meritocracy lies the reality of an educational system geared toward the reproduction of economic relations... Dominant classes seeking a stable social order have consistently nurtured and underwritten these ideological facades... (1976: 103).
21. A similar argument is made by Stacey Pigg (1992), who points to the connection between development discourse and the hierarchical structure of Nepali society.

Chapter 5

The Seminar: The Successful Failure of the Women's Empowerment Project

Manufacturing a Fictitious Success: The Seminar and Thapa's Class

The village teachers' training course (hereafter, the seminar) was the main and probably sole achievement of my stay in Nepal. The fact that some ten village women received formal certification from the Ministry of Education to teach other women in their villages, acknowledging their entitlement to carry out literacy training, turned out to be the peak of my activity as the irrigation project's foreign consultant on gender issues. This achievement stands out against the background of the profound and insistent objection to the women's program and the ongoing attempts of the irrigation project's local heads to prevent its implementation. In the present chapter I will demonstrate how this achievement symbolized the failure of my efforts to ensure that the women's program was carried out.

I will also reflect on some further gender perspectives relevant to the convoluted progress of the women program. It will be described how all parties became involved, to varying extents and in various ways, in the seminar, despite their intensifying resistance and efforts to prevent the implementation of the women's project. The daily interventions of high-ranking officials in the seminar could be read as a reflection of their commitment to and interest in the seminar's purpose, content, and outcomes. This surprising engagement of the irrigation project heads—both the locals and Leon—might have indicated that their reluctant attitude towards the seminar and to the whole women's project had changed. I will argue, however, that these interventions did not signify any change in their basic attitudes toward the implementation of the women's project. Rather, it appears that the seminar became, for a certain time, part of the daily machinations of the irrigation project. Thus, people's behavior in relation to the seminar should be understood within the broader social context of the irrigation project. In other words, once the seminar became a reality, the irrigation project staff's attitude toward it stemmed from their ongoing social relationships and from the existing power structure. As the irrigation project was controlled by men and oriented toward men's activities and interests, the seminar's affairs attracted their attention, and the seminar room became a female site which men exploited for the exercise of power.

The "exercise of power," as a discursive outcome of "instrument effects" in the context of development, has already been noted by James Ferguson (1990: 255). He argued that while development projects tend to end up as failures (in terms of their planners' intentions) political effects may be realized almost invisibly alongside this failure. Thus, "any intentional deployment only takes effect through a convoluted route involving unacknowledged structures and unpredictable outcomes" (ibid.: 276). The seminar provides an example of these political successful outcomes in the context of a failing women's development project.

My gender activities report (Hertzog 1997), presented to the local and Israeli heads of the irrigation project, indicates that the seminar was perceived by me as a success. In the report, I wrote:

> A 9-day preparatory seminar ended on 21.9.97. Ten village teachers, each of whom will facilitate literacy in her own village, were authorized by the district Ministry of Education to teach, and were provided with a formal certificate. All ten women were provided with transportation by the irrigation project's vehicles, with daily allowance and refreshments. The seminar was held in the conference hall of the irrigation project's headquarters lasting from 10.00 until 16.30 every day, including Saturday.
>
> The rate of the village teachers' attendance was almost 100%. According to the seminar's trainers, eight of the participants did well, and the other two had considerable difficulties because of language problems. One of these women has overcome great difficulties, including having her baby with her every day, managing to attend all class days and to fulfill all the tasks exercised in class.
>
> Feedback from the seminar participants so far suggests that the small size of the group (only 10 instead of 20–30 women) and having female teachers played an important role in its success. The two female trainers were provided on our request. Following this experience it is recommended to have women trainers in the next seminars too and also in other kinds of training for village women and WGOs, whenever possible. (ibid.: 3)

According to this report, the seminar was a considerable achievement. All the women managed to finish the seminar, attending most of the training days offered, including Saturday. They overcame distance problems (some of them had to travel for about two hours) and fulfilled all the tasks required of them. The seminar teachers reported that most of the village teachers did well. The fact that the Ministry of Education provided the participants with a teaching certificate, signed by the head of the district office, endowed the seminar with a sense of real worth. The participants expressed their satisfaction with the seminar, their teachers, and the venue (the conference hall, a small, relatively pleasant, and comfortable room). The irrigation project provided the participants with transportation, refreshments and allowances. In addition, the seminar offered some valuable constructive lessons in terms of assessment and recommendations for future implementation. One such recommendation was that women instructors were preferable to men instructors, for the purpose of training village teachers as well as for other activities intended for women. Apparently, this had not always been the case, and some groups of women farmers had received training from men. Another recommendation that emerged from the experience of the seminar was that small groups of women (ten per class) were preferable to bigger ones, as this enabled more personalized training.

Nevertheless, despite the seemingly positive outcome of the seminar, and notwithstanding its ambitious aims in terms of women's empowerment,[1] it cannot be regarded as having contributed to reducing village women's marginality or their experience of discrimination. Rather, it implicitly reflected, in Jo Rowlands's phrasing, "realities of power, inequality, and oppression" (Rowlands 1999: 149).

The seminar affair resembled, in many ways, Thapa's literacy class in Ekala. Both episodes served, in practice, as a deceitful means of conveying the impression of the irrigation project heads' sincere commitment to implementing the women's program. The women in the hut in Ekala were used as actors in a play staged to appease the worries of the World Bank about the seriousness of those in charge of implementing the women's project. It turned out to be very effective at proving to the Bank that the Nepali directors were reliable and could be trusted in financing their activities. Leon and the local heads of the irrigation project—Pandit, head of the farmer organization division; Gupta, a local consultant on farmer participation; and Acharya, head of the engineering division—repeatedly mentioned wanting the irrigation project to "look good" in Wolffenson's eyes. The women's project's success provided evidence of their personal achievements.

Analyzing NGO and INGO relationships in Nepal, Celayne Heaton Shrestha similarly demonstrates how a particular project's "'success story' was immediately earmarked as a 'showpiece'" (Shrestha 2004: 2) for a donor team's visit. She describes the local team's efforts to create "a good impression" on donors, including trying to ensure

> that the team had a pleasant visit. There was no sense that trying to portray a realistic field situation was the name of the game … nor was there ever a sense that we were "faking it." It all seemed as though the facts of the project, in spite of the stated visit aims, were not what the visit was about. The concerns on everyone's lips had to do with how best to receive the team and causing them as little hardship as possible … The [focus was on the] status of visitors/evaluators as guests, as persons-to-be-entertained. (ibid.: 12)

The seminar, too, had the appearance of a show. The classroom, the group of village women, the teachers, the opening and closing events, all served to convey the impression that the literacy program was about to take off. The subsequent opening of only ten classes, out of the 300 planned, following the conclusion of the "successful" seminar, exposed the deceitfulness of this show. This became apparent after I left Nepal, just as the Ekala literacy class was exposed as a sham once Wolffenson left Nepal. Nevertheless, in both cases all parties played their part in constructing the image of the forthcoming implementation of the women's program. The World Bank's people could not avoid noticing that the classes in Ekala were a bluff (as I suggested in Chapter 3). And I too must have realized, by the time the seminar started, that the women's program would not be carried out. Yet, I preferred to believe that my intensive efforts were not in vain. Concentrating on opening and running the one seminar enabled me to maintain my self-image of professional integrity and to conclude my visit to Nepal feeling that I had achieved something meaningful, however limited.

Manufacturing the image of a development projects' success is indeed not unique to the project under study. In his study of a farming project in India, David Mosse suggests that "the social production of development success" implies the cooperation of all developing parties in creating the deceitful image of a project's success (Mosse 2005: 157–83).[2] Joanna Pfaff-Czarnecka similarly argues that "many failures are not evaluated as failures, but are instead interpreted as successes" (Pfaff-Czarnecka 2004: 184). In her study of Nepal's Maoist rebellion, she elaborates on the deceitful character of development projects in Nepal and the wide cooperation of all parties in dissembling about their success. She argues: "Currently, even in the most remote areas of Nepal, villagers are well aware that the success of development cooperation has to rely upon representations of its success. What the villagers observe is that enthusiastic depictions of development interventions do not necessarily correspond with assessments at the grassroots" (ibid.: 185). Pfaff-Czarnecka tells the story of a village known "for being very successful in implementing development projects" and for its collective strategies of carrying them out. While, over the years, only a minor part of the project was implemented, and only the village leader benefited from it, the donors visited the village and produced a documentary film "to record its success." Nevertheless, although most of the villagers readily joined in the filming, in private discussions many of them said that they felt that "they have been made fools of" (ibid.: 187).

In considering the role of deceit in the context of the women's program, I follow Caroline Gerschlager and Monika Mokre's analysis (Gerschlager and Mokre 2002).[3] Drawing on Adam Smith's work on moral sentiments (Smith 1984), where he argues that a certain deception is inevitable in any social setting, Gerschlager (2002) argues that successful exchange is based on deceit. While standard "male stream" economic models ignore deception and imply that deception cannot succeed, Gerschlager considers deception as the key to understanding the functioning of exchange, and as an efficient aspect of exchange. Hence, I suggest that the role of deceit is not unique to the development context. Rather, it is embedded in this context, as in any other situation of hierarchical power relationships. Deceit, from this point of view, serves superiors as a way of calming resistance, removing the objections of subordinates (by promising unrealistic advantages, for instance), or for handling pressures exerted on superiors.

Both the Ekala literacy class and the seminar were the outcomes of pressure exerted on the local heads of the irrigation project. The World Bank applied considerable pressure on the Nepali heads of the irrigation project to demonstrate progress with gender development activities and, therefore, they were pleased to find that things "were working" as a result of their demands. Consequently, the local heads of the irrigation project could easily fool them: starting up one literacy class and hiring a new local consultant was enough to get the Bank off their backs. My own pressure on the local heads of the irrigation project, and on Thapa in particular, was daily and continuous. Evidently, the seminar opened as a direct outcome of my intensive urging.

Some of these pressures were described earlier (in Chapter 1) in relation to the demand that a male guardian provide a signature to approve his daughter's or wife's participation in the seminar. This demand was clearly a means of delaying the opening of the seminar, and consequently the implementation of the large-scale literacy program. When Pandit and Gupta were taken by surprise, realizing that the seminar was going to start the next day, they then mentioned, for the first time, that a woman's participation in the seminar would require male consent. This stalling tactic worked, and the seminar did not start the next day. Indeed, I found the negotiations very troublesome. It felt as though I was nagging Pandit, Gupta, and Thapa to accept something they opposed. When Pandit and Gupta eventually suggested starting the seminar on Thursday of the same week, it was clearly a gesture to calm me down. I realized, as my fieldnotes record, that "that was the farthest I could go with my pressures." Thapa and Pandit had done their best to prevent the opening of the seminar but ended up giving in to my continuous pressure, albeit only until the moment of my departure from Nepal.

Another point of comparison between the literacy classes in Ekala and the women's seminar concerns the urge to demonstrate personal achievement and competence to those in power. Thapa had to prove his competence to James Wolffenson and other representatives of the World Bank. Apparently, Thapa thought that the failure of the women's program would be seen as his own personal failure, which he clearly needed to avoid. Assuming that one class would be sufficient to create an image of his own success, as well as that of the women's program, he bankrolled the literacy class with his own money. Likewise, a single group of seminar graduates provided me with the illusion of achievement, and of contributing to the advancement of village women. It enabled me to prove myself worthy to the local heads of the irrigation project, to my Israeli employers, who paid for my time and work, and to myself as well. Anita's situation was even more complicated because she needed to ensure future employment, and therefore had to prove her vital contribution to the women's program. Feeling that both of us had to prove our worth to our superiors in the irrigation project, Anita said to me on the day before the seminar opened, "this is our first test."

However, there is a significant difference between Thapa's endeavors to demonstrate competence and reliability, and Anita's and mine. Anita and I both aspired to accomplish a great deal and to implement the full-scale women's program. In practice, however, we were expected to implement nothing. In my case it became evident that the less progress I made, in terms of opening classes, the more satisfied those in charge were (although they would not admit this openly). Thapa, on the other hand, did not want to implement the women's development project. Nevertheless, he was formally praised and respected for something on which he did not deliver.

Both Thapa and I manipulated and took advantage of the women's groups' visual and sentimental impact. The sight of the women, young girls and older women, sitting in a dark, tiny, muddy, clay hut, concentrating on their books, appearing eager to become literate, was a very persuasive and touching picture. No less persuasive and touching was the sight of the ten women, aged fifteen to over fifty, sitting around tables, watching the trainers carefully, writing diligently, and complying with the vigilant supervision of "important" males, who used to visit the seminar from time to time. The two delicate, petite teachers added also to the fragile atmosphere in the seminar. The diminutive female student, who brought her baby and her elder son, to look after the baby while she was studying, created a particularly moving sight. She came from a distant village and spoke a different Nepali dialect from that of her classmates and teachers. This additional obstacle must have made it nearly impossible for her to persevere in her studies. Nevertheless, she missed class only once, when the baby was sick, probably as a result of having been carried all the way to town on a rainy day. For my part, I often invoked this woman's eagerness to complete the seminar training as a powerful symbol of women's ambition to study and achieve economic and social mobility. The woman's devotion and fragility was used by me to convey my own feminist commitment and social sensitivity as well as the seminar's success, which was presented as my personal professional achievement. Indirectly and invisibly, then, I realized personal advantages, just as the men on the irrigation project staff did. Hence the "actual process proceeded" masked "by its contrast with the intentional plans, which appear bathed in the shining light of day" (Ferguson 1990: 276).

The Collaboration of the Project's Partners in Faking Progress

Clearly, neither the heads of the World Bank nor the Nepali and Israeli heads of the irrigation project were genuinely interested in any substantial progress in implementing the women's project. Therefore, one literacy class and one seminar group represented the minimum attainment needed for demonstrating progress and the maximum of what the women's project was allowed to achieve. It follows that the irrigation project directors' real purpose was "to look good," and to make believe that a great deal more was going to materialize. Similarly, Pfaff-Czarnecka argues that the common explanation offered by entrepreneurs and implementers for not fully and successfully implementing the projects they are in charge of is: "'what is not completed will be finalized in due course', whatever 'in due course' may imply" (Pfaff-Czarnecka 2004: 184).

This point is also compatible with Fenster's single workshop on gender awareness, carried out in October 1996, which she organized and attended. Her plan to provide some 27,000 women aged between 10 and 65 with literacy skills—a number that would have amounted to some 900 women's groups—followed by economic activities, ended up as unimplemented recommendations in her papers. The one gender awareness workshop which was held was highly praised and frequently mentioned as Fenster's achievement during her visit to Nepal.

The World Bank's cooperation with the pretense of the women project's success, by presenting the meager (and practically evanescent) accomplishments as "good work," was repeated with regard to the ten literacy classes that were opened after I left Nepal. In a letter some two months after I returned to Israel, Leon informed me about a visit by the Bank's supervising delegation. Its members' excited reaction was very similar to that of the previous Bank delegation to Ekala. He wrote:

> On the 5–6–7/11/97 a visit of a supervising delegation of the World Bank (IDA) took place in a literacy class in the village Bhawarabari, next to tube well EW/S. The visit lasted for half an hour. It was 19.00 and despite the very poor light, provided by a few lanterns, and the difficulty to read from the board, the head of the delegation, Mr Mint, was deeply impressed. He spoke with two students, one of whom was 16 and the other was at least 40, and praised the teacher who was doing, according to him, a "holy work."[4]

Thus, gaining the Bank's trust appeared to be a very easy task, and faking the implementation of the women's project was, in fact, welcomed by the Bank's representatives. It is apparent, therefore, that both parties were eager to present the only literacy class in Ekala and the one class in Bhawarabari as a success, even describing it in terms of "holy work," while in practice eliminating the women's project. Moreover, the delegation's head, Mr Mint, openly admitted to the Bank's disinterest in the women's project. According to Leon's letter, "Mint repeatedly stated that the project is mainly an agricultural irrigation project and that he is committed to complete it on time, as was scheduled in the contract, including from the financial perspective, and therefore his main efforts will focus on the civil assignments, the electric and mechanical."[5]

Mosse suggests that gender projects fail to be implemented and to become "part of the projects' self-representations," because they attain "neither internal support [within organizations] nor external demand for anything but the simplest notion of gender equity..." (Mosse 2005: 152). However, Mr Mint's statement, which suggests that there was no intention of implementing the women's program, demonstrates that no realistic chance existed for the women's project from the outset. The World Bank, the Israeli irrigation company, and the Nepali government never intended to carry out the women's project, despite their expressed enthusiasm regarding the women they met in the field. Therefore, Mosse's explanation for the failure of gender projects—that project consultants fail to gain support—is not supported by my ethnography. That is, gender consultants fail, according to my experience because they are not expected to succeed, but rather to provide the façade of empowering women.

The Seminar: The Exercise of Men's Power and the Use of Cultural Discourse

Despite the reluctance of the heads of the irrigation project to fully implement the women's program, as soon as the seminar became a reality they treated it as an inseparable part of the irrigation project's social life. Hence, some of them used it as a platform for displays of power. Important people from the irrigation project and outside it visited the class, and opening and closing ceremonies were organized. Several of the higher-ranked employees, whether directly or indirectly connected to the women's program, expected to be invited to talk, and some insisted on their "right" place in the line of speakers.

The negotiations over who would speak at the opening of the seminar started as soon as the date was fixed. After Mr Gurung, the district head of the Ministry of Education, accepted a request from Anita and myself to assume professional responsibility over the teachers and for the teaching certificates, I suggested that he present greetings at the opening of the seminar. Anita approved, explaining that, "after all, he is the director of the Ministry of Education in our region." When the two of us arrived later at the irrigation project offices, I informed Pandit that Mr Gurung had been asked to talk at the opening of the seminar and that he was pleased to accept the offer. Pandit was pleased and also agreed to my suggestion that he himself address the audience at the opening, immediately adding that Acharya should also be invited to join the greeting panel. Apparently, Anita had already spoken with Acharya about this. Pandit then suggested that I should also speak at the opening. I replied that Anita was the one who should be given this role. Pandit then insisted that I must speak as "an outside guest." I reacted jokingly: "Well, you are the boss, whatever you say." He did not like my remark, and replied: "No, I am not the boss. We are working in cooperation." Later on, I found out that my name appeared second on the list of speakers, right after Mr Gurung's.

On our way home, I asked Leon if he would come to the opening of the seminar. He replied instantly: "Of course, I have to replace Thapa, who will not be able to attend the opening." Uneasy at the growing number of people who were supposed to talk at the seminar opening, I went to Pandit to inform him that Leon would replace Thapa, and also suggested that I did not need to talk at the event. Indeed, I assumed that if Thapa were to attend the event he would certainly speak and therefore Pandit would not. Pandit responded instantly and determinedly that both of us should talk.

Ranju, one of the WGOs, convened the opening event. She asked Pandit to speak first. Pandit talked about the importance of literacy and the need to empower the village women. Then Ranju turned to me and asked me to talk. I used statistics published that same day in the *Rising Nepal*, a Nepali English-language paper, about rates of illiteracy in the world. The data suggested that some fifty years ago the rate of illiteracy in nineteen countries from around the world was over 45 per cent, whereas the current average rate had dropped to 23 per cent, while in Arab countries in Asia and Africa it was still 70 per cent.[6] I then concluded that, "our challenge should be to reduce the rate of illiteracy and provide women with a key to knowledge, information, and perhaps to economic wealth as well." When I finished, Ranju turned to Leon and asked him to talk. He turned to Acharya and suggested that Acharya speak before him, thus making him the last speaker, but Pandit told him that Ranju was the one who decided the order of speakers. As he was left with no choice, Leon started his talk saying: "The teachers will be inspected by us. We shall determine if they are doing a good job." Acharya spoke last, and he reflected on the importance of education for women.

Thus, the ten women had to listen to the four of us talking for almost an hour about the importance of literacy and education and about the vital challenge of disseminating knowledge and literacy. The women were also explicitly reminded (by Leon) of their dependence on "us," their superiors, who would be monitoring their progress.

At the closing event, the number of speakers grew to six. The list of speakers included Pandit, Anita, one of the graduating women, Leon, Gurung, and Thapa. When the important people had left the room, I gave a short speech, raising the number of speakers to seven. The closing ceremony further demonstrated the power differential between the female trainees and teachers, and the males who were addressing them. As the speakers finished talking to the women, and after the certificates were handed out, Gurung looked at the board and noticed a table indicating the students' grades in the tests. He then took the stage again to address the women for a second time, expressing dissatisfaction at the poor level of achievement of two students and reservations about their capacity to teach others. The women were obviously humiliated in front of their classmates and the speakers, all of whom, apart from myself, were males. Embarrassed by Gurung's comments, I tried to suggest quietly to him that perhaps it was not the proper time to talk about these women's grades. Gurung ignored my remark and continued to reprimand the women.

Later on when I discussed this episode with Thapa, he told me that having noticed the women's timidity at the opening of the seminar he had invited them to his office after it had ended. Then he asked them if they thought they could teach other women and they confidently replied that they could. Thapa concluded: "So I told them, you see that you can teach?!" Thapa might have wanted to ensure that the women's shyness would not undermine them in their teaching. It is also possible that he felt uncomfortable about Gurung's comments, and therefore he tried to make up for them. However, at my farewell party he used the incident to prove my lack of understanding of the local mentality, claiming that "Nepali people are not easily offended."

Signing the teaching certificates manifested another form of symbolic power. When this was done Leon insisted on signing them. Thus, his signature appeared side by side with that of Gurung (the ministry official) and my own, as representative of the women's development program.

Male domination pervaded the seminar from the outset. I have already mentioned the demand that men sign their spouses' or daughters' form to signal their approval of participation in the seminar (see Chapter 1). I argued there that this demand was a manipulative tactic aimed at stalling the implementation of the women's project. It also derived from a patriarchal discourse and culture. However, I would argue that traditional, cultural, patriarchal structures and norms were instrumentally used in this case to serve the male officials' needs. They probably assumed, consciously or unconsciously, that "cultural" explanations work well at convincing foreigners like myself that local culture and tradition impose unavoidable constraints. Moreover, employing "traditional" rhetoric turned me into an "outsider," one who was unable to express reservations concerning local norms. Doing so would imply my rudeness and arrogance.

Thus, cultural or traditional narratives served the male officials in justifying their rejection of an activity intended for women's advantage, and were conveniently manipulated to suit their needs. Moreover, cultural constraints are dynamic and can be dramatically changed by social, economic, and political conditions and crises, such as wars, immigration, and so on. Evidence of this can be found in studies of rural women's participation in Nepal's Maoist insurgency. For example, Mandira Sharma and Dinesh Prasain show that, despite "dominant cultural narratives in Nepal which portray women as weak and submissive," women comprised "between thirty to forty per cent of the Maoist cadres" (Sharma and Prasain 2004: 152). Other studies also suggest that women were conspicuously involved in the war and argue that their mass participation reflects the dynamic transformation of cultural identities in Nepal and the emancipatory potential of women's participation in a militarized movement (see, e.g., Gautam, Banskota, and Manchanda 2001; Manchanda 2004).

I would argue, therefore, that whereas the women's program was presented as a means to create a gender transformation, in practice it was sabotaged by male officials (in the irrigation project and outside it) who used "cultural" rhetoric to prevent its realization.

Bossing Women in the Hierarchical Setting of the Irrigation Project

The process of hiring the two seminar teachers provides another example of the gendered power relations embedded in the encounters that took place. Anita and I first met the two candidates who were to train the village teachers in the seminar at the district office of the Ministry of Education. The two women were in their fifties, and looked passive and gloomy. They were standing quietly in the corner of the room, waiting to be addressed, while Anita and I were talking with Gurung's assistant. He explained that the teachers were very experienced and that they used to teach in a high school. One of them had been an English teacher and the other had taught social sciences. We asked Gurung's assistant to approve our inviting the two women to our office, as we wished to speak with them in more detail about the seminar, and he agreed. However, none of us asked the women themselves if they could or wanted to join us. The teachers' inferior position was established by all parties, by Gurung's assistant as well as Anita and myself. While the official treated us as his equals, he seemed to perceive the two teachers as obedient employees. Nevertheless, Anita and I unintentionally collaborated with him. Thus, the bureaucratic encounter that took place at the district offices of the Ministry of Education fostered the teachers' invisibility and social vulnerability.

When the four of us arrived at Leon's office he was sat at his table. Leon attended the whole meeting, following our conversation quietly. I asked the teachers about their teaching technique, whether it was didactic or interactive. They explained patiently. As the teachers' English was very poor, they responded to some of my questions in broken English and to others in Nepali, which Anita translated. We found out that the two teachers had had only ten years of schooling. When I asked about their teaching materials, they opened up a worn-out envelope, from which they took out and displayed various items: cut-out letters, books, and booklets. Then they specified the items needed for the seminar. Anita and I were perplexed, as we had no idea how to organize all that was needed on time. We suggested various ideas for obtaining the books, but none seemed to be realistic.

I emphasized the need for focusing on training in practical literacy skills, such as filling out forms and reading newspapers. When I suggested that reading newspapers should be taught only in the last part of the literacy course, Leon intervened, after sarcastically requesting permission to interrupt. He turned to me and said in Hebrew, with an authoritative tone, that I was talking too fast and that the two women understood nothing of it. He added: "Although you ask them whether they understand you, they don't feel free to tell you that they don't understand." I reacted apologetically, saying (also in Hebrew) that "this is exactly what I am doing, I am speaking very slowly and I use Anita's help to clarify things." We went on to discuss other problems concerning the women program, such as the lack of books and instructional devices.

Leon intervened repeatedly, commenting on various subjects that came up in the conversation. He made skeptical observations, which he directed at me in Hebrew. He asked when and how the village women would learn, raising doubts concerning their ability to study at night after a full day's domestic work, as well as about the teachers' ability to teach at night after dark. Regarding the teachers' comments about their previous experience of working with women in the villages, he claimed triumphantly: "Even the teachers say that there is a significant drop-out rate of participants from classes that take place at night."

Leon's apparent interest in the seminar (and the literacy training) and his many interventions could be regarded as a genuine expression of concern for the seminar's (and the literacy program's) success. As Tahal's representative, he might have felt responsible for my professional performance and for the appropriate implementation of the program of which I was in charge. I suggest, however, that Leon was eager to convey to us (and, I suppose, to me in particular) that he was in control of things and that he knew much more than us, even in a field in which he was not an expert. He pretended to know everything, including how the teachers felt (their unease about admitting to their inability to follow me), the village women's difficulties (studying late at night), how I should talk (slowly), and how the teachers should teach. He behaved as if it was not only his right and duty, but also within his competency to instruct us—Anita, as well as the teachers and me—and to clarify to us the literacy program's constraints and limitations. Leon's repeated interference dictated the encounter's atmosphere and the social positioning of its participants. His skeptical comments not only revealed his doubts about the value of the women's program and his lack of belief about whether or not it would ever be realized, they also underscored the inferior position of the teachers, Anita, and myself. I assume that conveying an impression of his own superior bureaucratic and professional stance was particularly crucial to his attempt at putting me down.

It follows, then, that the encounters in Gurung's and Leon's offices established power differentials that were the outcome of bureaucratic structured domination. Although in Gurung's office Anita and I cooperated in the process of excluding the two teachers, it was that fact that we were on Gurung's territory and his assistant's formal authority which fostered the social distance between the two women and the rest of us. Whereas in the first encounter gender was relatively muted in relation to socioeconomic status, in Leon's office the gender dimension was clearly revealed. While the four of us interacted in a friendly, informal manner, Leon's aggressive and patronizing interventions, and his attempts to control our conversation, demonstrated a substantial difference between the four women and the single man in the room. Moreover, while the women involved in this encounter had some relevant professional credentials, Leon had no such background, and instead pretended to have expertise and authority in matters that we discussed.

Men's Supervision of the Seminar

The seminar attracted visitors, mainly senior irrigation project employees, who used to watch the women, and discuss among themselves what was going on and how things should work. Thus the group of teachers and students, who were never asked if they minded being observed or how they felt about the continuous intrusion, became an object of social exchange. These visits became part of the seminar from the first day. Leon's attendance at the seminar was particularly conspicuous. When the opening ceremony was over, Acharya was about to leave the room when he suggested that Leon escort him out. Leon replied that he wanted to stay to see how the seminar worked. Anita and I remained in the room, sitting among the students, and participated in the first assignment presented by the teachers. Later on that day, Anita and I discussed our impressions, following our participation in the introductory part of the seminar. Anita said that the teachers informed her that my partner during the exercise where we introduced ourselves in pairs was the weakest student in the group, and had language difficulties.

When I went to Leon's office after leaving the seminar room, Leon asked me why I had left. I told him that I did not want to burden the women with my presence. Leon was displeased and said, "It is important to see what the teachers' worth is and what the women are doing." I told him that I would visit the class again in a few days when the group assumed its working routines. Indeed, I did not voice any objection to Leon's demand that I attend the seminar class regularly and interrupt its routine. Instructing me to attend the class, to observe its activities, to evaluate the teachers' and students' performance, and probably to report to him about all of it, implied his control over the seminar through me. Indeed, it also implied his ambition to impose his control over me. Leon's pervasive engagement in the seminar, as revealed in his verbal and physical participation in the opening and closing events, was just one instance of male domination with regard to the seminar. Similarly, Gurung's reprimand of the women in front of all the other participants and Thapa's paternalistic attitude toward the two offended women also exposed the gendered power component of the irrigation project's setting. The assumed right to supervise, watch, evaluate, and gossip about the women's activities in the seminar was taken for granted, particularly by Leon but also by others, including Anita and myself. It seems that I considered Anita and myself to be directly responsible for the seminar and, therefore, I perceived our attendance at the classes to be more legitimate and justified.

Yet, I was evidently ambivalent about my attendance of the seminar. This emerges from my reaction to Leon's demand that I should attend the class regularly, and from the way in which Anita and I integrated into the class's activity. Both of us stayed in the class after the ceremonial part was over, not as observers but rather as full participants, taking part in the games of mutual introduction. The teachers handed everyone one half of a piece of paper, on which part of a proverb was written. Then every woman had to look for the missing part of the proverb. When the missing half of the proverb had been located, each member of the resulting pairs was then expected to find out details about their partner, following which they were asked to present themselves to the whole group. My partner and I had a proverb that said something like: "Between health and wealth—the first is preferred." She was a short woman, who seemed to lack self-confidence, repeatedly pulling her headscarf back.

I did my best to fit in with the group as one of the students. Nevertheless, the teachers' evident need to convey the message to me, through Anita, that my partner was "the weakest student in the group" suggests that my attendance was intrusive and threatening. Thus, despite my efforts at becoming a "regular" participant in the ongoing activities, the teachers perceived me as an outsider representing the authorities, with the power to influence their professional reputation and future prospects in the women's program and beyond it. The teachers may have thought that if I perceived the student I interacted with as representative of the others' learning capacities and potential, I would draw negative conclusions about the class, themselves, and of their chances at success.

I perceived Anita's daily visits to the seminar as an appropriate, even important, activity because she was local and spoke Nepali. Evidently, this enabled her to follow what was going on and to evaluate the teachers' performance and the progress made by the students. This implied, of course, that both students and teachers were being regularly observed and supervised, directly by Anita and indirectly by me (and consequently by Leon and other irrigation project staff).

Urged by Leon to attend the class, I joined Anita one day and found Gupta already sitting in the class. He seemed very satisfied. He told Anita and me afterwards that one of the students was an acquaintance of his, and said "she is a very talented woman." In response, I said that the woman who sat next to his friend was "very intelligent, she can sew and in fact is sewing clothes for her neighbors." Leon, who overheard the conversation, said, "I told them [the teachers] that they should not become anxious because of my presence, as I don't understand one word of Nepali. I said that because I felt that the teachers' voice lowered dramatically when I entered the class." Gupta and Leon laughed, enjoying the story. Leon's description of the influence he had on the teachers indicates clearly that he was aware of the impact of his intrusion into the class. However, he did not seem to care, as it was self-evident to him that he was entitled to enter the seminar room whenever he felt like it without asking for permission. Leon regarded the teachers as either naive or foolish because, according to him, they failed to realize that he did not speak one word of Nepali and needed an explicit mention of this fact.

It appears that the women were used, mainly by males (like Leon and Gupta) but also by Anita and me, as a resource in social interactions. Observing and discussing the women in the seminar enabled us to position ourselves as superior—professionally, socially, and personally. The interaction between the irrigation project staff, who controlled desired resources, and those who lacked them, and therefore depended on their benefactors, resembled, in some ways, a parent–child relationship. The teachers and their students were perceived and treated as protégées who needed watching, instruction, and compliments, and could be ridiculed when they were not present.

It is not surprising, therefore, that in this context of patronizing interactions the students bargained over refreshments. When offered one kind of refreshment, the women continuously demanded another kind until they achieved what they wanted. The students complained daily to Anita and me about the two biscuits they each received and demanded samosas instead. Anita and I were well aware of the need to please the women, as we were also depending on them to complete the seminar classes. Consequently, we did not give up until we managed to obtain samosas for the women.

No Books for the Seminar: Men's Stalling and Women's Anxiety

The lack of seminar textbooks led to a mini-drama in which Anita and I were the naive party at first, believing that Leon and Thapa were doing their utmost to provide the needed books on time. Early on in my involvement in the women's program I found out that there was a book shortage, and that the procedures involved in purchasing them were complicated. It was impossible to purchase the books on the free market and they had to be obtained from the Nepali government. In the district education office, Anita and I found a meager number of the books we needed for the literacy classes and seminar. The books were clearly not available in sufficient numbers for our large scale literacy program, and some of books needed for the advanced stages of the literacy studies were simply unavailable. Moreover, obtaining the books entailed long bureaucratic procedures, including having applications approved by officials in the district Ministry of Education, followed by the approval of the head of the informal education department in the main office of the ministry in Kathmandu. Only then, and after paying for the books, could they be supplied.

Anita and I were anxious to ensure that the books arrived before the seminar started. When we realized that the procedures involved were much more complicated than we had anticipated, we tried every possible way to overcome this unexpected delay. Thus, Anita suggested that during our joint visit to Kathmandu she would hand in the vital letters of application personally, and, if nothing else, return with the books needed for the seminar. With no check in hand from the irrigation project to pay for the 900 books needed (which we planned to start immediately after the first seminar ended), Anita could not purchase the books.[7]

Eager to ensure the opening of the literacy classes, and deeply upset about these delays and difficulties, I suggested that I would pay for the books out of my own pocket and get a refund from the irrigation project later. Thapa agreed to the idea and said that the money would be repaid by the irrigation project. However,

Leon's wife Hanna, with whom I spent some of my time while visiting Kathmandu, was startled by my suggestion, and warned me about the risk of losing my money. The effort of obtaining the books involved pursuing Thapa daily to sign a check for the books, but he was never available. Anita and I were repeatedly promised that we would get the check to us "in no time" and that Thapa would sign it as soon as he returned to his office. As Thapa was either absent or unavailable, we tried to get help from Pandit, hoping that he might find a way to obtain the books for the literacy classes before the seminar ended. Pandit exhausted all possible excuses for the continuous delay, always concluding our encounters by saying that everything depended on Thapa.

The problem of the books for the literacy classes was never resolved, since they were never purchased, and—except for the ten that opened after I left Nepal—the classes never started. The smaller problem of obtaining books for the seminar teachers and students was solved by Leon. The token contribution he offered us emphasized his general cynical attitude in relation to the literacy program. Feeling desperate about the chances of acquiring the books on the day before the seminar started, Anita said to me mischievously that Leon would buy the books. I expressed my doubts regarding this. Leon would not, I thought, pay for the 900 books for the literacy classes, but I suggested that he might, nonetheless, purchase the smaller number of books needed for the seminar. To my surprise, when I brought this idea up Leon agreed to buy the few books and materials needed for the seminar on his next visit to Kathmandu.

Nevertheless, he stated that he would need Thapa's approval in writing to ensure that he got his expenses reimbursed. Anita told him that Thapa's approval had been given over the telephone. This precondition was then followed by Leon recounting Thapa's problematic record in repaying debts. He told us that some time ago the local heads of the irrigation project had come to owe Tahal $12,000. "I had all the proofs for their debt," he said, "and I wrote Thapa a letter, titled: 'An Unpaid Debt.' Thapa was very angry and said that they did not owe that money to Tahal and that he never signed any document to that effect." After sharing with us his lesson, he said that he would get the books for the seminar. However, when he returned from his weekend in Kathmandu he did not bring the books. Eventually, Leon's contribution to solving the problem of the books was to acquire a single Stage II textbook for the teachers, which he brought from Kathmandu on the closing day of the seminar. Anita photocopied it for the two teachers.

Realizing that Leon's commitment to acquiring the books before the seminar opened was no guarantee of actually getting them, and as the seminar was about to start the next day, we went again to the district education offices to look for texts and materials that would be useful. Our search through the clutter produced only a few crumpled and detached pages from an old teacher-training textbook.

When the seminar started we still had no books or materials for the teachers. However, the teachers themselves had all they needed to start with. The ten Stage I textbooks for the seminar students were donated by PACT, an international literacy NGO, whose representative Anita and I had met in Kathmandu and whose services we intended to hire for training the WGOs. The Ministry of Education's district official provided ten Stage II books, but only after the seminar ended.

This mini-drama, in which Anita and I were determined to overcome whatever obstacle was put in our way, went on for weeks. Our persistent and stubborn efforts in confronting reluctant male officials revealed the literacy program to be a phantom and unveiled the gendered nature of power within the project. The male officials could pretend to the two of us that they supported the women's program and our efforts, while at the same time they avoided our requests for the books that we had been promised, and they lied to us, pledging their cooperation while simultaneously withholding it. Thus, it appears that our role in this affair placed the two of us in a vulnerable, absurd position, and fostered our grave dependence on the heads of the irrigation project, Thapa and Leon in particular. While they controlled the women's program budget, they encouraged us to believe that they intended to finance our (approved) plans and our negotiated agreements with potential partners.

The Seminar: Degrading and Disempowering Women

Leon's obsessive interest in the seminar was diametrically opposed to his explicit reservations regarding the entire literacy program, which he expressed these just a few hours before the opening of the seminar. Leon was expecting a letter from Israel regarding my estimated costing of the women's development project. Although I will discuss this episode in detail in the next chapter, at this point it may be relevant to mention that Leon's interest in the seminar had nothing to do with the actual implementation of the women's project. Apparently he considered his role in supervising it as self-evident. As Tahal's representative, he perceived himself as legitimately responsible for any activity that was carried out by its employees— in this case, Anita and me. It follows, therefore, that Leon's attitude to the seminar (and the whole women's program) was two-faced: objecting to any substantial resource-intensive activity on the one hand, and supervising ongoing activities on the other. Other high ranking officials, like Thapa, Gupta and Pandit, also revealed this self-contradictory attitude, yet Leon's overt statements made the deceitful component contained in these encounters more conspicuous.

The fax Leon received from Tel Aviv on the morning of the seminar opening was Tahal's approval of my estimated costing. Leon let me read the fax, which said that it is the client's business to decide on the extent and objectives of budget expenditure. "Now I am covered," he said, and then asked me to come and sit next to him. Looking very irritated he said to me:

> I explained to them [his superiors in Tel Aviv] that your proposed budget does not leave any room for Tahal to make a profit. I would never approve such a proposal. The only profit Tahal can gain here is perhaps from hiring the teachers or organizations that will carry out the women's project. However, in your proposal, there is no profit for Tahal, and they know that they should include in the budget the experts [i.e., those who work for the irrigation project] that would cost some $250,000 … [A]fter all, with all due respect to women, other things are higher priority. You heard Sonderman [from the Ministry of Agriculture] who said that the position of women here is not bad at all. I heard them [the local heads of the irrigation project] saying that they have invested too much money here and that they don't have any more money to invest here.

But it was not only Leon who was being duplicitous. Thapa, who had done his utmost to undermine the realization of the women development project, also behaved as if he supported the seminar. He addressed the women in the seminar very warmly and spoke positively about the importance of literacy for women. Moreover, Thapa made a sentimental gesture to the seminar teachers. When he came back from a holiday in India, he brought three small styrofoam folders. Showing us the folders, he explained to Anita and me that each of them had cost him $1. He suggested that these could efficiently replace the conventional classroom blackboard, and serve the village teachers when teaching in the villages, as most villages would not have any boards.

Anita and I expressed our enthusiasm, and I suggested to Thapa that he patent his idea. Thapa was very pleased at our childish excitement over his gesture. Thus, the styrofoam board encounter exposed further the fragile position and profound dependence of Anita and I. We needed to show appreciation and gratitude regarding Thapa's ridiculous gestures, while at the same time he denied us the most basic financial support, such as money for purchasing textbooks for the seminar and literacy classes.

Thapa's attitude revealed that he understood that we, the women, could be bought cheaply and that our submissive cooperation was ensured. His gestures symbolized paternalistic disrespect for all women, the seminar students, the teachers, Anita, and myself. This and other trivial, cheap gestures accentuated to the extreme the men's cynical attitude toward women. Just as Leon was only prepared to buy a single book for the seminar teachers to please Anita and me, Thapa found he could buy us off with a toy-like article for the seminar. The lion's share of the project budget was earmarked for "important" projects and people, as Leon's comment about "other things" being of a "higher priority" revealed. The local and national male executives of the irrigation project were the ones who benefited from the budget intended for the women's project, as will become clear in the next chapter.

In conclusion, the events described above demonstrate how the women's development project, formally aimed at women's empowerment, in practice disempowered women. The seminar affair is an example for how an activity that set out to advance women's interests was overtaken by male officials and exploited for exercising their power and for advancing their interests. In the end only ten women were trained as village teachers and only ten literacy classes were started; thus, the village teachers were given almost no chance to teach literacy, which was offered to some 300 village women instead of about 9,000 (or 27,000, according to one of the initial documents). It appears, then, that the women's development project was a project aimed at women's empowerment that failed because of the successful efforts of all parties: the World Bank, the Nepali government, and the Israeli irrigation company.

Gender policies, Sara Hlupekile Longwe suggests, have a "strange tendency ... to 'evaporate' within international development agencies" (Longwe 1999: 63). The evaporation of the women's empowerment project in rural Nepal provides an example of this phenomenon, which seems to reflect deep-rooted gendered power differentials in society, both at international and at local levels. Thus, a more general understanding that emerges from the seminar affair is that projects aimed at advancing women's empowerment, like other development projects designed to advance social equity, cannot bring about social change. Because these projects are embedded in the larger socioeconomic, cultural, and political power structures, which are eminently patriarchal and capitalist, they are taken over and absorbed by those in power to serve and preserve the prevailing power structures. This line of argument is in accord with Frank Youngman's study of a national literacy programme in Botswana, which "in fact served to reproduce the class, gender and ethnic inequalities within society" (Youngman 2000: 135). Moreover, Youngman too was aware of the fact that the literacy program served political interests, constituting "a strategy of state legitimation by demonstrating a welfare concern for providing the rural areas with social services. The overall consequence was to legitimate Botswana's capitalist development and social inequality" (ibid.: 135–36).

The kind of political interpretation of development that I offer echoes with other studies of educational policy. Such an analysis is offered by Malcolm Adiseshiah, who argues:

> Education is not politically neutral. It is an active supporter and faithful reflector of the status quo in society. If the status quo is predominantly unequal and unjust, and it is increasingly so, education will be increasingly unequal and unjust and there will be no place for non-formal education to improve the conditions of the poor ... If, however, society is moving in an equalitarian direction, then non-formal education can and will flourish. (Adiseshiah in Fordham1980: 21)

This optimistic understanding appears to be irrelevant to the context of the women's project and of development projects at large. This is so because non-formal education projects that take place in developing, colonized, or poor countries, by definition do not correspond to the preconditions suggested by Adiseshiah.[8]

For social change to produce greater equity—whether it be addressed at inequalities of gender, ethnicity, class, or whatever—power centers must be comprised of proportional representation of all (or most) relevant sectors in society. Education—whether formal, adult, informal, or non-formal—can generate social change when it is inseparable from comprehensive policies and practices of economic equality and social justice (Mulenga 2001). Thus, Wickens and Sandlin suggest, in the context of literacy: "For progressive shifts over literacy from colonialist Western control to local governance to significantly continue worldwide, financial structures must be reorganized. Local governments need the economic freedom to make wise decisions on the behalf of their own populace, rather than bending to Western mandates over free labor markets" (Wickens and Sandlin 2007: 290).

Notes

1. Jo Rowlands suggests that appealing terms such as "empowerment," "participation," "capacity-building," "sustainability," and "institutional development" are instrumental in ignoring or hiding "realities of power, inequality, and oppression" (Rowlands 1999: 149).
2. The development project studied by Mosse, described at one point as a "jewel in the crown," was two years later judged to be "very disappointing" or "negligible" (Mosse 2005: 183).
3. The volume edited by Gerschlager and Mokre (2002) contributes to an alternative feminist conceptualization of the embedded connection between exchange and deceit. Thus, for instance, Mokre's essay in the volume examines Adam Smith's considerations on exchange and deception as a concept of identity-building (see Smith 1984).
4. Letter from Leon, 10 November 1997.
5. Letter from Leon, 10 November 1997.
6. The data comes from an article titled "World Illiteracy Rate Falls," *Rising Nepal*, 9 September 1997, p. xx.
7. Each book cost 27 rupees (approximately $0.46). The total cost of the books was about $414.
8. The role of education in preserving power structures in society is also discussed in Chapter 3.

15. One of the WGOs with her motor-cycle

16. A bazaar in the village (organized by a women's organization)

17. Village women at the bazaar

18. A village woman making fun of me

19. A "field bank"

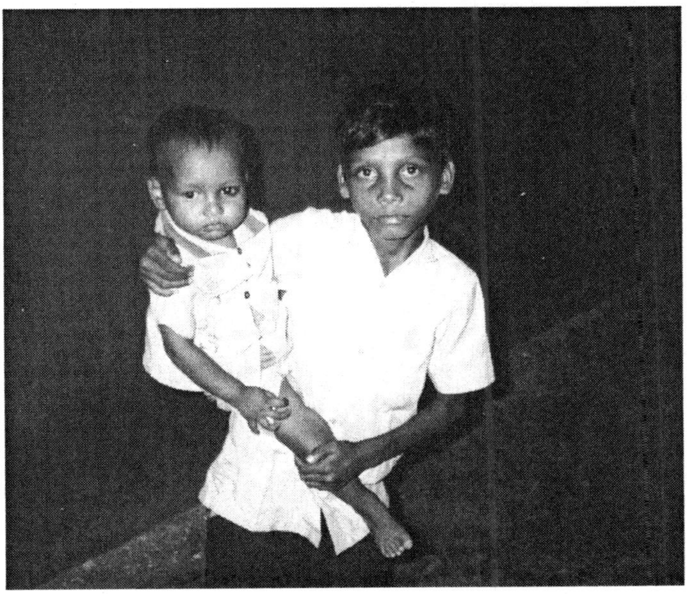

20. Baby-sitting his little brother while his mother studies at the seminar

21. At the seminar room

22. Addressing the seminar graduates at the closing ceremony of the seminar

23. Addressing the women at the closing ceremony of the seminar

24. Representing the seminar graduates in the closing ceremony

25. At the farewell party

26. At the farewell party

Chapter 6

Gender and the Phantom Budget

A Women's Budget in a Male-dominated Context

An examination of the "budget affair" exposes the essential features and the symbolic implications of the budget within the narrative of the women's development project. The budget affair began with Tovi Fenster's stay in Nepal during the summer of 1996 and continued during my stay one year later. In discussing Fenster's and my own cost estimation earlier (see Chapter 3) I indicated how the two budgets exposed our preference for literacy classes, for gender awareness workshops, and similar projects, while pushing aside economic activities. Another impact of the budget, described earlier, was the vibrant round of social engagements that evolved once word got around that generous funds were available, to which the near and more distant organizational environment (NGOs in particular) reacted excitedly. The women's program's budget also disclosed, while intending to conceal, the wide wage disparities between different categories of employees, which affected social relationships in many ways. Moreover, the budget reflected the complex relationships that existed between the Nepali officials and representatives of foreign agencies, the World Bank and Tahal in particular, in relation to spheres of administrative and professional responsibility. Indeed, the changes I made to the budget as a result of verbal and written interactions clearly reflected underlying power struggles as I sought to balance the women's project's budgetary needs against competing interests. The gendered power conflicts were probably the most significant social engagements that emerged as part of the budget drama.

In this chapter I will describe the conflicts and power struggles that ensued over the budget and argue that it did not and was not meant to represent a plan of action. I will elaborate on the social relationships and interactions at large and on gender relations in particular, which the budget affair revealed and set in train. I will also describe the futile effort invested in preparing and discussing the proposed budget with those in charge of the irrigation project. The irrigation project heads opposed in various ways the implementation of the women's project budget, and consequently ensured that the project had a negligible chance of being implemented.

Dealing with the budget of the women's project was an integral and significant part of my daily activities throughout my stay in Nepal. Some of my labor-intensive activities were: writing up the cost estimation for the implementation of the women's project; discussing and negotiating this over and over again with high ranking officials; continuously pressuring Thapa, the Nepali director of the irrigation project, to send the budget proposal to his superiors in the Ministry of Agriculture and to the World Bank for approval; interacting daily with heads of professional divisions within the irrigation project regarding their responsibility for implementing various parts of the program; negotiating with governmental officials and NGOs' representatives outside the irrigation project over their proposals, and more.

The fact that I was asked to produce a budget and report, though one had been submitted a year earlier (see Fenster 1996), implied, by definition, its needlessness. Evidently, I was expected to provide a new version of the budget (and report), since naturally I could not submit my predecessor's budget proposal. Nevertheless, none of the basic data concerning the target population, the time frame, or the general purposes of the women's project (as vaguely stated by the various parties) had changed during the year that had elapsed. Indeed, the process of producing a budget entailed ongoing bargaining over the preferred activities, their extent and their expense, the number of groups and total population to be included in the project, as well as the total sum, and so forth. To me the process seemed like a game played between parties of unequal power; the stronger player was allowed to invent new rules as they pleased while the weaker party was obliged to comply with these changing rules. Moreover, as power relations within this game were defined by gender, the budget indirectly reflected the way in which male players—whether working for the Nepali government, the World Bank, or Tahal—underestimated women's issues and interests. In this game women could be easily manipulated, whether intentionally or unintentionally. Thus, the budget portrayed the women's development project as a fictitious, simulated social affair within a male dominated context, characterized by "radically unequal power relations" (Ferguson 1990: 121–22).

A Flexible Budget and Feminine Compliance

My practical involvement with the budget began a few days after I arrived in Bhairahawa, and I started to prepare my own cost estimate for the women's development and economic activities program—a document that was attached as an annex to my report (see Hertzog 1997). I had first seen a budget for the project some time before I left for Nepal, when I read Tovi Fenster's report, which was handed to me by Tahal during a visit to their offices in Tel Aviv. While reading her report I was completely unaware of the centrality of the budget issue, its latent implications and the conflicting interests that lay hidden behind it. Thus, I concentrated on the descriptive part of her report. The fact that the cost estimate appeared as an annex to her main report further encouraged me to ignore its implications.

The point I wish to make about preparing a new cost estimate is that I was expected to produce something that was unnecessary and redundant. Nevertheless, I found out at a later stage that my cost estimate and final report were the only products that were actually expected from me by Tahal. In practice, all my other initiatives were, from Tahal's point of view (and even more so the point of view of the local irrigation project staff), clearly undesired and even irksome. The reports demonstrate, inadvertently, "the instrumental value of paper products" (Mosse 2005: 134).[1] I suggest that they were used to provide evidence of Tahal's suitability as an implementer of women's empowerment projects, presenting itself as professionally capable and committed to women's affairs. Tahal's presentation of itself as a competent executor of the World Bank's declared purposes with regard to empowering women (see, e.g., World Bank 1990, Murphy 1995),[2] offers an example of the way development agencies and practitioners adjust themselves to funders' and employers' "changing fads—environment one year, gender the next; decentralization today, impact-assessment tomorrow" (Eade 1997: 5). Judith Justice noticed in the early 1970s (in India) that "the priorities of international funding agencies shifted frequently, changing trends in international assistance" (Justice 1989: xi) with regard to health care. She suggests that the "competition for AID contracts is intense," and the "immediate focus of the consulting groups is often on obtaining the contract and meeting AID's requirements, while the realities of the recipient country's health needs may fall into the background" (ibid.: 28). Graham Hancock describes this tendency as "a genetic trait" (Hancock 1989: 72) of developers to present their expertise according to the prevailing fashions of the funders—the World Bank being a particularly conspicuous one. Sondra Hausner (2006), however, argues that this conduct of development institutions and donor agencies emerges from the inherent needs of organizations, rather than from a vague, irrational "fad" or "trait." She argues that development agencies will "continue to cast human rights, reproductive health, sexuality, empowerment, poverty, subjecthood, citizenship, identity, forests, water, and education (to name a few domains through which development processes affect people's lives) within certain heuristic frames. They must do so, in order to function as institutions" (ibid.: 318).

When Leon suggested, on one of my first days in Bhairahawa, that I prepare a cost estimate and final report, I did not express any reservations but obediently accepted his demand and started working on it. Moreover, I never questioned the fact that I had to prepare a cost estimate when there was one available already. Furthermore, while analyzing the ethnography, I found out that the first version of the women's project and budget was submitted by Fenster as early as February 1992. For a long time I assumed that her involvement in the women's project had begun in summer 1996. However, I noticed that a letter sent to me by Leon, some two months after I returned home, noted that her engagement with the women's project began some four years earlier. Recounting a visit of the World Bank delegation to the irrigation project, Leon wrote that he tried to convince the head of the delegation to support the women's project's implementation:

> I reminded Mr Mint that the issue of women's advancement in the [irrigation] project area was the Bank's "baby" and that Tovi Fenster had prepared, as early as February 1992, a program that included, in addition to the "literacy" constituent, [the recommendations concerning] developing and encouraging other skills with the purpose of creating income-generating sources for women, and that until now the Bank has not renounced its interest in these programs. The budget Tovi has prepared amounted to over $400,000.[3]

Thus, while I could have anticipated that my employers and their Nepali partners would expect a report concerning my visit, including proposed recommendations, this was not the case with regard to the women's project's budget. Surprisingly enough I did not mention this unexpected demand in my fieldnotes. It appears, therefore, that I accepted the demand of preparing a cost estimate as a taken-for-granted assignment, or as an assignment that I had no choice but to carry out. Although I was facing an unreasonable demand, I could not or would not dare refuse to comply with it, as I yearned to be professionally respected. Anxious upon my arrival in Bhairahawa, and throughout my stay, to "demonstrate professional competence" (Mosse 2005: 26)[4] and to be acknowledged as a professional gender consultant, I may have thought that writing a report and budget estimate were part of what was expected of me in my professional capacity. The fact that my fieldnotes do not mention any reluctance on my part concerning the unexpected demand can be explained as a denial, and as a means of maintaining my self-esteem. This understanding follows Herta Nöbauer's (2002) claim that self-denial strategies serve as a means to retain self-esteem in professionally structured power relations between men and women.[5] Moreover, following Beate Krais (1993: 172–73), Nöbauer (studying the academic sphere) argues that denial emerges from the "structural violence and symbolic violence women are confronted with in their working-relationships (Nöbauer 2002: 121).

The point to be stressed here is that potential violent behavior is embedded in all bureaucratic frameworks (Marx 1976). However, power differentials and the violent potential within organizations are closely connected to their gendered structure, as Kathy Ferguson (1984) suggests. The power structures of "bureaucratic capitalist society" are the "primary source of the oppression of women and men" (ibid.: ix) and "a machine in which everyone is caught, those who exercise power just as much as those over whom it is exercised" (Foucault 1972: 156). Nevertheless, the prominence of gender perspectives in power structures, which are revealed in my case study, demonstrates the role of "femininity as subordination" (Ferguson 1984: 92–99) in bureaucratic settings. It follows, as Ferguson argues, that "as long as there are groups of people who hold institutionalized undemocratic power over others, femininity will continue to be a trait that characterizes the subordinate populations" (ibid.: 122). Thus, my silent compliance with unreasonable demands imposed on me by Tahal through its representative—such as providing a report that was not needed—serve as an example of the "feminine" component of subordination in organizations.

Gender Consultants Accommodating to the Power of Men

Working on the budget entailed a process of deconstructing Fenster's categories and emphases, dividing activities into sub-sections, and calculating them in local money. Anita, who was a very practical and knowledgeable person, and familiar with the value of money and other essential information about alternative options, was very helpful in the process. My personal input into the revised cost estimate mainly concerned emphasizing vocational training such as agricultural training, small enterprises such as handicraft production, and a suggestion that economic activities be allocated similar sums to those given to the literacy classes.

However, the most significant change that I introduced into the budget was a substantial reduction in the total cost when compared to Fenster's own budget. Fenster's total proposed budget was about $440,000, and was calculated on the basis of 300 groups of women (about 9,000 women altogether) taking literacy classes. In my own cost estimate I reduced the budget to approximately $290,000, for the same 300 groups. Fenster allocated $300,000 for what she labelled vaguely as "development packages." As indicated earlier (see Chapter 3), this vagueness was instrumental in blurring the fact that literacy classes were the core of the whole program and budget. Thus, Fenster allocated the sum of about $300,000 out of the total $440,000 to literacy classes. Fenster's other major allocations were $15,000 for wages (for thirty WGOs and two WOs), $18,000 for gender workshops, and $60,000 for animal husbandry training (which was the only economic activity included in her budget). Fenster did not include village teachers' wages in her budget, while in mine $58,000 were allocated for the wages of thirty WGOs, two WOs, and 300 village teachers.

In my budget, I allocated the sum of $131,000 to economic activities; that is, nearly half of the total amount. Thus, $80,000 were allocated for sewing training, $34,000 for the economic activities fund, and $17,000 for the handicraft project. I indicated earlier that Fenster effectively disregarded women villagers' demands regarding economic resources, and suggested that this might betray her inadvertent compliance with her employers' expectations that the women's program should concentrate on literacy training (see Chapter 3).

The way in which the budget shrank in the process of revising Fenster's proposal offers further evidence of compliance with employees' expectations. Unknowingly, I became an accomplice, cooperating with the explicit and implicit expectations of

Tahal, my employer, on whom I depended heavily for my professional acknowledgement. I was unaware of the compelling control behind "innocent" casual comments (mainly expressed by Leon) and of my vulnerable situation (Nöbauer 2002: 119).[6] It appears that I inadvertently served Tahal's interests (and those of the local irrigation project heads) by significantly reducing the original budget, which the World Bank allocated for women's benefit. Thus, in practice, I served to legitimize the devaluation of women's expectations and to deprive them of potential economic resources. Hence, I was a "reluctant accomplice" (ibid.: 119), cautiously criticizing male patterns. Nevertheless, I adapted to them. In doing so, I "not only continue[d] to update traditional sex roles, but also, contribute[d] to a male dominated [academic] culture based on paternalism" (ibid.: 121).

My cooptation into the male dominated irrigation company provides what is for me an irritating example for Vilfredo Pareto's explication of "co-optation" (Pareto 1991) in the gender sphere.[7] Pareto argued that absorbing leaders of excluded groups into the ruling elite serves to perpetuate the existing power structure. In the gender context, feminist scholars have discussed co-optation as a patriarchal strategy, which enables a few women to be integrated into leadership positions of mainstream institutions, while excluding and discriminating women collectively (e.g., Ferguson 1984; Acker 1992; Chatty and Rabo 1997; Murthy 1999; Nöbauer 2002). Kathy Ferguson argues that individual women's success in "mov[ing] up in the organizational world often provides both material and social rewards for individual women … but there is nothing particularly feminist and certainly nothing radical about them" (Ferguson 1984: ix). Murthy points to the tendency of women's NGOs to "strike bargains with patriarchal structures" (Murthy 1999: 177). Organizations do not change as a result of few women's entrance into leading positions, neither can it promote women's equal opportunities, as liberal feminism has advocated (Ferguson 1984: 4).

Enjoying economic and social benefits while adhering to my employers' expectations to provide useless reports in my capacity as gender consultant, I clearly embodied the co-opted feminist professional.[8] Ferguson argues that people often resist the demands of an organization and "their resistance is either penalized or coopted, and they face real suppression if they lose" (ibid.: 19). Moreover, compliance is not based on "habit or the routinization of choice. Obedience is enforced" (ibid.: 19). Citing Gray and Roberts-Gray's study of bureaucratic compliance (Gray and Roberts-Gray 1979), Ferguson concludes that "enforcing agents plus sanctions for compliance are major contributors to the power of bureaucratic rules" (Ferguson 1984: 218 n.43).

Although I adapted reluctantly to the dictates of the project's males staff, I became the accomplice who cooperates with hegemonic power in order to prevent sanctions, to ensure personal benefits, and to avoid hassle.

Stimulating Hopes, Providing Vague Promises

I began to be aware of problems regarding the budget one week after my arrival at the irrigation project site, when I showed a draft cost estimate to Pandit. He made a few comments regarding aspects he thought were missing from the budget. Following a short discussion about hiring another coordinator (Anita was the only coordinator employed at that time), Pandit unwillingly approved the additional coordinator in the proposed budget. I explained that introducing 300 groups of village women to the project, within a short time span, made it crucial that another coordinator be employed. Pandit concluded: "It is up to Thapa to decide." At the time I did not pay much attention to this comment. I continued to discuss with him the cost estimate, and urged his cooperation in facilitating the implementation of the women's project. In retrospect it seems that Pandit was gently, but nevertheless firmly, suggesting, that he had no power to make significant decisions and that the right person to turn to was Thapa. Assuming that because he was the person in charge of the village group organizers and coordinators Pandit, had the power to make things work in the field, I failed to register his message.

Thapa played his part, convincingly reassuring me that the women's project had realistic prospects. This was revealed in a meeting with the representatives of a health NGO. Thapa told the visitors, who were eager to obtain a substantial part of the budget for health training included in the women's project, that the president of the World Bank was interested in projects for women and, therefore, there should be no problem of money. He mentioned the World Bank's financial commitment to women's advancement so as to reassure the health professionals that their efforts in "adjusting" (that is, reducing) their proposed training cost estimate to our demands would pay off eventually. At that point, apparently, Thapa needed to present the women's project as imminent and viable. Pandit, who attended the meeting, translated Thapa's reassuring sentences (which were spoken in Nepali) to me, probably with the intention of softening the impression made by his evasive response at our meeting the day before.

The pragmatic approach presented at the meeting by Lama, head of the irrigation project's agricultural division, was further cause for optimism in relation to the project. Lama suggested improving the village women's skills in growing garden vegetables, thus contributing to the improvement of nutritional standards. He said, "Women do 70 per cent of all agricultural work, except for the ploughing. We can also train women how to store seeds. A short training course can solve the problem. Varieties of trees, such as eucalyptus, and skills such as planting, are other topics suitable for women's training." Lama went on with other practical suggestions for women's training which could be incorporated into the village groups' activities. He also elaborated on facilitating sewage collection for the purpose of household gas production. Lama explained that such enterprises necessitated setting up groups in order to obtain a 75 per cent subsidy from the Agricultural Development Bank of Nepal. He stated that his department did not have enough workers to provide agricultural training for 300 groups of women.

However, specifying this number of women's groups implied a formal acknowledgement of the project's scope and targeted population. Consequently, the budget prospects were made to sound more realistic and tangible.

Indeed Thapa's negotiations with the health people clearly suggested that he took the women's project most seriously. This meeting, therefore, encouraged me to think that the irrigation project's heads were serious about their stated intentions and that the budget, even if modified, would serve as a solid basis for the implementation of the women's project.

Disillusionment Sets In: The Gradual Revealing of Real Intentions

The slim hope I tried to hold on to turned out to be an illusion. Three days later, on the day I travelled to Kathmandu, I was intensely occupied with improving the final version of the cost estimate. I was extremely anxious to submit it to Thapa for approval, after which the budget was to be sent to his superiors in the Ministry of Agriculture for review. Only then could the budget be sent on to the World Bank for its directors' final approval. As I depended on Raju, Leon's secretary, to type up the cost estimate for me, I became nervous when I found out that he was preoccupied with preparing Leon's monthly report for Tahal. Raju started to work on my revised budget proposal only at midday, just about the time when I had to get ready to leave for the airport. By that time, I realized that there was no chance that the budget proposal would be ready before I left. Nevertheless, I asked Raju to fax the revised version to me at Leon's home in Kathmandu. As soon as I arrived in the city, I went to Leon's house, hoping to find the budget proposal waiting for me there. To my disappointment, the revised budget had not arrived. I phoned Leon in his Bhairahawa office to find out why the budget had not been sent out. He explained that it was too late to do any more work, and that, "in any case, Thapa is about to leave Bhairahawa tomorrow and, therefore, he will have no time to go over the budget proposal. Moreover, it is important that the two of us go over the budget very carefully. Besides, Raju is very busy at the moment with my monthly report." I did not give up and insisted that it was most important that Raju finish working on my budget that day. I explained that I had to receive the corrected text, in order that I send it out for final alterations the next morning, just in time to hand the completed version to Thapa before he left Nepal. Leon acceded to my demand reluctantly. At 7 P.M., when Hanna and I returned from the garden party at the Shangri-La Hotel, the retyped, corrected budget was slowly coming out of the fax machine.

The following day, beginning early in the morning, I made several revisions to the budget, which I faxed at different intervals to the office in Bhairahawa in an attempt to persuade Leon to forward the budget to Thapa before his departure. Yet I was constantly met with criticisms of the budget and delaying tactics, until finally Leon reluctantly agreed to transmit the revised budget to Thapa. Returning to the office in Bhairahawa on Sunday afternoon, I continued to work with Raju on correcting the budget draft. The next day I worked with Anita on translating the costings into Nepali rupees and incorporating additional minor articles. She suggested changing the budget proposal's title to include women's development, which I willingly accepted. Leon was sitting nearby, studying the budget vigilantly and succeeded in finding a spelling mistake.

The next phase of the budget negotiating process began a short while after copies of it were distributed to Thapa, Gupta, and Pandit. Gupta entered our office a couple of hours after receiving my budget proposal. He made a few marginal comments to start with, and then presented his main concern over the proposed budget: "The project you suggest is not applicable. Its scope is too extensive for implementation. I told Tovi the same thing. In her project plan she related only to the dimension of the targeted population and much less to the operational capacity of the irrigation project people." He went on, pointing out to me that the 300 groups of women referred to in my budget did not exist in the irrigation project area. He added:

> Originally the total number of the project irrigation locales was 182 tube wells. As ten project locales were shut down, because the farmers were not interested in irrigation services from the wells, only 172 organized groups of farmers remained active around the tube well irrigation services. Thus, in fact only about half the amount of active farmers' groups, which Tovi Fenster and you refer to, exist. It would be very nice if we could generate half of the number of women's groups you propose.

Gupta was guilty of manipulating the numbers, since even if the "correct" number of groups was 172, this was still over half of the 300 groups in both Fenster's and my own cost estimates. He was clearly suggesting that the proposed budget was incorrect. In an attempt to convince him that the budget was reasonable, I replied:

> Implementing an ambitious project such as ours necessitates substantial funding. We need to take into account that some adjustments and changes will take place. We may, for example, decide that some of the groups will not receive literacy training but will rather be offered sewing training [which was supposed to take place only after the first phase of literacy training ended]; money will be needed for such changes.

This kind of response clearly reflects the self-justifying approach I assumed, facing the officials' decisive reservations. At this point in time I was almost begging Gupta and the other senior officials to take the women's program seriously.

The most dramatic event in the chronology of budget negotiations occurred that same night at the bachelor house, when Leon and I were chatting over dinner. Leon said:

> I am not the worst of sceptics, yet I am a sceptical person, and I cannot foresee the project being realized. They [officials at both local and national levels] all count on this budget for traveling overseas. Tovi's budget was huge and I let my superiors know what I thought of it at the time. Your budget and program for action are more serious and thorough, but I do not see how I can sign on a budget proposal of $300,000, which does not have any chance from Tahal's point of view. You should know that Tahal's plans are based on a project estimation of $400,000, half of which must be allocated for paying consultants and the maintenance of the tube wells.
>
> You see, everything [in the irrigation project] will fail or succeed on two things, marketing and maintenance of wells. Moreover, the planning of the irrigation project involved a serious fault. It did not take into account the limited extent of farmers' demand for the wells' water. If we had known from the beginning that the utilization of the wells' water would be so low, the depth of digging could have been reduced to a quarter [of what was dug] because the smaller amount of land [drawing water from the wells] would need a much smaller supply of water for adequate coverage. Consequently, the construction of roads, to facilitate the access of trucks to the well sites, would not be required and would not have been wasted on farmers, who are used to walking in the mud all their lives. There would also be no need to set up the electricity system, which was planned with the purpose of facilitating the full-scale irrigation plan of the whole project area.

As Leon was talking about the problems of the irrigation project—and inadvertently admitting to its failure[9]—I finally realized that neither he nor Tahal were genuinely interested in the ambitions of the women's program. I was stunned to find out that sending me to Nepal had little to do with actual aspirations for advancing women, whether in the spheres of vocational, agricultural, economic, or literacy training. At best, so I realized, the irrigation project's partners might accept the implementation of small bits and pieces of the women's development project, which would require only a small portion of its (allegedly) intended budget.

I was reflecting on this revelation when Leon said suddenly: "You look shocked." I quietly replied:

> I am only contemplating. My working assumption, which followed Fenster's budget proposal, was that the women's development project was allocated some $400,000. Tahal gave me Fenster's report and no one hinted that there was any other working assumption. Had I been told that it was a $50,000 project I would have dealt with the budget proposal accordingly. I think that this can even be described as deceit.

Leon said, "But I told you several times that the budget must cover the expenses of all the projects, not only the women's project." I replied, "You said at Thapa's office that the World Bank allocated the money for the sake of benefiting the women and that all we need to do is to send the budget proposal to the Bank." Leon replied: "Perhaps I was not concentrating at that time and was thinking about other things that were bothering me. It is also possible that I vaguely mentioned things that made you understand me wrongly. Consider your plan as a drawer project."[10]

Leon's reply infuriated me and I responded instinctively: "I am not one for working papers and I am not ready to become part of a bluff. If I find out that this is the situation I shall go back home." He looked anxious and intimidated, replying: "You should talk first to Tahal, before taking such a step. They might even demand that you repay them the money. You should know that if you go back before the term of your employment ends it might be considered a breach of contract." Although no such sanction was mentioned in the contract which I signed with Tahal, Leon succeeded in making me nervous, and I replied, "I certainly do not want to pay back any money but I do not want to be a part of a bluff." At the same time my threat to quit upset Leon very much. He threatened me, probably because he panicked, as a result of the trouble I might create. Leon tried then to soften the tone, and said:

> You see for yourself that people here [in Bhairahawa] are interested in implementing the project, you said that Anita and Pandit are interested. The World Bank is also interested in the project, as you said. So there are at least two positive parties, and perhaps a third one [i.e., Sonderman, Thapa's superior, head of the development department in the Ministry of Agriculture] would also approve the project. I can openly tell you that I could possibly approve a budget of $150,000. I simply know people around here so well; it takes them months to do things. Sometimes you have to sleep things over. I always discuss problematic situations with Hanna [Leon's wife], and she tells me that I have not come to save Nepal.

Leon then changed the subject and we talked about Gupta's claim concerning the number of groups involved in the irrigation project area. Leon said that Gupta's evaluation of the number of existing farmers' groups scattered around the tube wells was wrong. In any case, there was no direct connection between the 182 (or 172) wells in the project area and the potential number of organized women's groups.

It became clear that I, like my predecessor, unknowingly served as "a cog" (Weber 1978: 105) in the money-spinning machine that rolled budgets between the World Bank, Tahal, and the Nepali government. The irrigation project's parties concealed from me their intentions for as long as it was possible to avoid telling me the truth. Thus, I discovered bits of information gradually, only when Leon had no choice but to reveal some of the facts behind the contradictory and inconsistent messages I was receiving. It slowly became clear that the women's project budget was the subject of the rival claims of both the Israeli and Nepali partners in the irrigation project. The first hoped to use some $200,000 of the budget for remunerating their "more important" irrigation consultants and for paying for "the maintenance of the tube wells." The latter counted on the budget for traveling overseas.

Thus, it appeared that both parties were actively attempting to divert most of the budget to finance their preferred options; they may even have possibly intended to leave a small sum of money for the women's activities, to keep up an appearance of really implementing the women's project. Leon was well aware of the immorality of this conduct, as his quoting of Hanna implied. Hanna told him, so he said, that he did not "come to save Nepal," meaning that he did not have responsibility for changing the situation (of the country, of corrupt politicians, and so on). Her words implied he should rather look after his own interests and mind his own business. Suggesting that I adopt this attitude made it easier for him to ignore the moral ramifications of his part in the subterfuge regarding the women's budget. It follows that waiving responsibility serves in personal contexts, no less than it does in the public sphere, to accommodate organizational failures and deceitful conduct to ongoing activity and to one's peace of mind.[11]

Men's Games: Power, Aggression, and Devaluing Women's Issues

Shocked, hurt, and suddenly aware that I had been misled, I exposed my vulnerability and humiliation in a spontaneous, childish, feminine way, declaring that if I could not have what I had been promised I would break the rules of the game and leave. This, indeed, was the reaction of a weak, vulnerable person who felt powerless and cheated. Leon clearly provoked this immature, unbusinesslike reaction—my refusal to comply with my role in the game as a well-paid report producer. He reprimanded me for forgetting "facts," for not remembering things he had told me "a few times". He used evasive excuses for his contradictory messages (saying that he was preoccupied by things that were "bothering" him) and even threatened me by hinting at the possible implications of breaking my contract with Tahal. Leon also devalued my work, suggesting that I should consider it a "drawer project." By saying that I was not the kind of person who delivered "working papers," I was responding to Leon's implied lack of respect for my professionalism. My reply also reflects the realization that I was being used by Tahal.

This game has another angle: the irrigation project officials preferred to distance themselves from responsibility for problematic situations by transferring that responsibility to others. Avoiding responsibility for unsolvable difficulties that their clients or employers present, by involving others in sharing responsibility for those problematic situations, is a feature of bureaucratic settings (Handelman 1980).[12] Yet, the avoidance of personal responsibility also takes place inside organizations, by involving officials from varying positions and ranks. Thus, officials tend to ensure that when they take risky or problematic decisions they are supported by more senior colleagues. (Hertzog 2004).[13] This tactic was mentioned earlier in relation to Pandit and Gupta, who used to end discussions with me by remarking: "Thapa is the one who makes decisions." Similarly, Leon blamed the Nepali officials, "the people here," as responsible for delays and the dwindling chances of carrying out the women's project. However, when forced to do so by my emotional explosion, he revealed his active role in undermining my attempts to finalize the budget.

The power struggles surrounding the budget reflected the embedded gendered power relations within the context of the irrigation project. This was apparent in the relative importance attributed to the "women's project," as compared to the "men's" irrigation project. Leon's remark that the irrigation project's failure or success depended on the "marketing and maintenance of wells," and Gupta's comment that "this is an irrigation project" that has nothing to do with women's issues, as well as other comments, implied clearly that the women's project was not perceived by them as "really" important.

Gendered power differentials were also apparent in informal, personal encounters. Leon treated me as a weaker, harmless partner whom he could manipulate. He was not impressed by my "feminine" emotional explosion (cynically suggesting I consider my proposal a "drawer project"), and only when I appeared to be able to exercise some form of resistance (by threatening to quit) did he change his attitude. At that point, when he realized my determination to assert my power, Leon brought up some new (misleading) information. Whereas he initially suggested that the women's project could have a maximum budget of $50,000, following my ultimatum he raised the figure to $150,000, an amount which he "might approve."

The gendered power game, played out against the backdrop of the irrigation project, suggests that the budget was bargaining chip; the more one succeeded in presenting oneself as powerful, the better were one's chances of promoting one's interests. As a male-dominated site, the power game that took place within and around the irrigation project meant that men's rules dictated the social dynamic. In this ongoing game, actors were constantly trying to strengthen their positions and acquire benefits. They would use cynicism, lies, promises, devaluation, bribery, and avoiding taking responsibility in problematic situations to improve their chances.

Reliance on contracts is an institutionally formalized means used by those in power to exercise control and impose obedience. Marta Callas and Linda Smircich (1992) argue that the power of contracts to establish control over employees emerges from male dominance in organizations. They contend that the concept of commitment in the organizational context implies that individuals are subordinated to the organization. This conception of commitment is "tied to a concept of domination and control—culture over nature—associated with male rationality since the philosophies of the Enlightenment" (ibid.: 230). The role of the contract in my Nepali experience demonstrates the instrumental use of contracts at points of crisis, when a serious conflict between employer and employee rises. Failing to perform loyally and comply with my employers' expectations, even if justified by professional or moral commitments, was used as a means to threaten me. In fact, Leon used my contract to threaten me with possible sanctions (paying back money), to impose obedient cooperation, and to silence my criticism. My contract contained only one short article that related to the anticipated outcomes of my consultancy. An article setting out "general commitments" stated that "the worker is committed to perform loyally and with her best professional knowledge and experience her services to Tami (Tahal Engineers Consultants) within the spheres of the subject." Although no specific sanction was mentioned in my contract it appears that the vague term "loyalty" can be instrumentally used against "disloyal" employees. I assume that Leon was hinting at this when he warned me against breaking the terms of my contract.

"Drawer projects" is another term that illustrates the power of organizations in this power-constructed complex. To store a project in a drawer implies its uselessness, but it also implies that the project can be cancelled and its failure concealed, thus enabling those who initiated it not to be held accountable for its failure or redundancy.

Reacting emotionally to Leon's insult, feeling humiliated, and retreating from the power game can be perceived as my idiosyncratic reaction to the situation. However, it is reasonable to attribute this behavior to gendered socialization and prevailing power structures. This argument gains support from a number of studies that point to the extensive role played by political, economic, and cultural forces in fostering gendered power relations, which are revealed at personal, community, and state levels (e.g., MacCormack and Strathern 1980; Collier and Yanagisako 1987; Moore 1988; Hodgson 2001). Until the 1970s, organizational theories related mainly to the study of male society (Acker and Van Houten 1992: 16). Organization theory presented a gender-blind picture of organizations, and was "constructed as non-gendered. Written through a male perspective, culture and discourse, [organization theory] has espoused theories of empiricism, rationality, hierarchy and other masculinized concepts. In this way organization theory has been implicitly gendered" (Hearn and Parkin 1983: 149). Moreover, it appears that gender blindness has not vanished in up-to-date studies of organizations. Thus, for example, in his recent study of kibbutz leadership, Reuven Shapira (2008) offers a critical and comprehensive analysis of kibbutz research while completely ignoring any gender perspective.

Feminist studies on organizations since the 1970s have revealed the gendered elements of organizations. Joan Acker argues that "hierarchies are gendered and that gender and sexuality have a central role in the reproduction of hierarchies" (Acker 1992: 253). Ralf Lange argues further that, "structures, processes, practices and actors in organizations are always connected with hegemonic forms of masculinity" (Lange 1997: 114).[14] Similarly, Mats Alvesson and Yvonne Billing (1997) argue that masculinity is an inherent constant of organizations.

Becoming Part of the System: A Co-opted Feminist

My emotional reaction to Leon's remarks demonstrates Acker's claim that the "emotionality of women [is] outside organizational boundaries" (Acker 1992: 259).[15] It follows that resisting the implications of the objections to implementing the women's project by emotionally expressing my anger and humiliation could have no impact on my superiors and on the women's project's prospects. Therefore, I could either conform or retreat (Ferguson 1990: 19). I preferred to adjust myself to the compelling dictates that were forcefully unveiled.

In the dramatic encounter, Leon played the part of the "instrumental" (ibid.: 93) male in control and I assumed the part of the vulnerable, subordinate female. As I did not return to Israel, despite my threats, I adopted an idealist's stance, while complying, in practice, with the men's expectations and their perception of the situation. I argued continuously with Thapa and other irrigation project officials, trying to convince them of the potential advantages of the women's project. I put continual pressure on Thapa, in particular, urging him to facilitate the completion of the draft budget, although he was obviously stalling and causing repeated delays. Gupta was another person whose objections to the budget I tried to overcome and whose cooperation I desperately tried to gain. As Tahal's employee, Gupta seemed to associate himself with the company's interests more than other high-ranking officials who, except for Anita, were directly subordinate to Thapa. It was evident that Gupta was respected by both Thapa and Leon. My efforts, therefore, were directed at inspiring Gupta to support the budget.

The day after Gupta remarked that the number of women's groups outlined in my budget was unrealistic, I entered his room and tried to shift him from his antagonistic position. He calmly repeated his arguments and I, similarly, repeated my own. I said, "If the money is spent, more money will come in because the gender issue is 'in' now in the World Bank and in Nepal as well, if we are to infer from politicians' statements and from the numerous projects for women implemented by NGOs."[16] To convince Gupta further I referred to the context of Israeli local government, where "those mayors who spend beyond their approved budgets are rewarded with bigger budgets, whereas those who stick to their approved budgets are punished by cutting down their subsequent annual budget." Gupta was not impressed and did not change his mind. He patiently explained that the money was not a gift but rather a loan that must be repaid, "therefore those in charge are not keen on spending the money which they will need to repay." I asked what the rate of interest was and he said, "There is no interest to be paid, but the loan has to be repaid and that is why the heads of the irrigation project hesitate to spend it." When I asked why the Nepali government had not told the World Bank that they did not want the loan, he replied carefully: "No one would tell you this but the government is interested in the loan for other purposes, mainly for developing infrastructure.[17] But the Bank demands that they use the loan for women's advancement projects too. If it were for free they would take the money and spend it without hesitation."

Gupta also mentioned the pressure the World Bank applied, which he (like Leon) conceived as effective in getting things done. He also showed me the Bank's report on its delegation's visit to Ekala, pointing to the Bank's explicit satisfaction with the progress made in the women's project. Gupta was convinced that hiring Anita was a result of the Bank's pressures, but seemed to point to the issue of the World Bank's pressure in order to divert attention from his own and other local officials' responsibility, and from their objections to the women's project. In a way, he was suggesting that the World Bank was the right party to turn to, since only if the Bank demanded the implementation of the project firmly enough could things work. Indeed, as I have argued in previous chapters, the Ekala story did not demonstrate any substantial achievement in implementing the project, and, therefore, the Bank's pressures could hardly be seen as highly effective. Moreover, the pressure applied by the Bank to hire a new local gender consultant (Anita) and foreign gender consultants (Fenster and myself) worked out only because Tahal was deeply interested in hiring the local and expatriate gender consultants, as employing consultants provided Tahal with its main profits. Therefore, Tahal acceded to the World Bank's demands and itself put pressure on the Nepali officials.

Thus, I conclude that becoming part of the system was unavoidable. Despite the humiliation I was subjected to, and my awareness of the deceitful manner in which the women's project was viewed by those working for the irrigation project, I did not dare return home nor attempt any practical measures against Tahal. The shame of being marked a failure, the possible loss of money, and more besides, prevented me from taking a radical step. Consequently, I adopted "masculinized" (Hearn and Parkin 1983: 149) strategies like manipulative bargaining and instrumentally collaborating with officials to help me return home with my peace of mind and professional esteem relatively intact.

Manipulating Facts and Figures

The information Gupta unintentionally disclosed in our encounter revealed the extent of manipulation by project officials. According to the World Bank's report (issued following the Bank's delegation's visit to the irrigation project in 1996), which he showed me, the potential number of women's groups in the irrigation project area was 900. This number would mean some 27,000 women of working age attending the planned literacy classes. The target population of the irrigation project is well established in Fenster's report (Fenster 1996). Drawing on the 1990 district profile of Rupandehi, she reported that: "in 1992, the population in the Project area consisted some 86,000 people. Women consisted 49% of the total population i.e., 42,500 out of which some 27,000 are at the age between 10–65. This is the target puplation of this plan. This number consists of some 770 women groups (taken 35 women per group)" (ibid.: 17).

This information indicates that Gupta, like other heads of the irrigation project, was well aware of the basic facts, such as the number of women and of women's groups that could be considered as potential participants in the women's project. It follows that when Gupta criticized my budget, arguing that my calculations concerning the number of potential groups to be included in the women's project were unrealistic and did not correspond with the precincts of the tube wells, he deliberately misled me.

However, it appears that Gupta was not the only one to twist the facts to suit his argument and his employer's needs, for so too did other heads of the irrigation project. Thapa and Leon in particular also ignored the demographic data and stuck to the figure of 300 women's groups as the relevant figure in our discussions. Evidently the smaller the number of groups, the smaller was the required budget. Indeed, funding 900 groups instead of 300 would have meant multiplying the sums of money for the women's project. Hence, negotiating with me over the number of women's groups to be included in the women's project was the main tactic Leon and Gupta employed in order to reduce the sum allocated for women's activities in my budget. This maneuver was unveiled in a discussion with Leon, a short while after speaking with Gupta.

Entering his office, Leon said, with evident satisfaction, that he had heard from Gupta that I had agreed to reduce the number of women's groups to be included in my program. I replied spontaneously and decisively: "No way. I definitely have not agreed to any such thing. In fact I even noticed in the World Bank's report, which Gupta showed me, that there is the potential for 900 groups in the irrigation project area." Leon panicked and said: "There are not 900 groups. They [the Bank's people] relied on Tovi [Fenster]'s proposal, which mentions the figure of 27,000." I insisted that, "Nevertheless, they [the Bank people] speak of 900 groups and I cannot see how any other figure can be substituted as a basic assumption for the budget proposal."

Thus, two main figures were discussed and negotiated: 300 and 900. It should be noted that by this time my budget proposal was based on 300 groups (as I mentioned earlier), which I either took for granted, following Fenster's budget, when I began working on the budget, or adopted because I was not in a position to voice my objection.

This vagueness concerning the elementary data necessary for producing a budget is rather striking. No less surprising is the fact that I had not noticed the conspicuously different figures until my irritating encounters with Gupta and Leon, which took place at a rather late stage of my stay. Moreover, there appears to be an inconsistency in Fenster's proposal between her budget and her report in respect to these two figures. The number of women's groups she took into account in her budget was only 300, whereas the data she presented in her report indicated a "target population" potentially three times larger. Fenster explains this discrepancy with reference to the time constraints imposed on the women project's implementation schedule. She writes:

> The Project ends in December 1998. This is a very limited time for incorporating all women in this program, and thus we suggest to

> incorporate at least half of the target population, that is, 10,000 women farmers in 300 groups, until the end of 1998, and to enable local women already trained to disseminate the knowledge obtained in the project training to other women in the area. (ibid.: 17)

However, it seems that Fenster's basic target population was reduced by two thirds—from 27,000 to 10,000—and not by half, as she suggests. Moreover, Fenster's idea of disseminating knowledge to women through the mediation of other trained women who would had not enrolled in the program, while initially intriguing, is vague and unrealistic when seriously examined. How can women who took one literacy class disseminate their knowledge to others?

The fact that my proposal suggested training the same number of groups the following year (by the end of 1998) meant that by then some 600 groups could already have completed literacy training (the first 300 would have finished their training by the end of 1997). In other words, the time limitation was not necessarily the real explanation for not including many more women's groups in the women's project. It is probable that the final figures proposed in Fenster's budget (300 groups) were the outcome of pressures put on her to modify her plan of action (770), just like the pressures that were exerted on me. In fact, while discussing with me the alleged need to reduce the number of groups, Gupta mentioned discussions he had had with Fenster. Modifying Fenster's scope of the women's project was crucial because, as suggested above, it facilitated a dramatic reduction in the size of the budget. It also established a better starting point for future negotiations with me. Thus, by taking Fenster's budget for granted, and determining the figure of 300 groups as a self-evident baseline for my budget, I unwittingly contributed to a further reduction of the budget in later negotiations.

Another point of interest is the World Bank's role in the bargaining over the number of groups to be included in the project. The women's project was scheduled to end in December 1998, whereas Fenster's proposal was submitted in October 1996. As the Bank leadership must have been aware of the large scope of the women's project (as revealed in the report that Gupta showed me), it is surprising that the project's termination date was so tightly fixed. However, this might indicate that the Bank was only superficially interested in the women's project, mainly in order to convey the impression of doing things for the benefit of women. Project proposals and reports about the "successful" women's project were, apparently, sufficient to satisfy the Bank.

Once I became aware of the diminishing likelihood of either the approval of the budgetary or the implementation of the women's project, and after confronting Leon's and Gupta's growing antagonism to my budget, as well as realizing that Thapa had resisted the women's project from the start, I adopted a denial strategy. Ignoring the negative implications of Leon's and Gupta's excuses and fabrications, and Thapa's forestalling, I behaved as though business was proceeding "as usual." This strategy helped me not only to endure the humiliating and depressing situation I was trapped in, but also to resolve the moral conflict entailed in my continued stay in Nepal. It also encouraged me to believe that if I went on talking about the women's project with those in charge, I could somehow make things happen and convince them to change their attitude and allow the project to materialize.

My pragmatic adaptation to the frustrating situation, when I became fully aware of how those in charge of the irrigation project viewed the women's project, offers an example of the personal adaptation experienced by individuals who are trapped by organizational practices which they oppose. Complying with organizational goals and policies that contradict an individual's own moral standpoint is a familiar phenomenon in bureaucratic settings, as Max Weber (1948) noted long ago, and has more recently been discussed by Herbert Kelman (1973), Raoul Hilberg (1983), Zygmunt Bauman (1989), and Ariella Azulai (2000).

In my interaction with Leon, on the morning after we had our row concerning the budget, I adopted a business-as-usual attitude. While Leon was going over the budget in the office, he checked every figure very thoroughly and managed to find two minor errors. He found out that I had calculated the wage of the two coordinators at a higher rate of pay than it appeared in the budget part of Tahal's contract, and I changed the figures accordingly. Then Leon said: "Now we shall submit the budget and see if they [the Nepali partners] approve it and how much they approve. I think that they will approve around $150,000 at the most." I asked, "Is this your assumption or your position?" He replied, "I wish they would approve $500,000 but I assume they will approve only around $100,000 to $150,000."

These figures seemed to correspond with the one Leon had previously mentioned, when he revealed the fact that it was unlikely that the women's project would take off. Thus, it seemed that he was ready to compromise, and agreed that a sum of between $100,000 and $150,000 might be approved for the women's project. These figures could have reflected Leon's evaluation of what his Nepali partners in the irrigation project had in mind regarding the women's project, and more importantly in relation to the project's budget. Thus, if $150,000 out of the $400,000 budget, originally earmarked for the women's project would be used for implementing the women's program, the sum of $250,000 will be left for the irrigation project's purposes. Furthermore, if the whole $400,000 women project's budget would not be used for implementing the women's program, then the irrigation project's head will be able to use all of the money according to their priorities and needs. On the other hand, the figures could mean that Leon was taking good care of Tahal's interests, which were more likely to be served by employing experts and ensuring Tahal's high profits, rather than with underwriting a women's project which would yield a much smaller profit. I suggest that the latter explanation is the most likely. The interests of both Tahal and their Nepali partners were clearly not women-oriented, and from this perspective their preferred use (or rather misuse) of the budget were in accord.

Additional evidence for Leon's real motivation includes his manipulative attempts to reduce the budget to the minimum amount possible. This was apparent when he introduced a new minimal figure for the budget. In fact, the sum of $100,000 was mentioned here for the first time. When Leon uttered it in a casual manner—saying, "they will approve only around $100,000 to $150,000"—I failed to notice how he had managed to establish a newly reduced figure as the baseline for negotiating further reductions in the budget.

Leon made it clear on various occasions that Tahal's profits from the women's project were derived from employing Anita and myself, with extra profit derived from our per-diem expenses. This explains why Leon insisted that I seek Thapa's approval for an extra day in Kathmandu on my way home, "for the purpose of work meetings." Leon explained very clearly that it was very important, for my own sake, that I ask for the extra day in Kathmandu. "Tahal does not do anything for the sake of our beautiful eyes," he said. "You see, for every day that I stay in Kathmandu, Tahal collects its per-diem." Leon's insistence on my making two additional visits during the upcoming six months (as suggested in the project proposal and budget) also shows that hiring consultants was the most desirable activity from Tahal's point of view. This explains why, at the moment Leon realized that these visits would not be approved by Thapa, his willingness to support the women's project, or rather its budget, diminished. Thapa refused to approve both an extra day in Kathmandu on my way home and my two "working visits" to the capital in the middle of my stay. As my flight and hotel expenses, as well as Tahal's corresponding overheads, were billed to the irrigation project, it is clear why Thapa opposed agreeing to expenses that he perceived to be a squandering of "his" budget.

Interestingly, I only became aware of the existence of an earlier budget, which was part of the contract between Tahal and the World Bank, at a late stage of analyzing my fieldnotes. Noticing Leon's comment, that the coordinators' wages in the budget were "too costly," I realized that an earlier budget must have existed, one which preceded Fenster's and my own cost estimate. This earlier version of the budget—perhaps the "original" one, from Fenster's visit in 1992, mentioned in the beginning of this chapter—seemed to have specified details such as coordinators' salaries. Since a budget existed prior to both Fenster's visit in 1996 and my own in 1997, it follows that our "expertise" in preparing a budget, and even drawing up a plan for the whole women's project, was clearly not needed. We were hired by Tahal, it appears, in order to "professionalize" Tahal's entrance into the gender-activities field, and thus to establish its status as a provider of gender-expertise services, vis-à-vis the World Bank's formal commitment to, and funding of, this sphere. Graham Hancock, who discusses the manipulative and opportunistic characteristics of the development industry thoroughly, argues that it "uncannily adapts to the changing modes" of donor agencies and countries (Hancock 1989: 72). This conduct, he argues, is common to all institutions of development, as they have "a genetic trait that programs each and every one of them for survival" (ibid.: 72).[18]

Hiring Anita and myself improved Tahal's profit-making capacity by extending their ability to claim against the irrigation project for overheads and per-diem allowances. That is to say, Tahal took advantage of the commitment (genuine or not) of the World Bank to improve the lot of women in developing countries by providing gender consultants, who enabled them to obtain some extra profit at a point close to the termination of Tahal's involvement in the irrigation project.

The "real" total sum of the budget was an obscure figure. Its vague and flexible character served the negotiations over it and efforts to minimize it. Yet, the budget sometimes seemed to be much higher than the amounts previously discussed. One encounter with Leon in the office illustrates this. Leon seemed to feel uncomfortable about my dawning awareness of the facts behind the budget, and one day I watched him nervously searching through his files. Eventually he found a letter that he had sent to Tahal in response to Fenster's budget. In the letter Leon claimed that he had found a conspicuous inconsistency between her budget and a proposal submitted by an NGO (probably geared to carrying out "development packages"). According to his calculations, as detailed in the letter, incorporating the NGO's budget proposal into Fenster's "cost estimation" should have resulted in a total budget twice that of the one she submitted. Adding Tahal's overheads (10 per cent), the total sum of her budget should have been nearly $800,000! In his letter, Leon claimed that this wrongly calculated budget involved "big money," and he demanded that Fenster account for this. He said in frustration that he had never received a reply to this letter from his superiors.

Despite the confusing messages, and the discrepant figures of budget negotiations, this episode further reveals that Tahal's interests lay with the hiring of local and foreign consultants. Quite clearly, as Tahal could make more profit from a project with a bigger budget, it would have been in its interest to make sure that it materialized.

The confusion over the budget affair caused me to overlook the information Leon had revealed. While I was completely occupied with my struggle to get approval for at least part of the budget and to see it put to work, I missed the implications of what Leon had said. I could not resist the temptation of using the opportunity to point out the advantage of my own budget, indicating that it was reasonable and moderate, and saying that, "my budget is the lowest, to the extent that it undermines the women's project's goals." Unsurprisingly, Leon was not impressed by my remark. Caught up in his own worries, he repeated his line from the previous day: "This money must ensure experts' remuneration and the tube wells' maintenance." Hence, mesmerized by the belief that I could "save" the women's project by agreeing to a reduced budget, I missed the significance of what Leon had said.

The budget for the women's project did not involve, it seems, a closed, finalized, and agreed-upon figure. The funds could have come out of the irrigation project's budget, or extra funds could have been negotiated with the World Bank. Support for the first possibility comes from Leon's claim that the budget had to cover several projects, and not just the gender activities project. This implies that no definite budget had been earmarked for women's activities. Consequently, all options were open for negotiation and for ongoing efforts to advance competing interests. Thus, the vagueness of the women's project's budget enabled the Nepali and Tahal's officials to negotiate over the budget for the women's project in the light of their own competing interests. Meanwhile, the World Bank could play the role of an innocent party, passing the ball into the Nepali court, suggesting that they were the ones who should be responsible for decisions about the use of the budget for the sake of "their" women.

In light of these exchanges concerning the size of the budget, Leon's insistence on the accuracy and consistency of the budget as a whole and of every minor detail within it seemed to be confusing, not to say banal. Moreover, he inadvertently revealed the hidden agenda behind the budget negotiations, while relating to the budget as a highly important and "real" document (a concrete "work plan"). This contradictory attitude could reflect Leon's need to convince me that the women's project was genuine and that my efforts were not in vain, thus ensuring that I would cause no trouble. Another possibility is that the contradiction emerged from Leon's need to ease his conscience, as he was, in some way, aware of his participation in a deceitful project. A simple and trivial explanation might also be posited, namely that Leon did not have much work on his hands, and that scrutinizing the budget's smallest details provided him with a seemingly serious activity. This explanation suits my general impression of his daily routine in the office, and it also accords with his eagerness to join us on our visits to the villages.

Coping with Confusing Messages and Stalling Tactics

The confusing and contradictory messages concerning the approval of the budget, and consequently the implementation of the women's project, continued until the end of my stay in Bhairahawa. Thapa's attitude, in particular, was puzzling. After many days of stalling and avoiding my appeals, suddenly he responded eagerly to the budget proposal, making decisions and encouraging me to finish work on the final revisions. Depressed and anxious about the fading chances of the budget's approval, Thapa's positive attitude was warmly accepted by me and inspired new hopes.

Eight days before I left Nepal, Thapa invited Leon and I into his office to discuss the budget proposal. He stated that the Nepali party to the women's project would not pay for Anita's professional training, traveling, or other expenses, because she was Tahal's employee. He added, cynically, that he did not care if Tahal decided to hire more local consultants at their own expense. Thapa instructed us to add the health NGO's proposal to the budget. He explained that the option of training the WGOs as health instructors made the NGO's proposal appealing, even though it meant that the WGOs would be paid more for their services. More money should be allocated for books, he said, and for the village teachers' additonal training. He then announced that should I revise the budget by the following day he would send it to his superiors in Kathmandu.

The health NGO came later on that day to Leon's office, submitting another revised version of the health program and budget. I told them that we were awaiting the approval of our budget by the World Bank. They wanted to know when would it be approved, and I replied that the first round of the health training would start, hopefully, two weeks later, in October. Leon commented in response to their question: "If it depended on me I would approve it by tomorrow. But I have been in Nepal only a year and a half, so you should know things better than me." He was sarcastically implying that Nepali officials were inefficient, and that the chances that the budget would be approved quickly and made available for paying for their services were very slim.

Later on, when Anita, Leon and I went back to Thapa's room to finalize our discussion of the budget, I asked Thapa if it would be possible to purchase bicycles for the WGOs, who had to walk long distances to the villages and to the irrigation project site. Thapa replied: "I would like to do that but I cannot, as long as the budget has not been approved. Anyway, I suggested purchasing the bicycles for the WGOs and taking the cost off their monthly salaries, but they refused." I also asked him about purchasing the 900 books for the women in the literacy classes, and he promised to deal with the issue the next morning. That night I worked until late, adjusting the budget to meet Thapa's specifications.

The next morning, Raju diligently incorporated Thapa's modifications into the budget, and struggled with my handwriting. Thapa came into our room to discuss some problematic points in the proposed budget regarding the health training. He claimed that the number of monitoring visits to the villages included in the health NGO's proposal was too large and too costly. I suggested that the budget should first be approved and that later on we could negotiate further with the health NGO. Thapa eventually agreed, and a little later I handed him the completed budget.

When Anita and I returned from our visit to the villages that day, we entered Thapa's room and found that he had approved the budget. I took advantage of the optimistic atmosphere and asked Thapa about the books (which he had promised he would deal with that morning). Thapa turned to Anita and asked her why she did not remind him of that in the morning, and then said:

> In the morning there were so many things to do. Well, tomorrow morning I shall see that the check for the books be sent out. The budget proposal will also be delivered only tomorrow morning. We will send it first to the World Bank and only then to the government [i.e., to his superiors in the Ministry of Agriculture].

> The World Bank should approve it instantly but the government will take its time, because the budget must finance other things [besides the women's project].

Feeling optimistic and grateful I said: "Only a few days ago I discovered that the women's project is supposed to be financed by the World Bank's loan and not through a grant. I can sympathize with the government's reservations." Thapa then said that he had asked that the money for the women's project be allocated as a grant—and thus not repayable—but that he had not succeeded. He added: "Tovi Fenster put pressure on me to start implementing the women's project, but it was impossible, because politicians' vision is shortsighted and they do not understand the significance of the women's project for the future. I succeeded in obtaining my superiors' approval for only the first ten classes."

The overall impression that emerged in these encounters was that Thapa genuinely intended to go ahead with the women's project but his superiors prevented him from doing so. Thapa had convincingly negotiated with the health NGO over details in their proposal, insisted on cutting down trivial costs, and encouraged them to invest much time and energy in adapting and readapting their proposal to his demands. He also rejected the idea of purchasing bicycles for the WGOs, for what he defined as ethical norms in public management. Moreover, he showed his concern for grassroots people by demanding allocation of more money for the village women's books and for the ongoing training of the WGOs.

Nevertheless, Thapa was, in fact, a shrewd operator. He avoided me for a long time and then, when I had lost all hope, he pretended to be serious just a short time before I left, making me believe that things were going to progress smoothly. He blamed others, his superiors and certain anonymous politicians, for not understanding the women's project's importance and for preventing its implementation. Thapa's success in obtaining his superiors' approval for opening ten classes implied that his endeavors to implement the women's project went only that far. This limited achievement and the efforts invested in it can be better described as a manipulative means for preserving appearances rather than as making real progress toward implementation. Moreover, although he proudly claimed that the approval of the ten classes was the outcome of his own rather than Fenster's efforts, they did not begin until after I left Nepal. Thus, Thapa presented himself as sincerely willing to facilitate the women's project and even struggle for it, while he delivered almost nothing in actual fact. Thapa's performance was so convincing that I felt the need to show sympathy for his own and his superiors' situation, being offered loans instead of grants by the World Bank. This provided Thapa with another opportunity to present his efforts on behalf of the women's project in a good light, telling me that he had unsuccessfully tried to turn the loan into a grant. My sympathy might also have helped ease Thapa's discomfort in the face of my pressures, and possibly camouflaged his insincerity. Several events further support this interpretation.

My sympathetic response to Thapa's difficulties can be understood as an instance of feminine conduct. Ferguson contends that women's role in organizations is assumed to be in contrast to that of men's. While the latter are seen as "analytic, independent, rational, competitive, and 'instrumental,'" the roles "traditionally associated with the female [are] … supportive, nonassertive, dependent, attentive to others, and 'expressive'" (Ferguson 1984: 93). However, it is the occupation of the subordinate position, rather than the state of being a woman per se, that explains the appealing, appeasing, and flattering gestures women employ. It is the marginalized place of women in organizations, and their meager formal power as a collective, that means that they employ supportive and attentive behavior as a means of being accepted by those who dominate. From this point of view, feminization "refers to the spread of … feminine traits to bureaucratically defined subordinates" (ibid.: 93). Women possess the skills "necessary to cope with the[ir] subordinate status" (ibid.: 93)—that is, to "please men," who are their superiors (ibid.: 94).

Peanuts: Unveiling the Truth about the Budget and its Intended Use

Six days before I left Nepal the women's project proposal with its budget had yet to be sent out. Upon my return from a village visit I went into Thapa's room to ask him if he had sent out the budget proposal and the check for the books. As he was in a meeting, I left. Thapa came by later and informed me that he had sent the order for the books that morning, and that the budget proposal would be sent out the following morning. Thapa added that he told the World Bank's representative in Kathmandu that the budget proposal was about to be submitted.

I then went to Lama's room to ask for his opinion of the budget, and indirectly to gain his support for it. Lama replied that the women's project budget was "peanuts" considering the World Bank's overall budget for the irrigation project. The budget submitted for the overseas study tours, he said, was considerably larger than that for the women's project. Peanuts—Lama's turn of phrase blatantly exposed and symbolized the attitude and hidden intentions of the heads of the irrigation project. Lama disclosed the fact that the delay in approving the budget and implementing the women's project, as well as the officials' reservations concerning the implementation of the women's project, had nothing to do with lack of money.

The simple explanation of the persistent and manipulative delays that had been employed regarding the budget was the desire of the heads of the irrigation project in both Kathmandu and Bhairahawa to use the money allocated for the women's project—little as it was—themselves, to finance their overseas study tours. Thus, the delaying tactics and the rationale behind the ongoing negotiations reflected the attitude that women's activities were not really important, and therefore the budget allocated for them could be used by male project staff for their own purposes. In other words, the negotiations served as an organizational ritual for legitimizing the diversion of the budget away from its intended purpose, wiping out any moral implications and, eventually, for gaining full, open control over the entire budget. Such a process could take place only if all parties—the World Bank, Tahal, and the Nepali government—combined forces and supported it (implicitly or explicitly).

Indeed, as women who might observe and protest about this were absent from positions of power in these male-dominated organizations, it was easier to exclude women from projects and to prevent them gaining access to even meager economic resources. This might explain why Thapa and Leon did their best to hide the facts from me. If I had realized what was going on I might have posed a threat to the smooth process of gaining control of the budget, something in which they collaborated. Moreover, Thapa's surprising change of heart and sudden efforts toward ensuring the approval of the budget a short while before my departure were also the outcome of the need to have the budget approved by the World Bank. In order that the money be made available for the study tours, the project budget had to be approved. Diverting most of the money could take place safely when there was no one to notice and criticize this action. Therefore, Thapa needed my cooperation as I was the one who prepared and submitted the budget proposal and provided a professional and formal backing for the diversion of the budget.

Thapa himself confirmed the information revealed by Lama at a later stage when I visited him at home. I asked Thapa about the study tours, and he explained that there were three groups going overseas: the first was due to leave soon for China and India, the second would go to a few other places, and the third, consisting of the three highest officials in the development department of the Ministry of Agriculture, were to go to Brazil and Mexico. "Our superiors in Kathmandu," he said, "want to go to South America and we will have to let them go there." I asked whether women were included in those groups, and he replied, "No, as there are no women hired by the irrigation project on a permanent basis." That evening, when I spoke with Leon over dinner, I mentioned the study tours and Lama's use of the expression "peanuts" to describe the women's project budget. Leon did not like the expression but admitted that senior project officials were going overseas. "We are trying to reduce the number from twenty-two to fourteen," he said, and hinted at corruption among the senior officials, conveying his objection and contempt. Needless to say, Leon did not criticize Tahal's part nor the World Bank's in going-along with the "study-tours" (or with the whisky-presents for the senior officials in the Ministry of Argiculture, as described in chapter 2) to the officials, nor consider them to be accomplices in the Nepali officials' siphoning off funds. Neither would he admit to Tahal being responsible for benefiting a few men with overseas trips at the expense of resources promised to a large population of women. Indeed, he would not acknowledge his own part in this: laying obstacles in my path during the approval of the budget and the implementation of the women's project; panicking in response to my budget proposal; warning his superiors that my budget did not entail any profit for Tahal; continuously reducing the sums specified in my budget.

More than resenting the study tours themselves, Leon resented the fact that they would not produce any profit for Tahal. This became apparent during our chat, as we walked all the way from the bachelors' house to the office through the main street. I asked Leon what Tahal would gain from the study tours. He replied:

> Tahal will make no profit because they [the trips] have nothing to do with Tahal. At first, the senior officials were supposed to go to Israel but the Nepali officials demanded that Tahal absorb the overhead expenses and Tahal refused. Then the Nepalese brought up another plan: to travel to countries that have nothing to do with Tahal's projects. I said to Thapa: "When you were in Israel [in 1979] the Israeli government owned Tahal, and it paid for everything. Tahal is now a private company, and you know what that means." Before the privatization of the company, the state covered all the expenses, even the pocket money, which was more than their salaries in Nepal.

The study tours offered by the Israeli government in the 1970s were probably a means of rewarding Nepali senior government officials for doing business with Israel mediated by the World Bank loans. The study tours at the end of 1990s were probably imposed on the Israeli partner, as, according to Leon, Tahal would not make any profit from them. In any case, the study tours signified bargains, in which the politicians and senior officials took for granted their privilege to be personally rewarded for their involvement in overseas projects.

I discussed the phenomenon of corruption earlier (see Chapter 2). However, the study-tour episode offers some further insights into this phenomenon from a gendered perspective. It exposes a hidden but nevertheless fundamental implication of hierarchy: it constructs the basis for the gendered allocation of benefits. Senior positions in organizations such as those described here are constructed so that they provide social and economic benefits for the few at the expense of the many. Moreover, this state of affairs is not recognized by those who benefit from it, and who provide "rational" and "patriotic" justifications for their conduct (see, e.g., Nordstrom 2007: 80).[19] The gendered structure of organizational hierarchies conveniently works to marginalize half of the potential competitors over senior positions and privileges, through informal gendered division of roles, supported by social and cultural constraints. A budget allegedly intended for thousands of women could be easily transferred to a small group of senior male officials. Invisible as a result of the senior officials' structured distance from them, the women could be easily ignored. Moreover, women like Anita and myself were available to provide them, sometimes but not always unwittingly, with support for their actions, and so contribute to the pretence of advancing rural Nepali women's well-being.

No Budget for Women's Activities

I learned almost incidentally three days before I left Nepal that the budget had been sent to the World Bank's representative in Kathmandu, by which time I had stopped chasing Thapa and urging him to send it out. On that morning, Thapa entered our office and was very friendly. He pulled up a chair and sat next to Anita and me, looking at pictures that I had taken during my visits to the villages, and suggested that I should enlarge one of them for Anita to hang on the wall. On his way out, he mentioned somewhat nonchalantly that he would ask Leon to bring the books he had ordered from Kathmandu, and that he had sent out the budget. I was so surprised that I spontaneously apologized for suspecting his intentions, saying that I had given up hope that the budget would ever be sent out.

My surprise and confusion at Thapa's casual announcement can be easily understood against the background of the ongoing delays. Moreover, just three days earlier, Thapa admitted that the budget has not yet been sent out. I found this out when I went to give Thapa an invitation to my farewell party and used the opportunity to ask him if the budget had been submitted. Thapa said: "It has not been sent out yet because I am waiting for a letter from Pandit. I will send it probably tomorrow or the day after, because of the strike." I asked why it could not be sent by fax, and he replied, "It has to be sent from Kathmandu, and also there are too many pages for a fax, and they might come out unclear." I felt angry and upset, as it seemed that the prospect of the budget and the women's project were evaporating. My frustration was such that, as I came out of Thapa's room, I said to Anita, "Had I known a week ago that it was all just a game, in which I have taken part, I would have left then to go back home." Regretting the demoralizing impact my statement had on Anita, who was the one staying on, I added right away that I hoped things were not so bad. Although it should have been completely clear to me, when speaking with Thapa a couple of days earlier, that the women's project was doomed, Thapa's announcement about sending out the budget filled me with new hopes.

The fact that I did not give up hope even at this point, although all facts by then indicated clearly that the women's project would not materialize, contrasts with Mosse's experience when he states that, "gender consultants, being especially skeptical of management intentions to address gender, were unwilling to prepare materials that 'would not be speaking any truth and more of falsehoods'" (Mosse 2005: 152).[20] I went on pretending to myself and to Anita that there was a chance of things materializing, and I clung to my professional integrity by stating that I would leave "if I knew" that things would not.

Nevertheless, it appears that it was not easy to find out the real facts. I remained confused by things for a very long time after leaving Nepal, and I did not begin to understand things until I began analyzing my field data. Only then, far away from the irrigation project's premises, did I realize that Thapa and the other Nepali officials were deeply interested in the World Bank approving the women's project budget, but for reasons other than those that would benefit village women. The reason was to enable them to utilize the budget for their study tours. The approval had to be achieved in such a way that I would not become aware of the fact that most of the budget was diverted away from its intended purpose. Were I to become aware of this, I might of course criticize this, or even publicize it. Furthermore, Thapa's charming and friendly attitude was effective in gaining our cooperation. Thus, it appears that he was manipulatively using "feminine interaction skills," such as being "attentive to others" (Ferguson 1984: 93, 94), breaking hierarchical distance, expressing appreciation, and encouraging employees' initiatives.

Thapa's social proficiency worked well with local people no less. This was apparent in many engagements which I attended with irrigation project staff, NGO representatives, and even with Leon. One meeting with the health NGO's representatives can serve to illustrate Thapa's skills in dissembling by acting as if certain things were going to happen when he knew full well they would not. One afternoon, a few hours after Thapa admitted that he had not yet sent in the budget, Leon joined Anita and me in negotiating with the health NGO's representatives. The meeting assumed the form of a play, in which we conveyed the impression that the women's project was about to start shortly, while the only problem remaining before the health project could be incorporated was the finalization of certain trivial technical details.

Anita and I raised some practical questions concerning the hourly rate of pay for the lecturers, the number of monitoring visits needed for the WGOs, and the cost of overheads. We discussed various details for over half an hour and eventually told the two men that we were waiting for the approval of the budget proposal by the World Bank. One of them stated firmly that they would rather go to Thapa and conclude things with him. So the five of us went to see Thapa, who greeted us warmly, and the negotiations started all over again. Thapa discussed the number of monitoring visits and the cost of overheads, the exchanges being conducted in Nepali. The NGO representatives agreed to receive a 15 per cent overhead rather than 20 per cent, and to reduce the number of visits they had originally proposed. Thapa also proposed making the irrigation project's vehicle available for driving the NGO's lecturers to the villages, provided that the organization covered the cost of fuel. The discussions proceeded in a positive atmosphere, and when we were about to finalize things I asked Thapa when the project would start, as this was something the NGO representatives had already asked me. Thapa smiled and said, "As soon as the Bank approves the budget." Not content with this, I said, "I'm not referring to the budget but rather to when the first training course on health instruction for the WGOs can start." He repeated his answer: "When the Bank approves the budget in a week or so, there will be no problem to start things." On the way out I told Anita that it seemed that Thapa was sincere in his intentions to go ahead with the women's project.

It follows that we all convincingly played our parts in this play, negotiating, bargaining, compromising over a budget and project that were not going to take place. In their negotiations with Anita, Leon, and myself, the NGO people were just about to give up in their effort to participate in the women's project. Thapa's attitude not only convinced them to continue in their efforts, but also to reduce further their demands. Even though I asked Thapa exactly when the health training would start, he maintained the pretense that things were about to happen, and this convinced the NGO people to continue in their efforts.

However, despite my ambivalence about the real chances of the women's project being implemented, I felt that I needed to reassure Anita, who depended on the project for her living. This was not easy. Anita's mood shifted between hope and despair, and she often lost confidence in the project's future. Thus, she cautiously told me one day that Pandit had told her that it was not clear if the women's project would be implemented. When I said it seemed there was only meager chance that the project would materialize, she asked why had all the WGOs been hired? Thus, while we both felt profoundly frustrated we also continued to hold on to our hopes, and I would give Anita some practical advice that I believed might help make the project happen. I said, for instance, "You can initiate activities that would contribute to establishing the existence of the project de facto." It appears that when my departure was close, and I began to realize that there was nothing in my power to make Thapa or anyone else in charge of the irrigation project realize the women's project, I continued to hope and act as if there was still a chance of remedying the situation.

Thapa's manipulative maneuvers in relation to approving the women's project budget can be contrasted with his completely different attitude toward obtaining a marketing expert. His determination to have this expert start work immediately for the irrigation project actively engaged him in achieving this goal promptly. One morning, Thapa entered our office in a fury that I had never witnessed before. He demanded Leon come to his office, thus avoiding my witnessing the expected clash. When Leon returned after seeing Thapa he was very upset. He composed a letter, which Raju typed instantly. Then Leon said:

> when they want something it must be done on the spot. He [Thapa] wants to hire the marketing expert *now*. The file was sent back from Kathmandu after lying there for half a year, and now he wants us to provide his [the marketing expert's] CV and hire that expert from this minute to the next, but later this can lie dormant for another year without doing anything about it.

Leon explained that the expert was needed for a large-scale marketing project. The evident conclusion is that the budget affair had nothing to do with the Nepali officials' incompetence, or with objective constraints that prevented the smooth approval of the budget and the subsequent implementation of the women's project. Rather, the Nepali officials had their priorities, which did not include women's activities. Leon's rejection of my idea, that a marketing expert could help marketing women's enterprises as part of the women's project, illustrates a similar underestimation of the women's project on the part of the Israeli party. He said, "We are talking about a large-scale project [the marketing of agricultural products] and not just about small things." That is to say, neither the Israeli nor the Nepali party was willing to use the money for the purpose of village women's activities, which were considered "small things." Hence, it was not a question of unbearable costs, nor the fact that the money was provided as a loan which needed to be repaid. The women's budget was tempting prey for the male officials' desires.

I was confirmed in this understanding on my last day in Bhairahawa, at the small, informal farewell party for me in Acharya's office. On the morning of my last day, Leon announced that a row was imminent over the women's project budget for the sake of agricultural instruction. He said that the Nepali senior officials wanted $250,000 for agricultural instruction. In the afternoon, at the farewell party, the budget and the women's project were discussed again. Acharya explained that the project might get underway but that it would have to suffer major budget cuts and that only a small part of it would get off the ground. I was pleased with his positive attitude and the chance that the project might, in some form, be implemented, and said: "Well, the most important thing is to start. When the World Bank realizes that something like seventy groups have been launched by the end of this year it will probably offer more resources, and then other financial resources could be made available."

Leon objected to my claim, and seemed to stand up for the women's project instead of me, and said, "The project is important and no part of it can be cut." I praised Leon for standing up for the project better than I had. Then Anita said quietly, "It is basically referring to a meager sum of money for each woman." Leon then compared the sums of money allocated for the study tours and the women's project. He said, "We are speaking about $260,000 for twenty-three senior officials compared to $290,000 for 9,000 women." Acharya said, "This is really peanuts, but what can we do? Our superiors are the ones who decide. They want the money."

Apparently, the budget had been divided in two: a sum of $240,000 had been earmarked for agricultural instruction, some $260,000 for study tours for high-ranking officials, and virtually nothing for the women's activities. Amazingly enough, I expressed my appreciation for both Acharya, who informed me about the need for significant cuts in the budget and in the scope of the women's project, and for Leon, whose resistance to the women's project I knew so well, and who was now comfortable enough to please me, shortly before I left Nepal. I suppose that by this time I preferred to leave without revealing my bitter disappointment, and to depart while on friendly terms. It also appears that until the final hours of my stay in Nepal I eagerly wanted to believe in the women project's prospects. In any case, until the last minute I continued to try and convince the local heads of the irrigation project of the women project's importance, and of their ability and responsibility to make it happen.

The deceptive management of the budget, and the women's project more generally, went on for some time after I left Nepal. This became apparent from Leon's letters, which I received a couple of months after my return to Israel. Examination of these letters suggests that the gender discourse was kept alive within the context of the irrigation project's premises, by those involved in the women's project, for as long as this project lasted, namely the ten literacy classes that were opened after I left. In a letter, Leon wrote:

> On the last day of the Bank delegation's visit I spoke with Mr Mint one-on-one, and asked him what was his personal position and the Bank's position concerning the programs you have prepared, which have been submitted to him. He thought that the report and the programs were very good, but too grandiose and pretentious for Nepal's conditions generally and for the Tarai, in particular. The Bank has approved only $110,000 for 160 classes, specifically for literacy classes, including some agricultural training (vegetable horticulture) and basic concepts in personal hygiene and health. If we demonstrate, by March 1998, that 160 classes were really opened up and successfully carried out he will be ready to "reconsider" the approval of an additional budget.[21]

According to Leon, Mr Mint was not particularly interested in the women's project's prospects, and Leon had to remind him that the project was the Banks' "baby." Moreover, Leon told him that Tovi Fenster's budget, which had been submitted to the Bank previously, amounted to some $400,000. Mr Mint replied, so Leon wrote, that "although the facts I mentioned were correct, yet the Bank never approved Tovi Fenster's budget." However, Leon did not give up and urged Mr Mint to influence the Nepalese to approve the $110,000 budget as soon as possible, and to see that they release the money needed for the programs, most urgently for the seminar for the twenty village teachers as well as for the additional twenty literacy classes that were ready to begin.

A subsequent letter from Leon suggests that by the end of 1997 the women's project's prospects had dwindled even further. Thus, he wrote to me:

> Concerning the advancement of women's status in the project region, no concrete progress has been made. The partial budget of $110,000 has not been formally approved yet [by the Nepali officials] and I do not expect its approval in the near future. This may take at least three more months, if it is approved at all ... [W]ithout an approved budget which should facilitate the money flowing into the project area, the plan of opening 160 classes by the end of March 1998 is an impossible mission, and therefore we will not be able to prove to Mint that we have done a good job. Thus it will prevent the approval of additional budget, beyond the $110,000.[22]

Well aware of the fact that after two years only 10 classes out of the 300 planned had been started—the latter figure itself having been pared down from 900—Mint must have known that there was no chance that the other 290 classes would commence by March 1998. Indeed, if we accept the accuracy of Leon's reported conversation with him, Mint did not really care whether the classes commenced or not. Similar to the preceding one, this budget was also a fiction. Indeed, the constraints and conditions that were stipulated as necessary for obtaining additional monies are proof that the prospects of the nonexistent budget's realization were nil. Moreover, as much as the original budget was flexibly changed, it still existed, although it was used for other purposes than women's activities.

To conclude, there was no definite budget earmarked for the women's project. The various figures that were mentioned at various points in the process of budget negotiation were not ones to which the involved parties were obliged to commit themselves. Eventually some $500,000 was spent in two areas—agricultural instruction and study tours—activities which excluded women almost completely.

Notes

1. Mosse suggests that paper products such as the "huge number of visit reports, progress reports, annual reports," serve consultants' purposes (Mosse 2005: 134).
2. In response to the growing demands of the feminist movement to include women in development projects, at the beginning of the 1990s the World Bank demanded that its partners (governments and development agencies) should relate to women's needs and ensure the allocation of resources to them.
3. Letter from Leon, 10 November 1997.
4. The embedded and practical need of the foreign consultant to satisfy their employer is described by Mosse as follows: "Beyond personal commitment to particular development goals and to the new project as their vehicle, our broad ambition was to demonstrate professional competence and so secure an enduring relationship with the donor and project agency/area" (Mosse 2005: 26). Mosse was himself a member of a British foreign consultancy team.
5. Herta Nöbauer discusses the self-denial strategy in the context of academia. Based on her ethnographic research on social practices of the (re)production of academic knowledge at Austrian universities, she argues that women, who depend on male senior academics for their academic promotion and recognition, disclosed their efforts "to hide their wounds resulting from discrimination, disappointment, and violation, and repress these wounds even from themselves." She further suggests that, "These women were trying to maintain their dignity by evading a question" (Nöbauer 2002: 113).
6. Similarly, Nöbauer suggests that hopes and expectations of being "afforded respect and recognition as scholars… is a central issue for all women," and therefore they are "highly vulnerable in that aspect" (Nöbauer 2002: 119).
7. Co-optation as a means of preserving power in the hands of controlling groups and blocking the participation of peripheral sectors in sharing power has been recognized for some time. One of the earliest writers on this was Vilfredo Pareto (1991). He suggested that the dominating elite either eliminate threatening leaders of excluded groups or absorb their representatives into the ruling elite. The absorbed leaders accommodate themselves to the elite's demands and norms, and thus serve to perpetuate the power structure.
8. Consultants' compliance with the requirement of submitting needless reports is mentioned by Justice, who writes that, "Most agencies expect their staff to write their own reports, even if

another agency has already provided good coverage on the same topic" (Justice 1989: 114). However, she perceives this expectation as a taken-for-granted requirement (which often is wrongly implemented) and does not consider the possibility that these reports serve as other than "sources of information" (ibid.: 112).

9. It is interesting to note that, apart from the ethnocentric views Leon had of the Nepali villagers, in some ways what he described as "faults" or "problems" could be considered as Tahal's major, if not only, success in its engagement in Nepal. Such a view was expressed by Sam, a British consultant (see the Introduction and Chapter 4 for a discussion of this and other related issues).
10. A "drawer project" is a Hebrew expression meaning a plan, sometimes a hypothetical exercise, with no immediate practical use, intended for envisaging future scenarios. In common parlance it can also refer to disturbing or undesired initiatives that the organization prefers to bury.
11. This tendency of organizations to ignore responsibility when facing problematic situations or when failing to fulfill their commitments is discussed in Chapter 3, with regard to, for instance, the failure of government agencies to provide educational and health services (see Thapa and Sijapati 2004; Whelpton 2005).
12. Don Handelman (1980) describes this bureaucratic conduct with reference to social workers at a welfare agency and shows how they tend to involve other agencies in sharing responsibility over problematic situations.
13. In an examination of tens of cases in which "children at risk" were taken away from their homes and put in youth institutions by the welfare authorities in Israel, I found that the welfare officials who recommended taking the children away cooperated intensively with other social workers within their departments as well as with officials from other departments, and with senior social work officials. This procedure enabled them to justify their decisions by saying that they "consulted" with other colleagues and reached a responsible and professional decision (see Hertzog 2004).
14. For a more detailed review of the literature on organizational theory and how to read it through gendered lenses, see Bendl (source: http://www.wu.ac.at/gender/mitarbeiter/bendl/bendl_2/genderlogic_bendl.pdf (retrieved 8 October 2010).
15. Joan Acker argues that, "Gender, sexuality, reproduction, and emotionality of women are outside organizational boundaries, continually and actively consigned to that social space by ongoing organizational practices" (Acker 1992: 259).
16. During my stay in Nepal I noticed that the English-language daily the *Rising Nepal* regularly reported on projects for "women's empowerment," and quoted politicians' statements on women's affairs.
17. See the discussion of this issue in the Introduction.
18. In his comprehensive study of the development industry and of the central role the World Bank plays in it, Graham Hancock speaks of the opportunistic conduct of development agencies as follows: "if humanitarianism is in the air, then they will make humanitarian statements; if environmental movements seem to be gaining political support, then the agencies will inject some ecology into their rhetoric … Meanwhile, if welfare-statism is on the ascendant in the donor countries, the aid agencies will highlight their own role in the international redistribution of wealth … If conservative values are enjoying resurgence on the other hand, then notions like 'structural adjustment' will be promulgated, the virtues of private enterprise will be extolled and 'market forces' will be assigned a god-like omnipotence. The variations and possibilities are virtually infinite" (Hancock 1989: 72).
19. Nordstrom uses interviews with three elite people to show how corrupt conduct is justified as being for the good of their nation and society. A commander who used his position to run mining concessions, says "what I do, I do for the good of this country." The politician who replies to Nordstrom's question about diverting most of Angola's education budget to "scholarships for a few elite children to study at leading private schools and universities in the world," says "This nation desperately needs the best of minds." And the businessman who

tries to "gain a foothold in the difficult flux of transitional development and political turmoil," says "I am helping my country" (Nordstrom 2007: 80–81).

20. Indeed, the difference between our respective contexts—Mosse's, as opposed to Anita's and my own—accounts for our different evaluations.
21. Letter from Leon, 10 November 1997.
22. Letter from Leon, 19 December 1997.

References

Abadzi, H. 1996. *Adult Literacy.* Washington, DC: World Bank.

Abu-Lughod, L. 1990. "The Romance of Resistance: Tracing Transformations of Power through Bedouin Women," *American Ethnologist* 17(1): 41–55.

Acharya, M. 2001. "Women and the Economy: The Key Issues," in L.K. Manadhar and K.B. Bhattahcan (eds), *Gender and Democracy in Nepal.* Kathmandu: Central Department of Home Science, Women"s Studies Program, Tribhuvan University, pp. 24–59.

Acker, J. 1992. "Gendering Organizational Theory," in A, Mills and P. Tancred (eds), *Gendering Organizational Analysis.* Newbury Park, London, New Delhi: Sage Publications, pp. 248–60.

Acker, J. and D. Van Houten. 1992. "Differential Recruitment and Control: The Sex Structuring of Organizations," in A. Mills and P. Tancred (eds), *Gendering Organizational Analysis.* Newbury Park, London, New Delhi: Sage Publications, pp. 15–30.

Ahearn, L.M. 2001. *Invitations to Love: Literacy, Love Letters, and Social Change in Nepal.* Ann Arbor: University of Michigan Press.

____. 2004. "Literacy, Power, and Agency: Love Letters and Development in Nepal," *Language and Education* 18(4): 305–16.

Allen, M. (ed.). 1994. *Anthropology of Nepal: Peoples, Problems and Processes.* Kathmandu: Mandala Book Point.

Alvesson, M. and Y.D. Billing. 1997. *Understanding Gender and Organizations.* London, New Delhi: Sage.

Andrade, S.J. and A.G. Burstein. 1973. "Social Congruence and Empathy in Paraprofessional and Professional Mental Health Workers," *Community Mental Health Journal* 9(4): 388–97.

Apthorpe, R. 1997. "Writing Development Policy and Policy Analysis Plain or Clear: On Language, Genre and Power," in C. Shore and S. Wright (eds), *Anthropology of Policy: Critical Perspectives on Governance and Power.* London and New York: Routledge, pp. 43–58.

Ardener, S. 1964. "The Comparative Study of Rotating Credit Associations," *Journal of the Royal Anthropological Institute* 94(2): 201–29.

____. 1984. "Preface" and "Incorporation and Exclusion: Oxford Academics' Wives," in H. Callan and S. Ardener (eds), *The Incorporated Wife.* London: Croom Helm, pp. i–iii; 27–49.

———. 1995. "Women Making Money Go Round: ROSCAs Revisited," in S. Ardener and S. Burman (eds), *Money-Go-Rounds, the Importance of Rotating Savings and Credit Associations for Women*. Oxford: Berg, pp. 1–20.

Ardener, S. and S. Burman (eds). 1995. *Money-Go-Rounds, the Importance of Rotating Savings and Credit Associations for Women*. Oxford: Berg.

Attwood, G., Castle, J. and S. Smythe. 2004. "'Women are Lions in Dresses': Negotiating Gender Relations in REFLECT Learning Circles in Lesotho," in A. Robinson-Pant (ed.), *Women, Literacy and Development: Alternative Perspectives*. London and New York: Routledge, Taylor & Francis, pp. 139–58.

Azulai, A. 2000. *How Does it Look to You?* Tel Aviv: Bavel (Hebrew).

Bagele, C. 2005. "Educational Research within Postcolonial Africa: A Critique of HIV/AIDS Research in Botswana," *International Journal of Qualitative Studies in Education* (8)6: 659–84.

Barasch, M. 1986. *An Evaluation of the Comprehensive Integrated Approach in Developing Paraprofessional Manpower in Welfare Services as Implemented by ASI*. JDC – Israel, Monograph Series No. 1.

Basu, A. 1999. "Women's Education, Marriage and Fertility in South Asia: Do Men Really not Matter?" in C. Bledsoe, et al. (eds), *Critical Perspectives on Schooling and Fertility in the Developing World*. Washington DC: National Academy Press, pp. 267–86.

Bauman, Z. 1989. *Modernity and the Holocaust*. New York: Cornell University Press.

Behar, R. 1996. *The Vulnerable Observer, Anthropology that Breaks your Heart*. Boston: Beacon Press.

Ben-Ari, E. 1989. "Masks and Soldiering: The Israeli Army and the Palestinian Uprising," *Cultural Anthropology* (4): 372–89.

———. "Israeli Soldiers, Japanese Children: Fieldwork and the Dynamics of Participant-Observation and Reflection," unpublished paper.

Bendl, R. "Gender Logic in Organizational Theories: Preliminaries of a Project in Progress." Retrieved 8 October 2010 from http://www.wu.ac.at/gender/mitarbeiter/bendl/bendl_2/genderlogic_bendl.pdf.

Bennett, L. 1983. *Dangerous Wives and Sacred Sisters: Social and Symbolic Roles of High-Caste Women in Nepal*. New York: Columbia University Press.

Betts, J. 2004. "Creating the Gender Text: Literacy and Discourse in Rural El Salvador," in A. Robinson-Pant (ed.), *Women, Literacy and Development: Alternative Perspectives*. London and New York: Routledge, pp. 68–84.

Bhattachan, K.B. 2001. "Peace and Good Governance in Nepal: The Socio-Cultural Context," in *Quest for Peace, SAP – Nepal, Kathmandu South Asia Partnership Nepal*, pp. 73–88.

Boissevain, J. 1966. "Patronage in Sicily," *Man* 1(1): 18–33.

Boserup, E. 1970. *Women's Role in Economic Development*. New York: St. Martin's Press.

Bourdieu, P. 1996. "The Family as a Realized Category," *Theory, Culture & Society* 13(1): 19–26.

Bowles, S. and H. Gintis. 1976. *Schooling in Capitalist America: Educational Reform and the Contradictions of Economic Life*. New York: Basic Books.

_____. 2001. "The Inheritance of Inequality," *Journal of Economic Perspectives* 16(3): 3–30.

Brawley, E.A. and R. Schindler. 1986. "Paraprofessional Social Welfare Personnel in International Perspective: Results of a Worldwide Survey," *International Social Work* 29: 165–76.

Brown, P. 1990. "Big Man, Past and Present: Model, Person, Hero, Legend," *Ethnology* 29 (2): 97–115.

Brownfoot, J.N. 1984. "Memsahibs in Colonial Malaya: A Study of European Wives in a British Colony and Protectorate 1900–1940," in H. Callan and S. Ardener (eds), *The Incorporated Wife*. London: Croom Helm, pp. 186–210.

Burawoy, M. 1979. *Manufacturing Consent: Changes in the Labor Process Under Monopoly Capitalism*. Chicago and London: The University of Chicago Press.

Callan, H. and S. Ardener (eds). 1984. *The Incorporated Wife*. London: Croom Helm.

Callan, H. 1984. "Introduction," in H. Callan and S. Ardener (eds), *The Incorporated Wife*. London: Croom Helm, pp. 1–26.

Callas, M.B. and L. Smircich. 1992. "Using the 'F' Word: Feminist Theories and the Social Consequences of Organizational Research," in A.J. Mills and P. Tancred (eds), *Gendering Organizational Analysis*. Newbury Park-London, New Delhi: Sage Publications, pp. 222–34.

Carnoy, M. 1974. *Education as Cultural Imperialism*. New York: McKay.

Castiglione, C. 2005. *Patrons and Adversaries: Nobles and Villagers in Italian Politics, 1640–1760*. Oxford, New York: Oxford University Press.

Chambers, R. 1983. *Rural Development: Putting the Last First*. New York: Longman Scientific & Technical.

Chatty, D. and A. Rabo (eds). 1997. *Organizing Women: Formal and Informal Women and Groups in the Middle East*. Oxford & New York: Berg.

Chaudhary, M.A. 1999. *Justice in Practice: Legal Ethnography of a Pakistani Punjabi Village*. Karachi: Oxford University Press.

Chopra, P. 2004. "Distorted Mirrors: (De)centring Images of the 'Illiterate Indian Village Women' through Ethnographic Research Narratives," in A. Robinson-Pant (ed.), *Women, Literacy and Development: Alternative Perspectives*. London and New York: Routledge, pp. 35–56.

Chowdhury, G. 1995. "Engendering Development? Women in Development (WID) in International Development Regimes," in J.L. Parpart, and M.H. Marchand (eds), *Feminism Postmodernism Development*. London and New York: Routledge, pp. 26–41.

Collier, J. and S. Yanagisako (eds). 1987. *Gender and Kinship: Essays Towards a Unified Analysis*. Stanford: Stanford University Press.

Cowen, M. and R. Shenton. 1995. "The Invention of Development," in J. Crush (ed.), *Power of Development*. London and New York: Routledge, pp. 27–43.

Cramer, S. 2007. "Gaaro: Nepali Women Tell Their Stories," *ISP Collection*. Paper 134. Retrieved 14 October 2010 from http://digitalcollections.sit.edu/isp_collection/134.

Dahl, G. 1987. "Women in Pastoral Production: Some Theoretical Notes on Roles and Resources," *Ethnos* 52(1–2): 246–79.

_____. 2001. *Responsibility and Partnership in Swedish Aid Discourse*. Uppsala: The Nordic Africa Institute.

Davis, J. 1977. *People of the Mediterranean: An Essay in Comparative Social Anthropology*. London: Routledge and Kegan Paul.

Debert, G.G. 1997. "Controlling Processes – Tracing the Dynamic Components of Power," Comments on L. Nader in *Current Anthropology* 38(5): 711–37.

Dembour, M.B. 2000. *Recalling the Belgian Congo, Conversations and Introspection*. New York, Oxford: Berghahn Books.

Des Chene, M. 1996. "In the Name of Bikas," *Studies in Nepali History and Society* 1(2): 259–70.

De Sales, A. 2003. "The Kham Magar Country: Between Ethnic Claims and Maoism," in D. Gellner (ed.), *Resistance and the State: Nepalese Experiences*. New Delhi: Social Science Press, pp. 326–58.

Dighe, A. 1995. *Women and Literacy in India – A Study in a Re-settlement Colony in Delhi*. Education for Development, Occasional Papers. Series 1(2). Retrieved 5 October 2010 from http://www.cemca.org/cemca_womens_literacy.pdf.

Dollar, D. and A. Kraay. 2000. *Growth is Good for the Poor*. World Bank: Policy Research Department.

Eade, D. 1997. "Preface," in D. Eade (ed.), *Development and Patronage*. Oxford: Oxfam.

Easterly, W. 2002. *The Elusive Quest for Growth: Economists' Adventures and Misadventures in the Tropics*. Cambridge, Massachusetts: MIT Press.

_____. 2006. *The White Man's Burden: Why the West's Efforts to Aid the Rest Have Done So Much Ill and So Little Good*. London: Penguin Press.

Elson, D. 2000. *Progress of the World's Women*. New York: Unifem.

Emerson, R.M. 1962. "Power-Dependence Relations," *American Sociological Review* 27(1): 31–41.

Enloe, C. 1989. *Bananas, Beaches and Bases: Making Feminist Sense of International Politics*. Berkeley: University of California Press.

Epstein, S. 1973. *South India: Yesterday, Today and Tomorrow*. London & Basingstoke: Macmillan.

Escobar, A. 1988. "Power and Visibility: Development and the Invention and Management of the Third World," *Cultural Anthropology* 3(4): 428–43.

_____. 1995. *Encountering Development, The Making and Unmaking of the Third World*. Princeton, New Jersey: Princeton University Press.

Esteva, G. 1992. "Development," in W. Sachs (ed.), *Development Dictionary: A Guide to Knowledge as Power*. London: Zed Books, pp. 6–25.

Etgar, T. 1977. *Chonchim Ve Somchot, Services for Assisting and Advancing Families.* Jerusalem: Ministry for Welfare and Labor (Hebrew).

Feldman, S. 1997. "NGOs and Civil Society: (Un)Stated Contradictions," *Annals of the American Academy of Political and Social Science*, 554: 46–65.

Fenster, T. 1996. *Gender Activities in the Project Area, Bhairahawa Lumbini Groundwater Project*. Bhairahawa: Ministry of Water Resources, Department of Irrigation.

Ferguson, J. 1990. *The Anti-Politics Machine: "Development," Depoliticization, and Bureaucratic Power in Lesotho.* Cambridge: Cambridge University Press.

Ferguson, K.E. 1984. *The Feminist Case against Bureaucracy.* Philadelphia, PA: Temple University Press.

Ferrell, J. and M.S. Hamm (eds). 1998. *Ethnography at the Edge: Crime, Deviance and Field Research.* Boston: Northeastern University Press.

Fordham, P. (ed.). 1980. *Participation, Learning and Change.* London: Commonwealth Secretariat.

Forster, M.R. 1998. "Clericalism and Communalism in German Catholicism," in M. Reinhart (ed.), *Infinite Boundaries: Order, Disorder and Reorder in Early, Modern German Culture.* Kirksville, Missouri: Sixteenth Century Journal Publisher 40: 55–76.

Foucault, M. 1972. *Power/Knowledge: Selected Interviews and Other Writings.* New York: Basic Books.

_____. 1990. *The History of Sexuality* (Trans. Robert Hurley). London: Penguin.

Freire, P. 1971. *Pedagogy of the Oppressed.* London: Penguin.

Freierman, S. 1990. *Peasant Intellectuals: Anthropology and History in Tanzania.* Madison: The University of Wisconsin Press.

Gardner, K. and D. Lewis. 1996. *Anthropology, Development and the Post-Modern Challenge.* London: Pluto Press.

Garfinkel, H. 1967. *Studies in Ethnomethodology.* Englewood Cliffs NJ: Prentice-Hall.

Gartrell, B. 1984. "Colonial Wives: Villains or Victims?" in H. Callan and S. Ardener (eds), *The Incorporated Wife.* London: Croom Helm, pp. 166–85.

Gautam, S., Banskota, A. and R. Manchanda. 2001. "Where There Are No Men: Women in the Maoist Insurgency in Nepal," in R. Manchanda (ed.), *Women, War and Peace in South Asia: Beyond Victimhood to Agency.* London and New Delhi: Sage Publications, pp. 214–51.

Gellner, D. 2003. *Resistance and the State: Nepalese Experiences.* New Dehli: Social Science Press.

Gellner, E. 1977. "Patrons and Clients," in E. Gellner and J. Waterbury (eds), *Patrons and Clients in Mediterranean Societies.* London: Duckworth.

George, S. 1988. *A Fate Worse Than Debt: A Radical Analysis of the Third World Debt Crisis.* Harmondsworth, Middlesex: Penguin Books.

Gerschlager, C, and M. Mokre (eds). 2002. *Exchange and Deception: A Feminist Perspective.* Boston, Dordrecht, London: Kluwer Academic Publishers.

Gerschlager, C. 2002. "Adam Smith and Feminist Perspectives on Exchange," in C. Gerschlager and M. Mokre (eds), *Exchange and Deception: A Feminist Perspective.* Boston, Dordrecht, London: Kluwer Academic Publishers, pp. 13–26.

Gifford, E.W. 1929. *Tongan Society.* Honolulu: Bernice P. Bishop Museum, bulletin 61.

Gilsenan, M. 1996. *Lords of the Lebanese Marches: Violence and Narrative in an Arab Society.* Berkeley: University of California Press.

Gledhill, J. 1994. *Power and its Disguises.* London: Pluto Press.

Gluckman, M. 1967. "Introduction," in A.L. Epstein (ed.), *The Craft of Social Anthropology.* London: Tavistock.

Goetz, A.M. and R. Sen Gupta. 1996. "Who Takes Credit? Gender, Power, and Control over Loan Use in Rural Credit Programs in Bangladesh," *World Development* 24(1): 45–63.

Goffman, E. 1959. *The Presentation of Self in Everyday Life.* New York: Doubleday Anchor Books.

____. 1961. *Asylums: Essays on the Social Situation of Mental Patients and Other Inmates.* New York: Doubleday Anchor Books.

Graff, H.J. 1979. *The Literacy Myth: Literacy and Social Structure in the Nineteenth-Century City.* New York: Academic Press.

Gray, T. and C. Gray. 1979. "Structuring Bureaucratic Rules to Enhance Compliance," *Psychological Reports* 45: 579–89.

Greenberg, O. 1982. *Women in Israeli Prison.* Tel Aviv: Cherikover (Hebrew).

Griffiths, P. 2003. *The Economist's Tale: A Consultant Encounters Hunger and the World Bank.* London: Zed Books.

Grillo, R.D. and R.L. Stirrat (eds). 1997. *Discourses of Development: Anthropological Perspectives.* Oxford: Berg.

Gronemeyer, M. 1992. "Helping," in W. Sachs (ed.), *Dictionary: A Guide to Knowledge as Power.* London: Zed Books, pp. 53–69.

Gurung, S. 1994. "Gender Dimension of Eco-Crisis and Resource Management," in M. Allen (ed.), *Anthropology of Nepal: Peoples, Problems and Processes.* Kathmandu: Mandala Book Point, pp. 330–8.

Gusfield, J.R. 1980. *The Culture of Public Problems: Drinking-Driving and the Symbolic Order.* Chicago: The University of Chicago Press.

Haaland, G. 2004. "Smelting Iron: Caste and its Symbolism in South-Western Ethiopia," in T. Insoll (ed.), *Belief in the Past, the Proceedings of the 2002 Manchester Conference on Archaeology and Religion.* Oxford: Archaeopress, pp. 75–86.

Hachhethu, K. 2004. "The Nepali State and the Maoist Insurgency, 1996–2001," in M. Hutt (ed.), *Himalayan People's War: Nepal's Maoist Rebellion.* Bloomington & Indianapolis: Indiana University Press, pp. 58–78.

Hancock, G. 1989. *Lords of Poverty: The Power, Prestige, and Corruption of the International Aid Business.* New York: The Atlantic Monthly Press.

Handelman, D. 1980. "Bureaucratic Affiliation: The Moral Component in Welfare Cases," in E. Marx (ed), *A Composite Portrait of Israel.* London: Academic Press, pp. 257–82.

Harris, P. 2004. "Social Inclusion, Globalisation and the Commonwealth," in C.J. Finer and P. Smyth (eds). *Social Policy and the Commonwealth: Prospects for Social Inclusion.* London: Palgrave Macmillan.

Harrison, S. 1993. *The Mask of War: Violence, Ritual and the Self in Melanesia.* Manchester: Manchester University Press.

Hausner, S.L. 2006. "Anthropology in Development: Notes from an Ethnographic Perspective," *India Review* 5(3): 318–42.

Hayter, T. 1971. *Aid as Imperialism.* London: Penguin.

Hearn, J. and W. Parkin. 1983. "Gender and Organizations: A Selective Review and a Critique of a Neglected Area," *Organization Studies* 4: 219–42.

Henry, J. 1963. "Golden Rule Days: American Schoolrooms," in J. Henry, *Culture against Man.* New York: Vintage Books, pp. 283–321.

Hertzog, E 1997. *Gender Activities Report, Bhairahawa Lumbini Groundwater Project.* Bhairahawa: Ministry of Water Resources Department of Irrigation.

_____. 1999. *Immigrants and Bureaucrats: Ethiopians in an Israeli Absorption Centre.* New York and Oxford: Berghahn Books, pp. 68–101.

_____. 2001. "Gender and Power Relations in a Bureaucratic Context: Female Immigrants from Ethiopia in an Absorption Centre in Israel," *Gender and Development* 9(3): 60–9.

_____. 2004. "Bureaucratic Violence and Children's Wellbeing," in E. Shadmi and L. Eden (eds), *In the Pursuit of Justice: Studies in Crime and Law Enforcement in Israel.* Tel Aviv: Cherikover, pp. 257–94 (Hebrew).

_____. 2007. "Negotiating Bureaucratic Identities and Control: The case of an Israeli Absorption Centre for Ethiopian immigrants," in F. Moore and S. Ardener (eds), *Professional Identities, Policy and Practice in Business and Bureaucracy.* Oxford and New York: Berghahn.

_____. 2010a. "Introduction: At Women's Expense – Gender between Education and Society," in E. Hertzog and T. Walden (eds), *At Teachers' Expense: Gender and Power in Israeli Education.* Jerusalem: Carmel, pp. 11–36 (Hebrew).

_____. 2010b. "The Role of Diseases in Constructing Bureaucratic Patronage over Ethiopian Immigrants in Israel," *Anthropology of the Middle East* 5(1): pp. 71–92.

Hillberg, R. 1983. *The Destruction of the European Jews.* New York: Homes and Meier.

Hirsch, E. and D.N. Gellner. 2001. "Introduction: Ethnography of Organizations and Organizations of Ethnography," in E. Hirsch and D.N. Gellner (eds), *Inside Organizations: Anthropologists at Work.* Oxford: Berg, pp. 1–18.

Hirschman, M. 1995. "Women and Development: A Critique," in J.L. Parpart and M.H. Marchand (eds), *Feminism Postmodernism Development.* London and New York: Routledge, pp. 42–55.

Hodgson, D.L. 2001. *Once Intrepid Warriors: Gender, Ethnicity, and the Cultural Politics of Maasai Development*. Bloomington and Indianapolis: Indiana University Press.

Hoftun, M., Raeper, W. and J. Whelpton. 1999. *People, Politics and Ideology: Democracy and Social Change in Nepal*. Kathmandu: Mandala Book Point.

Horsman, J. 1990. *Something in My Mind Besides the Everyday: Women and Literacy*. Toronto: Women's Press.

____. 1996. "Thinking about Women and Literacy: Support and Challenge," in C. Medel-Anonuevo (ed.), *Women, Education and Empowerment: Pathways Towards Autonomy*. Hamburg: UNESCO Institute of Education, pp. 62–8.

Hossain, M. 1988. *Credit for Alleviation of Rural Poverty: The Grameen Bank in Bangladesh*. Research Report 65, Washington D.C.: International Food Policy Research Institute.

Hulme, D. and P. Mosley (eds). 1996. *Finance Against Poverty: Effective Institutions for Lending to Small Farmers and Microenterprises in Developing Countries*. London: Routledge.

Hunter, M. 2008. *Social Care Paraprofessionals Feel out of their Depth*. Retrieved 20 October 2010 from http://www.communitycare.co.uk/Articles/2008/04/09/107830/social-care-paraprofessionals-feel-out-of-their-depth.html.

Hutt, M. (ed.). 2004. *Himalayan People's War: Nepal's Maoist Rebellion*. Bloomington and Indianapolis: Indiana University Press.

Jansen, W.H. 1978. *Profiles of Poverty in Bangladesh: A Preliminary Report*. Program Office, USAID Mission to Bangladesh.

Jewish Agency. 1984. *A Model for the Absorption of Ethiopian Immigrants in Transition Frameworks*. Jerusalem: A Working Paper for the Planning Team, Directors of Absorption Centres for Ethiopians (Hebrew).

Justice, J. 1989. *Policies, Plans and People: Foreign Aid and Health Development*. Berkeley, Los Angeles, London: University of California.

Kabbani, R. 1986. *Europe's Myths of the Orient*. Bloomington: Indiana University Press.

Kabeer, N. 1994. *Reversed Realities: Gender Hierarchies in Development Thought*. London: Verso.

____. 1999. "Targeting Women or Transforming Institutions? Policy Lessons from NGO Anti-poverty Efforts," in D. Eade (ed.), *Development with Women*. Oxford: Oxfam GB, pp. 32–45.

Karim, L. 2001. "Politics of the Poor? Grassroots Political Mobilization in Bangladesh," *PoLAR: Political and Legal Anthropology Review* 24(1): 92–107.

Karki, A. and D. Seddon. 2003. "The People's War in Historical Context," in A. Karki and D. Seddon (eds), *The People's War in Nepal: Left Perspectives*. Delhi: Adroit Publishers, pp. 3–48.

Keating, M. 2001. "Rethinking the Region: Culture, Institutions and Economic Development in Catalonia and Galicia," *European Urban and Regional Studies* 8(3): 217–34.

Kelman, H.C. 1973. "Violence without Moral Restraint: Reflections on the Dehumanization of Victims and Victimizers," *Journal of Social Issues* 29(4): 25–61.

Khandker S.R. and O.H. Chowdhury. 1996. "Targeted Credit Programs and Rural Poverty in Bangladesh," *Credit Programs for the Poor: Household and Intrahousehold Impacts and Program Sustainability.* Vol. 2, Dhaka: The Bangladesh Institute of Development Studies.

Khandker, S.R. Khalily, B. and Z.H. Khan (eds). 1996. *Credit Programs for the Poor: Household and Intrahousehold Impacts and Program Sustainability.* Vol. 1, Dhaka: The Bangladesh Institute of Development Studies.

Khandekar, S. 2004. "'Literacy brought us to the Forefront': Literacy and Empowering Processes for Dalit Community Women in a Mumbai Slum," in A. Robinson-Pant (ed.), *Women, Literacy and Development: Alternative Perspectives.* London and New York: Routledge, Taylor & Francis Group, pp. 206–18.

King E.M. and A.M. Hill. 1993. *Women's Education in Developing Countries: Barriers, Benefits and Policies.* Baltimore and London: John Hopkins University Press.

Krais, B. 1993. "Gender and Symbolic Violence: Female Oppression in the Light of Pierre Bourdieu's Theory of Social Practice," in C. Craig, E. LiPuma and M. Postone (eds), *Bourdieu: Critical Perspectives.* Cambridge: Polity Press and Chicago: University of Chicago Press.

Kunda, G. 1992. *Engineering Culture: Control and Commitment in a High-Tech Corporation.* Philadelphia: Temple University Press.

Lange, R. 1997. *Geschlechterverhältnisse im Management von Organisationen.* München-Mering: Hampp Verlag.

Lankshear, C. and M. Knobel. 2006. *New Literacies: Everyday Practices and Classroom Learning.* Buckingham, UK: Open University Press.

Leach, F. 1999. "Women in the Informal Sector: the Contribution of Education and Training," in D. Eade (ed.), *Development with Women.* Oxford: Oxfam GB, pp. 46–62.

_____. 2000. "Gender Implications of Development Agency Policies on Education and Training," *International Journal of Educational Development* 20(4): 333–47.

Lechner, J.F. and J. Boli. 2004 (2000). *Globalization Reader*, Oxford: Blackwell Publishing.

Leve, L.G. 2007. "'Failed Development' and Rural Revolution in Nepal: Rethinking Subaltern Consciousness and Women's Empowerment," *Anthropological Quarterly* 80 (1): 127–72.

Levy, C. 1991. *Critical Issues in Translating Gender Concerns into Planning Competence in the 1990s.* Paper presented at the Joint ACSP and AESOP International Congress, 8–12 July. Planning Trans Atlantic: Global Change and Local Problems, Oxford, UK.

_____. 1996. *The Process of Institutionalising Gender in Policy and Planning: The "Web" of Institutionalisation.* Working Paper No. 74. London: Development Planning Unit, University College.

Lewis, A. 1979. *Power, Poverty and Education.* Ramat-Gan: Turtledove Publishing.

Li, T.M. 1999. "Compromising Power: Development, Culture and Rule in Indonesia," *Cultural Anthropology* 14(3): 295–322.

Longwe, H.S. 1999. "The Evaporation of Gender Policies in the Patriarchal Cooking Pot," in D. Eade (ed.), *Development with Women.* Oxford: Oxfam GB, pp. 63–76.

Luke, A. 2003. "Literacy and the Other: A Sociological Approach to Literacy Research and Policy in Multilingual Societies," *Reading Research Quarterly* 38: 132–41.

Lyon, S.M. 2004. *An Anthropological Analysis of Local Politics and Patronage in a Pakistani Village.* Lewiston, New York: The Edwin Mellen Press.

_____. 2002 "Power and Patronage in Pakistan," Ph.D. dissertation. Canterbury: University of Kent. Retrieved 20 October 2010 from http://sapir.ukc.ac.uk/SLyon/Lyon.pdf.

MacCormack, C. and M. Strathern (eds). 1980. *Nature, Culture and Gender.* Cambridge: Cambridge University Press.

Maiava, S.L. 2001. *A Clash of Paradigms: Intervention Response and Development in the South Pacific.* Aldershot: Ashgate.

Manchanda, R. 1999. "Empowerment with a Twist," *The Hindu,* 21 November.

_____. 2004. "Maoist Insurgency in Nepal: Radicalizing Gendered Narratives," *Cultural Dynamics* 16(2–3): 237–58.

Manzo, K. 1995. "Black Consciousness and the Quest for a Counter-modernist Development," in J. Crush (ed.), *Power of Development.* London: Routledge, pp. 228–252.

Maruna, S. and T.P. LeBel. 2003. "Welcome Home? Examining the 'Reentry Court' Concept from a Strengths-based Perspective," *Western Criminology Review* 4(2): 91–107.

Marx, E. 1976. "Appealing Violence," in E. Marx, *The Social Context of Violent Behaviour: A Social Anthropological Study in an Israeli Immigrant Town.* London: Routledge & Kegan Paul, pp. 63–74.

_____. 1985. "Social Anthropological Research and Getting Acquainted with Arabic Society," in A. Hareven (ed.), *To Get Acquainted with Neighbouring Nations.* Jerusalem: Van Leer Foundation, pp. 137–152. (Hebrew).

_____. 1996. How Israel Deals with Russian and Ethiopian Mass Immigration, Paper prepared for ESSHC, May 9–11, Noordwijkerhout, Netherlands.

Matin, I. 1998. "Mis-Targeting by the Grameen Bank: A Possible Explanation," *IDS Bulletin* (29)4: 51–8.

Maycock, M. 2003. *Whose Revolution: Can the Maoist Movement in Nepal lead to Women's Empowerment?* University of London: School of Oriental and African Studies.

Mazawi, E.A. 1995. "Changes in Teacher's Role Patterns in the Arab Palestinian Society and their Stratifying Implications," in A. Ben-Amos and Y. Tamir (eds), *The Teacher between Mission and Profession*. Tel Aviv: Ramot, Tel Aviv University, pp. 59–78 (Hebrew).

McGuire, J.S. and B.M. Popkin. 1990. "Helping Women Improve Nutrition in the Developing World: Beating the Zero Sum Game," *World Bank Technical Paper* (114) Washington, DC: World Bank.

McKillop, R.F. 1989. *Village Beef Cattle Development: The Melanesian Experience*. Islands/Australia Working Paper No. 89/2. Canberra: National Centre of Development Studies, Australian National University.

Mead, M. 1973. *Coming of Age in Samoa: A Psychological Study of Primitive Youth for Western Civilisation*. New York: William Morrow Company.

Merton, R.K. 1957. *Social Theory and Social Structure*. Glencoe, IL: Free Press.

_____. 1973. "The Perspectives of Insiders and Outsiders," in R.K. Merton, *The Sociology of Science: Theoretical and Empirical Investigations*. Chicago: The University of Chicago Press, pp. 99–138.

Metzler Philosophie Lexikon. 1996. Begriffe und Definitionen, Prechtl, P., Burkard, F. P. (eds), Stuttgart & Weimar: J. B. Metzler.

Mies, M. 1986. *Patriarchy and Accumulation on a World Scale*. London: Zed Books.

Millican, J. 2004. "'I will stay here until I die' A Critical Analysis of the Muthande Literacy Programme," in A. Robinson-Pant (ed.), *Women, Literacy and Development: Alternative Perspectives*. London and New York: Routledge, Taylor & Francis Group, pp. 195–205.

Milligan, J.B. 2004. "Democratization or Neocolonialism? The Education of Muslims under US Military Occupation 1903–20," *History of Education* 33(4): 451–67.

Mills, C.W. 1956. *The Power Elite*. Oxford: Oxford University Press.

Misra, R., Ghose, M. and D. Bhog. 1994. "Concretising Concepts: Continuing Education Strategies for Women," *Convergence* XXVII (2&3): 126–34.

Mohanty, T.C. (ed.). 1991. *Third World Women and the Politics of Feminism*. Bloomington and Indianapolis: Indiana University Press.

_____. 2003. *Feminism without Borders: Decolonizing Theory, Practicing Solidarity*. Durham: Duke University Press.

Momsen, J.H. 1991. *Women and Development in the Third World*. London and New York: Routledge.

_____. 2002. "Myth or Math: the Waxing and Waning of the Female-headed Household," *Progress in Development Studies* 2(2): 145–51.

_____. 2004. *Gender and Development*. London and New York: Routledge.

Moore, H.L. 1988. *Anthropology and Feminism*. Cambridge: Polity Press.

Moser, C. 1993. *Gender Planning and Development: Theory, Practice and Training*. London: Routledge.

Mosse, D. 2005. *Cultivating Development: An Ethnography of Aid Policy and Practice*. London, Ann Arbor, MI: Pluto Press.

Mulenga, D.C. 2001. "Mwalimu Julius Nyerere: A Critical Review of his Contributions to Adult Education and Postcolonialism," *International Journal of Lifelong Education* 20(6): 446–70.

Murphy, J.L. 1995. "Executive Summary," in *Gender Issues in World Bank Lending. A World Bank Operations Evaluation Study*, Washington DC.: World Bank.

Murthy, R.K. 1999. "Power, Institutions and Gender Relations: Can Gender Training Alter the Equations?" in D. Eade (ed.), *Development with Women*. Oxford: Oxfam GB, pp. 165–78.

Nader, L. 1972. "Up the Anthropologist – Perspectives Gained from Studying Up," in D.H. Hymes (ed.), *Reinventing Anthropology*. New York: Pantheon Books, pp. 284–311.

_____. 1997. "Controlling Processes – Tracing the Dynamic Components of Power," *Current Anthropology* 38(5): 711–37.

_____. 2002. *The Life of the Law: Anthropological Projects*. Berkeley: University of California Press.

Neipris, J. 1984. *Social Welfare and Social Services in Israel: Policies, Programs and Issues*. Jerusalem: the council of Social Work Schools (Hebrew).

Nöbauer, H. 2002. "Between 'Gifts' and 'Commodities': An Anthropological Approach to the Austrian Academic Field," in C. Gerschlager and M. Mokre. (eds), *Exchange and Deception: A Feminist Perspective*. Boston, Dorddrecht and London: Kluwer Academic Publishers.

Nordstrom, C. 2007. *Global Outlaws: Crime, Money, and Power in the Contemporary World*. Berkeley and Los Angeles, California: University of California Press.

Onesto, L. 2005. *Dispatches from the People's War in Nepal*. London: Pluto Press.

Ortner, S.B. 2006. *Anthropology and Social theory: Culture, Power, and the Acting Subject*. Durham and London: Duke University Press.

Osmani, L.K. 1998. "Impact of Credit on the Relative Well-Being of Women: Evidence from the Grameen Bank," *IDS Bulletin*, 29/4: 31–8.

Oxby, C. 1983. "'Farmer groups' in rural areas of the Third World," *Community Development Journal* 18(1): 50–9.

Oxfam. 2000. "Growth with Equity is Good for the Poor, Executive Summary," *Oxfam Policy Papers*.

Pareto, V. 1991. *The Rise and Fall of Elites: An Application of Theoretical Sociology*. New Jersey: Transaction.

Park, R.E. 1959. *Race and Culture*. Glencoe Ill.: The Free Press.

Parpart, J.L. 1993. "Who is the 'Other'? A Postmodern Feminist Critique of Women and Development Theory and Practice," *Development and Change* 24(3): 439–64.

Parpart, J.L. and M.H. Marchand. 1995. "Exploding the Canon: An Introduction/Conclusion," in J.L. Parpart and M.H. Marchand (eds), *Feminism Postmodernism Development*. London and New York: Routledge, pp. 1–22.

Parvati, C. 1999. "Women's Participation in the People's War in Nepal," in A. Karki and D. Seddon (eds), *The People's War in Nepal: Left Perspectives*. Delhi: Adroit Publishers, pp. 165–82.

Patel, I. 1991. *A Study of the Impact of New Communication Technologies on Literacy in India*. A Research Report Prepared for the Asian Mass Communication Research and Information Centre, Singapore.

Patel, I. and A. Dighe. 2003. "Gender Issues in Literacy Education," in T.B.G. Jandhyala (ed.), *Education, Society and Development: National and International Perspectives*. New Delhi: National Institute of Educational Planning and Administration (NIEPA), pp. 219–234.

Pearl A. and F. Riessman. 1965. *New Careers for the Poor: the Nonprofessional in Human Service*. New York: Free Press.

Pettigrew, J. 2003. "Guns, Kinship and Fear: Maoists among the Tamu-mai (Gurungs)," in D. Gellner (ed.), *Resistance and the State: Nepalese Experiences*. New Delhi: Social Science Press, pp. 305–25.

Pfaff-Czarnecka, J. 2004. "High Expectations, Deep Disappointment: Politics, State and Society in Nepal after 1990," in M. Hutt (ed.), *Himalayan People's War: Nepal's Maoist Rebellion*. Bloomington & Indianapolis: Indiana University Press, pp. 166–91.

Phillipson, R. 1992. *Linguistic Imperialism*. Oxford: Oxford University Press.

Pigg, S.L. 1992. "Inventing Social Categories through Place: Social Representations and Development in Nepal," *Comparative Studies in Society and History* 34: 491–513.

Rahman, A. 1999. "Micro-credit Initiatives for Equitable and Sustainable Development: Who Pays?" *World Development* 27(1): 67–82.

Rahman, R.I. and S.R. Khandker. 1996. "The Role of Targeted Credit Programs in Promoting Employment and productivity of the Poor," in *Credit Programs for the Poor: Household and Intrahousehold Impacts and Program Sustainability*. Vol. 2, Dhaka: The Bangladesh Institute of Development Studies.

Rahnema, M. and V. Bawtree. 1997. *The Post-Development Reader*. New York: Zed Books.

Ricento, T.K. (ed.). 2000. *Ideology, Politics and Language Policies: Focus on English*. Amsterdam/Philadelphia: John Benjamins.

Riessman, F. 1968. *Up From Poverty: New Career Ladders for Nonprofessionals*. New York: Harper & Row.

Ring, L.A. 2006. "Introduction: The Zenana Revisited," in L.A. Ring, *Zenana: Everyday Peace in a Karachi Apartment Building*. Bloomington: Indiana University Press, pp. 1–39.

Robinson-Pant, A. (ed.). 1995. "Literacy in Nepal: Looking Through the Literature," *Education for Development, Occasional Papers Series*. I no. 1.

____. 2004a. *Women, Literacy and Development: Alternative Perspectives*. London and New York: Routledge.

____. 2004b. "'The Illiterate Woman,' Changing Approaches to Researching Women's Literacy," in A. Robinson-Pant (ed.), *Women, Literacy and Development: Alternative Perspectives*. London and New York: Routledge, Taylor & Francis Group, pp. 15–34.

____. 2005. "The Social Benefits of Literacy," Paper commissioned for the *EFA Global Monitoring Report 2006, Literacy for Life*.

Rogers, A., Patkar, A. and L.S. Saraswathi. 2004. "Functional Literacy, Gender and Identities: Policy and Practice," in A. Robinson-Pant (ed.), *Women, Literacy and Development: Alternative Perspectives*. London and New York: Routledge, Taylor & Francis Group, pp. 117–38.

Rowan-Campbell, D. 1999. "Development with Women," in D. Eade (ed.), *Development with Women*. Oxford: Oxfam GB, pp. 11–31.

Rowlands, J. 1999. "Empowerment Examined," in D. Eade (ed.), *Development with Women*. Oxford: Oxfam GB, pp. 141–150.

Ruby, J. 1996. "Visual Anthropology," in D. Levinson and M. Ember (eds), *Encyclopedia of Cultural Anthropology*. New York: Henry Holt and Company, 4: 1345–1351.

Sachs, W. 1992. "Introduction," in W. Sachs (ed.), *The Development Dictionary, A Guide to Knowledge as Power*. London: Zed Books, pp. 1–5.

Sahlins, M.D. 1963. "Poor Man, Rich Man, Big Man, Chief," *Comparative Studies in History and Society* 5(3): 285–303.

Said, E. 1979. *Orientalism*. New York: Vintage Books.

Schindler, R. and E. Brawley. 1987. *Social Care at the Front Lines: A Worldwide Study of Paraprofessionals*. London: Tavistock.

Schuler, S.R., Hashemi, S.M. and A.P. Riley. 1997. "The Influence of Women's Changing Roles and Status in Bangladesh's Transition: Evidence from a Study of Credit Programs and Contraceptive Use," *World Development* 25(4): 563–75.

Sciama, L.D. 1981. "The Problem of Privacy in Mediterranean Anthropology," in S. Ardener (ed.), *Women and Space: Ground Rules and Social Maps*. London: Croom Helm, pp. 89–111.

____. 1984. "Ambivalence and Dedication: Academic Wives in Cambridge University," in H. Callan and S. Ardener (eds), *The Incorporated Wife*. London: Croom Helm, 50–66.

Scott, C.J. 1985. *Weapons of the Weak: Everyday Forms of Resistance*. New Haven: Yale University Press.

____. 1990. *Domination and the Arts of Resistance: Hidden Transcripts*. New Haven: Yale University Press.

Sen, G. and C. Grown. 1987. *Development, Crises, and Alternative Visions: Third World Women's Perspectives*. Brazil: New Feminist Library, DAWN.

Sewell, W.F. 1992. "A Theory of Structure, Duality, Agency, and Transformation," *The American Journal of Sociology* 98(1): 1–29.

Shachak, O. 1985. *Absence of Power and Negative Stigmatization as Central Components of Project Renewal in Yerucham.* Unpublished research report, Beer Sheva: Ben Gurion University of the Negev (Hebrew).

Shakya, S. 2003. "The Maoist Movement in Nepal: An Analysis from the Women"s Perspective," in A. Karki and D. Seddon (eds), *The People's War in Nepal: Left Perspectives.* Delhi: Adroit Publishers, pp. 375–404.

Shamgar-Handelman, L. 1986. *Israeli War Widows: Beyond the Glory of Heroism.* South Hadley MA: Begin and Garvey.

Shapira, R. 2008. *Transforming Kibbutz Research: Trust and Moral Leadership in the Rise and Decline of Democratic Cultures.* Cleveland, Ohio: New World Publishing.

Sharma, M. and D. Prasain. 2004. "Gender Dimensions of the People's War: Some Reflections on the Experiences of Rural Women," in M. Hutt (ed.), *Himalayan People's War: Nepal's Maoist Rebellion.* Bloomington & Indianapolis: Indiana University Press, pp. 152–65.

Sharma, R.S. 1985. "How Feudal was Indian Feudalism?" *Journal of Peasant Studies* 12(2): 19–43.

Shiva, V. 1986. *Staying Alive: Women, Ecology and Development.* London: Zed Books.

____. 1993. "The Impoverishment of the Environment," in M. Mies and V. Shiva, *Ecofeminism,* pp. 70–90.

____. 2001. "World Bank, WTO, and corporate control over water," *International Socialist Review.*Retrieved 17 September 2010 from http://www.thirdworldtraveler.com/Water/Corp_Control_Water_VShiva.html.

____. 2002. *Water Wars: Privatization, Pollution and Profit.* London: Pluto Press.

Shore, C. 1999. "Fictions of Fieldwork: Depicting the 'Self' in Ethnographic Writing (Italy)," in C.W. Watson (ed.), *Being There: Fieldwork in Anthropology.* London: Pluto Press, pp. 25–48.

Shore C. and S. Wright (eds). 1997. *Anthropology of Policy: Critical Perspectives on Governance and Power.* London and New York: Routledge.

Shrestha, B.K. 1983. "Technical Assistance and the Growth of Administrative Capability in Nepal," *IDS Foreign Aid and Development in Nepal.* Kathmandu. Nepal: Integrated Development Systems.

Shrestha, C.H. 2004. "Do NGOs 'shop around'? A View on Donor-recipient Relationships from NGO Workers in Nepal." Paper Presented at NGO Study Group Seminar, Oxford, 28 April 2004. "Ethnography of NGOs: Understanding Organisational Processes."

Shtrii Shakti. 1995. *Women Development Democracy, A Study of the Socioeconomic Changes in the Status of Women in Nepal (1981–1993).* Kathmandu.

Siegel, D. 1989. *Violent Husbands – The Causes of the Problem and its Treatment.* Tel Aviv University: The Institute for National Insurance (Hebrew).

_____. 1998. *The Great Immigration: Russian Jews in Israel.* New York: Berghahn Books.
Sinha, S. and I. Matin. 1998. "Informal Credit Transactions of Micro-Credit Borrowers in Rural Bangladesh," *IDS Bulletin* 29 (4): 66–80.
Smith, A. 1984 [1759]. *Theory of Moral Sentiments.* Glasgow edition, edited by D.D. Raphael and A.L. Macfie. Ann Arbor: Liberty Fund.
Smith, M.K. 1998/2001. "Informal and Non-formal Education, Colonialism and Development: The Place of Informal and Non-formal Education in Development – the Experience of the South," *Infed.* Retrieved 21 October 2010 from *http://www.infed.org/biblio/colonialism.htm.*
_____. 2007. "Adult Education and Lifelong Learning – Southern Critiques and Alternatives: What Can Northern Educators Learn from the Experience of the South?" *Infed.* Retrievd 21 October 2010 from *http://www.infed.org/lifelonglearning/south.htm.*
Spencer, T. 2006. *Gender Activities in the Project Area, Bhairahawa Lumbini Groundwater Project.* A Project Report, submitted to Tahal Consulting Engineers LTD.
Stiglitz, J.E. 2002. *Globalization and its Discontents.* New York: W.W. Norton.
Strauss A., et al. 1981. "Negotiated Order and the Co-ordination of Work," in A. Strauss, *Psychiatric Ideologies and Institutions.* New Brunswick and London: Transaction, pp. 292–315.
Street, B.V. 2004. "Implications of the New Literacy Studies for Researching Women's Literacy Programmes," in A. Robinson-Pant (ed.), *Women, Literacy and Development: Alternative Perspectives.* London and New York: Routledge, Taylor & Francis Group, pp. 57–67.
Stromquist, N.P. 1990. "Women and Illiteracy: The Interplay of Gender Subordination and Poverty," *Comparative Education Review* 34(1): 95–111.
_____. 1992. "Women and Literacy: Promises and Constraints," *The Annals of the American Academy of Political and Social Science* 520(1): 54–65.
_____. 1994. *Literacy for Citizenship: Gender and Grassroots Dimensions in Sao Paulo.* Los Angeles: University of Southern California, School of Education (mimeo).
Subedi, P. 1993. *Nepali Women Rising.* Kathmandu, Nepal: Sahayogi Press.
Summers, L.H. 1993. "Foreword," in E.M. King and A.M. Hill (eds), *Women's Education in Developing Countries: Barriers, Benefits and Policies.* Baltimore MD and London: Johns Hopkins University Press, pp. v–vii.
Tahal Consulting Engineers LTD., and His Majesty's Government of Nepal, Ministry of Water Resources, Department of Irrigation: Bhirahwa Lumbini Ground Water Irrigation Project. 1992. *Socioeconomic Survey.* Tel Aviv, Kathmandu (July).
_____. 1997. *Prequalification for Employment of NGOs for Provision of Services Related to Women Development Programs.* Kathmandu (30 January 1997).
Tamang, S. 2002. "The Politics of 'Developing Nepali Women'," in K.M. Dixit and S. Ramachandaran (eds), *State of Nepal.* Lalitpur: Himal Books.

Tannenbaum, A.S. 1967. *Control in Organizations*. New York: McGraw-Hill.

Thapa, D. 2003. *Understanding the Maoist Movement of Nepal*. Kathmandu: Martin Chautari.

Thapa, D. and B. Sijapati. 2004. *Kingdom under Siege, Nepal's Maoist Insurgency, 1996 to 2004*. Kathmandu: The Printhouse, London & New York: Zed Books.

Thomas, M.R. 1993. "Education in the South Pacific: The Context for Development," *Comparative Education* 29(3): 233–48.

Thomas M.R. and N.T. Postlethwaite. 1984. *Schooling in the Pacific Islands – Colonies in Transition: Primary and Secondary Education in Papua New Guinea, Fiji, Cook Islands, New Caledonia, Society Islands, Tonga, Micronesia, Samoa, New Hebrides*. Oxford: Pergamon.

Thompson, J. J. 1994. "'There are Many Words to Describe Their Anger': Ritual and Resistance among High-Caste Hindu Women in Kathmandu," in M. Allen (ed.), *Anthropology of Nepal: Peoples, Problems and Processes*. Kathmandu: Mandala Book Point, pp. 358–71.

Tittler, R. 1992. "'Seats of Honor, Seats of Power': The Symbolism of Public Seating in the English Urban Community, c. 1560–1620," *Albion* 24(2): 205–23.

Umbarger, C. 1972. "The Paraprofessional and Family Therapy," *Family Process* 11(2): 147–62.

UNDP. 1995. Human Development Report. Retrieved 14 October 2010 from http://hdr.undp.org/en/media/hdr_1995_en_contents.pdf.

UNESCO. 1988. *Literacy for Girls and Women*. Briefing paper for International Literacy Year.

Vincent D. 1998. *The Culture of Secrecy: Britain 1832–1998*. Oxford: Oxford University Press.

Watson, C.W. (ed.). 1999. "Introduction: The Quality of Being There," in C.W. Watson (ed.), *Being There: Fieldwork in Anthropology*. London, Sterling, Virginia: Pluto Press, pp. 1–24.

Weber, M. 1948. "Politics as a Vocation" and "Bureaucracy," in *From Max Weber: Essays in Sociology* (translated and edited by H.H. Gerth and W.C. Mills). London: Routledge & Kegan Paul, pp. 77–128, and 196–244.

_____. 1978. *Economy and Society: An Outline of Interpretive Sociology* (translated and edited by G. Roth and C. Wittich), Berkeley & Los Angeles, California: University of California.

Whelpton, J. 2005. *A History of Nepal*. Cambridge: Cambridge University Press.

Wickens C.M. and J.A. Sandlin. 2007. "Literacy for What? Literacy for Whom? The Politics of Literacy Education and Neocolonialism in UNESCO and World Bank Sponsored Literacy Programs," *Adult Education Quarterly* 57(4): 275–92.

World Bank. 1990. *Women in Development: A Progress Report on the World Bank Initiative*. Washington, DC: World Bank.

____. 2001. *World Development Report 2000/2001: Attacking Poverty.*

Youngman, F. 2000. *The Political Economy of Adult Education and Development.* Leicester, U.K.: National Organisation for Adult Learning.

Yunus, M. 1998. *Banker to the Poor: The Autobiography of Muhammad Yumus, Founder of the Grameen Bank.* Bodmin: Aurum Press.

INDEX